The Glannon Guide
to Torts

ASPEN PUBLISHERS

The Glannon Guide to Torts

Learning Torts Through Multiple-Choice Questions and Analysis

Richard L. Hasen
William H. Hannon Distinguished Professor of Law
Loyola Law School, Los Angeles

Wolters Kluwer
Law & Business

AUSTIN   BOSTON   CHICAGO   NEW YORK   THE NETHERLANDS

Aspen Publishers
Attn: Permissions Department
76 Ninth Avenue, 7th Floor
New York, NY   10011-5201

To contact Customer Care, e-mail customer.care@aspenpublishers.com,
call 1-800-234-1660, fax 1-800-901-9075, or mail correspondence to:

Aspen Publishers
Attn: Order Department
PO Box 990
Frederick, MD 21705

Printed in the United States of America.

1 2 3 4 5 6 7 8 9 0

ISBN 978-0-7355-8480-8

Library of Congress Cataloging-in-Publication Data

Hasen, Richard L.
    The Glannon guide to torts: learning torts through multiple-choice questions and analysis /
Richard L. Hasen.
        p. cm.
    Includes index.
    ISBN 978-0-7355-8480-8
    1. Torts—United States. 2. Torts—United States—Problems, exercises, etc. I. Title. II. Title:
Guide to torts.

    KF1250.Z9H375 2009
    346.7303076—dc22

                                                                                                2009003084

About Wolters Kluwer Law & Business

Wolters Kluwer Law & Business is a leading provider of research information and workflow solutions in key specialty areas. The strengths of the individual brands of Aspen Publishers, CCH, Kluwer Law International and Loislaw are aligned within Wolters Kluwer Law & Business to provide comprehensive, in-depth solutions and expert-authored content for the legal, professional and education markets.

CCH was founded in 1913 and has served more than four generations of business professionals and their clients. The CCH products in the Wolters Kluwer Law & Business group are highly regarded electronic and print resources for legal, securities, antitrust and trade regulation, government contracting, banking, pension, payroll, employment and labor, and healthcare reimbursement and compliance professionals.

Aspen Publishers is a leading information provider for attorneys, business professionals and law students. Written by preeminent authorities, Aspen products offer analytical and practical information in a range of specialty practice areas from securities law and intellectual property to mergers and acquisitions and pension/benefits. Aspen's trusted legal education resources provide professors and students with high-quality, up-to-date and effective resources for successful instruction and study in all areas of the law.

Kluwer Law International supplies the global business community with comprehensive English-language international legal information. Legal practitioners, corporate counsel and business executives around the world rely on the Kluwer Law International journals, loose-leafs, books and electronic products for authoritative information in many areas of international legal practice.

Loislaw is a premier provider of digitized legal content to small law firm practitioners of various specializations. Loislaw provides attorneys with the ability to quickly and efficiently find the necessary legal information they need, when and where they need it, by facilitating access to primary law as well as state-specific law, records, forms and treatises.

Wolters Kluwer Law & Business, a unit of Wolters Kluwer, is headquartered in New York and Riverwoods, Illinois. Wolters Kluwer is a leading multinational publisher and information services company.

To my dad, who always puts his family first, and
to my mom, whose love and dedication know no bounds

Table of Contents

Acknowledgments

Though my name is the only one on the cover, this book is possible only because of the tremendous support I have received from others. Jennifer Johnson provided excellent research assistance, working tirelessly and enthusiastically from beginning to end. Brian Harlan carefully parsed each sentence for accuracy and clarity at the proofreading stage. Marsha Battee, Carla Heidlberg, and the Loyola faculty support staff provided wonderful administrative support, and Lisa Schulz provided excellent library assistance. Loyola Law School, and particularly Dean Victor Gold, provides all the support I need for my scholarly and teaching pursuits. Lynn Churchill, Christine Hannan, and Troy Froebe of Aspen Publishers have provided wise editorial direction. I have also benefited greatly from the anonymous reviewers of the manuscript. Remaining errors are mine alone.

In addition to support at work, I receive love and encouragement from my family, especially my wife Lori, and children, Deborah, Shana, and Jared. The first people to support me in my studies were my parents, and it is to them that I dedicate this book.

Finally, I am grateful to the American Law Institute for permission to quote from various Restatements:

Restatement of the Law of Torts, copyright 1939 by The American Law Institute. Reprinted with Permission. All Rights Reserved.

Restatement, Second, Torts, copyright 1979 by The American Law Institute. Reprinted with Permission. All Rights Reserved.

Restatement of the Law, Third, Torts: Liability for Physical and Emotional Harm—Tentative Draft No. 5, copyright 2007 by The American Law Institute. Reprinted with Permission. All Rights Reserved. (As of the date of publication, this draft had not been considered by the members of The American Law Institute and does not represent the position of the Institute.)

Restatement of the Law, Third, Torts: Liability for Physical Harm—Proposed Final Draft No. 1, copyright 2005 by The American Law Institute. Reprinted with Permission. All Rights Reserved. (As of the date of publication, this draft had not been considered by the members of The American Law Institute and does not represent the position of the Institute.)

February 2009
Los Angeles, California

The Glannon Guide
to Torts

1

A Very Short Introduction

When I was a law student, Torts was my favorite first-year class. Many students enjoy Torts because policy plays such an important role in how courts decide cases. When one person accidentally or intentionally hurts another, who should bear the cost? Torts is also the home of bizarre hypotheticals. Torts professors love to dream up unlikely (and sometimes entertaining) scenarios to push students to see the limitations of their arguments and to hone students' emerging advocacy skills.

The purpose of this book is to assist first-year students in mastering the subject of Torts through the tool of multiple-choice questions. I have organized each chapter in the same way. I begin by explaining a rule in its relevant context. I then test you on your understanding of what you have just read with a multiple-choice question. Following the question, I identify the correct answer to the question and explain why that answer is better than the other answers. New material then follows in the chapter using the same format. Each chapter concludes with "The Closer," a question that tests you on one or more major concepts from the chapter. (The final chapter of the book contains "Closing Closers" that test you on materials across the chapters and are more illustrative of the kinds of questions many professors would ask on final examinations.) At the very end of each chapter you will find "Rick's picks," my answers to the multiple-choice questions within each chapter.

You can use this book in one of two ways: You can read the material that appears before each question and then answer each question, or you could simply go right to the questions, checking your answers against "Rick's picks" in the back of each chapter. You could then go back to the questions you did not answer correctly and read the explanatory material before and after those questions.

Either way, be sure to give *your answer first*: this book won't do you much good if you just passively read the multiple-choice questions and my answers. You need to *practice the skill* of answering multiple-choice questions, and nothing helps more on a real exam than practicing with actual questions.

I have a few tips for answering multiple-choice questions, and most of these tips are just common sense.

First, read the call of the question. In other words, make sure you are answering the right question. It is not enough to find a correct statement of law in a multiple-choice answer; it must be appropriate for the question asked.

Second, pay careful attention to all of the words of the question. The answer to the question may depend upon a single word, a word that your Torts professor is unlikely to highlight with italics or otherwise. You need to spot it and know it is important. When you see a word that could be important in answering the question, circle it.

Third, your task is not to find the *perfect* answer, but only the best among the four choices listed, which sometimes turns out to be simply the *least bad* of four bad answers. For this reason, it makes sense to begin by eliminating clearly wrong answers. Often it is easy to eliminate one or two incorrect answers, leaving you with a better chance of choosing the correct answer through a focus on the important differences among the remaining choices.

Fourth, if you have time, go back and review your answer. Multiple-choice questions can be tricky because so much can turn on the words of the question. (See the second point above.) For this reason, it is easy to miss an important fact the first time through. If you can come back to the question after you have finished the others, you might see something you have missed. The danger of going back is that you will lose confidence in your original answer — but your confidence should build over time as you learn when to trust your instincts.

I have tried to organize the material in a way that would be typical for a first-year Torts class. The six major parts of the book are intentional torts, negligence, causation, strict liability, products liability, and damages. If your instructor covers various torts and torts subjects in a different order, you should be able to begin with a different part. There is one important exception to this point: *You should read Chapter 2 before reading anything else.* (I put that point in italics because you may not have mastered the part yet about finding the important stuff that can get buried in a paragraph of text.) Chapter 2 provides the basic building blocks you will need to understand the language used in the remainder of the chapters.

One final note: writing multiple-choice questions is tricky business, and you may find a question here or there in the book that you think contains the wrong answer, even after you have read my explanation. If you find one of those questions, or if you have any other comments or suggestions, please send me an e-mail message, at rick.hasen@lls.edu. Good luck!

2

Torts Basics: The Prima Facie Case and Affirmative Defenses

CHAPTER OVERVIEW
A. **What is a tort?**
B. **Elements of all torts**
C. **Affirmative defenses**
D. **The Closer: Understanding the interaction of the prima facie case and defenses**
⬥ **Rick's picks**

A. What is a tort?

Before law school, if you heard the word "tort," you probably thought of some kind of delicious dessert. That's a *torte* (with an "e"), not a *tort*, and is a subject more appropriate for culinary school than law school. The topic here is Torts, which is typically defined as a "civil wrong independent of contract." Let's take this definition apart and impose an important caveat.

First, note the use of the term "civil." As you learn at the very beginning of law school, the U.S. legal system is split into two parts, civil cases and criminal cases. The law that is applicable to each section is different, subject to different rules, procedures, remedies, and burdens of proof. Thus, consider the situation in which Adam shoots Barbara, causing her to suffer serious personal injuries. That conduct may or may not subject Adam to criminal punishment, such as jail time or a fine. The very same conduct also may subject Adam to tort liability, requiring him to pay some sum of money as damages to Barbara. The first case would be brought in a criminal court by a prosecutor. The second case would be brought in a civil court by Barbara. In that civil suit we call Barbara the *plaintiff* and Adam the *defendant*. We will refer to those who a jury finds to have committed a tort as *tortfeasors* (not "criminals," though some tortfeasors may also be criminals), and say that the tortfeasors are *liable* (not "guilty") for the torts they have committed.

For most crimes, the prosecutor would have to prove Adam (also called the *defendant* in the criminal trial) committed all the elements of the crime under a "proof beyond a reasonable doubt" standard. In contrast, if Barbara sues Adam in tort, she will need to prove all the elements of the tort or torts she asserts against Adam under a "preponderance of the evidence" standard, which is a "more likely than not" standard.[1] This standard is less onerous than the criminal standard. Because the standard of proof is different and the elements may be different, the same conduct might be found to be both a crime and a tort, one but not the other, or neither. For this reason, it is important to "compartmentalize" your brain if you are studying Torts and Criminal Law at the same time, especially when studying topics using the same terms but different standards, such as a requirement that Adam had the requisite "intent" when he did the shooting.

We have talked about the term "civil;" now let's consider what the tort definition means by a *wrong*. The term "wrong" is not self-defining, and on the civil side of the law Tort law identifies what counts as a wrong. In the Adam-Barbara example above, it may look at first glance that Adam has wronged Barbara, but that is not necessarily the case. Suppose Adam shot Barbara because she was about to shoot him first. Or suppose that Adam was cleaning his gun very carefully and it nonetheless went off, causing Barbara's injuries. Tort law separates the circumstances in which we allow Barbara to recover damages from those in which the law concludes that Adam should not be liable to Barbara in tort. Much of what follows in the remaining chapters is tort law's attempt to identify those wrongs.

Finally, torts involve civil wrongs *independent of contract.* As you will learn in your Contracts course, the law on the civil side often allows for the recovery of damages (and other remedies as well) when one party to a contract breaches that contract by failing to do what that party has promised to do. With a few narrow exceptions that will come up later in this book, a breach of contract, standing alone, is not a tort. The tricky part is that people sometimes commit torts within contractual relationships.

Suppose Clarissa is a surgeon operating on Dylan. Clarissa and Dylan have a contract: Clarissa promises medical services in exchange for Dylan's

---

1. As we shall see in Chapter 23, in many jurisdictions if Barbara sought additional *punitive* damages against Adam she would have to prove Adam engaged in the requisite bad conduct under a standard more onerous than the preponderance of the evidence standard. But apart from this exception, everything else studied in this book will be under the preponderance standard. We will look more closely at the meaning of the preponderance standard elsewhere in the book, especially in the discussion of actual causation in Chapter 13.

promise to pay. If Clarissa does not perform the services, or if Dylan doesn't pay, that could well be considered a breach of contract. But suppose Clarissa operates on Dylan, and she does so while she is drunk, leaving a sponge inside Dylan's abdomen. (Yuck! Get used to these gory hypos early; you will see a lot of them in a Torts class.) Clarissa's conduct could be a breach of contract (under the theory that one of her implied promises was to perform the surgery carefully). But whether or not it is a breach of contract — and despite the fact that there is a contract between the parties — Clarissa's conduct most likely constitutes the tort of negligence. The fact that there is a contract between the parties does not immunize Clarissa from a tort claim by Dylan against her.

QUESTION 1. Reliving O.J. As you probably recall from your time well before law school, prosecutors charged former football star O.J. Simpson under the criminal law with murdering his ex-wife Nicole Brown Simpson and her friend, Ron Goldman. Simpson's defense was that he did not do it, and the jury acquitted him of the criminal charges. The families of Nicole Brown Simpson and Ron Goldman sued Simpson for the tort of wrongful death. If O.J. Simpson's lawyers argued to the judge in the tort case that the wrongful death case should not go forward because the jury in the criminal trial already determined that O.J. Simpson did not do it, the court should:

A. Accept the argument because proof beyond a reasonable doubt is a stricter standard than the preponderance of the evidence standard.
B. Accept the argument because the results of a criminal trial are binding in civil courts.
C. Reject the argument because the first jury could have been wrong.
D. Reject the argument because proof beyond a reasonable doubt is a stricter standard than the preponderance of the evidence standard.

ANALYSIS. The structure of these choices is typical of multiple-choice questions. You not only have to figure out the right *result* in the case (should the court accept or reject the argument of O.J.'s lawyers?), but you also have to figure out *why*.

Choice **A** is wrong, but it is tricky. Part of the answer states a correct principle of law: proof beyond a reasonable doubt *is* a stricter standard than the preponderance of the evidence standard. But because the criminal standard is a stricter standard, it would not be inconsistent in the civil case for a jury to conclude that O.J. Simpson committed a tort. In other words, though a prosecutor might not be able to prove that O.J. Simpson committed the crime beyond a reasonable doubt, the prosecutor might have been able to convince a jury (and the plaintiff in the wrongful death suit might be able to convince a civil jury) that O.J. Simpson caused the death of the others *by a preponderance of the evidence.*

Choice **B** is wrong because it states an incorrect principle of law. As noted in the section above, criminal and civil systems are subject to different rules, standards, and remedies. Though we will see instances in the course where criminal proceedings are relevant to Tort cases, the general statement of Choice **B** is incorrect.

Choice **C** is especially tricky. Yes, it is true that the first jury could have been wrong in its conclusion about O.J. Simpson's guilt, and it is also true that the judge should reject the argument that the civil case should not go forward. But the judge should not reject that argument *because* the first jury could have been wrong. The key here is not that one jury is right and the other is wrong, but that different standards and rules apply in criminal and civil cases.

Choice **D** is therefore the correct answer because it ties the right result (that the court should reject the argument) with a good reason why the court should do so (because the preponderance of the evidence standard is lower than the proof beyond a reasonable doubt standard). There may be other reasons as well why the judge should reject O.J. Simpson's argument. For example, what plaintiffs need to prove in a wrongful death tort case may have different elements from what the prosecutor needs to prove in the criminal case. But that's irrelevant: among the four choices, Choice **D** is the best answer.

B.   Elements of all torts

Every tort has the same structure. This is a line I repeat perhaps 100 times in my Torts course because students often forget it. In the exam world, and in the real legal world, it is important to resist the temptation to cut to the chase and to focus on or discuss only the most difficult or important issue. Instead one must be methodical, logical, and consistent in making legal arguments, and doing so in Torts requires understanding the structure of a tort suit.

The structure is simply stated. The plaintiff bears the burden of proving by a preponderance of the evidence all of the "elements" of each tort. We call this exercise plaintiff's proof of the *prima facie* case. If the plaintiff fails to prove each of the elements making up the prima facie case, the plaintiff loses. So if the defendant can convince the jury (or the judge, who sometimes might sit instead of the jury as a factfinder or who sometimes makes determinations that keep cases out of the hands of juries) that the plaintiff has failed to prove even one of the elements of the tort, the plaintiff will lose the entire case.

In addition, even if the plaintiff can prove all the elements of the tort by a preponderance of the evidence, the defendant can still win (or in some cases, discussed later in the book, split the liability with the plaintiff) if the defendant can successfully raise and prove by a preponderance of the evidence an *affirmative defense* (the topic of Part C of this chapter).

So what are the elements of each tort? Speaking generically, the plaintiff must prove:

1. That defendant engaged in the requisite tortious conduct
2. Actual causation
3. Proximate causation
4. Damages

Torts differ in the first element, the *requisite tortious conduct*. By this term I mean conduct that makes a defendant's actions wrongful under tort law. Return again to our example of Adam and Barbara. Suppose that Adam deliberately shot Barbara for no good reason and with no good excuse. Barbara likely would sue Adam for the tort of *battery*, discussed in the next chapter. To greatly oversimplify for our purposes now, the tortious conduct for battery requires proof that Adam engaged in an intentional, non-consensual contact with Barbara, causing damage. Now suppose instead that Adam accidentally shot Barbara while Adam was cleaning his gun. Barbara in that case would likely sue Adam for the tort of *negligence*, discussed in Part II of this book. Again to oversimplify, the tortious conduct required for negligence requires proof that Adam owed a duty to Barbara and breached that duty by engaging in unreasonable conduct, causing damage. The requisite tortious conduct for battery differs from the tortious conduct for negligence, and whether Barbara tries to sue Adam for negligence, battery, or both depends upon what she thinks she can prove by a preponderance of the evidence.

After a plaintiff proves the requisite tortious conduct, the plaintiff will also have to prove actual causation and proximate causation (both discussed in Part III of this book) and damages (discussed in Part VI of this book). A plaintiff needs to prove each of these additional elements by a preponderance of the evidence as well. A plaintiff may sue for multiple torts, and we will see some reasons in this book why plaintiffs sometimes have an incentive to do so. But for each tort, it will be necessary for the plaintiff to prove all of the elements of each tort.

QUESTION 2. It's Element-ary My Dear Barbara. Adam shoots Barbara, leading Barbara to sue Adam for battery and negligence. In Barbara's jurisdiction the tortious conduct portion of the prima facie case for battery requires proof of six elements. Barbara proves five of the six elements to the jury by a preponderance of the evidence, but the jury concludes that Barbara failed to prove one of the elements by a preponderance of the evidence. The court should:

A. Rule for Barbara on her battery claim because she proved 5 of 6 elements (a preponderance of the elements).
B. Rule for Adam on Barbara's battery claim so long as Adam raised no affirmative defenses.
C. Rule for Adam on Barbara's battery claim whether or not Adam raised any affirmative defenses.
D. Rule for Adam on Barbara's battery claim and negligence claim.

ANALYSIS. Choice **A** is incorrect because it confuses two different concepts. On the one hand, a plaintiff in a torts case must prove *each element* of each tort by a preponderance of the evidence. On the other hand, a plaintiff must prove *all the elements* of the tort by a preponderance of the evidence. It is not enough to prove most of the elements to make out the prima facie case.

Choice **B** is incorrect for a different reason. Though it is true the court should rule for Adam, that ruling will have nothing to do with whether or not Adam raised any affirmative defenses. If the plaintiff cannot prove each element of the prima facie case by a preponderance of the evidence, the plaintiff loses, regardless of any affirmative defenses that might be raised by the defendant.

Choice **D** is incorrect as well. Each tort has the same structure, but it has different elements. Barbara's failure to prove an element of the tort of battery says nothing about whether or not she can prove the elements of the tort of negligence. A court should not rule for Adam on Barbara's negligence claim because of her failure to prove the elements of a battery.

Choice **C** is the right answer for the same reason that Choice **B** is the wrong one: If the plaintiff cannot prove an element of her prima facie case for one of her torts, she loses on that tort whether or not the defendant has raised any affirmative defenses.

C.   Affirmative defenses

As noted in the last part, a defendant can win a torts case in two different ways. First, the defendant wins if the plaintiff cannot prove each of the elements of her case by a preponderance of the evidence. But even if the plaintiff can prove all the elements of her case, the defendant has a second chance to win (or, in some cases, to reduce or split the liability with the plaintiff). The defendant can do so by raising and proving an affirmative defense by a preponderance of the evidence.

Thus, suppose Barbara proves the prima facie case for battery against Adam: she can show proof of each element of the tort by a preponderance of the evidence. Her story, which the jury believes, is that Adam intentionally shot her without her consent. Barbara still may not win her case. For example, suppose Adam pleads "self defense" as an affirmative defense (discussed in Chapter 4). "Yes, I shot Barbara," Adam argues, "but she was about to shoot me first with her own gun!" If Adam proves he acted in self-defense by a preponderance of the evidence, Barbara will lose her battery claim. (Note that self-defense is not a defense to negligence, though it may be relevant to the question whether a defendant is liable for negligence.)

As we will see, different torts have different affirmative defenses, and courts need to determine which affirmative defenses are legitimate ones. If Adam argues, "Yes, I shot Barbara, but I did not like the T-shirt she was wearing," a court is not going to recognize "wardrobe offense" as an affirmative defense. Indeed, as Chapter 23 details, such an argument could open Adam up to additional punitive damages.

QUESTION 3. Indefensible. Evan and Frank get into a knife fight, in which Evan suffers serious cuts. Frank tells the police who investigate the fight that he was acting in self-defense and that Evan was the aggressor. Evan sues Frank for battery, presenting evidence meeting the prima facie case for battery. Neither side put on any evidence regarding Frank's claim to the police of self-defense. On Evan's battery claim, the court should:

A. Rule for Evan if he has proven all the prima facie elements of the tort by a preponderance of the evidence.
B. Rule for Evan whether or not he has proven all the prima facie elements of the tort by a preponderance of the evidence because Frank failed to prove his affirmative defense.
C. Rule for Frank if Evan failed to prove by a preponderance of the evidence that Frank was not acting in self-defense.
D. Rule for Frank because both parties were equally at fault.

ANALYSIS. Choice **B** is an incorrect statement of the law. An affirmative defense is relevant only if the plaintiff has already proven all the elements of his prima facie case. It is not helpful to Evan that Frank failed to prove his affirmative defense of self-defense if Evan cannot prove the prima facie case. In other words, a plaintiff proving the prima facie case is a necessary condition to win a torts claim, even if it is not always sufficient to do so.

Choice **C** is wrong because the burden is on the defendant to prove his affirmative defense by a preponderance of the evidence; it is not on the plaintiff to *disprove* a defendant's affirmative defense by a preponderance of the evidence.

Choice **D** is an easy answer to eliminate from contention. It gives a response that is not supported by the facts of the question—that both parties were equally at fault. We don't know that fact. All we know is that Evan has presented evidence of the prima facie case for battery and Frank offered no evidence on self-defense.

Choice **A** is the correct answer. From the fact pattern, we don't know that Evan will necessarily win. If, for example, he fails to prove one or more elements of the prima facie case for battery, Evan loses regardless of Frank's failure to put on evidence of an affirmative defense. Choice **A** is conditional, telling us that Evan wins *if* he can prove his prima facie case. Note that this answer says nothing about the affirmative defense, but it doesn't have to. You already know that Frank will bear the burden of proof on this issue, and Frank put on no evidence here. So Evan is going to win if he can make out his prima facie case.

D.   The Closer: Understanding the interaction of the prima facie case and defenses

Now that you have learned the distinction between the plaintiff's burden to prove all the elements of the prima facie case, and the defendant's burden to prove any affirmative defenses *if* plaintiff first proves the prima facie case, it is time to put your knowledge to the test.

> **QUESTION 4. Blowing Smoke.** Guadalupe lives near the Hi-Tech-Co computer chip manufacturing plant. As a by-product of the manufacturing process, the plant produces a great deal of chemical waste. Guadalupe contracts a rare cancer, and she believes that she contracted the cancer through exposure to the chemical waste at the Hi-Tech-Co plant. Guadalupe sues Hi-Tech-Co for the tort of negligence. Her lawyer knows that the hardest part of the prima facie case to prove is actual causation: it will be tough to demonstrate that it was exposure to the plant's chemicals, and not some other genetic or environmental factor, that caused Guadalupe's cancer. For this reason, Guadalupe's lawyer devotes all of her attention at trial to proof of "actual causation," one of the elements of the tort of negligence (and indeed of all torts). At the close of trial, the jury, after considering the evidence, concludes that indeed it was exposure to the chemicals at the plant, and not some other factor, that caused Guadalupe's cancer. The court should:
>
> A. Rule for Guadalupe unless Hi-Tech-Co proved an affirmative defense by a preponderance of the evidence.

B. Rule for Guadalupe whether or not Hi-Tech-Co raised an affirmative defense.

C. Rule for Hi-Tech-Co whether or not it raised an affirmative defense.

D. Rule for Hi-Tech-Co only if it proved an affirmative defense by a preponderance of the evidence.

ANALYSIS. Choices **A** and **B** are incorrect for the same reason. Guadalupe cannot win this case because she failed to prove *each* of the elements of the tort of negligence by a preponderance of the evidence. Guadalupe's lawyer fell into the trap that you must avoid: focusing on the hard issue in the case (in this example, actual causation) to the detriment of the rest of the case. It doesn't matter if Guadalupe's lawyer put on the best evidence imaginable on the question of actual causation if she did not put on proof meeting each and every element of the tort of negligence. The fact pattern tells us that the lawyer devoted "all of her attention at trial" to actual causation. On these facts, there's no way that Guadalupe can win because the jury must find for Hi-Tech-Co. Plaintiff has not put on proof of all the elements of her prima facie case.

Choice **D** is wrong because it provides that Hi-Tech-Co wins "only if" it put on proof of an affirmative defense. Because Guadalupe failed to prove all but one of the elements of her prima facie case for negligence, Guadalupe will lose even if Hi-Tech-Co does nothing at trial. Thus, Choice **C** is the correct answer: Hi-Tech-Co wins whether or not it put on any affirmative defenses at trial.

Indeed, in the real world, this case never would have gone to a jury. As you will learn in your Civil Procedure class, if plaintiff fails to put on any evidence to prove at least one of the elements of its cause of action, the defendant will make a motion at the end of the plaintiff's presentation of evidence (called the "case-in-chief") for the court to take the question of the defendant's liability away from the jury and rule for the defendant right there and then. Worse for Guadalupe's lawyer, she has opened up herself to a possible tort suit against *her* brought by Guadalupe for attorney malpractice! But now that you have analyzed this question, I am confident this is a mistake you will never make.

✸ Rick's picks

PART I

Intentional Torts

3

Physical Invasions: (Harmful) Battery, Trespass to Land, Trespass to Chattels, and Conversion

CHAPTER OVERVIEW

A. Introduction to (harmful) battery

Imagine that Ira is drinking in a bar and he doesn't like the way Jay—a stranger—is looking at him. Ira walks over to Jay and punches Jay in the nose, breaking Jay's nose. Jay has medical bills, misses time from work, and is in pain. Jay may demand compensation from Ira for his losses. If Ira does not pay, Jay may sue Ira in court, and if Jay does so, he is likely to sue for the tort of *battery* (and perhaps other torts as well).

Our intuition is that Jay should be able to recover damages for this harm. There are many reasons society would want to give Jay such a right. First, we might have a theory of *corrective justice* that says that when one harms another (perhaps especially when one does so for no good reason) one has a moral (and legal) obligation to *compensate* the injured person for the harm inflicted. Such arguments go back to Aristotle and the eighteenth-century philosopher Immanuel Kant, and are moral arguments about right and wrong. These corrective justice theories say that Ira owes Jay *compensation* regardless of the social consequences.[1] It is a judgment that punching someone for no good reason is morally wrong, and the person who does so should do what he can to put the injured person as much as he can back to where he was before the injury. (We might want to *punish* Ira for his bad conduct over and above any compensation — but that's a topic for later in the book and for a course on criminal law.)

Second, society might have some very practical reasons to want to allow Jay to be able to sue Ira for damages in such circumstances:[2]

- By giving Jay the right to sue, we make it less likely he will retaliate, thereby providing the law as an alternative to self-help that could escalate violence in society.
- The potential for a tort suit could *deter* people like Ira from acting on their violent impulses.
- If society did not give someone like Jay the right to sue, Jay and others would have to invest in defensive measures to prevent harm to themselves. Maybe Jay would stay home, or choose to buy a gun. These costs might be *inefficient* in that they cause people to invest in protection rather than put their resources toward more productive use. (We will see many more economic arguments like this later in the book.) A rule allowing Jay to recover damages will make him less likely to overly invest in protective measures.

As you can see, there are many arguments in favor of allowing Jay to recover damages for the punch in the nose; indeed, it is hard to see a policy argument against allowing Jay to do so. (Elsewhere in the book we will see conflicting policy arguments and will face a harder choice over tort rules.) Tort law takes that policy decision and translates it into specific rules aimed to separate cases in which someone like Jay can recover and cases in which someone like Jay cannot. It requires proof of the elements of the tort or torts that Jay wishes to pursue, along with any potential affirmative defenses.

---

1. Scholars sometimes describe such arguments as *non-consequentialist* on this basis. An even fancier word for theories based on obligation and not social consequences is *deontological.* I'll try to avoid such jargon in this book, but your Torts professor may not. So you may need to be familiar with such terms.
2. Scholars sometimes describe these practical reasons as *consequentialist* or *instrumental* because they choose a rule *based upon the social consequences* the choice will have.

QUESTION 1. **This Kant Be Right.**   With which statement about actions for battery is a corrective justice theorist most likely to agree?

A. Society should allow actions for battery to save the police money.
B. Whether or not allowing battery actions will save the police money is irrelevant to the question whether or not the law should allow such actions.
C. Society should allow actions for battery only if it can be proven that such actions promote economic efficiency.
D. Society should allow actions for battery to prevent violent escalations.

ANALYSIS.   Of all of these choices, three of them are about the *consequences* of allowing actions for battery: Choice **A** looks at cost savings, Choice **C** looks at the related question of economic efficiency, and Choice **D** says such a law is justified if it prevents additional violence. In contrast, Choice **B** rejects the consequentalist arguments about battery. To someone like a corrective justice theorist concerned about *right and wrong*, issues such as cost savings to the police are irrelevant to the moral question. Choice **B** is right.

B.   The elements of battery

As we saw in the last chapter, every tort has the same structure: the plaintiff must prove her prima facie case for each tort by a preponderance of the evidence and, if the plaintiff does so, the plaintiff wins unless the defendant can raise an affirmative defense. You will recall that the structure of the prima facie case for all torts requires plaintiff to prove that:

1. **Defendant engaged in the requisite tortious conduct**
2. Actual causation
3. Proximate causation
4. Damages

As we talk about different torts (or "causes of action") through the beginning of this book, we focus only on the first part of the prima facie case (which I have put in bold above): that the defendant has engaged in the requisite tortious conduct. We will leave the questions of actual cause, proximate cause, and damages for Parts III and VI of this book. For each tort, the tortious conduct portion of the prima facie case will differ: what it takes to prove the requisite tortious conduct for battery is different from that for negligence or trespass. Moreover, even for a particular tort, such as battery, jurisdictions do not always agree exactly upon the elements to be proven or exactly what they mean. Jurisdictions also sometimes differ regarding applicable affirmative defenses as well. I will highlight important jurisdictional splits on these issues throughout this book.

We begin with the tortious conduct portion of the prima facie case for the tort of battery. As with most of the torts covered in this book, our first step in considering the elements of the tort of battery is the approach of the Restatement of Torts. The Restatement is an effort by the American Law Institute (ALI) to codify the law. No state has adopted the Restatement as a whole as its law, but the Restatement's approach and analysis has been influential in the development of the law and its approach often is cited and discussed by courts considering issues addressed by the Restatement. ALI is in the midst of issuing various portions of the third iteration of the Restatement of Torts, and much of the analysis of this book draws from completed portions of the Restatement (Third) of Torts. When it comes to intentional torts, however, we will focus on the specifics rules of the Restatement (Second) of Torts, which have been reaffirmed in the Third Restatement.[3]

The Restatement divides the tort of battery into "harmful" battery and "offensive" battery. We begin with the formal statement of the elements — often termed the "black letter" — of the tort of harmful battery in the Restatement (Second) of Torts § 13:

> An actor is subject to liability to another for battery if
> (a) he acts intending to cause a harmful or offensive contact with the person of the other or a third person, or imminent apprehension of such a contact, and
> (b) a harmful contact with the person of the other directly or indirectly results.

Consider again the Ian-Jay hypothetical discussed at the beginning of this chapter. Under those facts, could Jay make out the tortious conduct portion of the prima facie case for battery as defined in Restatement section 13? In answering this question, you might be tempted to "eyeball" the rule, get the gist of it, and reach a conclusion. *Resist this temptation!* The only way you are going to succeed in answering a question like this is to carefully read and analyze the Restatement black letter, word by word, breaking it down into its elements. Even then, as we'll see, the analysis remains incomplete because an important part of the prima facie case for battery, plaintiff's lack of consent, is missing from the Restatement's black letter.

So if we broke down the elements of section 13 (and added the consent point), we would see that a plaintiff has to prove five elements to meet the requirements of the tortious conduct portion of the prima facie case for battery:

1. The defendant (referred to here as "an actor") has acted

---

3. The Third Restatement of Torts "does not address the specific intentional torts or their elements. That law has not undergone significant changes since the Second Restatement of Torts and remains governed by it." Rest. (3d) Torts: Liability for Physical Harm: Intro. (2005).

2. The defendant intended to cause

   a. a harmful contact; or
   b. an offensive contact; or
   c. plaintiff's imminent apprehension of harmful or offensive contact

3. with the person of the other or a third person
4. and harmful contact has resulted.
5. Plaintiff did not consent (this element is absent from section 13, but part of the prima facie case, as we will see).

This is a lot to consider, making the question much more complicated than your eyeballing of the question would show. We now turn to each of these elements, and explore them in detail.

1. The Act Requirement

An act is a "voluntary muscular contraction." A defendant does not act if the movement is involuntary. If the movement is the result of a seizure or reflex, it is no act. Similarly, if a person makes some movement while sleepwalking, it is not an act. But any voluntary movement is an act, even if there is no intention to make contact. On the facts of the Ian-Jay hypothetical, Ian certainly acted. He was not asleep or having a seizure. The movement of his hand was voluntary.

QUESTION 2. Kevin the Ping-Pong Ball.   Kevin is sitting on a bar stool between Lena and Maurice. Lena and Maurice start arguing, and Lena pushes Kevin into Maurice, knocking Maurice off his bar stool and onto the floor. Maurice gets up and shoves Kevin into Lena. Both Lena and Maurice later sue Kevin for battery. Will the lawsuits be successful?

A. Yes as to Maurice's suit against Kevin, because Lena was the aggressor.
B. Yes as to Lena's suit against Kevin, if Maurice provoked Lena.
C. Yes as to both Maurice and Lena's suits against Kevin.
D. No as to both suits against Kevin.

ANALYSIS. Kevin was a passive instrument of both Lena and Maurice. Kevin did not act because he made no voluntary muscular contraction. Without such an act, Kevin cannot be liable for battery because neither Lena nor Maurice can make out the first element of the tortious conduct portion of the prima facie case for battery. For this reason, Choice **D** is right. Choices **A**, **B**, and **C** are each wrong. Choices **A** and **B** are wrong because it is irrelevant who the aggressor is between Lena and Maurice for purposes of figuring out *Kevin*'s liability. (It could be very relevant, as we will see, if they sue each other for battery.) Choice **C** is wrong because Kevin cannot be liable for battery absent an act.

2. Intent

Intent is very tricky when it comes to intentional torts, making it the first difficult issue that many law students face in a Torts class. To be liable for battery (at least under the Restatement), a defendant must intend to make a harmful or offensive contact or to put plaintiff in imminent apprehension of such contact. Looking closely, there are at least two subquestions hidden inside the intent requirement. First, what is the mental state that is required to meet the intent requirement? Second, what does one have to intend to do?

On the mental state, it is certainly enough to show that a defendant acted with the *purpose* of causing a harmful contact. Thus, if Ian slugs Jay in the bar because he thinks Jay looked at him funny, that intent would surely be sufficient under the Restatement. But Jay need not prove purpose in order to meet the intent requirement. Under the Third Restatement, "a person acts with the intent to produce a consequence" if the person either has the "purpose of producing that consequence" or "acts knowing the consequence is substantially certain to occur." REST. (3D) TORTS: LIABILITY FOR PHYSICAL HARM § 1. Suppose Nancy, without any specific purpose to cause injury, shoots her BB gun into a crowd at a mall, hitting Oscar. Nancy has acted, by using a voluntary muscular contraction to pull the trigger, and she had the intent to cause a harmful contact with Oscar because even if she did not have the purpose to hit Oscar, she was substantially certain that harmful contact with someone in the crowd would occur. That would be enough to meet the intent requirement.

QUESTION 3. Floored.   Perry, a 10-year-old, is at a party for his great aunt's 80th birthday. One of his great aunt's friends, Quincy, is about to sit down on a folding chair. Quincy is very old and moving very slowly. Perry comes over as Quincy is in the process of sitting down and, while seeing Quincy starting to sit down, moves the folding chair away, sitting on it himself. Perry does so because he wants to sit down, not because he wants to hurt Quincy. Quincy falls to the floor, breaking his hip. If Quincy sues Perry for battery, can Quincy prove that Perry had the requisite intent?

A. No, because Perry did not act.
B. No, because Perry did not have the purpose to cause Quincy to hit the floor.
C. Yes, because Perry acted with the knowledge that Quincy was substantially certain to hit the floor.
D. Yes, but only if Perry could fully appreciate how harmful a fall can be to an 80-year-old person.

ANALYSIS.   The question asks you to focus on intent, not on the rest of the tortious conduct portion of the prima facie case for battery. Choice **A** is therefore incorrect because the question whether Perry acted is separate from the question whether or not he had the requisite intent. Moreover, Perry did act because his moving of the chair was a voluntary muscular contraction. Choice **B**, though correctly focused on intent, is incorrect for a different reason: it is not necessary for Perry to have the purpose to cause Quincy to hit the floor in order for Perry to have the intent necessary for battery. Choice **D** is wrong because it gives the wrong standard for intent. It is not necessary that Perry appreciate the harmfulness of his actions in order for him to have the requisite intent for battery. Note that the fact that Perry is a child does not relieve him of liability for battery: Only very small children who are too young to act with the knowledge (or have the purpose) that a consequence is substantially certain to result would be able to escape liability for battery on intent grounds. This leaves us with Choice **C**. Perry acted with the knowledge that Quincy was substantially certain to make contact with the floor. We know that because the fact pattern tells us that Perry acted to move the chair despite the fact that he saw Quincy starting to sit down. That's enough for the jury to infer that Perry had the knowledge that contact was substantially certain to occur. The fact that Perry did so for his own purposes — to be able to sit down on the chair — and not for the purpose of causing Quincy injury does not save Perry from liability for battery.[4]

We have now seen that the mental state required to meet the intent requirement for the intentional torts is that one acts with the "*purpose* to produce the consequence" or "*knowledge* that the consequence is substantially certain to occur." But what "consequence"? That consequence differs by tort. According to the Restatement, for a harmful battery a defendant must intend to cause a harmful contact, an offensive contact, or to put the plaintiff in imminent apprehension of a harmful or offensive contact. Let's look at each of these in turn, then look at an approach that rejects the Restatement's view of intention.

Harmful contact. A defendant may be liable for battery if he acts intending to cause a contact with someone else that causes *physical harm.* (It is true that emotional harm is also "harmful," but in this context *harmful* is a term of art limited to physical harm.) So when Ian punches Jay in the nose because Ian doesn't like how Jay looked at him, a jury is likely to infer that Ian intended to cause a harmful contact. How so? Isn't it possible that Ian did not intend a harmful conduct and was just interested in touching Jay's nose in a non-harmful way? No, that's not possible. This leads to an important lesson that first-year law students need to learn early: Don't check your common sense at the door of the law school. It is very easy to make a facially plausible but flatly wrong argument by imagining a world that

---

4. The facts of this case are based loosely upon *Garratt v. Dailey*, 279 P.2d 1091 (Wash. 1955), a staple in many Torts casebooks.

doesn't exist. Jurors live in the real world and know that if Ian walked over to Jay in a bar because of how Jay was looking at Ian and punched Jay in the nose, that Ian intended to make a harmful contact.

QUESTION 4. Off Key. Professor Neher, a music professor, is having dinner with Ms. White, one of his students, and her family. While White is sitting down, Professor Neher walks up behind her and touches her back with both of his hands in a movement later described as one a pianist would make in striking and lifting the fingers from the keyboard. Neher did so to show her the sensation of certain forms of playing. Unfortunately, Ms. White suffered severe nerve damage, requiring surgery. Did Professor Neher have intent to cause a harmful contact sufficient for a cause of action for battery under the Restatement approach?

A. No, because though Professor Neher intended to make contact with White, he did not intend harmful contact.

B. No, because Professor Neher did not intend contact with White.

C. Yes, because the contact resulted in harm.

D. Yes, because he engaged in a voluntary muscular contraction.

ANALYSIS. Under the Restatement approach, the relevant question is whether Professor Neher had the intent to cause a harmful contact with White. Choice **B** is incorrect because Neher certainly intended contact with White; there's nothing in the facts suggesting that he made contact *inadvertently* with her. Moreover, under the Restatement approach it is not enough for the defendant to intend *contact*. The defendant must intend to cause a harmful or offensive contact (or to put plaintiff in imminent apprehension of such contact). Choice **C** is a terrible distractor likely to trip up a number of students. You need to distinguish between the requisite *intent* and the requisite *result*. It is in fact true that for a successful battery a contact must result. But the question did not ask you about battery generally—it asked you if Professor Neher had the intent to make a harmful contact. So Choice **C** is wrong because it answers the wrong question. Choice **D** is wrong because it too answers the wrong question. Choice **D** is focused on the question whether or not Professor Neher acted. He did act, because his hand movements were a voluntary muscular contraction. But that does not tell us whether Professor Neher had the requisite intent. This leaves us with Choice **A**. Under these facts, unlike the situation of Ian and Jay in the bar, it is much less likely that the defendant here had an intention to cause a physical harm to the plaintiff. Here, it was a social setting, and it appears that Professor Neher was trying to exhibit the proper way to play a piano, not to cause any physical harm. Now this is not to say that Professor Neher cannot be liable for battery; as we will see, he still might be under a few different theories. But it seems most unlikely that White would be able to prove that Professor Neher intended a harmful contact when he touched her.[5]

Offensive Contact. A defendant may be liable for battery even if the defendant did not intend to cause a harmful contact. In particular, the defendant can be liable for battery if he intends to cause an offensive contact. One of the most famous American battery cases at least possibly involves such a scenario. In *Vosburg v. Putney*, 50 N.W. 403 (Wis. 1891), an 11-year-old and a 14-year-old sat across from each other in a classroom. The first bell had rung, but the teacher had not yet begun class. The 11-year-old moved his foot across the aisle to kick the 14-year-old in the shin. Unfortunately, the 14-year-old had a prior infection in his leg, and the kick caused the infection to spread, leading to permanent loss of use of the leg. Even though the jury found that at the time the 11-year-old kicked the 14-year-old he did not intend to cause harm, the Wisconsin Supreme Court held that the 11-year-old could still be liable for battery.[6] Its opinion is particularly unhelpful in its discussion of intent, which appeared to rely on a kind of circular logic.

In any event, today the case is read in at least two ways. One way of reading the case is that the 11-year-old can be liable because he intended to make an offensive contact. The Restatement defines "offensive" by a reference to community standards: Conduct is offensive if it "offends a reasonable sense of personal dignity." REST. (2D) TORTS § 19. At least arguably, a child kicking another across the table after the first bell had rung offends a reasonable person's sense of dignity. A second reading of *Vosburg* is that it was enough that the 11-year-old intended contact, and that the contact was nonconsensual. That's the approach that the Idaho Supreme Court took in the *White* case, the subject of Question 4 above. To that court, it did not matter that Professor Neher intended neither harmful contact nor offensive contact: he intended *contact* with Ms. White, contact that White did not consent to, and that was enough. So some jurisdictions reject the Restatement's intent standard for battery in favor of proof of an intent to cause contact.

QUESTION 5. Throw in the Towel. Rick invites Steve to his house for dinner. Rick and Steve are old friends, and they often play practical jokes on each other. Before Steve arrived, Rick took one of his bathroom hand towels out into his backyard and rubbed it in the mud. He carefully folded the

---

5. The facts here are based upon *White v. University of Idaho*, 797 P.2d 108 (Idaho 1990).
6. The court also held that it did not matter that the 11-year-old could not have foreseen the extent of the damage he was going to cause with his kick. Endorsing the "thin skull" or "eggshell" plaintiff rule, the court said that foreseeability of the extent of harm was not required for a defendant to be liable in tort. Rather, a defendant takes the plaintiff as he finds him. If you happen to knock Humpty Dumpty off the wall rather than a sturdier person, you will pay for all the damages that you cause. We will return to this issue when we consider proximate cause in Part III and damages in Part VI.

towel so that the dirt would not be visible. Before dinner, Steve uses the bathroom to wash up, and rubs the towel on his hands and face, getting dirt all over himself. Rick and Steve have a good laugh. Unfortunately, the dirt in the towel contained some powerful germs, and Steve got very sick from his exposure through the practical joke. Steve sues Rick for battery. Can Steve prove that Rick had the requisite intent for a battery claim?

A. No under the Restatement approach, because Steve and Rick were friends at the time of the incident.

B. No under the Restatement approach, because Rick did not intend that Steve have a harmful contact with the towel.

C. Yes under the Restatement approach, because Rick intended that Steve have a harmful contact with the towel.

D. Yes under the Restatement approach, even though Rick did not intend that Steve have a harmful contact with the towel.

ANALYSIS. Choice **A** is the easiest wrong answer to eliminate. Whether or not the two of them were friends before this incident is not relevant to the question whether Rick had the requisite intent at the time of the incident. Choice **B** is wrong because even though Rick did not intend to cause physical harm to Steve under the Restatement, he can still be liable if he intended an offensive contact or to put Steve in imminent apprehension of such contact. Choice **C** is the flip side of Choice **B**, but it is also wrong. By putting dirt on a towel, Rick did not intend that Steve have a harmful contact. Choice **D** is therefore the best answer. Even though Rick did not intend for Steve to have a harmful contact with the towel, he certainly intended that Steve had contact with the towel (that's why he put it back and folded it in its proper way), and there is a strong argument that placing a dirty towel in a bathroom for someone to use would cause a contact that would offend a reasonable person's sense of dignity. Now maybe it would not offend *Steve's* dignity, given that Rick and Steve have had a history together of playing practical jokes, but the standard here is a *reasonable person's* sense of dignity, an objective standard. The fact that Steve might not have been offended could be relevant to an element discussed below, lack of consent.

Imminent Apprehension of Harmful or Offensive Contact. Even if a defendant who makes a harmful contact did not intend to make a harmful contact or intend to make an offensive contact — indeed even if defendant did not intend to make any contact whatsoever — that defendant may still be liable for battery if he intended to put the plaintiff in "imminent apprehension" of a harmful or offensive contact. The words "imminent apprehension" are a term of art that we will discuss more fully in connection with the tort of assault. For now, read those words as "immediate expectation."

So suppose, back in the bar, Ian moves to punch Jay in the face, but he does not intend to make contact; he just wants Jay to *think* he's about to get punched. If Ian makes a mistake and actually punches Jay, Ian has the requisite intent for battery despite the fact he did not intend (harmful or offensive) contact. He intended to put Ian in imminent apprehension of a harmful contact, which suffices for battery.

QUESTION 6. Throw in the Towel . . . Take II.   Rick invites Steve to his house for dinner. Rick and Steve are old friends, and they often play practical jokes on each other. Before Steve arrived, Rick took one of his bathroom hand towels out into his backyard and rubbed it in the mud. He carefully folded the towel so that the dirt would not be visible. Steve uses the bathroom to wash up before dinner, but does not use the towel, drying his hands on his shirt. Rick then takes the towel out of the bathroom and shows it to Steve, and they both have a good laugh. Then Rick takes the dirty towel and acts as though he is going to shove it in Steve's face — he wants Steve to think the towel will touch him, but he does not intend to actually touch Steve with the towel. As Rick shoves the towel near Steve's face, Steve backs up and trips over a stair in Rick's house, falling and breaking his leg. Steve sues Rick for battery. Can Steve prove that Rick had the requisite intent for a battery claim?

A. No under the Restatement approach, because Rick did not intend contact with Steve.

B. No under the Restatement approach, unless Steve feared the towel would cause him physical harm.

C. Yes under the Restatement approach, even though Rick did not intend that Steve have a harmful contact with the towel.

D. Yes under the Restatement approach, because Rick intended that Steve have an offensive or harmful contact with the towel.

ANALYSIS.   Choice **A** is wrong because a defendant under the Restatement need not intend to make any contact in order to be liable for battery. It is enough that the plaintiff is put in imminent apprehension of contact. Choice **B** is wrong because imminent apprehension is not the same as fear (it is an expectation) and because it is enough to have an immediate expectation of *offensive* contact if not harmful contact. Choice **D** is incorrect because the facts tell us that Rick did not intend a contact, much less an offensive contact. Choice **C** is therefore correct because Rick can be liable for battery if he intended to put Steve in imminent apprehension of an offensive contact. Now you might have been thrown off because the ultimate contact that resulted in this question resulted from the trip and fall rather than touching the actual object held by Rick. That question is relevant to a different part of the prima facie case: whether contact *resulted* directly or indirectly. But look at the call of the question. It asks only if Rick had the requisite *intent* for battery, not whether Steve can prove the entire prima facie case for battery.

3. Person of the other or third person

Back to our bar fight between Ian and Jay: Imagine that all the facts are the same as our original hypothetical, except Ian punches Jay's dog Fido rather than Jay. Would that conduct meet the tortious conduct portion of the prima facie case for battery? The answer is no. It is true that Ian's conduct was an *act*; it was a voluntary muscular contraction. A jury could fairly determine as well that Ian intended harmful conduct: He wouldn't slug Fido in the bar if he were not intending harm. But it is required for a battery that the defendant's intention be directed to the "person of the other" or a "third person." By "person of the other," the Restatement means either a part of plaintiff's body or something so connected with his body that it is considered a part of him, such as plaintiff's eyeglasses or cane. "Third person" means another person. And as much as we like Fido, Fido is not a person. Intent to make a harmful or offensive contact with a dog (or to put a dog in imminent apprehension of such contact) will not result in a battery.

You might protest that such conduct *should* be a battery. After all, Fido belongs to Jay and it seems morally wrong to harm Jay's pet. We can also construct a whole set of instrumental reasons why such conduct should constitute a tort. These are good arguments, and it may well be that by striking Jay's dog, Ian has committed at least one tort. But what Ian has *not* done is commit a battery.

The "third person" concept comes into play when a defendant intends to make a harmful or offensive contact with one *person* (or to put that person in imminent apprehension), but actually hits another. So if Jay ducks when Ian takes a swing at him, and Ian accidentally hits Tina, another bar patron, Tina can prove the tortious conduct portion of the prima facie case for battery: Ian acted, intending to cause a harmful contact with a third person, Jay, and harmful contact resulted without Tina's consent.

Wait a minute, you might say. You said that Ian *accidentally* hit Tina; that means he did not intend to cause a harmful contact to her. Maybe that conduct should allow Tina to sue for another tort such as negligence, but why battery? The answer is that Tina can take advantage of the concept of *transferred intent*. The intent that Ian directed toward Jay goes to Tina's benefit in her battery claim against Ian.

QUESTION 7. **High Speed Chase.**   Ursula has just robbed a bank, and she is being chased by Vic, a police officer. Both are driving down the highway in their automobiles. Ursula exits, followed closely by Vic. Ursula ends up on a dead-end street. She stops and Vic pulls up closely behind her. Vic tells Ursula to step out of the car, but she doesn't. Instead, she puts her car into reverse suddenly and forcefully. Her car rams Vic's car, and Ursula gets away until she is caught a few minutes later by other police officers. Vic has sustained three broken ribs. Vic sues Ursula for battery. Can Vic prove the prima facie case for battery?

A. Yes, if a car is considered a "person of the other."
B. Yes, because Ursula intended harm.
C. No, because a person cannot commit a battery with an automobile.
D. No, unless Ursula intended to put Vic in imminent apprehension of harmful contact.

ANALYSIS.   Choice **B** is a very common wrong answer for students. It is not enough that a defendant sued for battery intended *harm*. There must be an intent to make a harmful contact (or an offensive contact, or to put the plaintiff in imminent apprehension of such contact). Ursula could ram her car into Vic's fence, intending him harm. But that would not be a battery because a fence is not a person of the other or a third person. Choice **C** includes an incorrect statement of the law: one certainly can commit a battery with an automobile. If Vic were standing outside his car, and Ursula intentionally ran into him with her car, every court in the country would say that the fact that Ursula used an automobile to create the harmful contact does not protect Ursula from the battery charge. Choice **D** is wrong. To be liable for battery, Ursula could have intended a harmful contact with Vic. She did not need to have intended to put Vic in imminent apprehension of contact. The strongest argument against Vic being able to make out the prima facie case for battery is that a car is so far removed from a person so as not to be considered—like eyeglasses or a cane—as part of the "person of the other." Choice **A** is right because it is conditional: Vic can prove the elements of the tortious conduct portion of the prima facie case for battery *if* the car is considered the "person of the other."

4. Harmful contact directly or indirectly results

We are back in the bar, and Ian is taking a slug at Jay. Ian, being a little drunk, tries to hit Jay in the face but misses him completely, avoiding contact. In such circumstances, Jay cannot sue Ian for battery. Ian acted, he intended to cause a harmful contact with Jay's face, which is part of the person of the other, but harmful contact did not result. In the absence of contact, there can be no battery.

That's not to say that Jay has no cause of action. As we will see in the next chapter, he likely has a case for the tort of assault. But it is not a battery.

Suppose that Ian's aim was slightly better, and his fist just grazed Jay's nose, causing no physical damage. In that case, the Restatement would say that this is not a *harmful* battery under Restatement section 13. By "harmful," the Restatement is referring to physical harm, not emotional or dignitary harm. However, as we will see in the next chapter, under the Restatement Ian's conduct could be considered an *offensive* battery so long as Ian's actions resulted in an offensive contact.

Though many batteries are the result of direct contact (as when defendant's fist connects with plaintiff's nose), contact may also occur indirectly. So the child who pulls the chair out from under the person who is about to sit down is liable for a battery when that action indirectly leads to the person's harmful contact with the floor.

> **QUESTION 8. You Could Have Knocked Me Over with a Feather.**
> Walter doesn't like Xavier very much. To annoy Xavier while he snoozes on a park bench, Walter puts a feather up to the tip of Xavier's nose and moves it around. The feather causes Xavier to wake up and sneeze a powerful sneeze, knocking Xavier off the bench and onto the cement on the ground. Xavier breaks his kneecap. Can Xavier prove the elements of the tortious conduct portion of the prima facie case for harmful battery?
>
> **A.** Yes, because Walter had a bad motive and Xavier was injured.
> **B.** Yes, because the contact resulted in indirect harmful contact.
> **C.** No, because Walter intended an offensive contact, not a harmful contact.
> **D.** No, because Walter did not directly cause Xavier's contact with the floor.

ANALYSIS.   Choice **A** is incorrect. "Bad motive" is not a required element of battery; the fact that Xavier was "injured" also is not specific enough. For there to be a harmful battery, Xavier must be injured through a direct or indirect harmful contact. Choice **C** is tempting, but it is wrong. As we saw above, a defendant may intend to make an offensive contact rather than a harmful contact; so long as it leads to a harmful contact, a harmful battery claim can be successful. Choice **D** is wrong because indirect contact is enough. Walter need not make the direct contact that causes the injury. Choice **B** is therefore correct; the conduct was an indirect harmful contact, which satisfies the tortious conduct portion of the prima facie case for battery.

5. No consent

If you look back at how the Restatement describes the tortious conduct portion of the prima facie case for battery, it looks like we are done. We have established that a plaintiff must prove that the defendant:

1. acted,

2. intending to cause a harmful contact, an offensive contact, or to put plaintiff in imminent apprehension of a harmful or offensive contact
3. with the person of the other or a third person, and
4. harmful contact results.

As they say on those infomercials, "but wait, there's more." You wouldn't know it from just reading the black letter law, but Comment "d" to Restatement section 13 explains that "the absence of consent is a matter essential to the cause of action [for harmful battery], and it is uniformly held that it must be proved by the plaintiff as a necessary part of his case." There is no excuse for the Restatement drafters to have failed to put into the black letter the requirement that plaintiff did not consent, but let's put that to the side. It is now time to master the rules related to proof of no consent.

We have been confident that if Ian intentionally punches Jay in the face at the bar, Jay would be able to prove the tortious conduct portion of the prima facie case for battery. But suppose that Ian and Jay were professional boxers. At that point, everything changes. True, Jay could still prove that Ian acted, intending to cause harmful contact with Jay's person, and, if the punch lands, that harmful contact resulted. Yet no court would allow the battery case to go forward because of Jay's *consent.* Two professional boxers voluntarily and knowingly agree to such contact, and in such circumstances, the prima facie case will fail.

Consent to contact can be *express* or *implied.* Express consent exists when a person in writing or orally agrees to the contact. For example, the professional boxers likely signed a contract releasing each other (as well as the fight's organizers and promoters) from liability from any damages resulting from harmful contacts.

Consent can also be *implied in fact* from the circumstances. In the *Vosburg* case, involving the kick across the desk that resulted in plaintiff's loss of the use of a leg, the court distinguished a kick in the classroom from a kick on the playground, noting the "implied license" of the playground. A child who goes onto a playground where other children are playing and touching each other impliedly consents to touching through the action of voluntarily going on the playground. Express consent through words is not necessary. Sometimes it may be a difficult question for the jury whether a person has impliedly consented to being touched.

Courts also sometimes speak of *implied in law* consent, but this is a misnomer. It is more proper to think of this situation as the court excusing defendants' touching of the plaintiff without plaintiff's consent *on policy grounds.* Imagine, for example, that Yolanda has a heart attack at a restaurant and is unconscious. Zelda, another restaurant patron who does not know Yolanda, performs CPR, breaking one of Yolanda's ribs. Whether or not Yolanda could prove the rest of the tortious conduct portion of the prima facie case for battery (you should see that meeting the intent requirement may be difficult), courts on policy grounds say that the prima facie case fails because consent to touching is "implied in law." This is a rule that makes sense: an unconscious person needing emergency first aid cannot consent to a touching, but virtually all such persons would want such aid to be given. A rule that prevents Good Samaritans like Zelda from being sued for battery will encourage the giving of emergency first aid.[7] The technical way the law protects people like Zelda is through the fiction that the unconscious person consented.

Even when a person expressly or impliedly consents to a touching, that consent may be limited in scope. The child on the playground impliedly consenting to a game of tag does not consent to a punch in the jaw, and the professional boxer who expressly consents to a punch in the jaw does not consent to being shot with a gun. As with the question whether or not a plaintiff has consented, the jury must decide in certain cases whether the defendant's touching exceeded the *scope of the consent*.

QUESTION 9. Doctor, Doctor.   Andre is having trouble with his hearing. He goes to Dr. Beth, a surgeon, who recommends surgery on Andre's left ear. Andre signs a consent form to surgery on his left ear. While Andre is under anesthesia, Dr. Beth examines both of Andre's ears closely. She determines that Andre's right ear is in worse shape than his left ear, and performs surgery on the right ear only. Unfortunately, the surgery does not go well and Andre's hearing is now worse than before.

Can Andre prove the tortious conduct portion of the prima facie case for harmful battery?

A. No, because Andre expressly consented to surgery on his right ear.
B. No, because consent is implied in law due to Andre's unconsciousness.
C. Yes, because express consent must always be in writing.
D. Yes, if Dr. Beth's actions went beyond the scope of Andre's consent.

ANAYLYSIS.   Choice **A** is wrong because the facts tell us that Andre expressly consented only to surgery on his left ear. As explained, there may be an argument his consent to surgery on the *right* ear should be implied in fact, but that would not count as express consent. Choice **B** is tempting, but wrong. This is not like the Yolanda-Zelda Good Samaritan situation where there was no ability to obtain the consent of the unconscious person. Dr. Beth could have asked Andre for broader consent before Andre was unconscious due to the anesthesia. Choice **C** misstates the law and is irrelevant on the facts. First, express consent can be oral; it need not be in writing. In any case, whether

---

7. As we will see in Chapter 11 on affirmative duties in negligence, under the common law Zelda could still be liable for negligence in breaking Yolanda's ribs. But most states have passed "Good Samaritan" statutes granting immunity to Good Samaritans whose negligence causes further injury.

express consent can be oral does not answer the question whether Andre can make his case. Choice **D** is the best answer. Andre's express consent extended only to his left ear; the question here is whether Andre impliedly consented to surgery on the right ear in the event Dr. Beth thought this was in his best interest. In *Mohr v. Williams*, 104 N.W. 12 (Minn. 1905), a case similar to this question, the court sided with the patient over the doctor, viewing the question as one of the patient's autonomy: she, not the doctor, had the right to decide who may touch her body and under what circumstances. Other courts could reach a different conclusion, viewing the decision to undergo surgery as an implied consent for the doctor to take reasonable steps during surgery in what the doctor views as the patient's best interest.

C.   Trespass to land

While battery is one of the torts that protects individuals against unwanted physical interference with their bodies (we will see more in the next chapter), trespass to land is a tort that protects a person's *land* from physical invasion. Under the Restatement (Second) of Torts, section 158, a person who "intentionally . . . enters land in the possession of the other, or causes a thing or a third person to do so" is liable for trespass, even if he does not "cause harm to any legally protected interest" to the other person.[8]

Act. As with battery, there must be an *act*: if Charlie pushes Dina onto Eva's land, Dina cannot be liable for trespass to land because she did not commit a volitional act. (Charlie could well be liable, however.)

Intention. A person must also *intend* to enter the land in possession of another (or cause a thing or a third person to do so). Significantly, the person entering the land need not know it is plaintiff's land. Such a person can be liable for trespass even if the person entering the land makes a reasonable mistake that the land is his, or that the possessor of the land consented, or that he has a privilege to enter the land. REST. (2D) TORTS § 164. It is enough for the defendant to have the intention to enter the land. So unlike (at least the Restatement's treatment of) battery, trespass does not require conduct we would necessarily consider wrongful. If Fred goes onto Gina's land in the reasonable belief it is Fred's land and he cuts down a valuable tree, he still will be liable to Gina.

Enters the Land. If defendant fails to enter the land, even if he intends to do so, there is no trespass (just like a defendant who tries to touch plaintiff's body but fails cannot be liable for a battery).

---

8. The Restatement also provides for liability for someone who "remains on the land" or "fails to remove from the land a thing which he is under a duty to remove," but we ignore these variations here.

No Requirement of Damages. As we shall see in Part VI of the book, in most tort suits a plaintiff must prove he suffered (or is about to suffer)[9] actual damages to succeed. Trespass to land is different, however, in that a trespass that causes no damages can still succeed. Upon proof of the tort, a plaintiff without damages may be awarded "nominal damages" (such as $1) to declare to the world that defendant has trespassed on plaintiff's land. Why allow such a suit to go forward? One reason for this exception is that it allows neighbors with a boundary dispute to resolve it through an action in trespass. It also allows a plaintiff who is consistently harassed by trespassers to obtain relief without proof of damage to the land.

QUESTION 10. Mending Fences.   Halle is driving down the street when her brakes fail. If she would have continued going straight, she would have crashed into a group of school children crossing the street. So she deliberately turns her wheel toward Ida's land, crashing into Ida's fence, and stopping on Ida's front lawn. Ida sues Halle for trespass to land. Can Ida prove the tortious conduct portion of the prima facie case for trespass to land?

A. No, because she did not intend to cause harm.
B. No, because she did not intend to enter Ida's land.
C. No, because by entering Ida's land she averted a greater loss to others.
D. Yes.

ANALYSIS.   Choice **A** is incorrect because one need not intend to cause harm in order to be liable for trespass to land; it is enough that Halle intended to enter the land. Choice **B** is a close second choice, but it is ultimately wrong. The facts tell us that Halle deliberately entered Ida's land. The fact that she has a good reason for doing so, or that she made the choice under the exigencies of the moment, does not defeat Ida's argument that Halle had the intent to enter her land. Choice **C** is tempting but wrong as well. Nothing in the prima facie case allows for such a balancing. Now you might find this terribly unfair because Halle did a good thing choosing to hit the fence rather than the kids. Though that is undoubtedly true, that fact will be relevant to *affirmative defenses* discussed in Chapter 5, and not to the prima facie case. In sum, Halle acted (she voluntarily got behind the wheel and then steered the car when the brakes failed), she intended to enter Ida's land, and in fact entered it. Choice **D** is right.

---

9. Sometimes a plaintiff sues to prevent the defendant from causing future damage. In that case, a court may grant an *injunction*, which is a court order telling defendant to do or not do something.

D.   Trespass to chattels

Chattels are items of personal property, such as shoes, cars, and pets. Just as one can commit a trespass to real property, one can commit a trespass to a chattel as well. A person who acts, intentionally interfering with a chattel in the possession of another, or who dispossesses that person of the chattel, is liable for trespass to chattels. REST. (2D) OF TORTS § 217. For example, I could be liable for trespass to chattels if I see your cell phone on the desk next to you, pick it up, and drop it, causing damage of $100. I *acted* volitionally, *intended* to "intermeddle" with a chattel in your possession, and I did in fact *intermeddle*, causing you *damage*. It does not matter if I believe the item to be mine. REST. (2D) TORTS § 244.

Unlike the tort of trespass to real property, trespass to chattels requires proof of actual damage. So if I pick up the cell phone, look at it for a few minutes, and then I return it to you undamaged, it is likely I will not be found liable for trespass to chattels. One cannot get nominal damages for interference with someone else's chattels. REST. (2D) TORTS § 218. (Perhaps the law has this different treatment of land and chattels because it is generally easier to protect one's chattels from invasion than one's land.)

Now suppose I take your cell phone and I keep it overnight. Depriving you of your personal property for a substantial period of time can be enough of an interference to count as a trespass to chattels, so keeping it overnight may be enough. But if I keep the property from you long enough — and certainly if I take it with no intention to return it — I could be liable for a more serious tort, *conversion*, discussed in Part E.

QUESTION 11. "Car"-ried Away. Jim is walking down the street and sees his friend Kevin's car parked along the curb near his house. Jim notices that the car is unlocked. Intending a practical joke, Jim puts the car in neutral and pushes it around the corner, parking it there. Kevin walks out of his house and cannot find his car. Thinking it is stolen, he calls the police and takes an hour giving the police a report. Then, taking a walk, Kevin notices his car parked around the corner. He is relieved to find his car and he calls the police embarrassed, believing he simply forgot where he parked his car. Jim later tells him about the joke. Kevin is not amused. Can Kevin prove the tortious conduct portion of the prima facie case for trespass to chattels?

A. Yes, if the court believes that by Jim's actions Kevin was deprived of possession for a substantial period of time.
B. Yes, because any intentional intermeddling with another's chattels is actionable as trespass to chattels.
C. No, because Jim intended his conduct as a practical joke.
D. No, unless the car was damaged by the move.

ANALYSIS. Choice **B** overstates the law. Some intentional intermeddlings, such as picking up the cell phone and immediately returning it, are not actionable as trespass to chattels. Choice **C** confuses intent and motivation. Jim may have been motivated, however wrongheadedly, by a desire to play a practical joke. But the question is whether he had the intent to intermeddle with Kevin's property, not his motive for doing so. Choice **D** is incorrect. Though damage to the car would be *sufficient* for the trespass to chattels claim, it is not *necessary*. It is enough if there is interference with a chattel for a substantial enough period of time. Choice **A** is therefore correct.

E.   Conversion

Conversion is closely related to trespass to chattels. A conversion occurs when a defendant intentionally exercises "dominion or control over a chattel which so seriously interferes with the right of another to control it that the actor may justly be required to pay the other the full value of the chattel." REST. (2D) OF TORTS § 222A. Like trespass to chattels, conversion may occur when a defendant does not know of the wrongfulness of the act, as when a defendant takes a plaintiff's cell phone thinking it is his own and then loses it. But conversion and trespass to chattels have two important differences:

1. Conversion requires *serious* interference, while trespass to chattels can arise for less serious interference with plaintiff's property rights. The Restatement gives six factors for determining if the interference is so serious as to count as a conversion.[10]
2. The result of a conversion determination is that defendant pays damages equal to the full value of the chattel. Trespass to chattels, in contrast, leads to damages measured by the loss in value of the item to plaintiff from the defendant's use along with the return of the item to the plaintiff. The Restatement allows mistaken converters (but not intentional converters) to return the item promptly upon discovery of the mistake and pay only trespass to chattel–type damages. REST. (2D) TORTS § 922.

---

10. They are:

    (a) the extent and duration of the actor's exercise of dominion or control;
    (b) the actor's intent to assert a right in fact inconsistent with the other's right of control;
    (c) the actor's good faith;
    (d) the extent and duration of the resulting interference with the other's right of control;
    (e) the harm done to the chattel;
    (f) the inconvenience and expense caused to the other.

REST. (2D) TORTS § 222A(2).

Many cases could be brought as either trespass to chattels or conversion. At the old common law, there were some additional complications, such as the rule that only conversion and not trespass to chattels would be appropriate if the defendant took plaintiff's item not from plaintiff's immediate possession but from the possession of a third party. But these rules have mostly disappeared today.

Some of the more interesting current issues on the scope of conversion relate to body tissue and intangible property. In *Moore v. Regents of the University of California*, 793 P.2d 479 (Cal. 1990), the California Supreme Court held that a person whose blood cells were used by his doctors to develop a commercial biotechnology product could not sue for conversion (though he could sue for two other torts, breach of fiduciary duty and lack of informed consent). Though courts traditionally held that conversion was not available for theft of intangible property, the law is changing. For example, recently the United States Court of Appeals for the Ninth Circuit held that a conversion claim could go forward based upon an Internet domain registrar who gave away plaintiff's valuable domain name (sex.com) after receiving a fraudulent letter directing it to do so. *Kremen v. Cohen*, 337 F.3d 1024 (9th Cir. 2003).

QUESTION 12. Sneaky Sneakers. Donald likes Mickey's brand new fancy sneakers. The shoes sell for $150. Donald takes Mickey's sneakers when he is not looking and wears them for a week, wearing them down and getting them dirty. Mickey then discovers what Donald has done. Mickey sues Donald for conversion. To what damages is Mickey entitled?

A. $150, the reasonable value of the shoes, unless a court determines that Donald's use of the shoes seriously interfered with Mickey's property rights.
B. In addition to return of the shoes, the loss in value of the shoes caused by the wear and tear, if the court determines that Donald's use of the shoes seriously interfered with Mickey's property rights.
C. Either A or B, but not both.
D. Neither A nor B sets forth the correct damages standard.

ANALYSIS. This is a tricky question, because it requires you to understand both the measure of damages for trespass to chattels and conversion *and* the substantive standard for each of these torts. The $150 amount would be correct if this were a conversion, because conversion gives the full value of the thing taken. But Choice **A** is incorrect because of the use of the word "unless." For a court to find conversion there must be such a serious interference with plaintiff's property rights that we award the entire value of the item to plaintiff. So Choice **A** would be correct if the word "unless" were "if." For similar reasons, Choice **B** is wrong. Loss in value of the shoes would be appropriate under trespass to chattels, which would result if the court did not find a serious interference with Mickey's property rights. Because both choices are incorrect, Choice **C** is also incorrect. Choice **D** is the correct answer.

F.   The Closer: Doggedly parsing the elements of torts

If you have worked your way through the examples in this chapter, you have already noticed the point I would like to highlight here: Sometimes conduct might not meet the tortious conduct portion of the prima facie case for one tort, but it might meet it for another tort. Moreover, as we will see in the next chapter, some conduct will satisfy the tortious conduct portion of the prima facie case for multiple torts.

There is one further wrinkle: there is some authority under the common law that intent can be transferred *between and among* the torts of battery, assault, false imprisonment, trespass to land, and trespass to chattels. *See* W. Page Keeton et al., Prosser and Keeton on Torts 36-38 (5th ed. 1984). Thus, one could intend to cause one of these torts and be liable if it leads to another. The Restatement, however, limits this possibility of transfer to assault and battery (more on that in the next chapter), and it is difficult to find any modern cases that actually have found transferred intent between torts outside the context of assault and battery. *See Alteiri v. Colasso*, 362 A.2d. 798, 801 (Conn. 1975).

Here is an example to get you to look at the elements for multiple torts simultaneously, something that is often a feature of multiple-choice exam questions in a Torts course.

> **QUESTION 13. Dogged Pursuit.**   Lauren, a 10-year-old, is playing in a public park. She sees Mark playing with his dog Fido. Lauren is bored, so she starts shooting her BB gun directly at Fido. One of the pellets hits Fido on his side. The pellet breaks one of Fido's ribs. Fido is in great pain, and because of the pain Fido bites Ned, who is jogging by in the park. Ned has to get stitches in his leg. Under the Restatement's approach, who can sue Lauren and for what tort?
>
> **A.** Ned can prove the tortious conduct portion of the prima facie case for battery and Mark can prove the tortious conduct portion of the prima facie case for trespass to chattels.

B. Ned cannot prove the tortious conduct portion of the prima facie case for battery but Mark can prove the tortious conduct portion of the prima facie case for trespass to chattels.

C. Ned can prove the tortious conduct portion of the prima facie case for battery but Mark cannot prove the tortious conduct portion of the prima facie case for trespass to chattels.

D. Ned cannot prove the tortious conduct portion of the prima facie case for battery and Mark cannot prove the tortious conduct portion of the prima facie case for trespass to chattels.

ANALYSIS.   Choices **A** and **C** are incorrect because Ned cannot prove the tortious conduct portion of the prima facie case for battery against Lauren. Lauren acted by voluntarily shooting the BB gun. But she did not intend to make contact with Ned or a third person—she intended to make contact with a dog, and a dog is not a person. Nor did she intend to put any person in imminent apprehension of such contact. Thus, although harmful contact indirectly resulted to Ned and Ned did not consent, the battery claim would fail. Nor does the Restatement allow for transferred intent between the torts of trespass to chattels and battery. (It is, however, at least theoretically possible that some jurisdictions, not following the Restatement, would allow for such transferred intent.)

Mark will have an easier time proving the tortious conduct portion of the tort of trespass to chattels. Lauren acted by intentionally shooting her BB gun at Mark's chattel, Fido. She intended to intermeddle (the facts don't give us any other reason for her to be shooting) and she caused damage, the broken rib. For this reason, Choice **B** is correct and Choice **D** is incorrect.

 # Rick's picks

1. This Kant Be Right	B
2. Kevin the Ping-Pong Ball	D
3. Floored	C
4. Off Key	A
5. Throw in the Towel	D
6. Throw in the Towel . . . Take II	C
7. High Speed Chase	A
8. You Could Have Knocked Me Over with a Feather	B
9. Doctor, Doctor	D
10. Mending Fences	D
11. "Car"-ried Away	A
12. Sneaky Sneakers	D
13. Dogged Pursuit	B

4

Emotional and Dignitary Torts: Assault, Offensive Battery, and False Imprisonment

CHAPTER OVERVIEW
A. Introduction: Why protect dignitary and emotional harms?
B. Assault
C. Offensive battery
D. Transferred intent between assault and battery, and the relationship between the torts
E. False imprisonment
F. The Closer: Choose your tort!
✦ Rick's picks

A. Introduction: Why protect dignitary and emotional harms?

We have already seen that tort law protects individuals from certain physical invasions, at least those constituting a harmful battery or a trespass to land or chattels. Such rules may be justified on the moral grounds of *corrective justice* and for more instrumental (or practical) reasons, such as reducing the overall level of violence in society.

These same interests may also apply when a plaintiff suffers no physical injury (such as a broken nose or a busted fence) but suffers some kind of emotional or dignitary harm. When Alice deliberately spits in Belinda's eye because she is angry with Belinda, at least some theories of corrective justice would require that Belinda be compensated: Just as a punch in the nose causes damage that needs to be redressed, an affront to dignity, or, for that matter, an action that causes emotional distress, arguably is a wrong that requires compensation as well. Instrumentally, the case is at least as strong. By giving Belinda the right to a tort action, we make it much more likely that the dispute between Alice and Belinda will be settled peaceably and not lead to an escalating spiral of violence.

But allowing compensation for emotional and dignitary harms raise two practical problems. First, it is harder to measure the proper amount of compensation. If Alice broke Melinda's nose, we could at least examine the medical bills and any potential lost wages caused by the need to take care of the nose. With a spit in the eye, the amount of compensation is less certain. There is no market in unconsented spittings to reference.

Second, with emotional harms, there is the danger of feigned or exaggerated claims. Belinda may not have been all that bothered by Alice's spit in the eye. But once she is in court, she could be tempted to say that she has suffered a great deal of emotional harm from Alice's conduct. Even assuming Belinda suffered some distress, there is no machine we can put on Belinda's brain to measure the extent of her distress, nor do we know how much money it would take to put Belinda back in the position she would have been in but for the wrong.

For these two reasons, the development of tort law related to dignitary and emotional harms has evolved more slowly. We will consider three such torts in this chapter, and in Chapter 6 we consider a more recent tort representing expansion in this area: intentional infliction of emotional distress.

QUESTION 1. Just Justice. Which of the following is *not* an instrumental argument in favor of allowing tort compensation for dignitary or emotional harms?

A. Compensation makes it less likely that victims will take revenge.
B. Compensation is warranted because intentionally inflicting such harm is wrongful.
C. Compensation prevents an escalation of violence.
D. Compensation is efficient because it decreases the need to invest in protective measures such as security guards.

ANALYSIS. Choices **A**, **C**, and **D** all raise instrumental arguments because they point to the supposed good consequences of allowing compensation: Victims won't take revenge, violence will not increase, or social efficiency will benefit. Only **B**, the correct answer, supports compensation regardless of the consequences. It says that compensation is warranted because intentionally inflicting such harm is "wrongful," a moral judgment.

B. Assault

The idea that one could recover for purely emotional or dignitary harm, at least in some circumstances, is an old one. Back in the fourteenth century, an English court agreed that a would-be patron of a tavern could be liable for an assault for swinging a hatchet near the head of the tavern owner, who stuck her head out to tell him that the bar was closed. Even though the hatchet did not touch her head, the court recognized that she had been harmed from experiencing the hatchet being swung near her head. *I de S. and Wife v. W. de S* (1348 or 1349), *reprinted in* Epstein, Cases and Materials on Torts 79 (9th ed. 2008).

Restatement (Second) of Torts section 21(1) sets forth the elements of the tortious conduct portion of the prima facie case for the tort of assault:

> **An actor is subject to liability to another for assault if**
> **(a) he acts intending to cause a harmful or offensive contact with the person of the other or a third person, or an imminent apprehension of such contact, and**
> **(b) the other is thereby put in such imminent apprehension.**

If in reading this section you are experiencing some déjà vu, it is because section 21 closely parallels the cause of action in section 13 for harmful battery, analyzed in detail in Chapter 3. The act requirement between the two torts is the same, as is the intent requirement. The sections differ in the result that is required: harmful battery requires that harmful contact result; assault requires that the plaintiff is put in imminent apprehension of harmful or offensive contact. In addition, the Restatement apparently doesn't require a plaintiff to prove lack of consent as part of the prima facie case for assault (as the plaintiff must do for harmful battery — see the last chapter). Instead, as with the other intentional torts besides battery, consent can serve as an affirmative defense, an issue we consider in the next chapter.

Let's consider each of the elements of assault in turn.

Act. As with battery, for there to be an assault a defendant must act, meaning the defendant must make a voluntary muscular contraction. Involuntary actions or reflexes do not count.

QUESTION 2. Shove It! In a hallway, Carl pushes Diana toward Edward. Edward sees Diana coming toward him and jumps out of the way. Edward sues Carl and Diana each (separately) for assault. Both defendants argue to the judge that the case cannot go forward because there was no act. How should the court rule?

A. The case can go forward against both Carl and Diana, because each acted.

B. The case can go forward against Carl who acted, but not against Diana, who did not act.
C. The case can go forward against Diana who acted, but not against Carl, who did not act.
D. The case cannot go forward against either defendant, because neither defendant acted.

ANALYSIS. When Carl pushed Diana toward Edward, this was an act on Carl's part. It does not matter that his actions toward Edward were indirect. Carl made a voluntary muscular contraction in pushing Diana. In contrast, Diana did not act. Though she moved, it was through no voluntary action on her part. She cannot be successfully sued for assault. Choice **B** correctly gives this answer, with Choices **A**, **C**, and **D** being incorrect.

Intent. As with a defendant facing a harmful battery claim, a defendant sued for assault may demonstrate the requisite intent in one of three ways: the defendant may

- intend to make a harmful contact with the person of the other or a third person;
- intend to make an offensive contact with the person of the other or a third person; or
- intend to put the plaintiff in imminent apprehension of harmful or offensive contact.

Any one of these is sufficient to meet the intent requirement for assault.

QUESTION 3. **Triggering Fear.** Francesca brings her antique gun collection to the public park to show her friend Gina. The guns are not loaded. Gina takes out one of the guns from the case, admiring it. She picks up the gun and holds it out as if she were going to shoot it to get the feel for the gun. When she picks up the gun, she sees no one around. But Henry is riding by on his bicycle and happens to pass right in front of Gina as Gina picks up the gun and holds it out. Henry becomes very afraid and nearly crashes his bike. Henry sues Gina for the tort of assault. Can Henry make out the tortious conduct portion of the prima facie case for assault?

A. Yes, because contact is not required for an assault.
B. Yes, unless Henry's bike actually crashed.
C. No, because Gina did not act.
D. No, because Gina did not have the requisite intent.

ANALYSIS. When Gina held up the gun, she was certainly committing an act. It was a voluntary muscular contraction. For this reason, Choice **C** is incorrect. Though it was an act, Gina did not act with the requisite intent. When she held out the gun she did not see anyone around. Therefore she did not have the purpose and did not act with the knowledge that she was substantially certain to make a harmful or offensive contact with Henry or a third person. Nor did she have the purpose or act with the knowledge that she would put Henry or a third person in imminent apprehension of such contact. Thus, Choice **D** is correct. Choice **A** is incorrect because, though it states a correct proposition of law (contact is not required for an assault), the assault claim fails because of a lack of intent. Choice **B** is wrong because whether or not Henry's bike crashed could be relevant to Henry's cause of action for battery, not assault.

> **QUESTION 4. Take a Stab at It.**   Jamie and Kira start arguing at a baseball game. Their tempers flare. Jamie takes out her knife and tries to stab Kira. Kira gets out of the way and the knife almost goes into Larry, who sees the whole thing. Though the knife does not touch Larry, it comes within an inch of his face, upsetting Larry greatly. Can Larry make out the tortious conduct portion of the prima facie case for assault against Jamie?
>
> **A.** No, because Jaime did not make contact with Larry.
> **B.** No, because Jamie did not intend to make contact with Larry.
> **C.** Yes, even though Jamie did not intend to make contact with Larry.
> **D.** Yes, unless the knife actually made contact with Larry.

ANALYSIS.   In this case, Jamie acted by voluntarily moving the knife. From the facts (we know there is an argument where tempers are flaring), it sounds like Jamie intended to make a harmful contact with Kira. Though Kira is not the plaintiff, to meet the intent requirement of battery it is enough for the defendant to intend contact with a third person. It appears that Larry was put in imminent apprehension of contact. Thus, it appears that Larry can make out the tortious conduct portion of the prima facie case for assault. Choice **C** accurately explains that Jamie can be liable for assault even if she did not intend to make contact with Larry. Choices **A** and **D** are incorrect because contact is not necessary for an assault. Choice **B** is incorrect because, though intent to make contact with Larry would be sufficient to meet the intent requirement for battery, it is not necessary.

Plaintiff Put in Imminent Apprehension. The plaintiff must also prove that she was put in imminent apprehension of harmful or offensive contact with herself; it is not enough that she believed someone else would suffer a harmful or offensive contact. *See* REST. (2D) TORTS § 26. "Imminent apprehension" is a term of art; it does not mean "fear." It means an immediate expectation of contact. A plaintiff can sue for assault even if she believes she can take evasive maneuvers to avoid the contact.

The contact that the plaintiff expects must be *immediate.* A threat to beat you up "a week from Tuesday" is not good enough. Some courts say that "mere words" are not enough to create an assault, on grounds that such words need to be accompanied by some evidence that the threat of contact could be carried out immediately in order for the plaintiff to be put in *imminent* apprehension of harm.[1]

Nor is a *conditional threat* enough, unless the condition is certain to occur immediately. In a famous old English case, two parties were arguing and one, putting his hand on his sword, said to the other "If it were not assize-time, I would not take such language from you."[2] The court said that such a threat did not amount to an assault, because the threat was conditional. *Tuberville v. Savage,* 80 Eng. Rep. 684 (K.B. 1669).

Finally, and perhaps to belabor the obvious, in order to win on assault, the plaintiff must actually experience the expectation of contact; it is not enough to learn of the near contact after the fact. Though that knowledge may be upsetting, it is not compensable under the tort of assault.

> **QUESTION 5. Triggering Fear, Take II.** Same fact pattern as in Question 3, with the following continuation: After Gina finishes looking at the gun, she hands it to Francesca. Francesca then holds the unloaded gun up to Gina's head and pretends she is going to shoot Gina. Ida, who is rollerblading nearby, sees the incident and becomes very upset over the thought that Francesca would shoot Gina. If Ida sues Francesca for assault:
>
> **A.** The court should rule for Francesca because Ida was not put in imminent apprehension of contact with her own person.
> **B.** The court should rule for Francesca because, by failing to actually shoot, Francesca did not act.
> **C.** The court should rule for Ida because Francesca attempted to put a third person in imminent apprehension of contact.
> **D.** The court should rule for Ida because Ida was put in imminent apprehension of harmful contact.

ANALYSIS. Francesca acted by holding the gun up to Gina's head; it was a voluntarily muscular contraction. So we can eliminate Choice **B** as a possible choice. Under these facts, Ida was never put in imminent apprehension of contact *with herself*; instead, she was upset that Francesca looked like she was going to shoot a *third person,* Gina. But in order to meet the imminent apprehension element of assault, Ida must have imminent apprehension of

---

1. As the Restatement puts it: "Words do not make the actor liable for assault unless together with other acts or circumstances they put the other in reasonable apprehension of an imminent harmful or offensive contact with his person." REST. (2D) TORTS § 31.
2. "Assize-time" was the time that the judges, riding circuit, were in town to hear cases.

contact with herself. (She might have a cause of action for intentional infliction of emotional distress, discussed in Chapter 6, but not assault.) For this reason Choice **A** is correct and Choice **C** is not. Choice **D** is incorrect because it is not enough that Ida was put in imminent apprehension of harmful contact. It must be imminent apprehension of contact with herself.

QUESTION 6. Your Money or Your Life. Mark is walking in a dark alley late at night when Ned pops out from the shadows. Ned tells Mark in a threatening voice: "I have a gun in my pocket. If you don't give me all of your money right now, I'll shoot you." Mark runs away and Ned is later captured. Can Mark prove the tortious conduct portion of the prima facie case for assault?

A. No, because Ned's threat was conditional.
B. No, because Ned's threat was not immediate.
C. Yes, if under the circumstances Mark was put in reasonable apprehension of an imminent harmful contact.
D. No, because Mark was able to run away.

ANALYSIS. Though Ned gave a conditional threat, it was a threat to do something immediately or face a harmful contact. In such circumstances, the fact that the threat is conditional does not let the defendant off the hook. Choice **A** is therefore wrong. The words in the threat "right now" make it clear that it was an immediate threat, removing Choice **B** from possible choices. Choice **D** is incorrect for a different reason: a defendant can still be liable for assault even if the plaintiff can take evasive action to avoid harmful contact. Choice **C** is the best answer. Though it is true that "mere words" sometimes do not count as an assault, if under the circumstances one is put in reasonable apprehension of harmful contact that is enough. A jury could well conclude that a threat like this in a dark alley late at night would suffice for the assault charge.

QUESTION 7. The 98-Pound Weakling. Prof, a weak and cowardly law professor, walks up to Arnold, a bodybuilder (and successful governor). Prof is angry with Arnold for his position on budget cuts. After lecturing Arnold, he tries to poke his finger into Arnold's chest for emphasis. Arnold steps out of the way and Prof falls to the ground. Security personnel take him away.

If Arnold sues Prof for assault:

A. Arnold should lose, because he was able to take evasive action to avoid offensive contact.

> **B.** Arnold should lose, because he was not afraid of Prof's attempted poking.
> **C.** Arnold should win, because he was put in imminent apprehension of offensive contact.
> **D.** Arnold should win, if he can prove he was actually afraid of being poked.

ANALYSIS.   Recall that to succeed on assault, a plaintiff must prove that he had an immediate expectation of a harmful or offensive contact to himself. It does not matter if the plaintiff can take evasive maneuvers to avoid the contact. Here, Prof arguably attempted to make an offensive contact with the person of the other; the fact that Arnold took evasive action is irrelevant. Choice **A** is therefore incorrect. Nor does it matter whether or not Arnold was actually *afraid* of the contact; it is enough that Arnold had an *immediate expectation* of contact. For this reason Choices **B** and **D** are wrong. Choice **C** correctly explains that Arnold wins, so long as he had an immediate expectation of offensive contact.

C.   Offensive battery

We finally consider the tort of offensive battery, which resembles the structure of harmful battery and assault. According to Restatement (Second) of Torts section 18(1):

> An actor is subject to liability to another for battery if
> (a) he acts intending to cause a harmful or offensive contact with the person of the other or a third person, or an imminent apprehension of such contact, and
> (b) an offensive contact with the person of the other directly or indirectly results.

Breaking down the elements — and adding in the point about plaintiff's lack of consent explained in Chapter 3 in relation to harmful battery — we can see the same familiar structure. A defendant is liable for battery if:

1. The defendant has acted
2. The defendant intended to cause

   a. a harmful contact; or
   b. an offensive contact; or
   c. plaintiff's imminent apprehension of harmful or offensive contact

3. with the person of the other or a third person
4. and *offensive* contact has resulted.
5. Plaintiff did not consent.

Given this parallel structure to assault and harmful battery, there's no need here to run through all of these elements again. (If you are unfamiliar with these elements, you need to go back and read the material in Chapter 3 on harmful battery.) The main difference here is the fourth element: the harm that results is *offensive contact*, rather than *harmful contact*. Before discussing the meaning of offensive contact, it is worth pausing for a moment to ask why the drafters of the Restatement created two separate sections, one for harmful battery and one for offensive battery. Why not just "and harmful or offensive contact with the person of the other directly or indirectly results"? The point appears to be an effort to separate two different kinds of harm. The harmful battery tort (section 13) protects against physical harm to the body. The offensive battery tort (section 18) protects against dignitary and emotional harm. By having the different sections, the Restatement emphasizes that each is a kind of harm worthy of compensation.

Offensiveness. Recall from the last chapter that we generally measure offensiveness using a reasonable person standard: the jury is to decide what would offend a reasonable person's sense of dignity. *See* REST. (2D) TORTS § 19. To use the example from the beginning of this chapter, society wants to compensate Belinda after Alice deliberately spits in Belinda's eye even if Belinda suffered no physical harm from the saliva entering her eye. Virtually all jurors would agree that such conduct is offensive.

The Restatement defines offensiveness using an objective reasonable person standard, rather than a subjective standard based upon what would offend a particular person. The Restatement punts on the question whether a defendant "is liable if he inflicts upon another a contact which he knows will be offensive to another person's known but abnormally acute sense of personal dignity." REST. (2D) TORTS § 19, *Caveat.*

QUESTION 8. Throw in the Towel, Revisited. Rick invites Steve to his house for dinner. Rick and Steve are old friends, and they often play practical jokes on each other. Before Steve arrived, Rick took one of his bathroom hand towels out into his backyard and rubbed it in the mud. He put it in his bathroom, making sure the dirt was visible. He thought Steve would see the towel before picking it up and get a good laugh. Steve uses the bathroom to wash up before dinner, and does not notice the dirt on the towel. He rubs the towel on his hands and face, getting dirt all over himself. Steve is very upset and sues Rick for battery.

Can Steve prove the tortious conduct portion of the prima facie case for battery against Rick?

A. No, because Rick didn't intend that Steve would actually put the dirty towel on his face.

B. No, unless Rick intended that Steve be put in imminent apprehension of offensive contact.
C. No, because Steve did not have a harmful contact with the towel.
D. No, because Steve did not notice the dirt on the towel.

ANALYSIS. Under these facts, there is no question that Rick acted (by putting the dirty towel in the bathroom). Nor is there any question that offensive contact resulted with Steve's face, part of the person of the other. The big question here is one of intent: from the facts, Rick did not intend that Steve would make contact with the towel ("He put it in his bathroom, making sure the dirt was visible. He thought Steve would see the towel before picking it up and get a good laugh."). So the only possible way that Steve wins here is if he can prove that Rick intended that Steve be put in imminent apprehension of offensive contact. That's Choice **B**, the correct answer here. Choice **A** is wrong because one need not intend that the plaintiff have an offensive contact to be liable for offensive battery. Choice **C** is wrong because plaintiff having a harmful contact is not necessary for battery; an offensive contact is enough. Choice **D** is wrong because whether or not Steve should have noticed the dirt on the towel is irrelevant for the elements of the prima facie case for battery.

QUESTION 9. My Cup Runneth Over. George has a strong aversion to Styrofoam cups, ever since he tried to eat one as an infant. Whenever he has contact with Styrofoam, he gets very upset. Haley knows about George's aversion and she does not like George very much. As George is about to sit down on a chair, Haley sneaks an empty and clean Styrofoam cup on the chair, causing George to sit down on it. As Haley expected, George became very upset. Can George make out the tortious conduct portion of the prima facie case for battery in a jurisdiction following the approach of the Restatement?

A. No, because Haley did not know for certain that George would sit down on the cup.
B. No, because George did not suffer physical harm.
C. No, unless the jurisdiction determines that offensive contact includes contact which would offend a sensitive person's, but not necessarily a reasonable person's, sense of personal dignity.
D. No, unless George actually saw the cup before sitting down on it.

ANALYSIS. This question directly tests you on knowledge of the Restatement caveat. A reasonable person's sense of personal dignity is not offended by sitting on an empty and clean Styrofoam cup (contrast that with sitting on a pile of worms!). But George has an abnormally acute sensitivity to Styrofoam, which Haley knows about and exploits to inflict emotional distress on George. The Restatement does not answer the question whether a person like George should be able to recover for battery in these circumstances. This idea is accurately conveyed in Choice **C**, the correct answer.

Choice **A** is wrong because from the facts it appeared that Haley had the purpose of causing George to make contact with the cup, and by putting it there she was at least substantially certain such contact would occur. (If you do not understand this, you need to review the material on intent in Chapter 3.) Choice **B** is incorrect because for an offensive battery a plaintiff need not suffer physical harm; emotional or dignitary harm is enough. Finally, Choice **D** is wrong because whether or not George saw the cup before he sat on it could be relevant to the question of *assault* (being put in imminent apprehension of a possibly offensive contact) but not to the question of *battery* (which is about whether the possibly offensive contact actually occurred).

Note that in a jurisdiction that would not count Haley's conduct as constituting an offensive battery, it might be possible for George to sue Haley for a different tort discussed in Chapter 6: intentional infliction of emotional distress.

D. Transferred intent between assault and battery, and the relationship between the torts

The Restatement's parallel structures for the intent portion of the tort causes of action for harmful battery (section 13), assault (section 21), and offensive battery (section 18) are no accident; instead, the parallel treatment allow for transferred intent not only between persons but also *between these torts*. For example, if Michael intends to put Nancy in imminent apprehension of a punch and, to his surprise, actually lands the punch, Michael can be liable for battery. Similarly, if Michael intended to hit Nancy but missed, Nancy can bring a tort suit for assault.[3]

In the situation where Michael surprisingly lands the punch, he could be liable for *both* assault *and* harmful battery. Why should this be so? Wouldn't

---

3. As we saw in the last chapter, under the common law, but not under the Restatement, some jurisdictions recognize that intent can be transferred across a range of common law torts: assault, battery, false imprisonment, trespass to land, and trespass to chattels. But I have not found any modern cases allowing such transferred intent as the basis for a tort.

this give Nancy a double recovery? If the jury is properly instructed, it would not. The battery tort should compensate Nancy for her physical harm (doctor's bills, bandages, lost wages) as well as the pain she endured from the punch. The assault tort compensates only for the emotional harm and/or the dignitary harm occurring when Nancy anticipated Michael's blow landing on her face.

Now, it might be that the harm from the assault is pretty minimal in this case. But if Nancy has a good lawyer, she will ask for both. Not only might the jury grant additional damages for this assault that it would not have compensated for had there been only a battery; in the event Nancy seeks punitive damages (more on that in Chapter 23), pointing out more bad conduct by Michael can help Nancy in that portion of her case.

QUESTION 10. **Offensive Kiss.**   While Nancy naps in the park, Paul, an acquaintance of Nancy who likes Nancy a great deal, quietly walks over to her and gives her a kiss on the lips in front of many people. Nancy sleeps through the whole thing. When Nancy awakes, she learns about Paul's actions and is very upset. She sues Paul for assault and battery. In evaluating whether Nancy can make out the prima facie case for each tort, the factfinder should conclude:

A. Nancy can make out the prima facie case for assault, but not battery.
B. Nancy can make out the prima facie case for battery, but not assault.
C. Nancy can make out the prima facie case for both assault and battery.
D. Nance cannot make out the prima facie case for either tort.

ANALYSIS.   The way to approach a problem like this that asks you about the success for multiple torts is to consider the elements for each tort separately, reach your conclusions, and then look for the multiple choice answer that matches your conclusions. Without doing so, there is no way you can use the process of elimination to help you here because the four choices represent the four permutations in answering such a problem.

Considering assault, there is no question that Paul acted through his voluntary muscular contraction leading to the kiss on Nancy's lips. In kissing an acquaintance who is unconscious, he certainly intended contact, and there is a strong case he intended offensive contact, because kissing a stranger or even an acquaintance who is sleeping is likely to offend a reasonable person's sense of dignity. (As noted earlier, it doesn't matter that Paul doesn't think it would be offensive to Nancy.) The contact was intended to be with Nancy's lips, part of the "person of the other." The assault case falls apart, however, because Nancy was not put in imminent apprehension of contact. Recall that "imminent apprehension" means an immediate expectation of contact. Nancy did not learn of the kiss until afterward, and that's not good enough for assault, even if, as is the case here, she suffered emotional distress upon learning about what happened.

We have now established that Nancy cannot prove the tortious conduct portion of the cause of action for assault, meaning we can eliminate Choices **A** and **C**. Now consider battery. The first three elements discussed above are the same: Paul acted, and he intended to cause an offensive contact with the person of the other. To succeed on battery, Nancy will also have to prove that offensive contact resulted and lack of consent. She can prove these as well. A group of people saw Paul kiss Nancy while she was sleeping, contact which offends a reasonable person's sense of dignity. A person who is sleeping cannot give consent. (Contrast this with a person who gives consent to a touching before becoming unconscious, as with a patient who consents to surgery.) Because Nancy can prove the tortious conduct portion of the prima facie case for offensive battery but not for assault, Choice **B** is the correct answer.

E.   False imprisonment

The final intentional tort protecting plaintiffs from emotional and dignitary harms that we consider in this chapter is false imprisonment. We will turn to intentional infliction of emotional distress in Chapter 6 after we consider affirmative defenses in Chapter 5.

Under Restatement (Second) of Torts section 35(1):

> An actor is subject to liability to another for false imprisonment if
> (a) he acts intending to confine the other or a third person within the boundaries fixed by the actor, and
> (b) his act directly or indirectly results in such confinement of the other, and
> (c) the other is conscious of the confinement or is harmed by it.

As with the other torts, it is necessary to break this down into the elements to see the tortious conduct portion of the prima facie case for false imprisonment.

Act. In order to be liable for false imprisonment, the defendant must commit a volitional act. Aside from a sleepwalking defendant, it is hard to imagine scenarios in which a plaintiff's false imprisonment claim would fail on the act requirement, but the next question is my feeble attempt to do so.

QUESTION 11. Locked In.   Quincy, an Acme Bank employee, is working in his branch's vault when a robbery takes place. Roger, a security guard, is standing by the vault when Suzanna, the robber, runs by. She shoves

Roger on her escape. Roger falls against the door of the vault, causing the door to close. Quincy is locked into the vault for five hours. Quincy sues Roger and Suzanna for false imprisonment. Each defendant claims that Quincy's case cannot go forward because Quincy cannot prove each defendant acted. (Consider each defendant's conduct separately.) How should the court rule?

A. The case against Suzanna and Roger cannot go forward because neither directly acted.
B. The case against Suzanna cannot go forward because she did not act directly, but the case against Roger can go forward because he was the direct cause of Quincy's confinement.
C. The case against Suzanna can go forward because she directly acted, but the case against Roger cannot go forward because Roger did not act.
D. The case against both Suzanna and Roger can each go forward because both Suzanna and Roger acted.

ANALYSIS. This should be an easy question once you determine if either or both of the defendants have acted. Suzanna shoved Roger; this was the result of a voluntary muscular contraction on Suzanna's part. Suzanna therefore acted, meaning Choices **A** and **B** are wrong. In evaluating whether Suzanna acted, it does not matter whether the result of confining Quincy occurred directly or indirectly.

Roger was pushed into the vault and did not make any voluntary muscular movement to close the vault. Roger did not act. For this reason, Choice **D** is wrong and Choice **C** is correct.

Note that there's a good chance—as discussed immediately below—that Quincy's false imprisonment claim against Suzanna could fail because of a lack of the requisite intent. But the question asked you to focus only on the act requirement.

Intent. Under the Restatement the defendant must "intend to confine the other or a third person within the boundaries fixed by" the defendant. Note that this intent requirement for false imprisonment is different from the intent we have seen with assault and battery (there, a plaintiff had to prove a defendant's intent to make harmful or offensive contact, or to put the plaintiff in imminent apprehension of such contact).

Considering the last example, unless Quincy can prove that Suzanna shoved Roger *with the intent of confining* Quincy (or Roger) in the vault, the false imprisonment claim likely fails for lack of intent.[4] Transferred intent

---

4. The claim wouldn't fail if the jurisdiction allowed transferred intent between the torts of battery and false imprisonment. See footnote 1. Don't feel too bad for Quincy. At the least, he likely has a good negligence claim against Suzanna, as we will see in Part II of this book.

between persons is possible here: If Suzanna shoved Roger with the intent to confine him in the vault but actually ended up confining Quincy, Quincy could prove that Suzanna had the requisite intent. But if the shove just posed an unreasonable risk that Quincy (or Roger) would be confined, that would fail the purpose or knowledge with "substantial certainty" standard for intent in intentional torts.

The defendant's intention must be to confine *within boundaries fixed by* the defendant. Suppose, for example, a shop is about to close for the night and the owner locks the door of the shop. A person on the outside of the shop who wishes to come into the shop cannot raise false imprisonment, because the person on the outside is not confined within any boundaries. In contrast, a customer locked in the store could prove this element of the prima facie case, so long as the shop owner knew of the customer's presence in the store.

QUESTION 12. Trapped! Tina parks her car on a street corner, with one of her tires covering a steel plate on the street. Unbeknownst to Tina, Uma is working in the sewer system below the plate. The only way for Uma to get out is by moving the plate, which she was able to do until Tina parked her car on top of it. Uma is stuck underground for 24 hours, until Tina happens to move her car. Uma caught pneumonia from being stuck under the ground. If Uma sues Tina for false imprisonment:

A. Uma's claim will fail because Tina did not act.
B. Uma's claim will fail because Tina lacked the intention to confine Uma.
C. Uma's case will succeed because Uma was harmed by the confinement.
D. Uma's case will succeed if she can prove she was actually confined.

ANALYSIS. Uma's claim for false imprisonment has a problem: Tina did not know that Uma was under the steel plate that sat under Tina's car. Without such knowledge, we cannot say that Tina had the purpose or had the knowledge with substantial certainty that she was confining Uma. Choice **B** reflects this answer. Choice **A** fails because Tina did act when she drove her car onto the steel plate: Be sure not to confuse the act and intent requirements. Choice **C** fails because whether or not Uma was harmed by the confinement does not solve Uma's problem proving that Tina had the requisite intent. Choice **D** fails for a similar reason: It won't be a problem for Uma to prove she was actually confined, but that does not solve Uma's problem with proving intent.

Actual confinement. The plaintiff also has to prove that she was actually confined by defendant's actions. If there is a reasonable means of escape, then there is no actual confinement. Of course, what constitutes an easy means of escape can, in certain circumstances, become a question of fact for the factfinder. The Restatement gives the example of no confinement when "an athletic young man" is locked "in a room with an open window at a height of four feet from the floor and from the ground outside." Rest. (2d) Torts § 36, Illus. 1. But change the facts a bit and things are harder. What if plaintiff is an old man, or the height is 8 feet, or the "athletic young man" saw that the defendant had a gun and was likely standing outside?

QUESTION 13. Curses, Soiled Again!   Walter, an athletic young man, is dressed in a tuxedo for his wedding day. Vera, his former girlfriend, forces Walter at gunpoint into her tool shed behind her home. She locks Walter into the tool shed. The back of the shed has an open window. Walter can easily climb out of the window, but if he does so, he will get his tuxedo covered in mud. Rather than do so, he bangs on the tool shed door, begging Vera to let him out. After three hours — after the starting time of Walter's wedding ceremony — Vera lets him out.

If Walter sues Vera for false imprisonment:

A. Walter can make out the prima facie case if a jury agrees that climbing through the window was not a reasonable means of escape.
B. Walter can make out the prima facie case only if he proves he was in imminent apprehension of harmful contact.
C. Walter cannot make out the prima facie case because he was confined for only three hours.
D. Walter cannot make out the prima facie case because Vera failed to act by opening the door.

ANALYSIS.   We can start by eliminating Choice **B**. It may be that Walter has a great claim for assault against Vera, which would require proof that he was put in imminent apprehension of contact (or another variant under the assault/battery intent standard). But imminent apprehension is not an element of the prima facie case for false imprisonment. Choice **C** is incorrect for a different reason: There is nothing in the prima facie case that imposes a lower time limit on bringing such a claim. Of course, if the imprisonment was for an extremely short time, it may be difficult for a plaintiff to prove damages. But being confined for three hours on one's wedding day certainly does not seem like a frivolous confinement. Choice **D** is incorrect because Vera acted by confining Walter to the shed. The fact that Vera failed to open the door after confining him is irrelevant to the prima facie case. Choice **A** is the best choice. The relevant question for the jury is whether climbing out of the shed window into the mud is a reasonable means of escape, especially for someone in a tuxedo on his wedding day.

Consciousness of the Confinement or Harm. The final element of the tortious conduct portion of the prima facie case is consciousness of the confinement or harm caused by the confinement. Let's take the consciousness requirement first. Suppose that Xavier is traveling on a passenger train from New York to California. During the night, while Xavier sleeps, Yolanda, a train worker, locks Xavier in his train compartment for five hours, intending to keep him in his room while she searches other rooms for valuables to steal. She then unlocks Xavier's compartment. Xavier has slept through the whole thing, and learns about the confinement later. Under the Restatement, Xavier has no cause of action for false imprisonment. Although Yolanda acted by locking the door, did so to confine Xavier, and he was actually confined, Xavier was not conscious of it at the time, and therefore suffered no compensable harm. (This is akin to the person who sleeps through what would have counted as an assault.) The fact that he learns about what happened later and is very upset is not grounds to allow his claim to go forward.

As an alternative to proving consciousness, a plaintiff who was not aware of the confinement at the time can still recover in some jurisdictions if he was physically harmed by the confinement. For example, an infant that is locked in a vault for two days and suffers dehydration and malnourishment can still recover damages for false imprisonment even though the infant's brain is too undeveloped to be conscious of the confinement. *See* REST. (2D) TORTS § 42, Illus. 3.

QUESTION 14. Like a Bad Neighbor. Zane is a five-year-old boy who lives across the street from Adam, an 80-year-old man. Zane is always making noise playing in the street, and this bothers Adam, who values his peace and quiet. One day, when Zane was playing out in the street, Adam called him over. "I have some candy in my basement. Come on over and have some," Adam tells Zane. Zane goes in the basement and Adam quickly locks him in there alone. "I won't let you out unless you promise to never make noise in front of my house again," Adam tells Zane. Zane starts to cry and does not answer Adam, yelling that he wants to see his mommy. After an hour, Adam lets Zane out of the basement. Adam has suffered from nightmares ever since.

If Zane sues Adam for false imprisonment:

A. Zane cannot prove the prima facie case because he did not suffer physical harm.

B. Zane cannot prove the prima facie case because infants are not aware of their confinement.

C. Zane can prove the prima facie case only if the nightmares count as harm.

> **D.** Zane can prove the prima facie case whether or not the nightmares count as harm.

ANALYSIS. To answer this question, first consider each element of the tortious conduct portion of the prima facie case for false imprisonment. Adam acted by using words (the promise of candy) to lure Zane into the basement and by locking the door. Adam intended to confine Zane to the boundaries of his basement. Zane was not allowed out for an hour, showing actual confinement. Finally, Zane was conscious of the confinement; he was crying and asked for his mother. There seems no question he can prove the tortious conduct portion of the prima facie case. Choice **C** is therefore wrong because proving that the nightmares count as harm is not necessary. It is enough that Zane has suffered this dignitary and emotional harm to be entitled to compensation for false imprisonment. For similar reasons, Choice **A** is wrong: It is not necessary to prove physical harm if the plaintiff can prove consciousness of the confinement. Choice **B** is incorrect because though there may be very small infants who are unaware of their confinement, on these facts Zane was well aware of his confinement. This leaves us with the correct choice, Choice **D**: Zane can recover whether or not nightmares count as harm.

F.   The Closer: Choose your tort!

A common skill tested on multiple-choice questions (and essay questions as well, for that matter) is to figure out which tort or torts could be viable claims brought by a plaintiff. It is a good skill to test, because it is one that is more like the real world. A client will not come into your office and say: "I'd like to sue for trespass to chattels." Instead, the client will tell you a story, and it will be up to you to figure out the relevant facts and which tort or torts would be worth pursuing. Of course, we haven't seen the entire case yet. We cannot fully evaluate the likelihood of success of a tort without looking at both the entire prima facie case for the tort (including actual cause, proximate cause, and damages) and potential affirmative defenses. But you still have enough knowledge to answer some of these questions (indeed, you already answered one in the "Offensive Kiss" question). Before trying to answer the question, make sure you know the tortious conduct portion of the prima facie case for all the torts covered thus far (harmful battery, trespass to land, trespass to chattels, assault, offensive battery, and false imprisonment).

> **QUESTION 15. Choose Your Tort!** Brian knows that his archenemy Craig is having breakfast in his dining room. Brian can see Craig through a pair of binoculars. Craig's house is at the bottom of a steep hill, behind a wooden fence and a long grassy yard. Brian has transported a heavy boulder in his truck to the top of the hill above Craig's house. Brian honks the horn repeatedly until Craig looks out the window. Then he sets the boulder in motion straight toward Craig's fence and home. Brian is hoping to damage Craig's property and run him over with the boulder. Craig sees the boulder coming toward him, but knows it is way too small to be able to hit him in his home. The boulder knocks down Craig's fence and comes to a stop in the middle of Craig's lawn.
>
> For which tort or torts can Craig prove the tortious conduct of the prima facie case against Brian?
>
> **A.** Trespass to land
> **B.** Assault
> **C.** Both A and B
> **D.** Neither A nor B

ANALYSIS.   Rather than an open-ended essay type question asking you to identify the tort or torts that might come into play in a problem like this, here the issue is much more discrete: To answer a question with two choices, followed by a "both" and "neither" option, you want to consider each option separately and then reach your conclusion.

Can Craig prove the tortious conduct portion of the prima facie case for trespass to land? Yes. Brian acted by setting the boulder in motion. He intended to cause the boulder to enter into his land. ("Then he sets the boulder in motion straight toward Craig's fence and home. Brian is hoping to damage Craig's property and run him over with the boulder.") The boulder in fact entered the land. All of the elements are met.

What about assault? Again, Brian acted by setting the boulder in motion. Brian also acted with the intent to cause a harmful contact with Craig: he wanted to "run him over with the boulder." The problem for Craig's assault claim is lack of proof of imminent apprehension. The facts tell us that "Craig saw the boulder coming toward him but knew it was way too small to be able to hit him in his home." Without that immediate expectation of harmful or offensive contact on the part of the plaintiff, assault fails. For this reason, Choice **A** is the correct answer.

Rick's picks

1.	Just Justice	B
2.	Shove It!	B
3.	Triggering Fear	D
4.	Take a Stab at It	C
5.	Triggering Fear, Take II	A
6.	Your Money or Your Life	C
7.	The 98-Pound-Weakling	C
8.	Throw in the Towel, Revisited	B
9.	My Cup Runneth Over	C
10.	Offensive Kiss	B
11.	Locked In	C
12.	Trapped!	B
13.	Curses, Soiled Again!	A
14.	Like a Bad Neighbor	D
15.	Choose Your Tort!	A

5

Affirmative Defenses to Intentional Torts

CHAPTER OVERVIEW
A. Introduction to affirmative defenses
B. Consent
C. Insanity
D. Self-defense and defense of others
E. Defense of property
F. Recapture of chattels
G. Necessity
H. The Closer: Choose your (defensive) weapon
✦ Rick's picks

A. Introduction to affirmative defenses

As you may recall from Chapter 2, the defendant has two ways in which to win a tort case. First, the defendant wins a cause of action if the plaintiff cannot prove by a preponderance of the evidence *all* of the elements in a tort case. In some tort cases, the defendant's defense consists primarily of putting on evidence demonstrating that the plaintiff cannot prove one or more of these elements. But even if the plaintiff can prove all of the elements of the tort by a preponderance of the evidence, the defendant can still win by raising an *affirmative defense* and proving it by a preponderance of the evidence. For example, a plaintiff who was shot by defendant might be able to prove all the elements of a harmful battery, but if the defendant can prove that the shooting was in self-defense, plaintiff's battery claim will fail.

Affirmative defenses can sometimes be tricky. Not all defenses work with all torts. And some defenses, such as *necessity* against a trespass claim and *comparative negligence* in a negligence claim result in a *sharing of liability* rather than an either/or split. This chapter focuses on affirmative defenses that sometimes may be raised against intentional torts. As this book considers other causes of action in later parts, I will discuss applicable affirmative defenses in subsequent sections as well.

QUESTION 1. Burden of Proof. Barbara shot Andy in the leg. Barbara admits that she did the shooting and that Andy can prove the prima facie case for harmful battery, but claims she shot Andy in self-defense. Which is an accurate statement about how the jury must consider the self-defense claim?

A. Andy wins, unless he can prove by a preponderance of the evidence that Barbara did not act in self-defense.

B. Andy loses, unless he can prove by a preponderance of the evidence that Barbara acted in self-defense.

C. Barbara wins, unless she can prove by a preponderance of the evidence that she acted in self-defense.

D. Barbara loses, unless she can prove by a preponderance of the evidence that she acted in self-defense.

ANALYSIS.   This is a straightforward question, but with multiple-choice answers worded in a tricky way. The way affirmative defenses work is that the defendant must prove the affirmative defense by a preponderance of the evidence. It is not the job of the plaintiff to *disprove* an affirmative defense of the defendant. Choice **D** is the only choice that accurately explains this concept. Barbara has already conceded that Andy can prove the prima facie case for harmful battery, so she is going to lose unless she can prove the affirmative defense of self-defense by a preponderance of the evidence. The other choices are wrong. Choice **A** is a completely wrong statement of the law: He wins unless *Barbara* proves she did act in self-defense. Choice **B** is incorrect because he does not bear the burden of proof on these questions. It would also be illogical for Andy to prove this point. If Andy proves the prima facie case and both parties do nothing, Andy wins. Choice **C** has it backward: Barbara wins *if* she can prove the affirmative defense, rather than she wins *unless* she can prove the affirmative defense.

B.   Consent

We have already examined the issue of consent in Chapter 3 because lack of consent is an element that the plaintiff must prove as part of the prima facie case for battery. For other intentional torts, however, lack of consent is not an element of the plaintiff's case. Instead, the defendant must raise and prove consent as an affirmative defense.

For example, suppose that Carlos drives onto Davina's driveway and breaks some of the pipes underneath the ground. Davina could sue Carlos for trespass to land: Carlos acted, intended to enter Davina's land, and in fact did so, causing damage. It looks like Davina could make out the tortious conduct portion of the prima facie case for trespass to land. But suppose that Davina *invited* Carlos to come onto the driveway. In that case, Carlos could raise Davina's consent to the entry of the land as an affirmative defense, and if Carlos proves that Davina in fact consented, then Davina recovers nothing in her trespass claim. (Whether Davina could sue for negligence or some other tort is a different question.)

As discussed in Chapter 3, there are basically two kinds of consent. *Express* consent exists when a person in writing or orally agrees to the conduct. In our example, if Davina gave written or oral consent to go onto the land, that would be express consent.

Consent can also be *implied in fact* from the circumstances. For example, if Davina opened her gate as Carlos approached, a jury might view her conduct as impliedly consenting to Carlos's entry onto the land. The question is one of fact under the circumstances.

The question of consent focuses upon the plaintiff's actions, not the defendant's perception of them. If Carlos makes a mistake — even a reasonable one — about whether or not Davina consented by opening her gate, he can be liable. The rationale behind this rule appears to be that if the defendant has doubts about whether the plaintiff has consented, the defendant can always ask for express consent.[1]

Finally, as with the case of battery (as noted in Chapter 3), there are rare circumstances in which the court creates a fiction of consent, termed *implied in law* consent, to relieve a defendant of liability for an intentional tort on policy grounds. In the battery context, we saw that when a person renders first aid to an unconscious person in an emergency, the court will recognize this fiction of implied in law consent and bar the plaintiff's battery claim if the plaintiff was injured by the first aid. One controversial use of implied in law consent occurred in the context of a false imprisonment case, *Peterson v. Sorlien*, 299 N.W.2d 123 (Minn. 1980). Parents of an adult child in college had her kidnapped and "deprogrammed" after her parents believed she had joined a religious "cult." Though the adult child was kept involuntarily for three days, she then stayed voluntarily for the next ten days, until she ultimately decided to return back to her fiancé and the religious organization. She sued the deprogrammers and her father for false imprisonment. Though

---

1. This is a rule that is not always followed. For example, in *O'Brien v. Cunard Steamship Co.*, 28 N.E. 266 (Mass. 1891), the plaintiff received a vaccination as part of a mass vaccination program for immigrants. When plaintiff approached the doctor, she held out her arm and received the vaccine. When she became ill and later sued for battery, the court rejected the claim, noting that any "unexpressed feelings" of an unwillingness to consent were irrelevant; it was the "overt acts" that counted.

the opinion is not entirely clear, and refers to the ten-day consensual period as somehow waiving any objections to the earlier nonconsensual period, the case is best understood as excusing the lack of consent in such circumstances on policy grounds, here, the ability of parents even of adult children to take steps the parents view as necessary to protect them from harm.

QUESTION 2. Eddy the Great.   Eddy the Great is a magician who escapes from chains and does similar tricks. Eddy calls up an audience member, Frederica, at one of his shows, and asks her to inspect a trunk Eddy is about to enter. Frederica does so, and confirms the trunk appears solid, with no trapped doors. Eddy tells Frederica: "Lock me in this trunk, and do not let me out no matter how much I beg and plead." He gives her the only key. Eddy then has his assistant lock his hands with some chains and goes inside the trunk and yells to Frederica to lock it. Frederica locks the trunk before it is then lowered into a larger glass cage containing rattlesnakes. Unfortunately for Eddy, the usual trick he uses to get out of the chains (a key hidden in his mouth) does not work (because he accidentally swallowed the key) and Eddy cannot get out. Eddy pleads with Frederica for the key, but she does not give it. The audience roars with laughter as Eddy's pleas get more serious. Soon, a rattlesnake gets into the trunk and bites Eddy. The show ends, and Eddy, who miraculously survives, sues Frederica for false imprisonment. In ruling on Eddy's tort claim, a court should:

A. Reject the claim because Eddy expressly consented to being confined.
B. Reject the claim because Eddy was partially at fault.
C. Reject the claim because Frederica's mistake as to consent was reasonable.
D. Accept the claim because Frederica's mistake as to consent was unreasonable.

ANALYSIS.   Eddy can probably prove the tortious conduct portion of the prima facie case for false imprisonment. Frederica acted, she intended to confine Eddy by locking him in the trunk, and he was actually confined: He could not get out of the trunk and ended up getting bitten by the rattlesnake. The question is whether Frederica can successfully raise the affirmative defense of consent. In this case, it looks like she can. Before Eddy got into the trunk, he gave express consent to being kept in there against his will: "Lock me in this trunk, and do not let me out no matter how much I beg and plead." This express consent should bar Eddy's false imprisonment claim. Choice **A** correctly explains this point. Choice **B** is incorrect because whether Eddy is partially "at fault" or not is not relevant to the tortious conduct portion of the prima facie case of the defense of consent. Choices **C** and **D** are incorrect because Frederica did not make a mistake, reasonable or otherwise, about whether or not Eddy consented: Eddy consented at the time

Frederica took the action confining him. What happened after that does not go to the question of the initial consent.

C.   Insanity

Insanity is generally *not* accepted as a defense in intentional torts. So if I hit you with a stick because I believe you are a CIA operative sent to spy on me, I can be liable for a harmful battery. I acted, I intended to cause a harmful contact with your person, harmful contact resulted, and you did not consent. Thus, the treatment of insanity under tort law differs from the treatment under the criminal law, which absolves defendants of some criminal liability under certain circumstances.

Why doesn't tort law recognize insanity as an affirmative defense to intentional torts? Courts have offered a few reasons, most notably the corrective justice claim that if someone suffering from a mental disease or defect is free to participate as a member of society, that person should have to pay for the damage he causes. Some courts also recognize the instrumental argument that liability will encourage those who are charged with caring for people with such mental diseases or defects to take steps to prevent them from injuring others. On the other hand, failure to recognize such a tort defense may seem unfair if we think that only people who are at fault should pay for the damage they cause. (Much more on this fault/cause debate to come in Chapter 7 on the choice between negligence and strict liability.)

Though courts generally do not recognize insanity as an affirmative defense, it is possible that a mental disease or defect could be relevant in determining whether a defendant had the requisite intent for the particular tort. For example, as we saw in the last two chapters, in order to be liable for battery or assault under the Restatement, a defendant must intend to make a harmful or offensive contact with the person of the other or a third person, or to put the plaintiff in imminent apprehension of such contact. Suppose that a person suffering from a delusion believes he is squeezing a lemon, when in fact he is actually choking someone around the neck. If the person believes he is squeezing a lemon, he lacks the intent to make a harmful contact *with the person of the other or a third person* because a lemon is not a person.

If a court would allow the defendant to be relieved of liability in the "Lemon Head" example, it is roughly equivalent to allowing the affirmative defense of insanity. But note that this allowance treats people suffering from a mental disease or defect differently *depending* upon the nature of the delusion. The CIA delusion does not absolve the defendant of liability because such an agent is a person; the Lemon Head delusion does. For this reason, some courts may simply refuse to allow defendants to testify as to the nature of their delusions, allowing the jury to infer that the defendant intended harmful contact with the person of the other to allow an action for battery.

Failure to allow the insanity defense also treats the person with the insane delusion more harshly than the sane person who sleepwalks and commits an intentional tort. The sleepwalker is not engaged in a voluntary muscular contraction and therefore there is no act. The delusional person generally engages in a voluntary act.

QUESTION 3. The Dream Police.   Gary had a dream he was a police officer who was trying to catch some robbers. In his dream, his police dog Mutts was secretly working for the bad guys. Gary had to restrain Mutts in order to stop him from aiding the robbers' escape. In reality, Gary was sleepwalking during this dream and choked his neighbor Ian's dog, Scraps, seriously injuring the dog. Ian sues Gary for trespass to chattels.[2] Gary's strongest argument against liability for this tort is that:

A. A person suffering from an insane delusion is not liable for his torts.
B. Gary did not have the intent to make contact with a *person*.
C. Gary did not act.
D. Gary is not responsible for his actions.

ANALYSIS.   Gary interfered with Scraps, Ian's chattel. (Sorry dog lovers — and I'm one of them — dogs are property, not people.) The question is whether he is liable for the injuries he inflicted. We can easily eliminate Choice **A** as a possible choice: Not only is it an incorrect statement of the law ("insane" people are generally liable for their intentional torts); there is no indication that Gary was acting under an insane delusion. Instead, he was sleepwalking. Similarly, we can eliminate Choice **D**. A generalized argument that Gary is not responsible for his actions may be a good policy argument, but a stronger argument will tie the responsibility point to the prima facie case or affirmative defenses. Choice **B** is incorrect because intent to make contact with a person is not an element of the tort of trespass to chattels (it is relevant for battery, a different tort). The best choice is Choice **C**. Because Gary moved in his sleep, he did not make a voluntary muscular contraction sufficient to meet the act requirement of every intentional tort.

---

2. From Chapter 3, you should recall that a person who acts by intentionally interfering with a chattel in the possession of another, or who dispossesses that person of the chattel, is liable for the tort of trespass to chattels.

D.   Self-defense and defense of others

One obvious affirmative defense that courts recognize is self-defense. If someone is about to attack me, I have a right to defend myself. In doing so I could take actions that might otherwise be considered a battery, assault, false imprisonment, or some other tort. If a defendant raises self-defense as an affirmative defense and a jury agrees the defendant has proven it by a preponderance of the evidence, the plaintiff must bear his own costs of injury, and the defendant is obligated to pay nothing.

A person may not use self-defense against *any* use of force or threatened use of force, only against *unprivileged* force or threatened use of force. So if a police officer is about to use force for the legitimate purpose of capturing a suspect, the police officer has a privilege to do so, and a suspect's use of force against the officer will be a battery not subject to the affirmative defense of self-defense.

Two key issues can arise in cases in which a defendant raises the defense of self-defense.

First, who was the aggressor? In cases where both plaintiff and defendant have threatened and hit each other, there may be a question as to who acted first and who acted second in self-defense. There is not much *law* on this question, though it is going to be centrally important in many real-world cases raising issues of self-defense. In most instances, this is a *factual* question to be resolved by a jury.

The second question is one of proportionality. Suppose you tell me that you are going to spit in my face because you don't like me, and you get ready to spit. At that point you have committed an assault (review from the last chapter: you acted, intending to put me in imminent apprehension of an offensive contact, and I was put in imminent apprehension of such contact). I then would be justified in taking some action in self-defense: I might even be able to make a nonconsensual intentional touching (which would otherwise be a battery) to prevent you from doing so, such as pushing you away. But I couldn't use disproportionate force, such as stabbing you.

The idea of proportionality appears throughout the Restatement's treatment of this subject. For example, Restatement (Second) of Torts section 63(1) provides that a person is "privileged to use reasonable force, not intended or likely to cause death or serious bodily harm, to defend himself against unprivileged harmful or offensive contact or other bodily harm which he reasonably believes that another is about to inflict intentionally upon him."

The Restatement allows for the infliction of "force intended or likely to cause death or seriously bodily harm" only in limited circumstances: Such force must be in reaction to a reasonable belief that the other is about to inflict intentional contact or other bodily harm that puts the person "in peril of death or seriously bodily harm or ravishment, which can safely be prevented only by the immediate use of such force." REST. (2D) TORTS § 65(1). But even then, such force cannot be used if the person about to be attacked can safely retreat (if attacked somewhere other than his home). *Id.* § 65(3)(a). (There is no requirement to retreat when one is going to use reasonable, non-deadly force to repel an attack. *Id.* §63(2)(a).) Force cannot be used for other reasons, such as punishment or future deterrence.

QUESTION 4. Assize-Time Updated.   John and Kevin get into an argument in a bar. John puts his hand on his gun and says: "If there wasn't a cop at the end of this bar, I'd blow your brains out!" (You should recall from last chapter's discussion of assault and the *Tuberville* case that this is a conditional threat that does not count as an assault.) Kevin punches John in the face, breaking his jaw. John sues Kevin for harmful battery. Assuming John can prove all the elements of battery, can Kevin successfully raise the affirmative defense of self-defense?

A. No, because Kevin used disproportionate force.
B. No, because Kevin was not justified in using any force.
C. Yes, because John had a gun.
D. Yes, because Kevin did not use deadly force.

ANALYSIS.   A court is going to find that Kevin was the aggressor here. Though John did put his hand on the gun, he coupled it with a comment which, under the law governing assault, constituted a conditional threat that is not considered an assault. Given that John has not assaulted Kevin, Kevin cannot commit what would otherwise be a battery against John. (That's actually the holding of the old *Tuberville* case, by the way.) For this reason, Kevin cannot use any force and therefore Choices **A**, **C**, and **D** are incorrect. Choice **B** correctly states the law.

QUESTION 5. Take That!   Mona doesn't like Nancy very much. They see each other walking on the public street. Mona walks up to Nancy and slaps her in the face. She then walks away in the opposite direction. Nancy, angry at Mona and concerned that Mona might slap her again the next time they see each other, catches up to Mona and slaps her very hard, knocking Mona to the ground.

If Mona sues Nancy for harmful battery:

A. Nancy will lose because she used disproportionate force.
B. Nancy will win because she used proportionate force.
C. Nancy will lose because she did not act in self-defense.
D. Nancy will win because she acted in self-defense.

ANALYSIS.   Under these facts, Mona had already walked away after the slap, so it does not appear that Mona was about to make another contact with Nancy. For this reason, Nancy could not have been acting in self-defense. Instead, she acted out of anger and to deter Nancy from future bad conduct. That is an impermissible motive and does not count as self-defense, regardless of the amount of force that was used. For this reason, Choice **C** is correct and the other choices are wrong.

Reasonable Mistake. Note that under the Restatement's test, as well as under the common law in many jurisdictions, a person can use reasonable force in self-defense if that person "reasonably believes" the other is about to inflict offensive or harmful contact or other bodily harm upon him. A corollary of this idea of "reasonable belief" is that a person can take actions in self-defense if the person makes a *reasonable mistake* as to the need for self-defense.

Note how the treatment of self-defense differs from the treatment of consent. As we saw earlier in this chapter, generally speaking, a reasonable mistake as to plaintiff's consent is not good enough; unless the plaintiff has actually consented, consent may not serve as an affirmative defense to an intentional tort.

Why the difference in treatment? One possible answer is that when issues of consent arise, it is always possible to get clarification from the would-be plaintiff before committing the would-be tort. ("Would it be okay for me to drive onto your driveway?") With self-defense, in contrast, the situation is urgent. In most circumstances, there is no ability to get clarification from the would-be plaintiff before committing the would-be tort. ("Are you really going to shoot me, or are you just joking in pointing that gun at my head?")

Note also the tension between the reasonable mistake idea in self-defense and the lack of an affirmative defense for insanity. We let the person who inflicts bodily harm on another off the hook if he did so in mistaken self-defense, but we don't let the person suffering from the mental disease or defect off the hook for committing a tort that the person had no ability to control or prevent.

QUESTION 6. CIA Delusion.   Lara is under a delusion caused by mental illness that she is being chased by CIA agents. In fact, she is not. She sees Mary walking down the street, and honestly believes that Mary is about to spray a poison in her face that will kill her. Lara picks up a big rock and throws it at Mary's head. Mary suffers a concussion and is hospitalized for a week. Mary sues Lara for battery, and Lara raises self-defense as an affirmative defense. How should the court rule?

A. Lara's affirmative defense should be accepted because she had an honest belief that she was being attacked by CIA agents.

B. Lara's affirmative defense should be accepted even though she did not have a reasonable belief she was being attacked by CIA agents.

C. Lara's affirmative defense should be rejected despite the fact that she had an honest belief that she was being attacked by CIA agents.

D. Lara's affirmative defense should be rejected because Lara used disproportionate force.

ANALYSIS. Lara was not actually under attack, so the battery claim brought by Mary should succeed unless Lara can argue she made a reasonable mistake as to the need for self-defense. An *honest* belief is not the same as a reasonable one. Nothing in the facts indicates that Lara's belief was reasonable. For this reason, Choices **A** and **B** are incorrect. Given that Lara did not have a reasonable belief as to the need for self-defense, she could not use *any* force. The issue of proportionality does not arise. For this reason, Choice **D** is incorrect. This leaves us with the correct answer, Choice **C**: even though Lara had an honest belief, the affirmative defense should be rejected because it was not a reasonable belief.

Innocent Third Parties Hurt Along the Way. The self-defense principle says that a person under attack can use reasonable force to repel the attack, and in the case of an attack threatening death or serious bodily injury, the person under attack may even use similar measures in return in some circumstances. But suppose that in taking similar measures an innocent third party is injured. The Restatement's position is that the person under attack is not liable for battery unless the person under attack "realizes or should realize that his act creates an unreasonable risk of causing such harm." REST. (2D) TORTS § 75. To put this standard in terms that will become familiar in the next part of the book, it is permissible to take steps in self-defense except when doing so would be negligent.

QUESTION 7. Rude Awakening. Orly is walking down a deserted street late at night. Peter jumps out of the bushes with a gun and tells Orly: "I'm going to kill you." Orly takes out a gun from her purse and tries to shoot Peter, who runs away. The bullet from Orly's gun misses Peter but hits Quentin, who was sleeping in his bed in an apartment right next to the street. If Quentin sues Orly for harmful battery:

A. Quentin should win, if, in shooting at Peter, Orly should have realized that she created an unreasonable risk of harming an innocent bystander.

B. Quentin should win because Orly intentionally shot the gun.

C. Quentin should lose because Orly intended to shoot Peter, not Quentin.

D. Quentin should lose because Orly meant no harm to Quentin.

ANALYSIS.   Recall that to prove the tortious conduct portion of the prima facie case for harmful battery, Quentin can succeed if he shows, as he can on these facts, that Orly acted, intending to cause a harmful contact with a third person (in this case, Peter), and harmful contact resulted to Quentin without Quentin's consent. Orly will try to win the case by claiming self-defense. Under the applicable rules, she can successfully raise the defense unless she realized she was creating an unreasonable risk of harm to third parties. That's the standard set forth in Choice **A**. Choices **B** and **D** are incorrect statements of the law: intention to shoot a gun is not enough to establish liability for battery, and a defendant's lack of intent to cause harm to *plaintiff* is not enough if she intended harm to a third person. Choice **C** similarly ignores the possibility of transferred intent.

Defense of Others. Related to the privilege to take actions in self-defense is the privilege to defend an innocent third party from attack. In order for the privilege to apply, it must be that the person about to be attacked would himself have the privilege to act in self-defense, and the other person's intervention must be necessary. Under the Restatement, defense of others is a valid defense even if the defendant makes a reasonable mistake as to the need for defending the other. REST. (2D) TORTS § 76.

QUESTION 8. Slapstick Tragedy.   Moe sees Larry holding Curly in a headlock. Moe should have realized they were just joking around, but Moe stabs Larry with a knife, causing serious personal injuries. Larry sues Moe for battery, and Moe raises defense of others in self-defense. Which is *not* an argument Larry can make against Moe's affirmative defense?

A. Moe acted unreasonably in believing Curly was really under attack.
B. Moe used disproportionate force in repelling Larry.
C. Moe could not have acted in defense of Curly because Curly was not privileged under these circumstances to use force in self-defense against Larry.
D. Only the person under attack, and not a third party, may use force against an attacker.

ANALYSIS.   A defendant may claim defense of others only when the other is actually under attack or the defendant has a reasonable belief that person was under attack. Here, we are told that Moe should have known that Curly was not really under attack. For this reason, Choice **A** states a correct argument that Larry could raise against the defense of others defense. Similarly, Choice **C** also raises a good argument: If Curly could not have acted under these circumstances, Moe could not either. Finally, Choice **B**

states a correct principle. One can only use proportionate force in repelling an attack, whether the defense is self-defense or defense of others. Stabbing someone to break up a headlock appears to be disproportionate force. This leaves us with Choice **D**, the only one that states an incorrect principle of law, and therefore represents the right answer here.

E.   Defense of property

The affirmative defense of defense of property parallels the defenses of self-defense and defense of others. The main difference is that, unsurprisingly, the amount of force used to defend property can never be deadly force. A human life is worth more than property, even valuable property. This is subject to an important caveat, however: If a person makes an unprivileged entry onto someone else's land while the landowner is present, in certain circumstances the landowner can rely upon the more general affirmative defense of *self-defense*, rather than merely the defense of defense of property.

Here is the main Restatement (Second) of Torts provision, § 77, concerning defense of property:

> An actor is privileged to use reasonable force, not intended or likely to cause death or serious bodily harm, to prevent or terminate another's intrusion upon the actor's land or chattels, if
> (a) the intrusion is not privileged or the other intentionally or negligently causes the actor to believe that it is not privileged, and
> (b) the actor reasonably believes that the intrusion can be prevented or terminated only by the force used, and
> (c) the actor has first requested the other to desist and the other has disregarded the request, or the actor reasonably believes that a request will be useless or that substantial harm will be done before it can be made.

Note the following important features:

- The force must be reasonable force, never rising to the level of deadly force.
- If the intrusion is privileged (as we will see with some necessity hypotheticals coming up later in the chapter), force cannot be used.
- If there are ways to terminate the intrusion without force, those means must be used (that seems to be a corollary of the earlier point that only *reasonable* force can be used).
- The land or property owner must first consider whether it is prudent to ask the intruder to leave before using force, and must do so unless the owner reasonably believes the request will be useless or the intruder will commit the harm before the request is made.

QUESTION 9. **Don't Tread on Me.**   Rafi is riding his bike through some fields on the outskirts of town. As he is riding he is listening to music through headphones. He cannot hear a thing. Stan owns land near where Rafi is riding. He sees Rafi riding with the headphones on and sees that, despite the "No Trespassing" signs posted on Stan's property, Rafi is about to enter Stan's land and run over Stan's flower garden, which contains many rare and valuable flowers. Stan calls to Rafi to stop but Rafi does not hear him. As Rafi crosses his property line, Stan takes his shotgun and shoots a hole in Rafi's front bike tire. Rafi falls off the bike and breaks 6 bones. He sues Stan for battery. Can Stan successfully raise the defense of defense of property?

A. No, because one can never use a gun to defend property.
B. No, because Stan failed to warn Rafi again before shooting.
C. No, if the jury finds the amount of force used by Stan was unreasonable.
D. Yes, because the value of the flowers exceeded the value of the bike tire.

ANALYSIS.   On these facts, Stan would be justified in using reasonable force to keep Rafi from going onto his property and ruining his flowers. Stan tried to warn Rafi, but Rafi could not hear. The big question here is whether Stan used an unreasonable amount of force in trying to stop Rafi; shooting at a tire of a moving bicycle could inflict some heavy damage on the bike rider. Choice **C** accurately explains the difficult issue before the jury — whether the amount of force used was justified. Choice **A** states an overly broad and incorrect principle of law. Choice **B** is incorrect because it is enough that Stan tried to warn Rafi once. Given the headphones and the speed of the bike, a further warning would have been useless and likely too late. Choice **D** is incorrect because it is the wrong comparison in judging the reasonableness of the force: It is not just the risk to the bike, but also the risk to Rafi, that Stan must weigh in the comparison.

Spring Guns and Other Defensive Devices. A person who owns property cannot always be around the property to protect it, and the law allows reasonable defensive measures to protect the property, such as barbed wire, especially if the landowner takes steps to warn any potential intruders of the defensive measure. *See* REST. (2D) TORTS § 84. More extreme defensive measures, such as "spring guns" set to automatically fire when an intruder trips a wire on the landowner's land, generally are not allowed because such devices can inflict death or serious bodily injury. *See* REST. (2D) TORTS § 85. Such a policy is unsurprising; it is just an extension of the idea that one cannot use such force in defense of property.

When it comes to devices such as spring guns, there is a temptation to treat "bad" trespassers, such as a person who enters defendant's land to steal property,[3] more harshly than "good" trespassers, such as a trespasser who is chasing a neighbor's lost animal to recapture it.[4] The distinction is not formalized in the law, but it could influence judges and juries.

QUESTION 10. Tammy L'Orange.   Val had been having a lot of trouble with thieves, so she set a trap. Tammy breaks into Val's house to steal Val's plasma television while Val is away. In entering Val's property Tammy trips a wire that causes a paint gun to go off. Tammy is sprayed with bright orange paint that is nearly impossible to remove for many weeks. After Tammy leaves the house, Val calls the police and the police pick up Tammy in the neighborhood; she was easy to spot because she was covered with bright orange paint. Tammy sues Val for battery. Can Val successfully defend herself using the defense of defense of property?

A. Yes, because any steps taken to deter thieves are acceptable means of defending property.

B. Yes, because the paint gun trap involved a reasonable use of force under the circumstances.

C. No, because any kind of mechanical device constitutes an unreasonable defense of property.

D. No, because Tammy was not present at the time.

ANALYSIS.   Though Tammy set a spring gun, it does not appear to be the type of spring gun that would inflict death or serious bodily injury on an intruder. Instead, it appears likely to inflict at most an offensive contact — hard-to-remove paint — which may make it easier to identify the intruder. A court would likely accept this as a reasonable use of force against an intruder. Choice **B** accurately captures that idea. Choice **A** states the law incorrectly; it is not true that *any* steps, especially steps involving deadly force, may be taken to defend property. Choice **C** similarly misstates the law. You can probably think of all kinds of mechanical devices, such as burglar alarms, set up to defend property that are not unreasonable defenses of property. Finally, Choice **D** is incorrect because one may take reasonable steps to defend property even if one is not home at the time.

F.   Recapture of chattels

Closely related to the affirmative defense of defense of property is the defense of recapture of chattels. If someone takes your personal property (chattel) by

---

3.   *See Katko v. Briney*, 183 N.W.2d 657 (Iowa 1971).

4.   *See Bird v. Holbrook*, 4 Bing 628, 130 E.R. 911 (C.P. 1825). *See generally* EPSTEIN, TORTS §2.12.2.

force, you can use reasonable force within a reasonable amount of time to recapture the chattel. The rules on the amount of force allowed parallel the rules that apply to defense of property. Similarly, the owner must ask the chattel-taker to return the property before using reasonable force, unless it would be useless or dangerous to do so. The reasonable time requirement is going to be a jury question.[5]

Recapture of chattels is not available if the person in possession of the chattel had taken it under a "claim of right." In *Kirby v. Foster*, 22 A. 1111 (R.I. 1891), defendant employer gave plaintiff, an employee, money to distribute to other employees. On the advice of counsel, the plaintiff kept some of that money for himself, claiming he was owed it by the employer. The employer's agent then made contact with the plaintiff in an effort to get the money, injuring the plaintiff in the process. Plaintiff sued for battery, and the defendant employer raised the defense of recapture of chattels. The court held the defense could not be used in this case:

> [T]his right of defen[s]e and recapture involves two things: first, possession by the owner, and, second, a purely wrongful taking or conversion, without a claim of right. If one has [e]ntrusted his property to another, who afterwards, honestly though erroneously, claims it as his own, the owner has no right to retake it by personal force.

The appropriate step for the employer in such circumstances is to file an action in court seeking a return of the money.

It is not necessary that the chattel-taker forcibly take or steal the chattel from its owner. If the chattel-taker obtains the property through duress or fraud, the owner can seek to recapture the chattels using reasonable force in a reasonable time.

QUESTION 11. MP3 Rip-off. Wendy is studying in the law school library while listening to music on her MP3 player, which has a "skin" (or covering) that is bright pink. She leaves for the day, forgetting her MP3 player in the library. When Wendy returns, it is not there. A few minutes later, Wendy is walking on the law school campus and sees Zeta, another student, listening to music from an MP3 player with a bright pink skin. Wendy sneaks up behind Zeta and rips the MP3 player from Zeta's hand. The attached headphones also come off, causing Zeta to get a nasty cut on her ear. Zeta sues Wendy for battery and Wendy raises the defense of recapture of chattels. The MP3 player was indeed Wendy's. How should the court rule on Wendy's defense?

---

5. According to Professor Epstein, recapture of chattels must be done in "hot pursuit" of the chattel-taker. EPSTEIN, CASES AND MATERIALS ON TORTS 67 (9th ed. 2008). Under the Restatement's approach, the amount of time can be longer, even sometimes a few days. *See* REST. (2D) TORTS § 103. I have found no modern American cases discussing the question.

A. Wendy's claim fails because her attempt to recapture was not timely.
B. Wendy's claim fails because she did not first ask Zeta if the MP3 player was Wendy's and Wendy cannot demonstrate it would have been useless or dangerous to ask before using force.
C. Wendy's claim fails because Zeta did not use fraud or duress to capture the chattel.
D. Wendy's claim succeeds because the MP3 player belonged to her.

ANALYSIS.   Though a chattel owner like Wendy has the right to recapture chattels taken from her within a reasonable time, she must first make a demand for the chattel unless she reasonably believes it would be useless or dangerous to do so. In this fact pattern, there are no facts suggesting it would be useless or dangerous to ask Zeta first. For this reason, Wendy's defense should fail, meaning Choice **B** is correct. Choice **A** is wrong because, though there is a debate over timeliness requirements, waiting a few minutes would not be seen as too short a time by any court. Choice **C** is incorrect because it is not necessary that the item be taken through fraud or duress for the owner to have the right of recapture of chattels. Choice **D** is wrong because there are limits on the defense of recapture to chattels even when an owner is sure that she has discovered her property in the hands of another. One of those requirements is the requirement to make a demand for the item's return unless it would be useless or dangerous to do so.

G.   Necessity

The final affirmative defense to intentional torts that we consider in this book is *necessity*. Necessity is different from the other affirmative defenses in that (except in its form as *public* necessity) it is a conditional, or incomplete, defense. To understand what this means, consider this hypothetical: Abe is hiking alone in the woods and gets lost. He is tired and hungry. He comes across a cabin in the woods that is locked. He breaks into the cabin and eats a can of beans from the cupboard. The cabin belongs to Beth, who returns to find Abe eating the food at her kitchen table.

Let's now consider two possible continuations of this story to see how necessity functions as an incomplete defense.

Scenario 1. *Beth versus Abe for Trespass to Land and Conversion.* Beth lets Abe finish his food and leave. She later sues him for trespass to land and conversion. Beth could easily make out the tortious conduct portion of the prima facie case for these torts. Abe acted, he intended to enter Beth's land, and he entered Beth's land, causing damages. He also seriously interfered with her food by eating it. Abe could raise the affirmative defense of necessity, giving him a privilege to use Beth's property because of the exigent circumstances. But — and here's the tricky part — even if the jury agrees that Abe acted out of necessity, Abe still must pay for the damage he caused (in this case the broken door and value of the food). That's what makes it a *conditional* or *incomplete* defense.

So what good is the defense of necessity if Abe still has to pay? First, a jury finding of necessity would mean that this would not be an appropriate case for the award of punitive damages.[6] Second, a finding of necessity is relevant in letting Abe take what he wants and pay for it later. To understand this second point, consider our alternative scenario.

Scenario 2. *Abe versus Beth for Battery.* Imagine now that Beth comes back to her cabin to find Abe in there. Beth tells Abe to leave, but Abe says: "I'm so sorry. I'm hungry and tired and got lost in the woods. May I please eat some of your food?" Beth says no, but Abe ignores her. Beth then picks Abe up and throws him out of the cabin. In Abe's weak state, he falls and breaks his leg. He later sues Beth for battery.

Abe can likely make out the prima facie case for battery. Beth acted, she intended contact (one dispute might be if she intended harmful or offensive contact) with Abe, harmful contact resulted, and there was no consent. Beth would like to defend herself by claiming defense of property, arguing that her use of force was reasonable. However, and here is the key point, a court will *not* let Beth raise the affirmative defense of defense of property if Abe was acting out of necessity.[7]

To put it another way, when someone acts out of necessity in committing what would otherwise be a tort such as trespass to land or conversion, the owner of the property does not have the right to interfere with the intruder. The intruder is privileged to take what he or she needs, subject to payment afterward. As the Minnesota Supreme Court put it in a famous necessity case, *Vincent v. Lake Erie Transportation Co.*, 124 N.W. 221 (Minn. 1910), "Theologians hold that a starving man may, without moral guilt, take what is necessary to sustain life but it could hardly be said that the obligation would not be upon such person to pay the value of the property so taken when he became able to do so."

The idea of making necessity an incomplete or conditional defense is a brilliant legal solution to an economic problem, that of a *bilateral monopoly*. In most transactions, there are many buyers and many sellers, and if one buyer or seller offers an unreasonable price, there is competition. In this environment we expect market prices to emerge. In conditions of emergency, however, there are not many buyers and many sellers. Think of how much Beth might charge Abe for a can of beans if Beth were unscrupulous. When

---

6. More on the standards for awarding punitive damages in Chapter 23.
7. This is essentially the holding of one of the most famous necessity cases, *Ploof v. Putnam*, 71 A. 188 (Vt. 1908).

there is one buyer and one seller, a bilateral monopoly, we don't expect competitive prices to emerge. By allowing Abe to take what he needs and then pay market rates afterward, tort law mimics the conditions that would have occurred had there been a competitive market at the time Abe needed the can of beans.

QUESTION 12. Lend Me a Hand. Carol is swimming in public waters near Dario's dock when a storm comes in. Carol calls Dario for help, and Dario, standing on the edge of the dock, refuses to help. Carol grabs onto the dock to try to pull herself up. Dario steps on her fingers and Carol falls into the water. She loses consciousness and later washes up on shore with serious personal injuries.

If Carol sues Dario for battery:

A. Carol wins because she was privileged to come up onto Dario's dock.
B. Carol wins, but only if she can prove she would not have caused any damage to the dock.
C. Carol loses because Dario used reasonable force to defend his property.
D. Carol loses because Dario used reasonable force in self defense.

ANALYSIS. Without any claim of necessity, Carol would be liable for trespass to real property (even if she did not cause any damage — see Chapter 3). But Carol was drowning and could have claimed necessity to justify the trespass. For this reason, Dario was not privileged to use *any* force to prevent her from entering his dock. He was not obligated to help her, but he couldn't hinder her entry. And certainly the use of force that could kill her — in this case stepping on the fingers that were clinging to the dock — was unreasonable in any case. Choice **A** correctly explains that Carol's battery case will succeed because she was privileged to go onto Dario's property. Choice **B** is wrong. Carol can trespass because of the necessity even if she would have caused damage. Choice **C** is wrong because Dario is not allowed to use any force, much less the unreasonable force he used here, because of Carol's claim of necessity. Choice **D** is wrong because Carol was not attacking Dario, nor could he reasonably think so under these facts. So self-defense will not be successful.

As a final aside on this hypothetical, imagine if Carol tried to pull herself out of the water by grabbing not onto the dock, but onto Dario's *leg*. The question would then be whether or not a person could commit a *battery* out of necessity. On this question, the Restatement (Second) of Torts § 73, *Caveat*, takes a pass: "The Institute expresses no opinion that there may not be a privilege to inflict a comparatively slight bodily harm upon another for the purpose of protecting the actor or a third person from a disproportionately greater bodily harm, as for instance, death, threatened otherwise than by the conduct of the other."

Public Necessity. Though necessity ordinarily is an incomplete or conditional defense, when a person acts to further the public good, *public necessity* serves as a complete defense. In cases of public necessity, the person taking or destroying others' property need not pay for the damage caused.[8]

What counts as *public* necessity?

> Cases of public necessity arise when natural forces or third parties require the destruction of the property of some to save the lives or property of other people. These actions are usually undertaken by a public official charged with the welfare of the community and not an individual property owner for her own benefit.

RICHARD A. EPSTEIN, TORTS 65 (1999).

QUESTION 13. Down Dog. Evan, an animal control officer with the City of Pacificana, is on patrol when he sees an apparently rabid dog threatening a crowd of people. Evan shoots the dog with a tranquilizer gun. The dog collapses upon being shot, and dies of a heart attack. Frannie, the owner of the dog, sues Evan for trespass to chattels. What result?

A. Evan can successfully claim necessity, but he will have to pay for the reasonable value of the dog.

B. Evan can successfully claim necessity, and under applicable tort law he need not pay for the reasonable value of the dog.

C. Evan cannot claim necessity unless the dog was threatening Evan.

D. Evan cannot claim necessity because it was not necessary to shoot the dog.

ANALYSIS. This fact pattern presents a classic case of public necessity. Evan was a public official acting in the interest of the public welfare by shooting a rabid dog threatening a group of people. Because he can make a claim of *public* necessity, tort law will not require him to pay compensation. Choice **B**, and not Choice **A**, makes the dual points that Evan can raise the necessity defense and that he need not pay. Choice **C** is wrong because public necessity may be raised to assist others. Choice **D** is simply wrong on the facts; a public official has every right to shoot a rabid dog threatening a group of people.

---

8. When the person doing the taking is a public official, there may be issues as to whether the Fifth or Fourteenth Amendments to the U.S. Constitution requires the payment of "just compensation" for the taking. But that is an issue for a Constitutional Law course, not a Torts course.

H.   The Closer: Choose your (defensive) weapon

As this chapter demonstrates, even when a plaintiff can prove the tortious conduct elements of an intentional tort, defendants have a number of possible affirmative defenses that might be raised, depending upon the facts. One of the jobs of a defense lawyer is to consider the various affirmative defenses and decide which are viable, and which ones are worthy of presentation to the jury. This is a skill you can start to develop by examining this chapter's Closer.

> **QUESTION 14. Choose Your (Defensive) Weapon.**   Gerry is suffering from paranoid schizophrenia, and without medication he can be violent. Gerry buys a gun and goes into the middle of a crowd in Times Square, threatening to shoot passersby. Hal sees what is happening and shoots Gerry in the leg. Police apprehend Gerry and Gerry later sues Hal for battery. What is Hal's strongest defense to the battery claim?
>
> **A.** Defense of others
> **B.** Public necessity
> **C.** Insanity
> **D.** Consent

ANALYSIS.   Off the bat, you should be able to eliminate Choices **C** and **D**. Choice **C** is incorrect for two reasons. First, it is arguably the plaintiff, not the defendant, who is "insane." Second, insanity is generally not a defense to intentional torts. Choice **D** is wrong because there is no reason to believe that Gerry had given any kind of consent to being shot. The harder question is between Choices **A** and **B**. Choice **A** is a better choice. By his actions, Gerry was assaulting members of the crowd. A person with a gun threatening to shoot in a crowd presents an imminent threat of harm. Hal could take defensive and proportional measures (perhaps not actions likely to lead to Gerry's death, but serious actions) to save members of the crowd. Choice **B** is tempting, because in many ways the fact pattern in this example mirrors the one in Question 13 about the rabid dog. But, as was explained above in the discussion of necessity, public necessity is generally about the use or destruction of property for public benefit, not taking actions against *persons* who threaten harm to others. When the public danger is a person and not property, the appropriate defense is self-defense/defense of others rather than necessity.

Rick's picks

1. Burden of Proof	**D**	
2. Eddy the Great	**A**	
3. The Dream Police	**C**	
4. Assize-Time Updated	**B**	
5. Take That!	**C**	
6. CIA Delusion	**C**	
7. Rude Awakening	**A**	
8. Slapstick Tragedy	**D**	
9. Don't Tread on Me	**C**	
10. Tammy L'Orange	**B**	
11. MP3 Rip-off	**B**	
12. Lend Me a Hand	**A**	
13. Down Dog	**B**	
14. Choose Your (Defensive) Weapon	**A**	

6

Intentional Tort Frontiers: Intentional Infliction of Emotional Distress

CHAPTER OVERVIEW
A. Introduction: Why a new tort protecting against emotional harm?
B. The elements of IIED
C. Special rules for bystanders
D. Affirmative defenses to IIED: Must-see TV
E. First Amendment concerns
F. The Closer: When IIED, and when other intentional torts?
✦ Rick's picks

A. Introduction: Why a new tort protecting against emotional harm?

The idea that a plaintiff suffering emotional distress may, in some circumstances, recover damages in tort is not new. After all, as we saw in Chapter 4, early assault cases date back to the fourteenth century in England. But courts have been wary about damages for emotional distress for two reasons: first, the lack of a market measure for such damages and, second, the possibility that plaintiffs would lie or exaggerate the amount of their distress in order to recover large damages from a jury.

For this reason, until relatively recently in tort law emotional distress damages were available only when they could be recovered as part of another tort. So if the defendant committed a battery, assault, false imprisonment, or another tort that caused some emotional distress, these damages could be recovered as *parasitic to* the initial tort action. But if the plaintiff could *not* prove the prima facie case for one of these torts, the plaintiff could recover no damages. This led courts sometimes to find a minor technical violation of one of these torts in order to allow the recovery of more significant emotional distress damages. *See Bouillon v. Laclede Gaslight Co.*, 129 S.W. 401 (Mo. App. 1910) (defendant committed technical trespass to land and caused significant emotional distress damage by berating plaintiff, causing her to have a miscarriage; court allowed emotional distress damages as parasitic to the nominal damages for trespass). Under the logic of these old cases, a plaintiff suffering similar emotional distress could not recover any damages absent the serendipity of at least the technical violation of another tort. Be sure to review the causes of actions for the other intentional torts so that you can see when they will work and when they won't work as a hook for emotional distress damages.

Beginning at the end of the nineteenth century, with the case of *Wilkinson v. Downton*, 2 Q.B. 57 (1897), courts began recognizing the tort of intentional infliction of emotional distress ("IIED" for short). In *Wilkinson*, the defendant played a practical joke on a woman, telling her that her husband was involved in an accident at work and was lying there with both of his legs broken, urging her to get to his worksite with a couple of pillows. The woman suffered serious emotional distress. Though the court could have found that the defendant committed the intentional tort of fraud on the plaintiff (a tort not discussed in this book), the court instead recognized a new tort, which would not require proof of another tort as a "hook" for emotional distress damages. Many other courts, and the Restatement, later followed suit, but with strict limits placed on the tort to deal with the problem of spurious or exaggerated claims. We will turn to the elements of the tort next.

QUESTION 1. Emotional Hang-Up.   Every night for a month, Andrea has been getting phone calls in the middle of the night. The caller says in an ominous voice: "I'm watching you." The caller then hangs up. Andrea is upset and frightened. The police discover the calls have been made by Bill, her neighbor, who is upset that Andrea put up a fence along their property lines. Andrea would like to sue Bill in tort. Which is her strongest cause of action?

A. Assault
B. Harmful battery
C. Offensive battery
D. None of the above

ANALYSIS.   This question is aimed at making you realize that defendants can intentionally inflict all kinds of emotional harm without doing so through one of the categories of intentional torts. Reviewing the torts from Chapters 2 and 3, there is no assault here. Though Bill acted, he did not intend to put the plaintiff in imminent apprehension of a harmful or offensive contact, and did not intend to cause a harmful or offensive contact with the plaintiff. The battery claims fail for the same reason, plus the fact that no physical contact, harmful or offensive, ever resulted. This means that Choice **D**, none of the above, is the correct answer and Choices **A**, **B**, and **C** are incorrect. If Andrea is to recover for a common law tort (as opposed to a statutory cause of action for telephone harassment, as now exists in a number of jurisdictions), it will have to be for IIED.

B.   The elements of IIED

The Restatement (Second) of Tort's treatment of intentional infliction of emotional distress has been very influential. The core of the Restatement approach is section 46(1):

> One who by extreme and outrageous conduct intentionally or recklessly causes severe emotional distress to another is subject to liability for such emotional distress, and if bodily harm to the other results from it, for such bodily harm.

As with the other intentional torts we have considered, it is necessary to break this down into the elements of the tortious conduct portion of the prima facie case:

1. A defendant must engage in extreme and outrageous conduct.
2. The defendant must do so intentionally or recklessly to cause serious emotional distress.
3. The plaintiff must suffer severe emotional distress.

Let's consider each of these elements in turn.

Extreme and Outrageous Conduct. Life is full of lots of indignities, and many of us suffer emotional distress from various sources on a regular basis. The IIED tort is not designed to turn every insult into a lawsuit. Instead, the conduct is limited to behavior that goes beyond all bounds of decency.

Students often express frustration that the Restatement defines outrageous in an apparently tautological way: "Generally, the case is one in which the recitation of the facts to an average member of the community would arouse his resentment against the actor, and lead him to exclaim, 'Outrageous!'" REST. (2D) TORTS § 46 cmt. *d*. At first glance, a definition defining the term "outrageous" by using the term "outrageous" is itself outrageous! But the point of the Restatement section is that the standard of outrageousness is going to be judged by community standards and not fixed in time. The Restatement itself offers some (dated and sometimes sexist) examples of outrageous conduct, including a hypothetical based upon the facts of *Wilkinson,* a situation in which the defendant gives the plaintiff a dissolving bathing suit that causes plaintiff to become naked at a swimming party at an exclusive resort, and one involving the principal of a high school summoning "a schoolgirl [to his office] and abruptly accus[ing] her of immoral conduct with various men," and then "bully[ing her] for an hour, and threaten[ing] her with prison and with public disgrace for herself and her parents until she confesses." REST. (2D) TORTS § 46 illus. 1, 3, & 6.

Some kind of conduct is outrageous only if a plaintiff is particularly susceptible to emotional distress by reason of some physical or mental condition or peculiarity, and the defendant acts in the face of such knowledge. Many of the examples given by the Restatement in this context are outdated and would be almost quaint if they weren't offensive,[1] but the general principle remains good law. Note that even under these circumstances, "major outrage" is essential to the tort. Calling "an otherwise normal girl who is a little overweight, and quite sensitive about it" a "hippopotamus" is not outrageous enough to justify damages, even if the girl is "embarrassed," "angry," "brood[ing]," and "made ill." REST. (2D) TORTS § 46 cmt. *f* & illus. 13.

QUESTION 2. Emotional Hang-Up, Take II. Every night for a month, Andrea has been getting phone calls in the middle of the night. The caller says in an ominous voice: "I'm watching you." The caller then hangs up. Andrea is upset and frightened. The police discover the calls have been made by Bill, her neighbor, who is upset that Andrea put up a fence along their property lines. Andrea sues Bill for intentional infliction of emotional distress. Can Andrea prove the tortious conduct portion of the prima facie case for IIED?

A. Yes, if the jury concludes Bill's conduct was extreme and outrageous.
B. No, because Bill did not make a threat of physical violence.
C. No, because one cannot engage in outrageous conduct by telephone.
D. No, unless Bill knew that Andrea was extra sensitive to phone calls in the middle of the night.

ANALYSIS. Andrea will argue that calling someone up anonymously in the middle of the night every night for a month to say "I'm watching you" is extreme and outrageous conduct. This will end up being a question for the jury. Certainly this conduct is more extreme than calling an overweight and sensitive person a "hippopotamus," but it is not nearly as extreme as some

---

1. Here is one that shows the Restatement's age (the final draft of the Second Restatement was issued in 1965): "A, an eccentric and mentally deficient old maid, has the delusion that a pot of gold is buried in her back yard, and is always digging for it. Knowing this, B buries a pot with other contents in her yard and when A digs it up causes her to be escorted in triumph to city hall, where the pot is opened under circumstances of public humiliation to A. A suffers severe emotional distress and resulting illness. B is subject to liability to A for both." REST. (2D) TORTS § 46 illus. 9.

other examples of outrageous conduct. Choice **A** correctly states that the question whether the conduct was extreme and outrageous is a jury question. Choices **B** and **C** are wrong for the same reason: they state incorrect categorical rules about what counts as outrageous conduct. Choice **D** is wrong because a jury could conclude that Bill's conduct is extreme and outrageous even absent proof that Andrea was extra sensitive to phone calls in the middle of the night. Understanding why Choice **A** is better than Choice **D** goes back to a point I made in Chapter 1. Don't leave your common sense at home. Most of us would be freaked out by middle-of-the-night phone calls as Andrea has endured. In the real world, it would not be surprising for a jury to consider this conduct extreme and outrageous even absent proof of extra-sensitivity.

Intent. IIED has a different intent structure than we have seen with the other intentional torts. For the other intentional torts, the defendant had to act either with the *purpose* of causing the consequence relevant to the tort (such as entering plaintiff's land, for trespass to land) or with the *knowledge* that the consequence is substantially certain to occur. Under IIED, in contrast, purpose, knowledge, or *recklessness* is enough. Recklessness here refers to an action taken "in deliberate disregard of a high degree of probability that the emotional distress will follow." REST. (2D) TORTS § 46 cmt. *i.*

IIED expands the level of intent necessary to meet the tortious conduct portion of the prima facie case to deal with, among other things, the problem of the cruel practical joke, as in *Wilkinson.* It might be difficult for a plaintiff to prove that when the defendant played the practical joke in telling plaintiff her husband had suffered a terrible accident and broken both of his legs, he actually acted with the purpose to cause severe emotional distress or even with the knowledge that such emotional distress was substantially likely to result. Likely the defendant thought in his own demented way that he was being funny, and did not actually consider the high risk that his actions would in fact lead to these results. The recklessness standard captures these kinds of cases as well.

QUESTION 3. Killing Fields.   Carl is very depressed and decides to kill himself. He goes out of town to the woods in a place he thought was very isolated. He shoots himself in the head, but does not die. Carl did not know it, but he had shot himself next to a campsite. A group of campers from a junior high school class come upon him. Carl is rushed to the hospital, and survives after surgery. Some of the students have been suffering from severe emotional distress since the incident. If the students sue Carl for IIED, can they prove the tortious conduct portion of the prima facie case?

A. Yes, because Carl acted with the purpose to cause emotional distress to the students.

B. Yes, because Carl acted with knowledge that emotional distress was substantially certain to occur to the students.

C. Yes, because Carl was reckless that emotional distress would occur to the students.

D. No.

ANALYSIS. Even assuming that this attempted suicide in a place where Carl could be discovered constitutes extreme and outrageous conduct, the students' tort claim will fail. The facts tell us that Carl went out of town to a place he thought was isolated. He did not know of the campsite. On these facts, he did not have the purpose of causing emotional distress to others who would happen upon him, nor did he have the knowledge that such emotional distress was substantially certain to occur. Nor, given the facts, was he deliberately disregarding a high probability that he would cause emotional distress to others. So there is no purpose (Choice **A** is wrong), knowledge (Choice **B** is wrong), or recklessness (Choice **C** is wrong).[2] That leaves us with Choice **D**, a simple "No."

Plaintiff Suffers Severe Emotional Distress. It is not enough that a defendant engages in extreme and outrageous conduct with the purpose, knowledge, or recklessness of causing serious emotional distress to the plaintiff. It is also necessary that the plaintiff suffer severe emotional distress. So if Bill has made those harassing phone calls to Andrea and Andrea is supremely annoyed but does not suffer severe emotional distress, Andrea can recover nothing for IIED. (Again, she might have a statutory cause of action in some states for telephone harassment, but she won't be able to get damages for IIED.) Moreover, it is not enough that the plaintiff suffers real emotional distress, it must be *severe*. The severity requirement serves at least two purposes. First, it eliminates suits over relatively minor incidents (think "hippopotamus"), which would clog the courts if they were allowed. Second, it deals to some extent with the problem of feigned or exaggerated claims. It will be harder to fake "severe" emotional distress because such distress will usually have consequences that would have been observable by others. Did the plaintiff go to see a therapist? Lose his job? Lose weight?

There is no set rule on how the plaintiff must demonstrate that he suffered severe emotional distress. As the Restatement section 46 makes clear, it is not necessary that the plaintiff suffer any "bodily harm," such as vomiting, to signal the credibility of the claim. But whatever evidence the plaintiff can muster will strengthen the argument and the claim for damages.

---

2. Contrast illustrations 15 and 16 of the Restatement (Second) of Torts section 46, which give examples of similar activities meeting the knowledge and recklessness requirements.

And the more outrageous the conduct, the less the plaintiff will have to demonstrate: "in many cases the extreme and outrageous character of the defendant's conduct is in itself important evidence that the distress has existed." REST. (2D) TORTS § 46 cmt. *j.*

QUESTION 4. Dog Day Afternoon.   Diane doesn't like her neighbor Emily very much. One afternoon, she leaves a dead and decomposing dog on the public sidewalk in front of Emily's house. Emily sues Diane for IIED. Emily has not gone to therapy, nor has she missed any work or shown any physical manifestations of emotional distress. Can Emily prove the tortious conduct portion of the prima facie case for IIED?

A. No, because she did not have any objectively verifiable proof that she suffered severe emotional distress.
B. No, because she did not suffer bodily harm.
C. Yes, if the jury concludes she suffered severe emotional distress.
D. Yes, so long as Emily suffered any emotional distress.

ANALYSIS.   There seems little doubt that a jury would consider the conduct of Diane to be extreme and outrageous, and it appears to have been done with the requisite intent: Even if Emily cannot prove purpose or knowledge, she should be able to prove at least that Diane acted recklessly about causing severe emotional distress. Even though Emily did not seek professional help, suffer bodily harm, or have any other outwardly measurable symptoms, a jury could still conclude that she suffered severe emotional distress. The question will be one of credibility. Choice **C** explains this point: Emily can prove IIED but only *if* the jury concludes she suffered severe emotional distress. Choices **A** and **B** are incorrect because there are no bright-line rules requiring objectively verifiable proof or bodily harm in order to allow the question of severe emotional distress to go to a jury. Choice **D** contains an incorrect statement of the law. It is not enough that the plaintiff suffer "emotional distress." It must be severe.

C.   Special rules for bystanders

The same concerns that cause courts to be cautious about allowing IIED actions at all — the lack of a market measure for emotional distress damages, and the fear of false or exaggerated claims — apply especially to claims of *bystanders* that have suffered severe emotional distress from witnessing conduct directed at another person. There is no question that such emotional distress can occur; imagine a parent witnessing the shooting of his or her child, for example. But allowing bystander claims could greatly expand tort liability.[3] For this reason, the Restatement and courts have put limits on bystander recoveries for emotional distress. These limits can lead to somewhat arbitrary results in similar cases, as we shall see. Here is the relevant Restatement provision, from Restatement (Second) of Torts § 46(2):

> Where [extreme and outrageous] conduct is directed at a third person, the actor is subject to liability if he intentionally or recklessly causes severe emotional distress
>
> (a) to a member of such person's immediate family who is present at the time, whether or not such distress results in bodily harm, or
>
> (b) to any other person who is present at the time, if such distress results in bodily harm.

Under this section, for a bystander to recover for IIED, the bystander most prove the following elements as the tortious conduct portion of the prima facie case:

1. The defendant engaged in extreme and outrageous conduct *toward a third person.*
2. The defendant engaged in this conduct purposefully, with knowledge, or recklessness about the emotional distress to be caused *to the plaintiff.*
3. The plaintiff was *present at the time* that the defendant engaged in extreme and outrageous conduct toward the third person.
4. The plaintiff suffered severe emotional distress.
5. The plaintiff is either a member of the third person's immediate family or the plaintiff's distress resulted in bodily harm.

The elements here are similar to, but not identical, to the usual action for IIED.[4] Note that while the extreme and outrageous conduct must be directed to a *third person,* the defendant must be at least reckless about the possibility of causing emotional distress to *the plaintiff.* So imagine that Defendant is about to shoot Husband. If the Defendant knows that Wife is present, or at least is reckless about her presence, then Defendant could be liable to Wife for IIED. But if the Defendant does not know of Wife's presence (even if the Defendant should have known), Defendant cannot be liable to Wife for IIED.

---

3. We will see courts considering a similar issue in the context of *negligent* infliction of emotional distress. See Chapter 12.
4. The new draft RESTATEMENT OF THE LAW THIRD TORTS: LIABILITY FOR PHYSICAL AND EMOTIONAL HARM section 45 (Tentative Draft No. 5, April 4, 2007), comment *l,* would change the bystander rules somewhat: allowing "recovery for emotional harm to 'bystanders' who are close family members and who contemporaneously perceive the event." Assuming this new section is permanently adopted by the Restatement drafters, it could change the way courts view bystander claims, narrowing the category of bystanders able to recover but allowing family members who "contemporaneously perceive" the event to recover, even if they are not "present."

Note also that the bystander claiming IIED must be *present* at the time of the extreme and outrageous conduct. It is not enough that Wife discovers her shot husband later, or witnesses it on television. (Presumably the Restatement drafters thought that being present either would make it more likely a bystander actually suffered emotional distress, or were otherwise looking for a way to limit liability.)

Finally, another check on the floodgates of such litigation is that those plaintiffs who are not immediate relatives must experience severe emotional distress that results in *bodily harm*: that is, some physical manifestation of the emotional harm, such as "shock" or "illness." *See* REST. (2D) TORTS § 46 cmt. *k*. Bodily harm is not required in a non-bystander case, and it is not required for bystanders who are immediate relatives (who presumably are more likely than a stranger to suffer emotional distress upon witnessing extreme and outrageous conduct perpetrated on a loved one).

QUESTION 5. Plaintiff Bingo. Fidel shoots Gerald for no good reason in front of Harry, Ivan, and Jessica. Harry is a friend of Gerald. Ivan has never met anyone before and happened to be passing by. Ivan has been vomiting since the incident because he is so upset. Jessica is Gerald's wife. Kim, Gerald's daughter, hears a shot from her apartment across the street from the shooting. She runs over and sees her father in a pool of blood. Harry, Ivan, Jessica, and Kim sue Fidel for IIED. All of them are extremely upset about the shooting, but no one besides Ivan has manifested any physical symptoms. Which of these plaintiffs can prove the tortious conduct portion of the prima facie case for IIED?

A. Jessica and Harry
B. Jessica and Ivan
C. Jessica and Kim
D. Jessica, Harry, and Kim

ANALYSIS. This is a question that requires application of Restatement (Second) of Torts § 46(2). Off the bat, we can eliminate Kim as a possible bystander. She was across the street in her apartment at the time of the shooting, and therefore she was not present at the time. (Perhaps being in the next room might be considered "present," but not an apartment across the street.) We can therefore eliminate Choices **C** and **D**, which both contain Kim. Harry also will not be allowed to recover as a bystander, because he is a friend, not an immediate family member, and he did not suffer any bodily harm. Choice **A** is therefore wrong. Jessica can recover because she is an immediate family member present at the time who suffered severe emotional distress. Ivan can recover as well. He is not an immediate family member (not even a friend), but he was present at the time and his severe emotional distress resulted in bodily harm. This makes Choice **B** correct. Note that this rule leads to some arbitrary results: Harry, the friend, cannot recover because he had no physical manifestations of his distress, but Ivan the stranger can recover because he was lucky enough (?) to vomit. Jessica gets to recover but Kim does not because she was down the block—even though Kim comes on the scene and likely suffered a great deal of emotional distress from seeing her father in this state.

D.   Affirmative defenses to IIED: Must-see TV

Until recent years, and certainly at the time of the Restatement, it likely seemed odd to talk about affirmative defenses to IIED. After all, what affirmative defense could the defendant in *Wilkinson* possibly point to in order to justify his "practical joke" of telling plaintiff her husband had broken both of his legs in a workplace accident?

In recent years, however, we have witnessed the rise of reality television series and confrontational talk shows such as *The Jerry Springer Show*. The entire purpose of many of these shows appears to be to put participants in embarrassing or humiliating situations and confrontations for the viewing pleasure of the audiences. Oftentimes the participants on these programs do so willingly either for monetary compensation or for notoriety. By partici- pating voluntarily (almost always including the execution of signed waivers of liability), these participants often have signed away their right to sue for IIED in the event they are placed in extreme and outrageous situations that cause their severe emotional distress. In such circumstances, *consent* may serve as a valid affirmative defense to defeat a claim for IIED. After all, a person who goes on *Jerry Springer* and gets humiliated—at least a person who has ever seen *Jerry Springer*—could hardly be surprised.

As we saw in earlier chapters' discussion of consent, however, just because someone consents to something doesn't mean he consents to everything. A professional boxer cannot sue an opponent for a left jab, but can for a stabbing in the boxing ring. Similarly, a person might consent to appear in one of these sensationalist television shows, but the activities that occur could go beyond the scope of the consent. Moreover, if the consent was secured through fraudulent statements, then a court might find the consent to be invalid, and the action for IIED could go forward.

QUESTION 6. Secret Crush. Jonathan was asked if he wanted to appear on the Valentine's Day episode of *The Jenny Jones Show*, a television show that often features people discussing embarrassing or personal issues and relationships. The producer of the show told Jonathan that he had a "secret crush" whose identity would be revealed on the show. Jonathan agreed to appear on the show. When he appeared, it turns out his "secret crush" was Scott, another man, who was a friend of his. Jonathan, who was not gay, was humiliated on the television program because he was embarrassed by questions about his sexual orientation. Can Jonathan sue *The Jenny Jones Show* for IIED?[5]

A. Yes, if the conduct in not revealing the gender of Jonathan's secret crush constitutes extreme and outrageous conduct.
B. Yes, if the conduct of *The Jenny Jones Show* went beyond the scope of Jonathan's consent.
C. Yes, if both A and B are true.
D. No, because Jonathan consented to any kind of treatment by agreeing to appear on the show.

ANALYSIS. The two main questions here are (1) whether the conduct of the show in keeping the gender of the "secret crush" secret constitutes extreme and outrageous conduct; and (2) whether the conduct of the show went beyond the scope of the consent that Jonathan gave when he agreed to appear on the show. Choice **C** correctly points out that Jonathan would have to prove both of these points in order to prevail on this cause of action. Choice **D** is a worse choice because it contains too broad a statement of the law. By agreeing to appear on the show, Jonathan did not consent to "any treatment." Certainly there would be some heinous activities that the show could engage in that would go beyond the scope of Jonathan's consent, even if this one did not.

The facts of this question arise out of a real world dispute that led to tragedy. A few days after Scott revealed himself as Jonathan's secret crush on *The Jenny Jones Show*, Jonathan shot and killed Scott. It does not appear that Jonathan sued the producers of *The Jenny Jones Show* for IIED. But Scott's family sued Jonathan and the producers of *The Jenny Jones Show* for a number of torts, including wrongful death. Jonathan, who had been convicted of murder and sentenced to 25-50 years in prison, settled the case. The case against the producers led to a $29 million verdict in favor of Scott's family. An appellate court reversed that judgment, holding that the producers were not responsible for Jonathan's actions. *Graves v. Warner Bros. Inc.*, 656 N.W.2d 195 (Mich. App. 2002).

---

5. Don't worry here about a lawsuit against an entity, *The Jenny Jones Show*, rather than a person. In Chapter 17, we will consider when one person (or entity) can be held responsible for the tort of another.

E.   First Amendment concerns

Another defense to IIED that may arise in rare circumstances is a First Amendment defense. As you will learn in a Constitutional Law course, the First Amendment to the United States Constitution bars the government from, among other things, "abridging" freedom of speech. In rare contexts in which a tort arises out of what a defendant *says or writes*, First Amendment questions can arise and bar a torts suit from going forward. The key example is a U. S. Supreme Court case, *Hustler Magazine Inc. v. Falwell,* 485 U.S. 46 (1988). Here is how the Court described the facts of the case:

> Petitioner Hustler Magazine, Inc., is a magazine of nationwide circulation. Respondent Jerry Falwell, a nationally known minister who has been active as a commentator on politics and public affairs, sued petitioner and its publisher, petitioner Larry Flynt, to recover damages for invasion of privacy, libel, and intentional infliction of emotional distress. . . .
>
> The inside front cover of the November 1983 issue of Hustler Magazine featured a "parody" of an advertisement for Campari Liqueur that contained the name and picture of respondent and was entitled "Jerry Falwell talks about his first time." This parody was modeled after actual Campari ads that included interviews with various celebrities about their "first times." Although it was apparent by the end of each interview that this meant the first time they sampled Campari, the ads clearly played on the sexual double entendre of the general subject of "first times." Copying the form and layout of these Campari ads, Hustler's editors chose respondent as the featured celebrity and drafted an alleged "interview" with him in which he states that his "first time" was during a drunken incestuous rendezvous with his mother in an outhouse. The Hustler parody portrays respondent and his mother as drunk and immoral, and suggests that respondent is a hypocrite who preaches only when he is drunk. In small print at the bottom of the page, the ad contains the disclaimer, "ad parody — not to be taken seriously." The magazine's table of contents also lists the ad as "Fiction; Ad and Personality Parody."

The Supreme Court held that it violated the First Amendment for an IIED suit to go forward against the magazine for an obvious parody, concluding:

> [P]ublic figures and public officials may not recover for the tort of intentional infliction of emotional distress by reason of publications such as the one here at issue without showing in addition that the publication contains a false statement of fact which was made with "actual malice," *i.e.,* with knowledge that the statement was false or with reckless disregard as to whether or not it was true.

Otherwise, political satire and commentary would be chilled.

I leave to Constitutional Law courses and books any further exploration of when the First Amendment defense to IIED or other torts is viable.

QUESTION 7. *Hustler v. Falwell II.*   Larry, the publisher of a pornographic magazine that often criticizes leaders of the Christian right, goes over to the house of Jerry, a leader of the Christian right who has often criticized Larry. Larry pours garbage all over Jerry's lawn, throws eggs at his windows, and blares music from his car. Larry does this every day for a month. Can Jerry successfully sue Larry for IIED?

A. No, because Jerry is a public figure and the case is therefore barred by the First Amendment.

B. No, whether or not Jerry is a public figure, because the case is barred by the First Amendment.

C. Yes, if Larry's conduct constituted extreme and outrageous conduct, Larry was at least reckless about causing Jerry severe emotional distress, and Jerry actually suffered severe emotional distress.

D. Yes, because publishers of pornography can never assert a First Amendment defense to IIED.

ANALYSIS.   Larry may be a publisher and Jerry may be a public official, but the First Amendment should be irrelevant to this case because Larry did not *say or write* anything that could potentially bring up a First Amendment defense. Throwing eggs, blaring music, and dumping garbage might have been politically motivated, but it is not political speech raising a First Amendment issue. Instead, whether or not Jerry can recover will depend upon meeting the prima facie case for the tort, as set forth in the correct answer, Choice **C**. Choices **A** and **B** both incorrectly conclude that the First Amendment should bar the tort in this case. Choice **D** states an incorrect proposition of law that is contradicted by the actual *Hustler v. Falwell* case.

F.   The Closer: When IIED, and when other intentional torts?

As we saw, courts recognized the tort of intentional infliction of emotional distress to deal with those situations in which defendants engaged in wrongful conduct likely to cause serious emotional distress but that did not fall within the tortious conduct of other intentional torts. Today, IIED exists alongside other intentional torts, which raises the following question: If a plaintiff could recover all of her emotional distress damages as parasitic to a traditional intentional tort (such as battery), should the plaintiff also try to prove a cause of action for intentional infliction of emotional distress? For example, suppose Lance deliberately shot Monica for no good reason, and Monica had a great deal of pain and suffering as a consequence. Is there any reason for Monica to sue for IIED in addition to battery?

Because a plaintiff can only get one recovery for all damages, filing an additional cause of action should not matter. But here are a few reasons why Monica's lawyer might list a cause of action for IIED in addition to one for battery:

1. Lance could have engaged in other conduct besides the battery itself that could be outrageous and an opportunity for additional damages.
2. If Monica is worried that she could not prove one or more of the elements of the cause of action for battery, she might try IIED as a backup, as it has different elements.
3. Psychologically, if Monica can prove that Lance's conduct violated more than one tort, perhaps a jury would increase the amount of damages.
4. Proof of IIED could be relevant in the jury's determination of the appropriateness of and the amount of punitive damages.

QUESTION 8. When IIED? Nancy and Oliver got into a fight, and Nancy stabbed Oliver. Fortunately, it was not a life-threatening wound. Oliver sues for battery and IIED, claiming $3,000 in medical bills, $10,000 in pain and suffering associated with the stabbing, and another $10,000 for emotional distress under the IIED tort. Nancy claims that even if Oliver can prove the elements of both torts, he cannot recover the additional $10,000 in emotional distress damages under the IIED tort. How should the court rule?

A. Nancy is right because the IIED damages simply duplicate a portion of the damages Oliver is seeking for the battery.
B. Nancy is right because emotional distress damages must always be parasitic to another tort besides IIED.
C. Nancy is wrong because bodily harm is not required to recover for the tort of IIED.
D. Nancy is wrong because a plaintiff can get more damages for the same injury by proving that the defendant committed more than one tort in the same action.

ANALYSIS. From the facts, it appears that Oliver is trying to recover the same damages twice for the same injury: the emotional distress he has suffered as a consequence of the stabbing by Nancy. Whether he gets those damages in battery or in IIED, he cannot get them twice. Choice **A** correctly explains this concept. Choice **B** is incorrect because the tort of IIED proves that emotional distress damages need not be parasitic to another tort besides IIED. Choice **C** is wrong even though it is a correct statement of the law: It is true that a plaintiff need not suffer bodily harm in order to recover for IIED (except for non-immediate family members seeking to recover as bystanders). But that point is irrelevant here. Oliver has suffered bodily harm and emotional distress. The question is not whether Oliver can be compensated for the emotional harm, but whether he can recover for the same emotional harm twice. Finally, Choice **D** is incorrect because it states an incorrect principle of the law. Regardless of the number of torts that a defendant has committed, a plaintiff can recover only once for each kind of damage that the defendant has caused to the plaintiff. To allow the plaintiff to recover multiple times would move tort damages away from the goal of compensation and toward the principle of punishment. If indeed Nancy's conduct is worthy of punishment, Oliver may ask the jury to award additional punitive damages for Nancy's bad conduct.

 # Rick's picks

1. Emotional Hang-Up	D
2. Emotional Hang-Up, Take II	A
3. Killing Fields	D
4. Dog Day Afternoon	C
5. Plaintiff Bingo	B
6. Secret Crush	C
7. *Hustler v. Falwell II*	C
8. When IIED?	A

PART II

Negligence

7

Introduction to Negligence: Corrective Justice, Efficiency, and the Choice Between Strict Liability and Negligence

CHAPTER OVERVIEW

A. Introduction: The choice between strict liability and negligence

The first part of this book considered some of the most important intentional torts that an injured plaintiff could raise against a defendant: battery, trespass to real property, trespass to chattels, conversion, assault, false imprisonment, and intentional infliction of emotional distress. If a plaintiff could prove the prima facie case, and the defendant was unable to raise any affirmative defenses, the plaintiff could recover damages. But suppose a defendant injured plaintiff in a way that did not meet the tortious conduct portion of the prima facie case for these torts. For example, imagine that the defendant, without intending to do so, poked a stick into the plaintiff's eye, damaging the eye.[1] Under what circumstances could a plaintiff still recover damages? To make out the tortious conduct portion of the prima facie case, should it be necessary for plaintiff to prove that the defendant's conduct was somehow *blameworthy* (for example, to show that the defendant was acting carelessly), or should it be enough for plaintiff to demonstrate that the defendant *caused* the plaintiff's injury?

Historically, under the old English common law, the answer was not clear. In order to sue for damages, a plaintiff had to use the right form of action, or "writ." The writs for tort cases were *trespass vi et armis* (trespass by force of arms, or "trespass" for short), and *trespass on the case* (or "case" for short). Don't confuse the old English trespass writ with the modern cause of action for trespass to real property. The old English writ of trespass was the technical form used to sue in tort for any kind of *direct harm* that the defendant inflicted on the plaintiff (it could be a modern case of battery, assault, false imprisonment, trespass to real property, or some other tort). In contrast, the old English writ of case was used for *indirect harm,* such as when a defendant left a roadblock in the road that plaintiff later tripped over. The writ system created a trap for plaintiffs: If the plaintiff sued using what the court later deemed to be the wrong writ — for example, if the plaintiff sued in trespass for a harm caused by the defendant that the court concluded was indirect — plaintiff would lose the lawsuit on the grounds that he filed the wrong writ. *See Scott v. Shepherd*, 90 Eng. Rep. 525 (K.B. 1773).

Over time, English courts directed plaintiffs seeking compensation for unintentional harm, such as the inadvertent poke in the eye, to bring suit through the writ of case (rather than trespass). However, these early English cases did not always require plaintiff to prove the defendant's "fault" before allowing recovery in cases of unintentional wrongs; there were some successful lawsuits under the writ of case in which the courts allowed a plaintiff to recover damages caused by the defendant *without proof of fault.* The old English courts, fixated on the technical forms of action, did not focus on the "fault versus cause" debate posed by the choice between negligence and strict liability. Eventually, however, as the writ system disappeared in both the English and American legal systems, courts had to set out the circumstances in which a plaintiff who could not prove the prima facie case for any of the intentional torts could nonetheless recover damages for unintended wrongs.

---

1. From Part I, you should know that this conduct does not constitute a battery. Though the defendant acted, he did not have the intent to cause a contact with the plaintiff. Without such intention, plaintiff could not prove the tortious conduct portion of the prima facie case for battery and would lose.

Modern American and English courts both settled on a general rule of *negligence* for cases of unintentional harms, leaving certain small areas of law under a strict liability rule. For the poke in the eye, described above, the rule was one of *negligence*: a defendant would not be liable for unintentional harm unless the defendant was somehow *at fault* in causing the harm to plaintiff. For limited types of conduct, such as those that involved "abnormally dangerous" activities, the courts adopted special rules of *strict liability*: in these "pockets" of strict liability, a defendant could be liable for plaintiff's damages only upon proof that the defendant's actions *caused* plaintiff's injury (putting aside for now the question of affirmative defenses).

In the remainder of this chapter, we consider policy arguments in the negligence versus strict liability debate. In the next chapters in this part, we consider in detail the rules that apply in negligence cases. In Part IV, we examine the most important pockets of strict liability: abnormally dangerous activities, nuisance, conversion, and vicarious liability.

QUESTION 1. Less Fun Than a Poke in the Eye with a Sharp Stick. Perry and Raj bring their dogs to a dog park. Unfortunately, their dogs start fighting. Perry picks up a stick and tries to separate the dogs so that they would stop fighting. Even though Perry was trying only to separate the dogs, he inadvertently poked Raj in the eye. Raj can no longer see out of that eye, and he wishes to sue Perry in tort in a modern American court. His best cause of action is one for:

A. Battery
B. Negligence
C. Strict Liability
D. *Trespass vi et armis*

ANALYSIS.   As explained in footnote 1 (and as should be clear to you if you started this book with Part I), Raj does not have a good cause of action for battery. Though it is true that Perry acted (his picking up and moving the stick was a voluntary muscular contraction), he did not intend to make a harmful or offensive contact with Raj, nor to put the plaintiff in imminent apprehension of such contact. (He intended contact with the dogs, which cannot be transferred to a person.) Because Perry lacks the requisite intent for battery, Choice **A** is incorrect. Choice **D** is incorrect because the question asks you about how a "modern American court" would consider the question. The old English forms have been abolished, so the suit would not be brought for *trespass vi et armis*. This brings us to the choice between strict liability and negligence. As explained above, the inadvertent poke in the eye case is governed by the general rule for unintentional harms, negligence.

Strict liability is reserved for special pockets of activity discussed further in Part IV. For this reason, Choice **B** is correct and Choice **C** is not.

B.   Corrective justice issues

The two main theoretical frameworks for analyzing tort rules are corrective justice theories, which are non-instrumental arguments[2] based upon what is morally right, and efficiency theories, which are instrumental arguments advocating the choosing of legal rules that promote overall social happiness or wealth. We will consider the wealth-based Kaldor-Hicks efficiency theory in the next section of this chapter. Here, we consider corrective justice theories.

As noted in Part I, theorists going back to the time of Aristotle have considered questions of the moral basis for tort liability. For intentional torts, widespread consensus exists that as a matter of justice those who intentionally inflict harm on another must compensate the other for the harm caused. On the question of unintentional conduct leading to harm, there is much less consensus among corrective justice theorists: On the one hand, some scholars have taken the view that whoever *causes harm* should compensate for the harm caused regardless of fault. If you have ever walked into a store displaying fragile items and seen the sign "you break it you pay for it," you understand the impulse behind a cause-based theory of liability.

On the other hand, other scholars have taken the view that *proof of fault* is necessary (in addition to proving causation) before a person causing harm to another is morally obligated to pay for the harm. As Justice Oliver Wendell Holmes put it, to require a defendant who caused harm to a plaintiff without fault to pay for it is no more justified than requiring the defendant to pay if the plaintiff is struck by lightning. In the absence of fault, this argument goes, there is no moral requirement of compensation.

Both arguments have some normative appeal. On cause-based theories, we could say that between two innocent parties, one who caused the harm and the other who did not, it is fairer to put the cost on the party that caused the harm. This argument makes clear an important point that Torts students often overlook: a conclusion that a defendant need not compensate plaintiff for a loss is also a decision that plaintiff will bear the loss himself or herself;[3] it is not as though the loss disappears. On fault-based theories, the argument is that we should not expect more from people than that they act reasonably

---

2. On the meaning of instrumental and non-instrumental tort theories, see Chapter 2.
3. In some such cases in which plaintiff has purchased insurance against certain kinds of harm, plaintiff does not bear the loss (or all of the loss) herself. But that is a matter of contract between the plaintiff and the plaintiff's insurer, and not the defendant.

under all the circumstances. If a defendant conforms her conduct to the standard of reasonableness expected by society, there is no moral basis to require that defendant to compensate plaintiff for the wrong. Either plaintiff should have to bear the cost himself, or society as a whole should bear the cost though some kind of social insurance program.

Obviously, a debate that has divided philosophers for centuries is not going to be resolved in this book. Students interested in this topic could take courses in jurisprudence, and consult numerous works on corrective justice and tort law.[4] For our purposes, it is important that you understand what the debate is about and keep your eye on the following question: Is tort law *consistent* in its treatment of the question of liability for unintentional torts? In fact, what you will see is that tort law is inconsistent. It adopts a fault-based standard generally, but then enacts exceptions to that principle, both in carving out pockets of strict liability (such as for abnormally dangerous activities) and, as we will see in the next chapter, within the negligence rules themselves.

QUESTION 2. Correct Corrective Justice. A corrective justice theorist declares: "Between two innocent parties, one who caused the harm and the other who did not, it is fairer to put the cost on the party that caused the harm." Such a theorist is likely to favor which theory of tort liability for unintentionally caused injuries?

A. Negligence
B. Strict liability
C. Kaldor-Hicks efficiency
D. All of the above

ANALYSIS. This is a straightforward question if you have done the reading or are already familiar with these concepts. For nonintentional torts, the two competing corrective justice ideas are those that favor fault-based liability, or negligence, and those that favor cause-based liability, or strict liability. The statement made by the corrective justice theorist in this question is one that supports cause-based liability, or strict liability. For this reason, the correct answer is Choice **B**, strict liability, rather than Choice **A**, negligence. Choice **C** is incorrect because Kaldor-Hicks efficiency is about promoting social wealth, not about choosing the fairest rules. Because we have eliminated choices **A** and **C**, the "all of the above" Choice **D** is also incorrect.

---

4. For a good place to start, *see* JULES COLEMAN, MARKETS, MORALS AND THE LAW (2002).

C.   Economic efficiency issues

1. Understanding Kaldor-Hicks efficiency

In contrast with non-instrumental corrective justice theories, which ask which tort rules are the *fairest*, economic efficiency theories are instrumental theories that look to evaluate the best results for *society as a whole*. The efficiency theory that has had the most influence in American law is *Kaldor-Hicks efficiency*, which uses *social wealth* as its rubric for evaluating legal rules. (Kaldor and Hicks were nineteenth-century economists who had come up with this measure of efficiency.) Under Kaldor-Hicks efficiency, society should choose legal rules which *maximize overall social wealth, regardless of its distribution*.[5] In the context of tort law, which primarily concerns losses in wealth (as opposed to contracts, which concerns potential gains in wealth), Kaldor-Hicks efficiency requires choosing rules that minimize social losses.

For those unfamiliar with economics, the ideas in the last paragraph are probably tough sledding. To make the ideas clearer, we begin with an admittedly unrealistic example of a choice between two rules governing automobile accidents between drivers and pedestrians. Rule 1 says that drivers should take care; Rule 2 says that pedestrians should take care. Let's assume further that if drivers follow Rule 1 or if pedestrians follow Rule 2, all accidents between drivers and pedestrians are avoided, that there are no costs of following these rules on anyone else, and that there are an equal number of drivers and pedestrians.[6] Here is a chart showing the average annual cost (in dollars) under each rule.

Rule	Cost to Driver	Cost to Pedestrian	Total Cost (Social Cost)
Rule 1	10	0	10
Rule 2	0	3	3

An economist using the Kaldor-Hicks criterion and choosing between Rule 1 and Rule 2 as the best tort rule for drivers and pedestrians would

---

5. Another important efficiency theory is Pareto efficiency, named after another nineteenth-century economist, which says that society should choose rules that make at least one person better off and no one else worse off. As we shall see, under Kaldor-Hicks efficiency, some rules will make some people worse off.

6. Economics is full of unrealistic assumptions, as we shall see in this chapter and the next when we consider the value of economic models to the crafting of negligence law. Consider this joke that some attribute to the Nobel Prize–winning economist, Paul Samuelson: a physicist, a chemist, and an economist are stranded on a desert island with no food. A crate of canned food washes ashore. The three try to figure out how to open the cans. The physicist suggests building a set of pulleys and levers to hoist the cans high enough and have them drop with just enough force to open the cans without spilling the food. The chemist thinks this plan is too risky and suggests heating the cans to a certain temperature to cause them to open at the seams. The economist responds that both the physicist and chemist have made this too difficult: "Simply assume a can opener."

choose Rule 2 over Rule 1, because Rule 1 costs society $10 while rule 2 costs society only $3. A few things to note about this choice:

- Unlike the corrective justice theorist, who chooses a rule that he believes is morally right, the economist applies a standard not concerned with morality, but rather with overall wealth.
- Value is measured in dollars, and economists assume it is equal to each person, even though to a poor person those first dollars are worth more (because they can be used to buy items essential for living).
- The economist chooses the rule on overall efficiency grounds regardless of its possible distributional inequity. Under Rule 2, pedestrians bear the entire cost for the rule for society (just as under Rule 1, drivers bear the entire cost for society).

An economist met with a fairness objection to one party bearing all of the social burdens would say the following: Don't use the law to try and promote distributional fairness. Choose the rule that makes the wealth of society greatest, and then use the *taxing power* to deal with such problems. The point for the economist is that it is cheaper for society to put the burden of taking care on pedestrians. If society believes that drivers should pay those costs, it is better *to tax the drivers $3* to pay for the pedestrians to take care than to force the drivers to take a $10 precaution.[7]

A Complication: Transaction Costs and the Coase Theorem. To this point, I have said that an economist would choose Rule 2 over Rule 1 to promote economic efficiency. That's not necessarily true, however. Suppose that society for some reason chooses Rule 1 rather than Rule 2. What would happen? Imagine first a society with just one driver and one pedestrian, who know each other and can communicate easily with one another. If society chooses Rule 1, the driver could say to the pedestrian: "Look, it costs me $10 to take care to prevent accidents between us. You could do it for only $3. Why don't I pay you $5? That way, you are better off (even after you spend the $3 on precautions, you'll have $2 more than you've had before). I'm better off because instead of it costing me $10, I pay only $5." Pedestrian could well agree to the deal, leading to the parties bargaining around Rule 1 to put Rule 2, the efficient rule, into effect.[8]

This insight is so important that economist Ronald Coase won the Nobel Prize for it.[9] Coase said, in what has come to be known as the

---

7. One counterargument is that economists do not explain how society is going to fairly decide to impose such a tax on drivers. Indeed, other economic theories suggest that drivers might be politically successful in preventing such taxation.
8. Now you might say that Rule 2 is not put in effect, because the pedestrian is not paying for it. But again, distributional issues are irrelevant to the economist. The question is not whether the driver or pedestrian pays for implementing Rule 2. The question instead is whether Rule 2 rather than Rule 1 is implemented.
9. *See* RONALD COASE, THE PROBLEM OF SOCIAL COST (1960).

"Coase Theorem," that in the absence of "transaction costs," the parties will bargain to an efficient result regardless of the underlying legal rule. That is, if there were no costs between parties to bargain (including the possibility of strategic behavior — such as pedestrian holding out for more than $5 from driver), it doesn't matter if society chooses Rule 1 or Rule 2; if society chooses the inefficient rule, the parties will have an incentive to bargain around it to the efficient legal rule.

In legal areas such as Contracts, the Coase theorem suggests that the law should be structured to facilitate such bargaining between parties, and without unnecessary regulation, so that parties can privately bargain to efficient legal rules. In Torts, however, such bargaining often will be unrealistic. That is, rather than having one driver and one pedestrian, there are millions of each (and many of us can be either one depending upon the circumstances). When there are a large number of parties, transaction costs are prohibitively high and we cannot expect the parties will bargain to an efficient legal rule without government intervention. Instead, society will have to choose the rule that appears the most efficient, by an estimate of the costs and benefits of each alternative. In the next section, we consider how economists suggest doing so in Tort law.

> **QUESTION 3. Coase-ing to Victory.** An economist seeking to promote Kaldor-Hicks efficiency through law would agree with which of the following statements?
>
> A. Legal rules should be chosen based upon the non-instrumental moral judgments.
> B. Legal rules should be chosen that make at least one person better off and no person worse off.
> C. Courts should always choose the most efficient legal rules because parties can never bargain to efficient results.
> D. When there are no transaction costs, the parties will bargain to an efficient result regardless of the underlying legal rule.

ANALYSIS. Recall that the Kaldor-Hicks efficiency criterion says that society should choose the legal rule that promotes overall social wealth regardless of its distribution. It is an instrumental theory looking at social costs and benefits. For this reason, Choice **A** is wrong (the worst of the four answers); non-instrumental, moral judgments have no place in the economic analysis of law. Choice **B** does set forth an efficiency criterion, but it is the Pareto criterion (see footnote 5) and not the Kaldor-Hicks criterion. Under Kaldor-Hicks, as we saw from the driver/pedestrian example, there can be winners and losers, and there is no requirement that the winners compensate the losers for their losses. Choosing between Choice **C** and Choice **D** is more difficult. The Coase theorem says that in the absence of transaction costs, the parties will bargain to an efficient result regardless of the underlying legal rule. Choice **D** correctly states the Coase theorem. Choice **C**, in contrast, states that parties can *never* bargain to efficient results, and therefore the Coase theorem is irrelevant. An economist would be less likely to believe in that statement, believing, for example, that in contract law the law's job should be to make transaction costs lower so that parties can bargain to efficient outcomes. That is, when the market comes close to Coase's conditions, the parties may in fact be able to bargain to an efficient result.

2. Efficiency and the choice of strict liability versus negligence

As we saw in the last section, Tort law is principally an area of high transaction costs. When transaction costs are high, we do not predict that the parties would bargain to an efficient result on their own. Economists would say that the next best solution to private bargaining is for society to choose the most efficient legal rule, the one that the parties would bargain to if transaction costs were not prohibitively high.

Judge (and former Yale Law School dean) Guido Calabresi made an early attempt to describe how to choose tort rules for unintentional harm. He suggested that society should place liability on the party that could most cheaply avoid accidents (the party he termed the "cheapest cost avoider").[10] Using the example from the last section, he would say that the burden should be put on pedestrians, not drivers, because the pedestrian rather than the driver could more cheaply avoid driver-pedestrian accidents ($3 per pedestrian per year rather than $10 per driver per year).

Calabresi's theory was a great step forward in efficiency analysis, but it had some problems. How would we identify the cheapest cost avoider? Where would such data come from? What if both parties could take precautions that could reduce the cost of accidents?

As economic scholars considered the issues further, they said that the choice between a rule of negligence and a rule of strict liability should turn on reducing the sum of three types of costs:

- Precaution costs
- Accident costs
- Administrative costs

Precaution costs are costs taken to prevent accidents. For drivers, it includes having working brakes, driving slower, and other precautions. These precautions have social costs. Accident costs are the costs to individuals when accidents actually do happen. For example, a pedestrian hit by a

---

10. Guido Calabresi, The Cost of Accidents: A Legal and Economic Analysis (1970).

driver will have medical expenses, will lose work, and will have other costs. Finally, there are the costs of administering the tort system that allows for compensation for accidents.

How can these costs be minimized? Let's put aside administration costs for the moment. Suppose we were trying to minimize the sum of precaution costs and accident costs. How to do so? We want potential injurers (such as drivers) to invest in some precautions. Some of the first precautions a driver takes (such as having working brakes) are very cost effective. You can prevent a lot of injuries with working brakes. So when the driver spends a little on precaution, accident costs drop a lot. But then if we continue to insist that the driver take more precautions, those additional precautions cause accident costs to drop at a lower rate. Imagine at the extreme that the driver slows down from driving 10 mph to 5 mph. That additional precaution imposes lots of costs on the driver (he now has to spend twice as long getting somewhere), but it is not likely to prevent a lot of accidents. Even at 10 mph, a driver would likely be able to avoid most accidents, and those that do occur are more likely to be more minor than accidents occurring at a much higher speed.

An economist would say that we want the driver to keep investing additional dollars in precaution until the last dollar invested in precaution gives back only one dollar in accident savings. (In economic talk, the driver should keep investing in precaution until the marginal cost of doing so equals the marginal benefit in saved accident costs.)

Under this model, a negligence rule can be efficient. Negligence sets a level of reasonable care to which a potential injurer such as a driver must conform. If society sets that level of care at the point where the marginal costs of precaution equal the marginal benefits of accident savings, negligence can induce drivers to take the cost-justified amount of precaution. Why? If the driver takes that precaution, he pays *only* the precaution costs; in the event a pedestrian is injured, the pedestrian bears her own accident costs. However, if the driver takes less than the cost-justified level of precaution and an accident occurs, the driver must pay not only for the precaution costs he actually incurred; he must also pay for the costs of the accident. Under a negligence rule, then, it is economically rational for the driver to comply with the negligence rule.

Perhaps surprisingly, strict liability too induces potential injurers such as drivers to take the cost-justified standard of care. Unlike the negligence rule, which sets a definite standard of care and imposes liability only when the defendant's conduct goes below that standard of care, under strict liability, a defendant pays all accident and precaution costs. In such a system, the defendant is going to set his standard of care so that it is at the point where the sum of precaution and accident costs are the lowest: This is the *very same point* as the point identified by the negligence standard. So under a strict liability standard, a rational defendant chooses the same cost-justified standard of precaution as under the negligence rule.

At first look, then, it appears that the choice between strict liability and negligence from the point of view of Kaldor-Hicks efficiency is a wash; either standard promotes economic efficiency. In general, it is true that even today economists continue to debate which standard is the more efficient one for unintentional harms. But there are a few additional points to keep in mind in this debate, points that might sway you one way or another in thinking about the efficiency question.

- *Administrative Costs.* Generally speaking, strict liability systems are cheaper to administer than negligence systems, because under both strict liability and negligence, a plaintiff must prove both causation (the defendant caused plaintiff's injury) and damages. In a negligence case, however, the plaintiff also has to prove that the defendant was at fault, which adds to the costs of litigation. On this basis, strict liability is economically preferable to negligence.

- *Activity Level Effects.* Another argument in favor of strict liability from the economic viewpoint comes from what economists call "activity level effects." Negligence works by setting a standard of care; for example, do not drive faster than 65 mph. Suppose that a person driving 65 mph is expected to have an accident once every 20,000 miles. A driver considering the negligence rule will consider only whether or not he will be liable in the event of an accident, and will conform to the 65 mph speed limit whether he drives 20 miles in a year, 20,000 miles, or 200,000 miles. So negligence does not control *how much* of an activity a defendant engages in. In contrast, because a defendant in a strict liability system pays all costs of liability, that defendant will consider not only what level of care to use (e.g., drive no faster than 65 mph) but also how much to drive (e.g., the driver is less likely to have to pay for an accident by driving fewer miles). Only strict liability controls activity levels.

- *Plaintiff's Conduct.* A negligence rule could induce potential injured persons (such as pedestrians) to take more care than a strict liability rule. Recall that under a negligence rule, if the defendant conforms to the set standard of care, the defendant is not liable even when he causes an injury to a plaintiff. That cost is going to be borne by the plaintiff. For this reason, a plaintiff may decide to take extra precaution under a negligence rule so as to avoid the cost of accidents that are not paid for by the defendant. Under this argument, plaintiffs take less care under a strict liability rule, knowing that defendants will pay no matter what happens. (One problem with this argument is that it assumes damages fully compensate tort victims; if in fact potential tort victims prefer being uninjured to being injured with a sum of money for compensation, they have ample incentive to take care even under a strict liability regime.) This argument points in favor of a negligence rule, or perhaps a rule of strict liability with an affirmative defense of plaintiff's negligence that would bar plaintiff's recovery.

In sum, despite these many pages of economic analysis, the choice between strict liability and negligence on efficiency grounds is indeterminate. We will return to economic analysis in the next two chapters, as we consider how economists would say that courts should set the standard of care in negligence cases.

QUESTION 4. Law and Econ 101. In the economic analysis of the choice between strict liability and negligence on efficiency grounds, which statement is *untrue*?

A. Only strict liability induces potential injurers to take the cost-justified standard of care.

B. Though both negligence and strict liability induce potential injurers to take the cost justified standard of care, strict liability better controls activity levels as well.

C. Negligence cases are more expensive to administer than strict liability cases.

D. Under a rule of negligence, plaintiffs have an incentive to take care to avoid paying for accidents occurring when defendants comply with the set standard of care.

ANALYSIS. One of the interesting and counterintuitive findings of the economic analysis of the choice between negligence and strict liability is the idea that both negligence and strict liability can induce potential injurers to take the efficient level of care. Choice **A** incorrectly states that only strict liability can do so. Choice **A** is therefore the right answer here — remember, we are looking for the statement the economist would disagree with! Choice **B** states the economic view that strict liability better controls activity level effects compared to negligence; that is, it affects not only how much care a person takes, but also how much of an activity one engages in. Choice **C** correctly states the point that negligence cases are more expensive to administer because there is another thing to prove: lack of reasonable care (an issue absent from strict liability prima facie cases). Finally, Choice **D** recognizes the point that under a negligence rule, there will be cases in which plaintiffs are injured by defendants but defendants are not ordered to pay damages. Under such a regime, plaintiffs have an extra incentive to take care.

D.   The Closer: Theory and reality

Where does all this theory leave us? The earlier sections of this chapter demonstrate that consensus has not emerged from either corrective justice theorists or economists over whether negligence or strict liability is a preferable rule for regulating unintentional conduct. Though the theorists have not reached consensus, the *law* has developed, perhaps surprisingly, in a pretty stable way. It has established negligence as the general rule to use in cases of unintentional conduct, and it has carved out special pockets of strict liability for use in narrowly defined categories. In addition, as we shall see in the next chapter, courts sometimes appear to impose liability without fault even in some negligence cases (as when a defendant simply cannot conform his conduct to a reasonable standard of care).

I will highlight these inconsistencies in the law as they arise in future chapters. We can then consider whether insights from corrective justice theories or economics might be used to justify the choices that the law has made. Ask yourself now whether you favor a rule of negligence or strict liability for cases of unintentional conduct causing injury, and see if your views change as you see the issue arise again in future chapters.

> **QUESTION 5. Theory and Reality.**   Which of the following statements is true about tort theories and the choice between negligence and strict liability for unintentional conduct causing injury?
>
> A. Corrective justice theories favor a strict liability approach while economic theories favor a negligence approach.
> B. Both corrective justice theories and economic theories favor a negligence approach.
> C. Neither corrective justice theories nor economic theories suggest a uniform approach to the strict liability versus negligence question.
> D. The law has followed corrective justice theories but not economic theories in choosing between negligence and strict liability.

ANALYSIS.   Among both corrective justice theorists and economists, no consensus has emerged over whether strict liability or negligence is the preferred approach to tort liability for unintentional conduct. For this reason, Choices **A** and **B** are both incorrect. Choice **D** is also incorrect. The law has gone its own way, choosing negligence as the general approach for unintentional wrongs, but preserving pockets of strict liability. Corrective justice does not suggest this approach. This leaves us with Choice **C**, which correctly explains that neither theory has a uniform approach to the question of liability for unintentional conduct causing harm.

✶ Rick's picks

1. Less Fun Than a Poke in the Eye with a Sharp Stick	B
2. Correct Corrective Justice	B
3. Coase-ing to Victory	D
4. Law and Econ 101	A
5. Theory and Reality	C

8

Breach: The Reasonable Person Standard

CHAPTER OVERVIEW
A. Introduction: The prima facie case for negligence, and a note about "duty"
B. Breach: Objectivity and context
   1. The reasonable person standard
   2. Adjusting the standard for age, physical disability, expertise, and other reasons
C. The meaning of reasonable care
   1. Common sense approaches
   2. Balancing, including the Hand formula
D. The Closer: Is the Hand formula the Holy Grail of negligence or deeply flawed?
✦ Rick's picks

A. Introduction: The prima facie case for negligence, and a note about "duty"

As explained in Chapter 2, every tort has the same structure. The plaintiff must prove the prima facie case by a preponderance of the evidence, and if plaintiff does so, the defendant can raise affirmative defenses. If plaintiff fails to prove all the elements of the prima facie case by a preponderance of the evidence, the defendant wins. As we shall see, in a negligence case if plaintiff proves all the elements of the prima facie case and the defendant proves one or more affirmative defenses, there is a sharing of the liability between the plaintiff and the defendant.

The generic structure of the prima facie case is:

1. That defendant engaged in the requisite tortious conduct
2. Actual causation

3. Proximate causation
4. Damages

Each tort differs in the first element, the *requisite tortious conduct*. For negligence, the requisite tortious conduct has two elements:

1. Duty
2. Breach

The plaintiff must prove *both* duty and breach in order to meet the tortious conduct portion of the prima facie case for negligence. Though duty comes before breach in the prima facie case — and is generally a policy question for a judge rather than a factual question for a jury — we will consider breach before duty. The reason for reversing the order is that students often confuse duty and breach issues. By focusing first on breach, it makes it easier to understand duty. (Trust me; I've been doing this for a while.) So we are going to make a temporary simplifying assumption about duty, which we will eventually relax in later chapters:

A defendant has a **duty** *(or responsibility) to everyone to avoid creating unreasonable risks of harm to others.*

Having given this temporary and oversimplified view of duty, we can now turn to a definition of breach, which is sometimes referred to alternatively as a defendant's "negligence" or fault.

A defendant **breaches** *a duty to a plaintiff when, judged from the perspective of a reasonably prudent person in the defendant's position, the defendant failed to use reasonable care to avoid a reasonably foreseeable risk to the plaintiff.*[1]

The remainder of this chapter and the entire next chapter aim to explain in great detail this definition and what it means for a defendant to "breach" a duty to the plaintiff for purposes of a negligence case.

QUESTION 1. Half-a-Loaf?   Allan sues Becky for negligence arising out of an automobile accident. The case goes to trial before a jury. After Allan has put on his evidence and before Becky gets to raise any affirmative defenses, Becky asks the judge to direct a verdict in her favor (that is, to rule for Becky and not let the jury decide the case), because Allan did not

---

1. Here is how the Restatement (Third) of Torts: Liability for Physical Harm § 3 (P.F.D. No. 1, 2005) defines negligence: "A person acts negligently if the person does not exercise reasonable care under all the circumstances. Primary factors to consider in ascertaining whether the person's conduct lacks reasonable care are the foreseeable likelihood that the person's conduct will result in harm, the foreseeable severity of any harm that may ensue, and the burden of precautions to eliminate or reduce the risk of harm." This definition is somewhat more specific than the one I use because it focuses on *balancing* as the way of proving negligence. We will return to the balancing issue later in this chapter.

put on any evidence establishing that Becky breached. Allan concedes the point, but argues that he established without question that Becky owed Allan a duty, and because Allan proved half of his case Becky should be liable to Allan for half of his damages. How should the judge rule?

A. Accept Allan's argument, letting the case go to the jury for half of Allan's damages.
B. Accept the argument, letting the case go to the jury for half of Allan's damages, except that Allan will get to recover nothing if Becky can prove at least one of her affirmative defenses.
C. Reject the argument because Allan must prove all the elements of his prima facie case in order to recover anything at trial.
D. Reject the argument because breach is a more important element of the negligence tort than duty.

ANALYSIS. In order for a plaintiff to win anything in any tort suit, the plaintiff must prove *each* of the elements of his prima facie case by a preponderance of the evidence. A plaintiff who proves only half of the elements is not entitled to half of the damages. For this reason, Choice **A** is wrong. Choice **B** is wrong for two reasons. First, it is wrong for the reason that Choice **A** is wrong: one cannot get half the damages for proving fewer than all of the elements of the prima facie case. Second, it is wrong because in a negligence case, proof by a defendant of an affirmative defense is not automatic grounds for the plaintiff to get nothing; instead, as noted above and as we will see in detail in Chapter 10, there is generally a *sharing* of the liability between the plaintiff and the defendant. Choice **C** correctly explains the principle that the plaintiff must prove *each* of the elements of the prima facie case by a preponderance of the evidence in order to prevail in the suit. Choice **D** reaches the right result — the court should reject Allan's argument — but for the wrong reason. Some elements of the prima facie case are not more "important" than others. It is necessary to prove all of the elements of the tort if the plaintiff is going to prevail at trial.

B. Breach: Objectivity and context

1. The reasonable person standard

You will recall from Part I that when it comes to intentional torts, a crucial element in the prima facie case is intent. For example, if a defendant who hit a plaintiff did not intend to make contact with plaintiff or to put the plaintiff in imminent apprehension of such contact, the defendant cannot be liable for battery even if the defendant in fact made contact with plaintiff that caused injury. Negligence is different from these intentional torts because proof of intention is not required. Indeed, many negligence cases arise precisely because the defendant was not even aware that the plaintiff was in any danger from defendant's actions, as when a defendant falls asleep while driving.

Indeed, not only is it unnecessary for the plaintiff to demonstrate defendant's *intent*, a plaintiff sometimes commits breach by *failing* to take a certain precaution. For example, a defendant driving a car carelessly who fails to apply the brakes and thereby causes injury to plaintiff can be just as liable for negligence as a defendant who applies the brakes too late or incorrectly.

Rather than a focus on intent, the essence of the breach element of the negligence tort is the *failure of the defendant to use reasonable care.* The standard is *contextual;* it is one of *reasonableness under the circumstances.*

In defining reasonableness, we generally apply an *objective* standard, asking what a reasonably prudent person ("RPP" for short) would do in similar circumstances. We do not apply a *subjective* standard, asking whether this particular defendant acted honestly or in good faith. To understand this distinction, consider one of my favorite torts cases, *Vaughan v. Menlove*, 132 Eng. Rep. 490 (C.P. 1837). In *Vaughan*, a not-very-smart landowner had a lot of hay on his land stacked near his neighbor's land. His neighbor warned him repeatedly that the hay could catch on fire, and that he should remove it. Instead, he said he would "chance it" and he made an "aperture or chimney" down the middle of his pile.

As you might expect, the hay caught fire and caused damage to the neighbor's property. As anyone who has ever made a fire could tell you, the chimney the landowner built likely made it easier for the fire to spread, because it provided a path for oxygen to get to the fuel in the fire.

The neighbor sued the landowner for negligence. (The landowner couldn't be liable for trespass to real property, because he did not *intend* to cause the fire to start or to go onto his neighbor's land. See Chapter 3 for more on the trespass tort.[2]) The neighbor argued that the landowner failed to use reasonable care to avoid a reasonably foreseeable risk to him. The neighbor's case was especially strong because the landowner ignored warnings about the danger of keeping the stacked hay.

The landowner's lawyer defended him against the negligence charge by arguing that he had acted in good faith; he just wasn't the brightest candle in the village and honestly didn't realize the danger he was putting other people in. Now we may doubt this claim, especially given the warning that the landowner chose to ignore. But let's assume for the moment that, in fact, we

---

2. Traditionally, courts also imposed strict liability for intentionally started fires that got out of control. More about that in Chapter 15.

were faced with an honest but stupid person, trying the best he could and injuring others. *Should* he still be liable?

The court said the landowner was liable, and that the standard for negligence liability was an *objective* one based upon comparing defendant's conduct with what an RPP would do under the circumstances. In *Vaughan*, the court said the jury could have concluded that an RPP would have cleared the hay, especially upon hearing of the danger. As to the argument that the defendant could not conform his conduct to the standard of an RPP because he was too stupid, the court concluded that a person will be held to the standard of an average person in like circumstances, and someone who cannot do so acts at his own peril.

That decision may seem sensible enough — after all, none of us would want this landowner as a neighbor — but note the curious echoes of the corrective justice debate over negligence versus strict liability in the last chapter. The corrective justice argument for negligence, you will recall, is that it is not fair to hold a person liable for an unintentional wrong unless the person was somehow at fault or *blameworthy*. Generally speaking, a person who fails to conform her conduct to the average standard of care is acting in a blameworthy fashion. But not the stupid landowner in *Vaughan*. Is he really to blame if he is too stupid to know how to conform his conduct to that of the average person?

My point in returning to the corrective justice debate over negligence versus strict liability is to show you that even negligence can sometimes impose liability without fault, as when it holds people to an "average" or "reasonable" standard of care to which they honestly cannot conform. Does that fact convince you that the landowner should not have been held liable? That strict liability should apply across the board to injuries caused unintentionally?

QUESTION 2. Dumb Joe. Joe is a kindergarten teacher. He lives in a dangerous neighborhood and he keeps a gun at home for protection. One day he accidentally takes the gun to school. Rather than keep it in his backpack, Joe takes it out of the backpack and shows it to the children. It was bright and shiny. "Now kids, I know this gun looks really cool but it is dangerous, so don't touch it." Joe leaves it on desk so he could keep an eye on it. But he forgets to put it away when he has to step out of the classroom for a few minutes. Unfortunately, one of the children picks up the gun and shoots himself in the foot. The child and his parents sue Joe for negligence. Joe claims that he honestly believed the children wouldn't touch the gun. Should the jury find that Joe breached a duty to the injured child?

A. No, if the jury believes Joe honestly was as careful as he could be.
B. No, if the jury believes Joe acted like a reasonably prudent person under the circumstances.

C. Yes, if the jury finds that Joe was telling the truth.
D. Yes, if the jury finds that Joe acted reasonably.

ANALYSIS. This is a tricky question because of how it is worded, but it is not conceptually difficult. In order to be found to have breached a duty, a defendant must fail to act as a reasonably prudent person under the circumstances. If a defendant acts like a reasonably prudent person, then there is no breach. Choice **B** correctly explains that if the jury believes Joe acted reasonably, there is no breach. You may have been put off by this answer because on these facts you believe Joe acted unreasonably. I do too, but you have to pick the best choice, and here are the reasons why the other choices are worse: Choice **A** is wrong because *honest* subjective beliefs do not protect a defendant from a finding of breach if the defendant fails to act like an RPP. Choice **C** is doubly wrong: First, subjective beliefs are irrelevant. Second, a jury is not *more* likely to find breach if it finds that the defendant acted honestly. Choice **D** is wrong because a jury's finding that Joe acted reasonably provides grounds for concluding Joe did *not* breach, and not grounds for concluding that Joe *did* breach.

2. Adjusting the standard for age, physical disability, expertise, and other reasons

Recall the definition of breach given earlier is this chapter, and pay attention now to the bolded portion of the definition:

*A defendant breaches a duty to a plaintiff when, **judged from the perspective of a reasonably prudent person in the defendant's position**, the defendant failed to use reasonable care to avoid a reasonably foreseeable risk to the plaintiff.*

The idea of judging reasonable care from the perspective of an RPP *in the defendant's position* means that a factfinder should take *context* into account in judging reasonable care. But that idea is in tension with the objective standard that we apply to the question of reasonable care. After all, as we saw in the last section, a stupid defendant is cut no slack under the breach standard: We ask about what a reasonably prudent person would do under the circumstances, and not what an honest but imprudent person would do. Sometimes the law does allow for context, however. For example, when a person faces a sudden emergency not caused by his own misconduct, the law tells the jury to judge reasonableness from the perspective of a person facing the emergency:[3] A decision to drive onto someone's lawn would

---

3. *See* REST (3D) TORTS: LIABILITY FOR PHYSICAL HARM § 9 ("If an actor is confronted with an unexpected emergency requiring rapid response, this is a circumstance to be taken into account in determining whether the actor's resulting conduct is that of the reasonably careful person.").

ordinarily be considered unreasonable, but not so if a driver did so to avoid hitting a child who suddenly dashed into the street. In this section we consider three areas in which context does matter for purposes of breach: age, physical disability, and expertise.

Age. We saw in Part I of this book that children may be liable for intentional torts such as battery, so long as they are old enough to form the requisite intent. The rule is somewhat different for the tort of negligence. In some jurisdictions, a child under the age of five simply cannot be liable for negligence. *See* REST. (3D) TORTS: LIABILITY FOR PHYSICAL HARM § 10(b) (P.F.D. No. 1, 2005). That means that the person injured by a child under five must bear the cost of her own injuries, unless she could sue the parents of the child for their own negligence in failing to supervise their child adequately.[4]

For children above the age of five, most jurisdictions use a sliding scale in evaluating the reasonableness of a child's conduct. Generally speaking, a child is held to the standard of a "reasonably careful person of the same age, intelligence, and experience." *See id.* Note how contextual the standard is: It is not just the standard of a "reasonably careful 8-year-old" (and as the parent of three kids, I can tell you what an oxymoron that sounds like to me!). It is a standard that allows the jury to "ratchet down" the definition of reasonableness for children of lower intelligence (think *Vaughan v. Menlove Jr.!*) and inexperience. Note that the more context that is added to the standard, the more the approach resembles the subjective, rather than objective, standard for judging breach in a negligence case.

Why does the law cut kids this kind of slack? The Restatement's explanation is that children are "less able than adults to maintain an attitude of attentiveness toward the risks their conduct may occasion" and less able "to understand risks, to appreciate alternative courses of conduct with respect to risks, and to make appropriate choices among these alternatives." REST. (3D) TORTS: LIABILITY FOR PHYSICAL HARM § 10(b) cmt. *b* (P.F.D. No. 1, 2005). But this rationale would apply to the defendant in *Vaughan* too: If we contextualize for children, why not for the less intelligent? A better answer might be that the law wants to encourage children to take *some* risky behavior as necessary for human development and the process of moving from childhood to adulthood. A tough standard of tort liability could inhibit such experimentation and be bad for society.

Though most jurisdictions ratchet down the standard of care for children using a kind of sliding scale based upon age, intelligence, and experience, some jurisdictions create an exception to this rule when a child engages in an "adult activity," such as driving. *See* REST. (3D) TORTS: LIABILITY FOR PHYSICAL HARM § 10(c) cmt. *f* (P.F.D. No. 1, 2005) ("The special rule

---

4. Contrary to the expectations of many first-year law students, parents are not vicariously (or automatically) liable for the torts of their minor children. See Chapter 17 for more on vicarious liability.

[taking into account a child's age, intelligence and experience in determining breach] does not apply when the child is engaging in a dangerous activity that is characteristically undertaken by adults."). The adult activity exception raises two questions: (1) why the exception? and (2) which activities count as "adult" activities?

On the first question, the Restatement justifies the exception on grounds that people can usually make adjustments to avoid being injured by children (such as by staying out of the way of the skateboarding kid careening down the street), but it is harder to do so when a child is engaged in these activities. *Id.*, cmt. *f.* Whether or not that is true depends upon the nature of the activity and more on the question whether the activity is dangerous than whether the activity is usually engaged in by adults (think of a child snowboarding quickly and dangerously down an icy hill). Perhaps a more honest answer would note that it is a question of social balance: Yes, we don't want to overdeter children as they take risks as part of their human development, but some overdeterrence is in order when the child, if careless, is likely to cause great bodily harm.

On the second question, the answer of what counts as "adult" activity can differ depending upon the region of the country in which the activity takes place. Some jurisdictions consider using a firearm to be an adult activity (the position of the Third Restatement); other jurisdictions say that it is not an adult activity and therefore a person injured by a child using a firearm must prove negligence under the contextual standard. At the heart of this question is the amount of subsidy society wants to provide for children engaging in these kinds of activities. The Restatement takes the position that if an activity is engaged in widely by both adults and children, whether it is entitled to an exception depends upon how dangerous it is.

QUESTION 3. Playing with Fire. Jonah is a 7-year-old who is always getting into trouble. The police had been to his house a few times to talk to Jonah about his dangerous activities and to warn him to be more careful. His parents and teachers consider him very immature and not all that bright. IQ tests confirmed he was of below-average intelligence. One day Jonah was playing with a book of matches that he found in his kitchen. He took the matches to an open field which was full of dry hay thanks to a recent drought. Jonah was lighting the matches and seeing how long he could hold them without dropping them. His friend Ken told him that it was probably not a good idea to play with matches there because he could start a fire in the field. Jonah replied that he'd chance it. Sure enough, one of Jonah's matches lit the hay on fire, and the spreading burned down the nearby house of Lois. Lois sued Jonah for negligence.

In considering whether Jonah's conduct constituted a breach:

A. A jury may consider the fact that Jonah was of below-average intelligence and consider that the police had talked with Jonah in the past about being more careful.
B. A jury may consider the fact that Jonah was of below-average intelligence but may not consider that the police had talked to Jonah in the past about being more careful.
C. A jury may not consider the fact that Jonah was of below-average intelligence but may consider that the police had talked to Jonah in the past about being more careful.
D. A jury may not consider the fact that Jonah was of below-average intelligence, nor may it consider that the police had talked to Jonah in the past about being more careful.

ANALYSIS. In considering a child's negligence (when the child is over five years of age and is not engaged in an adult activity), a jury should evaluate the child's reasonable care taking into account the child's age, intelligence, and experience. The fact that Jonah was of below-average intelligence is relevant to this question, obviously. This means we can eliminate Choices **C** and **D**, which state that the jury could not consider this fact. The issue of the police talking to Jonah to tell him to be more careful goes to the question of Jonah's experience, and therefore it is relevant as well. Choice **A** is correct and Choice **B** is therefore wrong.

QUESTION 4. Snowed Over. Mark, a 15-year-old, is on a winter vacation with his family and friends in a mountain area. One evening, Mark and his friends buy some beer and Mark becomes intoxicated. He and a friend went riding on Mark's father's snowmobile. Unfortunately, Mark accidentally crashes his snowmobile into a parked car where Noreen was sitting. Noreen suffers serious personal injuries, and sues Mark for negligence. In proving that Mark breached his duty of care to Noreen in a majority of jurisdictions:

A. The jury should judge Mark's behavior under the standard of a reasonably prudent intoxicated snowmobile driver of similar age, experience, and intelligence.
B. The jury should judge Mark's behavior under the standard of a reasonably prudent adult snowmobile driver, if snowmobiling counts as an adult activity.
C. The jury should judge Mark's behavior under the standard of a reasonable child of any age.
D. The jury should judge Mark's behavior under the standard of a reasonably prudent adult snowmobile driver, whether or not snowmobiling counts as an adult activity.

ANALYSIS. The ordinary standard for children under the age of 18 is ratcheted down to reasonable care for a child of similar age, intelligence, and experience. In some jurisdictions, a child engaging in an "adult activity" is held to the standard of a reasonably prudent adult engaging in the activity. It is not clear whether snowmobiling counts as an adult activity in those states that have an adult activity exception. Both children and adults engage widely in the activity, but it is a potentially dangerous activity, similar to driving, in that it involves a motorized vehicle that can cause a great deal of harm in an accident. (On the other hand, unlike driving, a license is not required in many places to operate a snowmobile.)

Choice **A** is incorrect because it talks about the standard of a reasonably prudent *intoxicated* driver of similar age, experience, and maturity. Even if the adult activity exception does not apply, we do not ratchet down for a minor's intoxication (consider the terrible policy implications of doing so). Choice **C** is incorrect because we do not apply a single child standard for "a child of any age." We compare activities to children of similar ages. This brings it down to Choices **B** and **D**. Choice **B** is a better one, because it recognizes that whether or not the adult standard applies depends upon whether or not the adult activity exception applies to snowmobiling. In only a minority of jurisdictions would a child be held to the adult standard regardless of whether or not the child was engaged in an adult activity.

Physical Disability. Though children definitely get the benefit of a ratcheting *down* when it comes to the question of breach, those with physical disabilities face a different kind of contextualization: They must act as a reasonable person with the same or similar disability. *See* REST. (3D) TORTS: LIABILITY FOR PHYSICAL HARM § 11(a) (P.F.D. No. 1, 2005) ("The conduct of an actor with physical disability is negligent only if it does not conform to that of a reasonable person with the same disability."). This is not simply a ratcheting down but an imposition of a contextualized standard of care, given the disability — a standard which could raise or lower what is expected of the disabled person, depending upon circumstances.

While it would certainly be negligent for a sighted person to fail to look both ways before crossing a street, we would not expect such conduct of a blind person, which would be literally impossible to achieve. But we would expect a blind person to take *precautions reasonable for a blind person* before crossing the street, such as relying on a sight dog to assist with the crossing, or to use a crossing that provides audible signals for the blind that it is safe to cross the street.

Courts adopt a similar standard for a person who has a *sudden physical incapacitation,* such as an unexpected heart attack while driving, causing injury to others. It is not negligence to drive despite knowing that each of us has the possibility of having such a sudden physical incapacitation. But if one has forewarning of the dangers of such incapacitation — for example, a doctor warns a patient that driving is dangerous because the patient has a heart condition that could well render the patient unconscious while driving — then the incapacitation is not taken into account in evaluating breach.

Both the general rule for physical disabilities and the specific rule for sudden physical incapacitation are justifiable on fairness grounds. We contextualize to take into account physical conditions that are out of the control of defendants who injure others. But again, the question arises how this compares to our failure to contextualize for the person of below average intelligence such as the defendant in *Vaughan v. Menlove*. Indeed, the Restatement follows the majority of courts in determining that "[a]n actor's mental or emotional disability is not considered in determining whether conduct is negligent, unless the actor is a child." REST. (3D) TORTS: LIABILITY FOR PHYSICAL HARM § 11(c) (P.F.D. No. 1, 2005). That hardly seems fair: the blind person gets a break, but not the person with a mental illness such as schizophrenia.

The Third Restatement is quite defensive on this point, recognizing that "modern society is increasingly inclined to treat physical disabilities and mental disabilities similarly, [an] inclination . . . supported by the recognition that many mental disabilities have organic causes." *Id.*, cmt. *e*. But it nonetheless follows the majority of courts for these reasons:

- *Administrability*—Looking at the criminal justice system, the Restatement says courts have a difficult time determining when a mental disorder is so serious as to negate liability.
- *Fairness Argument I*—"While modern society has tended to resolve these doubts [about a person's ability to function in society with a given mental disorder] in favor of deinstitutionalization, there is nothing especially harsh in at least holding such a person responsible for those harms that the person's clearly substandard conduct causes."[6]
- *Fairness Argument II*—Physically disabled people are still held to a standard of reasonableness given their disability, but those with a mental disability simply cannot be expected to act rationally. "Therefore, in mental-disability cases the law is often unable to implement the balanced approach that it applies to problems of physical disability." Convincing?
- *The Mitigating Effect of Comparative Responsibility*—As we shall see in Chapter 10, when both a defendant and plaintiff act negligently, there is a sharing of responsibility. In allocating shares of responsibility, a jury can take a mental disorder into account even though the jury cannot do so in determining whether there is negligence in the first place.

---

6. In other words, the Restatement says: Stop griping that defendants with physical disabilities get a better deal under the tort system: Be happy we didn't lock you up. Now pay up!

QUESTION 5. Roll On.   Noreen is wheelchair-bound thanks to her earlier collision with Mark and his snowmobile. Noreen is going down Main Street in her wheelchair and about to cross at the corner of Main Street and Elm Street. The light is green, but in Noreen's experience unless she waits to cross exactly at the time the light turns green, she cannot make it across the street in time in her wheelchair. She's in a hurry, and decides to cross the street anyway. Oswald, who is driving down the street carefully, must swerve to avoid hitting Noreen, who is still in the crosswalk as the light turns red. Oswald suffers serious physical injuries, and he sues Noreen for negligence. In evaluating whether Noreen breached her duty of due care to Oswald:

A. The jury should judge Noreen's conduct under the standard of a reasonably prudent person without taking into account any physical disabilities.
B. The jury should judge Noreen's conduct under the standard of a reasonably prudent person, taking into account Noreen's physical disabilities only if she is a child.
C. The jury should judge Noreen's conduct under the standard of a reasonably prudent person in a wheelchair.
D. The jury should conclude that Noreen did not breach, since she has a physical disability.

ANALYSIS.   A person with a physical disability is not judged under the same standard for negligence purposes as a person without such a disability. But that person must act as a reasonable person would with the same disability. That standard applies whether the person with the disability is an adult or a child. For these reasons, Choices **A** and **B** are incorrect. Choice **D** is incorrect because it implies that a person who has a physical disability cannot be found to have breached. This is wrong. Choice **C** correctly explains that Noreen should be judged under the standard of a reasonably prudent person in a wheelchair—the question is whether or not such a person reasonably would have crossed the street when she did so, rather than waiting for the next cycle of green lights.

QUESTION 6. Double Standard.   Pauline suffers from schizophrenia and often has delusions. Pauline is walking down Main Street and about to cross at the corner of Main Street and Elm Street. Though the light is about to turn red, Pauline is under a delusion she is being chased by bad guys, and she runs across the street. Oswald, who is driving down the street carefully, must swerve to avoid hitting Pauline's. Oswald suffers serious physical injuries, and he sues Pauline for negligence. In evaluating whether Pauline breached her duty of due care to Oswald:

A. The jury should judge Pauline's conduct under the standard of a reasonably prudent person without taking into account any mental disabilities.

B. The jury should judge Pauline's conduct under the standard of a reasonably prudent person, taking into account Pauline's mental disabilities only if she is a child.

C. The jury should judge Pauline's conduct under the standard of a reasonably prudent person with schizophrenia.

D. The jury should conclude that Pauline did not breach since she has a mental disability.

ANALYSIS. The parallels between this question and Question 5 are obvious and intentional. This question is meant to reinforce for you the difference in the treatment of physical and mental disabilities for purposes of evaluating breach. The general rule is that mental disabilities are not taken into account except for children. We do not evaluate any standard of reasonableness taking into account the disability (contrast this with how the law treats physical disabilities). For this reason, Choice **B** is correct. It is a better choice than Choice **A** because the facts do not tell you whether or not Pauline is a child and therefore **B** is a more complete answer than **A**. Choices **C** and **D** are wrong because the law does not adjust the standard of care to take mental disabilities into account, except for children.

Expertise. We have seen that the law often ratchets *down* the standard of care for children, ratchets *differently* the standard of care for those with physical disabilities, and refuses to ratchet differently the standard of care for those with mental disabilities. In the case of experts, however, the law ratchets *up*. A professional accountant who makes a mathematical error filling out a tax return is not held to the standard of a reasonably prudent person. Instead, we hold that person to the standard of a reasonably prudent professional accountant. *See* Rest. (3d) Torts: Liability for Physical Harm § 12 (P.F.D. No. 1, 2005) ("If an actor has skills or knowledge that exceed those possessed by most others, these skills or knowledge are circumstances to be taken into account in determining whether the actor has behaved as a reasonably careful person."). Though we ratchet up for experts, we don't ratchet down for beginners (unless those beginners are children).

The standard of expertise certainly applies to professionals, such as accountants and those who run power plants. But it also applies to those who possess expertise in something such as a sport, for example an expert amateur marksman who injures someone else. Note that unlike the other examples in this section, the law's decision to take context into account works against, not for, a defendant sued for negligence.

QUESTION 7. Going Downhill. Rayna, a 25-year-old, is a novice skier. After taking a couple of lessons, she decides to give it a try on a double diamond expert run. Unsurprisingly, Rayna collides into another skier, Sal, causing serious personal injuries. Assume Rayna owes a duty of care to Sal.[6] In determining whether Rayna breached, the jury should evaluate Rayna under which standard?

A. A reasonably prudent novice skier.
B. A reasonably prudent 25-year-old novice skier.
C. A reasonably prudent skier of similar experience.
D. A reasonably prudent skier.

ANALYSIS. Rayna is a novice and an adult. Because she is an adult, we do not ratchet down the level of care in her skiing because of her lack of experience. (We would do so if she was a child.) She is held to the standard of a reasonably prudent skier. The law recognizes that although there is a learning curve for certain activities, a person who engages in those activities cannot expect a subsidy through the tort system putting the cost of such accidents on the victims rather than the persons causing the injury. Of the four choices, Choice **D** simply and accurately states the relevant standard. Rayna will be evaluated against the standard of a reasonably prudent skier. Choice **A** is incorrect because beginners are not cut any slack. Choice **B** is wrong for that reason and the fact that we do not take age into account for adults, only children. Choice **C** is incorrect because that choice ratchets for experience as well. Though we ratchet up for great experience, we do not ratchet down for beginners.

C.   The meaning of reasonable care

1. Common sense approaches

We focus now on a different aspect of the definition of breach:

*A defendant breaches a duty to a plaintiff when, judged from the perspective of a reasonably prudent person in the defendant's position, **the defendant failed to use reasonable care to avoid a reasonably foreseeable risk to the plaintiff.***

What does the law mean by a failure to use reasonable care? As we shall see, there are five different ways that a plaintiff may try to prove that the

---

6. There's a good chance Rayna does not. See Chapter 11.

defendant failed to use reasonable care, two of which are discussed in the remainder of this chapter, and three of which we take up in Chapter 9:

1. Common sense
2. Balancing
3. Custom
4. *Negligence per se*
5. *Res ipsa loquitur*

The common sense approach simply trusts jurors to use their knowledge of the world to decide what is reasonable under the circumstances. We would all say that driving down the road with a blindfold on is unreasonable. In some situations, then, a plaintiff need do no more than tell the jury the story of what defendant did to prove breach.

This kind of approach is limited in many modern negligence cases, however. Consider an airplane mechanic who adjusts an engine to certain specifications. The plane crashes, and the injured plaintiffs claim that a reasonably prudent airplane mechanic would have used different specifications. In evaluating such a claim, jurors simply cannot rely upon common sense because issues of airplane engine specifications are beyond the normal experience and knowledge of jurors.

Nonetheless, some cases involving experts could be resolved using a common sense approach. Consider a doctor leaving a sponge in a patient during an operation. Even though details on appropriate medical procedure are beyond the normal experience and knowledge of jurors, a jury applying common sense could conclude that the doctor was negligent in such circumstances.

How does common sense work? Probably jurors do a bit of implicit *balancing* of costs and benefits (it is implicit in that jurors would not think in these terms). The risk of driving while wearing a blindfold is high, and the cost of removing the blindfold is negligible. Under any kind of balancing of risks and benefits, driving with a blindfold on is likely to lead to a high number of accidents without any offsetting social benefits. In simple cases like the blindfold case, a juror can simply "eyeball" the situation and reach the conclusion that the defendant's conduct is unreasonable.

> **QUESTION 8. Going Downhill, Take II.** Rayna, a 25-year-old, is a novice skier. After taking a couple of lessons in which an expert ski instructor skied backward while holding onto Rayna, she decides to try skiing down the mountain backward herself. Unsurprisingly, Rayna crashes into Sal, another skier. Assume Rayna owes a duty of care to Sal. In proving that Rayna breached, Sal presents no evidence other than the facts of what Rayna did. May the jury nonetheless determine that Rayna breached?

A. No, because Sal presented no evidence that compared the costs of Rayna skiing backward against the benefits of doing so.
B. No, because Rayna is a novice and is not held to an average standard of care.
C. Yes, because the jury can use common sense in deciding that Rayna's actions were unreasonable.
D. Yes, because Rayna is an adult and adults are strictly liable for the unintended injuries that they cause.

ANALYSIS.   The question here focuses on the burden that a plaintiff has in proving that a defendant breached a standard of care. In limited circumstances, a plaintiff need not present any specific evidence showing that defendant's conduct was negligent; the jury can simply use common sense based upon the facts of the situation. This looks like one of those cases: A novice skier should not attempt to ski down a hill backward in an attempt to emulate the skiing of her expert instructor. Because Sal did not need to present specific evidence of costs and benefits of skiing backward in order to prove breach, Choice **A** is incorrect. Choice **B** contains an incorrect statement of law: novices are held to a reasonable (average) standard of care. Choice **D** also presents an incorrect statement of the law: With limited exceptions discussed in Part IV of this book, people are not strictly liable for the unintended injuries that they cause. Choice **C** presents the correct answer: The jury can use common sense in concluding that Rayna failed to use reasonable care when she, a novice, decided to try to ski down the mountain backward.

2. Balancing, including the Hand formula

If common sense can get a jury only so far, what is the alternative? Overwhelmingly, negligence cases are about *balancing* of risks and benefits. We expect people to take some, but not all, precautions against accidents: Drivers should have cars with working brakes and lights, should drive at a reasonable rate of speed given the circumstances, and should pay attention to the road. Even with these precautions, some accidents still happen. All of those would be prevented if we banned driving, and most of them would be prevented if we required drivers to go no faster than 5 miles per hour in cars covered with thick layers of foam.

These latter absurd examples are meant to bring home a point: Tort law does not require people to take every conceivable precaution to prevent accidents; life is precious, but we do not treat it as priceless, preventing people from taking *any* risks that could injure others. The reason we require working brakes but not 5 mph speed limits is that we engage in *balancing* of costs and benefits.

Oftentimes that balancing is implicit. After a car accident, a jury considering a negligence case brought by an injured pedestrian is told that the driver was fiddling with the car radio and not paying attention to the road. No one bothers to explicitly compute the additional risks of driving that come with a failure to pay attention; the jury can figure it out for itself implicitly from its life experience. But sometimes the balancing is more explicit, especially when the risks are taken by large entities such as corporations or the government and the balancing requires more than intuition and basic knowledge of how the world works. Imagine that one of these entities releases very small amounts of a certain chemical into the local river. Likely the entity or some government agency performed some kind of cost-benefit analysis before the entity made the decision to release the chemical.

One of the most respected federal judges of the last century, Learned Hand, wrote a very influential opinion on balancing in negligence law. In *United States v. Carroll Towing Co.* 159 F.2d 169 (2d Cir. 1947), the judge put the balancing decision into a basic algebraic equation:

A person is negligent for failing to take a precaution B, if B < *PL*.

A person should take a precaution if the burden of taking that precaution, B, is less than the expected accident losses if the precaution is not taken. The expected losses are expressed as the probability of harm if the precaution is not taken, P, multiplied by the gravity of the harm to occur if the precaution is not taken, L. The Third Restatement appears to endorse this approach as the way of determining breach. *See* Rest. (3d) Torts: Liability for Physical Harm § 3 (P.F.D. No. 1, 2005) ("Primary factors to consider in ascertaining whether the person's conduct lacks reasonable care are the foreseeable likelihood that the person's conduct will result in harm, the foreseeable severity of any harm that may ensue, and the burden of precautions to eliminate or reduce the risk of harm.").

To understand how the "Hand formula" (also sometimes referred to as the "*Carroll Towing* formula") works, consider this example. To save costs, an airline decides to cut down on engine inspections, cutting inspections by 50 percent. The inspections save $200,000 per year in precaution costs. The inspections increase the annual risk of accidents by 1 percent, and if an accident with an airplane occurs, it is expected to cost $5 million in damages. The airline fails to discover an engine problem that would have been detected by the inspection, and an accident occurs. Was the airline's failure to inspect as frequently negligent?

We compare

$$B, \$200,000$$

with

$$P, .01, \text{ multiplied by } L, \$5,000,000, \text{ or } \$50,000.$$

Because $200,000 > $50,000, the airline would not be negligent under the Hand formula. In other words, the Hand formula would lead to the conclusion here that the additional inspections were not a cost-justified precaution.

If we changed the facts so that the expected accident cost is $50,000,000 rather than $5,000,000, however, then it *would* be negligent for the airline to fail to take the precautions, because the $200,000 cost saves $500,000 in expected accident savings.[7]

Torts students often resist the Hand formula, finding it heartless that the law would not require the airline to take a precaution that would reduce the probability of a terrible accident. Life is priceless, the argument goes. Of course life is priceless to each of us, but tort law does not treat it that way: If it did then we would all be riding around in foam cars that do not go faster than 5 mph. But, as we shall see in the next section, even if one accepts the idea that balancing is inevitable or required in tort law, there are a number of important criticisms of balancing as set out by the Hand formula.

QUESTION 9. Lend a Hand (Formula). Tina, a pleasure boat operator, does not have a working radio on board her tug to warn her of approaching storms. The cost of the radio is $100. The failure to have working radios increases the risk of injury to passengers by 5 percent per year. The average pleasure boat injury imposes $30,000 in damages. Tina's boat gets into an accident that would have been prevented if Tina had a working radio on board. Her passenger Uma suffers serious personal injuries totaling $50,000 and sues for negligence. Under the Hand formula, was Tina negligent in not having a working radio?

A. Yes, because the precaution cost is $1,400 less than the expected accident costs.

B. Yes, because the precaution cost is $2,400 less than the expected accident costs.

C. Yes, because $100 is less than $30,000.

D. No.

ANALYSIS. This question is very easy if you know the Hand formula and can figure out B, P, and L. It is very difficult if you cannot do both of those things. Here, the burden of taking the precaution — in this case the working radio — is $100. The probability of harm if the precaution is not taken is 5 percent (or .05), which is multiplied by the gravity of harm if an accident does occur, or $30,000. (This is viewed at the time the precaution is taken, not later on — so the actual accident costs do not matter.) .05 × 30,000 is $1,500. Once you compute this figure, and know that the precaution cost is $100, you can answer the question. Choice **A** correctly states that the

---

7. Those of you who read the last chapter carefully will note that this comparison is applying a Kaldor-Hicks efficiency standard. The question is total social costs, not who pays for precautions or who bears the costs of accidents.

precaution cost is $1,400 less than the expected accident costs. Choice **B** is incorrect because it is based upon the $50,000 in actual damages figure. We don't use actual damages, but we use estimates taken in advance (what economists call *ex ante*). Choice **C** is incorrect because the Hand formula does not simply compare *B* and *L*. One must compare *B* with *P* multiplied by *L*. Choice **D** is incorrect because here the precaution is cost-justified. Therefore, the failure to take the precaution counts as a breach.

D.   The Closer: Is the Hand formula the Holy Grail of negligence or deeply flawed?

For some, the Hand formula simply puts into mathematical form the job that juries should do in deciding upon breach. For others, the Hand formula is deeply flawed. Here are some of the major criticisms that can be raised against the Hand formula. You can decide for yourself how the formula stacks up against these criticisms:

- *The formula assumes risk neutrality, rather than risk aversion.* It assumes society is indifferent between a $500 precaution and a 1 percent chance of a $50,000 loss. In fact, people tend to be risk averse, and would be willing to pay a premium to eliminate even small chances of large losses (this is the reason that insurance is so popular). Whereas the Hand formula would say not to take a $500 precaution to prevent the 1 percent chance of the $49,999 loss, society may wish to call the failure to take such a precaution unreasonable.
- *The formula assumes individual rationality, and that individuals have enough information to calculate costs and benefits.* Psychologists have described all kinds of human systematic miscalculation of risk, and have explained that people evaluate risks differently when it comes to averting losses rather than realizing potential gains. The Hand formula assumes perfect human rationality. It also assumes that individuals have enough information to calculate costs and benefits, and that jurors can look backward and figure out whether a precaution that a defendant failed to take would have been cost-justified.[8]

---

8. A more sophisticated economic analysis of the Hand formula notes that it uses *total* costs and benefits in determining whether a precaution is cost-justified but that a more accurate formula should use *marginal* costs and benefits. *See* RICHARD A. EPSTEIN, CASES AND MATERIALS ON TORTS 211 (9th ed. 2008). In other words, to promote efficiency, a potential injurer should keep investing additional dollars in precaution costs until the last dollar in precaution costs yields exactly one dollar in accident savings. For students well versed in economics, this point probably makes perfect sense. For others of you, this point may require some additional discussion with your Torts instructor (if she cares about such issues).

- *The formula treats small probabilities of high loss events equivalent to high probabilities of low loss events.* Under the Hand formula, a 1 percent chance of a $50,000 loss is treated the same as a 10 percent chance of a $5,000 loss and a 50 percent chance of a $1,000 loss. Society might decide instead that in cases where either *P* or *L* is very high, it may be unreasonable to fail to take a precaution even if under the Hand formula such a precaution would not be cost-justified.

- *The formula assumes that "reasonableness" can be reduced to a mathematical formula.* This criticism goes further than the other formula in rejecting the equation of reasonableness with economic efficiency. Under a corrective justice or moral theory, the requirement of what it means to be reasonable is judged under a community standard that is not connected with costs and benefits. (I confess I have a hard time understanding how such a decision is to be made without considering costs and benefits at some level.)

QUESTION 10. Hands Down.   Which is *not* a criticism of the Hand formula?

A. The Hand formula assumes risk neutrality, while people tend to be risk averse.

B. The Hand formula requires comparing the burden of taking precautions with expected accident losses in determining breach.

C. The Hand formula assumes reasonableness can be reduced to a mathematical formula.

D. The Hand formula assumes perfect rationality and perfect information, conditions which do not occur in the real world.

ANALYSIS.   If you read and understood this section of the chapter, this is a straightforward question to answer. As described in the text, Choices **A**, **C**, and **D** each describe criticisms that some have raised against the Hand formula. Choice **B**, in contrast, simply explains how the Hand formula works: It is not a criticism of the formula.

 Rick's picks

1. Half-a-Loaf?	C
2. Dumb Joe	B
3. Playing with Fire	A
4. Snowed Over	B
5. Roll On	C

6. Double Standard	**B**
7. Going Downhill	**D**
8. Going Downhill, Take II	**C**
9. Lend a Hand (Formula)	**A**
10. Hands Down	**B**

9

More Ways of Proving Breach: Custom, *Negligence Per Se*, and *Res Ipsa Loquitur*

CHAPTER OVERVIEW
A. **Custom**
    1. **The general custom rule**
    2. **Medical cases: The medical case exception**
    3. **Medical cases: The informed consent digression**
B. *Negligence per se*
    1. **The general rule**
    2. **Excuses**
C. *Res ipsa loquitur*
D. **The Closer: Choosing a way to prove breach**
 ❂ **Rick's picks**

A. Custom

1. The general custom rule

The last chapter looked at the question of breach and provided the following statement of the elements:

> A defendant **breaches** a duty to a plaintiff when, judged from the perspective of a reasonably prudent person in the defendant's position, the defendant failed to use reasonable care to avoid a reasonably foreseeable risk to the plaintiff.

As we saw in the last chapter, two primary ways of proving breach are the use of common sense (recall the sponge left in the patient's abdomen) and balancing, whether it is done informally or through something more formal such as the Hand formula. In this chapter, we consider three additional ways a plaintiff may try to prove that a defendant breached: custom, *negligence per se*, and *res ipsa loquitur*. In connection to custom, we will also consider some special rules in the medical malpractice area.

We begin with custom. By "custom," I mean an industry standard, such as a decision of most airlines in the airline industry to inspect plane engines once every 50,000 miles. I do *not* mean an action that a person does often or habitually. ("I have a 'custom' of driving while blindfolded" doesn't count as custom for our purposes.) The question we consider is what role an industry's custom in facing certain risks should play in a negligence case.

Consider again the plane engine inspection hypothetical. Suppose that to cut costs, an airline, which had inspected its engines every 25,000 miles, changes its inspection plan to inspections every 50,000 miles, which is the standard most other airlines use. An accident occurs because of an engine failure, which the plaintiff says would have been discovered had the airline stuck with its 25,000-mile inspection schedule. Under the analysis of the last chapter, a plaintiff could try to prove breach through some sort of balancing test (common sense would be beyond the ordinary understanding of jurors here). But what if the defendant airline wished to defend by claiming that it did not breach — that is, the airline acted reasonably — because it followed the industry custom of inspections every 50,000 miles? How should courts treat the evidence of custom in the breach case?

Traditionally, courts took one of three approaches to the question of breach. One approach was to hold that the evidence was *dispositive* of the question of breach (by "dispositive" I mean that it resolved the entire question). *Titus v. Bradford B. & K. R. Co.*, 20 A. 517 (Pa. 1890). Under this rule, if a defendant could prove that it complied with industry custom, then the defendant could not be found liable for breach.[1] The idea here is that if the industry adopted a certain practice, it must be a reasonable one.

The second approach was one holding that evidence of custom was *inadmissible and irrelevant* in proving breach. *Mayhew v. Sullivan Mining Co.*, 76 Me. 100 (1884). Under this rule, whether or not a defendant could prove it complied with industry custom was not relevant to the question whether the defendant failed to use reasonable care to avoid a reasonably foreseeable risk to the plaintiff. The idea here is that an entire industry could lag behind reasonable conduct.

---

1. This is sometimes referred to as a defendant using compliance with custom as a "shield" against a claim of breach. A different question arises if a defendant fails to comply with an industry custom, and a plaintiff wants to use the defendant's lack of compliance as a "sword" to prove breach.

The third approach, and the one that has dominated tort law (outside the area of medical malpractice) is that evidence of custom is *admissible and probative of the question of breach*, but not dispositive. Under this rule, evidence that the defendant complied or failed to comply with custom would be admissible in a negligence case and a jury could consider it in determining whether or not a defendant breached, but such evidence alone did not resolve the entire question.

The leading case adopting this middle position is the *T.J. Hooper* case, 60 F.2d 737 (2d Cir. 1932), another famous torts case by Judge Learned Hand. In the case, a tug crashed because of the failure to have a radio on board to hear of approaching storms. Judge Hand rejected the argument that because there was no custom to have a working radio on board,[2] the defendant could not be found negligent: "There are yet, no doubt, cases where courts seem to make the general practice of the calling the standard of proper diligence; we have indeed given some currency to the notion ourselves. Indeed in most cases reasonable prudence is in fact common prudence; but strictly it is never its measure; a whole calling may have unduly lagged in the adoption of new and available devices." The Restatement (Third) of Torts follows *The T.J. Hooper* on the question of the role of custom in a negligence case.[3]

QUESTION 1. Lend a (Customary) Hand. Tina, a pleasure boat operator, does not have a working radio on board her tug to warn her of approaching storms. The cost of the radio is $100, and most tug operators equip their tugs with such radios. The failure to have working radios increases the risk of injury to passengers by 5 percent per year. The average pleasure boat injury imposes $30,000 in damages. Tina's boat gets into an accident that would have been prevented if Tina had a working radio on board. Her passenger Uma suffers serious personal injuries totaling $50,000 and sues for negligence. Tina asks the judge for an order preventing the jury from hearing evidence about industry practice regarding radios. How should the judge rule?

A. Exclude the evidence as inadmissible because custom can never be admitted into trial to prove breach.

B. Exclude the evidence because there is ample evidence of breach under a balancing test.

---

2. Perhaps it is fairer to say that Judge Hand rejected the argument *assuming* there was no custom to have a working radio on board. According to the lower court opinion, there *was* such a custom. *See The T.J. Hooper*, 53 F.2d 107 (S.D.N.Y. 1931) ("Radio broadcasting was no new or untried thing in March, 1928. Everywhere, and in almost every field of activity, it was being utilized as an aid to communication, and for the dissemination of information. And that radio sets were in widespread use on vessels of all kinds is clearly indicated by the testimony in this case."). Why might Judge Hand have chosen to ignore this fact? Perhaps he wanted to make a broader pronouncement about the use of custom in negligence cases.
3. RESTATEMENT (THIRD) OF TORTS: LIABILITY FOR PHYSICAL HARM § 13 (P.F.D. 2005).

C. Allow the evidence in because a jury is not bound by strict mathematical balancing in determining breach.

D. Allow the evidence in because the plaintiff also has evidence of balancing to present to the jury.

ANALYSIS. Under the rule set forth in the famous *T.J. Hooper* case, the general rule regarding custom in negligence cases is that such evidence is admissible and probative on the question of breach, but not dispositive. This is true regardless of whether there is other evidence of breach, such as the balancing evidence presented in this question. Choices **A** and **B** are incorrect because they incorrectly state that evidence of custom is inadmissible to prove breach. Choice **D** is wrong because in order to present custom evidence, it does not matter whether there is also evidence of balancing. Choice **C** presents the correct choice: A jury can consider the evidence of custom and need not be bound by any calculation under a balancing test in determining breach.

QUESTION 2. Sword or Shield? Same facts as in Question 1, except assume that most tug operators do *not* equip their tugs with radios. Tina wants to admit this fact into evidence and Uma moves to exclude it. How should the judge rule?

A. Exclude the evidence because evidence of custom is admissible as a sword but not a shield.

B. Exclude the evidence because evidence of custom is admissible as a shield but not a sword.

C. Exclude the evidence because evidence of custom is inadmissible as either a shield or a sword.

D. Allow the evidence.

ANALYSIS. The purpose of this question is to get you familiar with the terminology of "sword" and "shield," and to make sure you see the parity of the rule between plaintiffs and defendants. When a defendant complies with an industry custom and wishes to use evidence of compliance to show that plaintiff can't prove breach, the defendant is using custom as a "shield" against liability. When a defendant fails to comply with industry custom and a plaintiff wishes to use the failure to comply to prove breach, the plaintiff is using custom as a "sword" to establish liability. Either way, evidence of industry custom is admissible and probative, but not dispositive. For this reason, Choices **A**, **B**, and **C** are incorrect and Choice **D** is correct.

2. Medical cases: The medical case exception

The general rule of *The T.J. Hooper* — that custom is admissible and probative to prove breach, but not dispositive — is subject to an important exception in medical malpractice cases. In such cases, custom evidence usually is *dispositive* in proving breach in most medical cases. (We'll see one of the exceptions in the section of this chapter on *res ipsa loquitur* below.) This means that when there is evidence of medical custom presented, a jury is bound by it, and it cannot engage in its own balancing to decide whether or not a medical defendant (usually a doctor, dentist, nurse, or hospital) acted negligently.

One of the rare cases rejecting custom in the medical malpractice context is *Helling v. Carey*, 519 P.2d 981 (Wash. 1974). In that case, the defendant ophthalmologist failed to give plaintiff a test for glaucoma on grounds that it was not customary to do so for patients under the age of 40. Plaintiff contracted glaucoma, and sued the doctor for medical malpractice. The trial court on this evidence directed a verdict for the doctor, but the Washington state supreme court reversed, saying that a jury could consider the costs and benefits of giving such tests to patients under the age of 40. In other words, the position of the state supreme court was that evidence of custom was admissible, but not dispositive: Even in the face of evidence that the defendant complied with medical industry custom, the jury could still find the defendant to have breached.

The Washington state legislature reversed *Helling* by statute, R.C.W. §4.24.290, and courts in other jurisdictions have rejected it too. The overwhelming authority in the United States holds that custom is in fact dispositive in medical cases.

You might be wondering (or at least I hope you'd be wondering) why the law has developed different rules for doctors. Is this merely favoritism for doctors, who can use custom as a shield to prevent medical malpractice suits brought by patients who are unhappy with bad outcomes of certain medical procedures? Is it justified because medical care is very technical, and juries cannot competently engage in the balancing of costs and benefits? Because doctors, more than others, can be trusted to act reasonably?

I don't find these explanations persuasive. The first justification tends to assume doctors would have special power over courts or legislatures, out of proportion to, say, the interests of the trial lawyers for whom medical malpractice litigation is very important. The second justification does not seem right either: Medical questions can be complicated, but no more complicated than other issues of negligence that juries consider, such as litigation over airline maintenance policies. The final answer seems to have an overly rosy view of doctors compared to the rest of us.

A better explanation might be found in the economic analysis of negligence.[4] Richard Epstein has argued that in competitive industries, the customary standard of care that emerges is likely to be an efficient standard of care.[5] Think of the tug industry in the 1920s and tug operators deciding

---

4. This analysis assumes you are familiar with the concepts and terminology presented in Chapter 7. If not, you may want to read the section on economic analysis in that chapter before continuing here.
5. Richard A. Epstein, *The Path to* The T.J. Hooper, 21 J. LEGAL STUD. 1 (1992).

whether or not to buy radios to hear storm warnings. If having a radio is efficient (the benefits of having the radio exceed the costs), then the market will favor those tug operators that buy radios. Those who don't buy radios will have more accidents, and, in a competitive industry, be driven out of business. Eventually, only those tug operators with radios will be in business, and the "custom" of having a radio will be established. Using this reasoning, Epstein argues for the use of custom as a dispositive standard, and one that is more likely to lead to efficient choices than having juries do after-the-fact balancing of costs and benefits.

Epstein's argument is open to criticism. For one thing, if industries don't pay for all of the costs their choices impose (what economists call "externalities"), they may not adopt efficient customs. For another thing, it is hard to know when an industry is competitive, and when members of the industry have enough information about costs and benefits so that we can say with confidence that the customary standard that has emerged is an efficient standard.

But if you think about Epstein's argument and the medical profession, it makes a lot of sense. How do customs emerge in the medical field? Medical care is the subject of intensive research using carefully designed experiments, statistical analysis, and epidemiological studies. The medical field establishes custom by engaging in detailed balancing of costs and benefits. At its best, in the medical field (perhaps in others as well), the customary standard of care that emerges is likely to be an efficient standard.[6] If nothing else, allowing medical malpractice cases to be tried exclusively though a customary standard will save administrative costs, and jurors do not have to consider detailed evidence of costs and benefits of various medical procedures.

> **QUESTION 3. Lend a (Medical) Hand.**   Dr. Veronica, a surgeon, decides to perform back surgery on Warren after examining Warren's medical history of back problems. Most doctors would not have recommended such surgery because of its risk of paralysis, preferring instead to use a "conservative treatment" of bed rest for two weeks to see if Warren's back improved. Dr. Veronica goes ahead with the surgery, and unfortunately Warren becomes paralyzed. Warren sues Dr. Veronica for medical malpractice, and Dr. Veronica wishes to introduce evidence that the benefits of such surgery for patients such as Warren exceed the risks. Warren asks the judge for an order preventing the jury from hearing evidence of these costs and benefits. How should the judge rule?

---

6. Indeed, some have criticized the *Helling* case for using incorrect figures in its cost-benefit analysis. *See* Jerry Wiley, *The Impact of Judicial Decisions on Professional Conduct: An Empirical Study*, 55 S. CAL. L. REV. 345, 388 (1982).

A. Exclude the evidence as inadmissible because custom is dispositive in most medical malpractice cases.
B. Exclude the evidence because Warren is paralyzed.
C. Allow the evidence in because evidence of custom is admissible and probative, but not dispositive in determining breach.
D. Allow the evidence in because Dr. Veronica would be using it as a "shield," not a "sword," in disproving breach.

ANALYSIS. Although the usual rule is that custom is admissible and probative but not dispositive in proving breach, the standard in most medical malpractice cases is different: Custom is indeed dispositive in proving breach, whether used as a sword by the plaintiff or a shield by the defendant. When there is a custom in a medical malpractice case, evidence of balancing should be excluded by the judge as irrelevant. Choice **A** correctly sets forth this standard. Choice **B** is an easy one to eliminate: Why should the fact that plaintiff is paralyzed have any bearing on the breach question? Choice **C** is wrong because it states the general standard for custom in cases *besides* medical malpractice cases. Choice **D** is wrong because whether or not the evidence is used as a "sword" or "shield" is irrelevant to the question of custom's role in a negligence case.

Which custom in medical malpractice cases? Given the central role that custom plays in medical malpractice cases, it should be no surprise that litigation has sometimes focused on *which* custom matters. Two principal issues arise here.

First, there may be *two (or more) schools of thought* over how to deal with a particular medical issue. Some doctors may recommend one course of treatment, and other doctors recommend something different. So long as a medical professional follows the custom of a *recognized school of thought* (even if it is not the approach taken by a majority of professionals in the field), compliance with that custom will defeat a negligence claim. There must be a large enough group of medical professionals (not just a handful) to constitute a recognized school of thought.

Second, there may be issues related to *the resources of particular areas, such as rural areas.* The court used to recognize a different standard of care for different locations (the so-called locality rule), but in the modern era of cheap and easy communications about medical advances, courts have rejected the locality rule. *Brune v. Belinkoff,* 235 N.E.2d 793 (Mass. 1968). Courts still recognize that different localities have different resources. Thus, a small-town doctor would not be negligent for failing to have an expensive MRI machine available to diagnose certain problems. But he would be negligent if he did not refer a patient in need of an MRI to a larger hospital with access to such a machine.

QUESTION 4. Lend a (Medical) Hand, Take II. Dr. Veronica, a surgeon, decides to perform back surgery on Warren after examining Warren's medical history of back problems. Most doctors would not have recommended such surgery because of its risk of paralysis, preferring instead to use a "conservative treatment" of bed rest for two weeks to see if Warren's back improved. Dr. Veronica goes ahead with the surgery, and unfortunately Warren becomes paralyzed. Warren sues Dr. Veronica for medical malpractice, and Dr. Veronica wishes to argue that she follows her own "school of thought," the "Cut 'Em and Hope for the Best" strategy of dealing with back problems. No other doctors are part of this school of thought. Dr. Veronica argues that because she complied with this school's teaching, a jury could not find that she breached.

How should the court rule on this argument?

A. The court should accept the argument because custom is dispositive in medical malpractice cases.
B. The court should accept the argument because Dr. Veronica followed a recognized school of thought in medical malpractice cases.
C. The court should reject the argument because evidence of custom is admissible and probative, but not dispositive in determining breach.
D. The court should reject the argument because Dr. Veronica did not follow the custom of a recognized school of thought.

ANALYSIS. In medical malpractice cases, evidence of custom is dispositive in most cases. When there is more than one "school of thought" over proper medical care, a defendant can follow any recognized school of thought. One doctor cannot make up her own recognized school of thought. (This of course makes sense: If the rule were otherwise, any doctor could claim a "custom" of one doctor to defeat the breach portion of the negligence case.) In this case, Dr. Veronica is a school of one; she is not following any recognized school of thought. Accordingly, the court should reject Dr. Veronica's argument. Choice **D** correctly states this choice. Choice **C** reaches the right result, but for the wrong reason: Custom usually *is* dispositive in medical malpractice cases. Here, Dr. Veronica did not follow any recognized custom. Choices **A** and **B** are wrong because though following the custom of a recognized school of thought is enough to disprove breach in a medical malpractice case, Dr. Veronica did not do so in this case.

3. Medical cases: The informed consent digression

We now consider an issue that doesn't comfortably fit here, but it doesn't comfortably fit anywhere else in this book: The issue of informed consent in medical cases. (Its connection to the question of custom will become apparent in a moment.) Suppose a doctor recommends a certain treatment to a patient for the patient's illness. In so doing, the doctor fails to disclose some major risks associated with the treatment. The patient undergoes the treatment and, unfortunately, the risk that the doctor failed to disclose materializes. The patient wants to sue the doctor for failing to disclose the risk.

We could conceive of the patient's claim either as a battery or negligence.[7] You will recall from Chapter 3.B.5 that when a doctor fails to obtain *any* consent before touching a patient, the patient may have a good battery claim against the doctor (unless the patient was unconscious and facing an emergency). But the kind of case described in the last paragraph is different: The patient has given his consent, but has done so without full information. Many courts treat such a "lack of informed consent" claim as a special kind of negligence case.

In an informed consent case, the equivalent of the breach element is plaintiff's proof that the defendant medical professional failed to disclose a material risk to the plaintiff. In such a case, in many jurisdictions evidence of medical custom about what risks are disclosed is *not dispositive*. In other words, even if most doctors would not disclose the risk of a certain treatment to most patients, a jury can still find that the doctor breached by failing to disclose a material risk.

The reason custom is treated differently in informed consent cases compared to normal medical malpractice cases is the different interests involved. In informed consent cases the law is concerned about the patient's autonomy: The patient, not the medical professional, should have the ultimate say about the patient's treatment options and care. The informed consent rules protect the patient's right to bodily integrity and autonomy. A rule that leaves the issue in the hands of the physician is unduly paternalistic. In contrast, the question of how a medical professional performs her job raises issues of competence that the law evaluates under the customary standard of care; questions of patient autonomy do not arise.

Informed consent rules require that medical professionals disclose *material* risks. What counts as such a risk? "[A]ll risks potentially affecting the decision [whether or not to undergo a certain treatment] must be unmasked." *Canterbury v. Spence*, 464 F.2d 772 (D.C. Cir. 1972). A patient, for example, should be told the risks of paralysis that accompany back surgery because that is a fact that a patient would want to know.[8]

Courts have recognized a few exceptions to the disclosure requirement. First, and most obviously, a doctor need not obtain informed consent if the patient is unconscious and there is no family member to give consent on the

---

7. Whether we call it battery or negligence might matter for a number of procedural reasons; for example, there may be a different statute of limitations applicable to the two claims.
8. In informed consent cases, a large question is one of causation: Did the doctor's failure to disclose a material risk make a difference in the patient's decision? We consider this question in Chapter 13.

patient's behalf. Second, if a particular patient is particularly sensitive to bad medical news, a doctor may make an individualized assessment that it would be medically counterproductive to fully disclose risks. But this is a narrow exception for very sensitive individuals, and a doctor fails to disclose so at his peril: A jury could well find that the patient could have handled the information. The informed consent rules could well be causing medical professionals to over-disclose potential risks of various treatments.

QUESTION 5. Lend a (Medical) Hand, Take III. Dr. Veronica, a surgeon, decides to perform back surgery on Warren after examining Warren's medical history of back problems. Dr. Veronica fails to disclose to Warren that the surgery has a 1 percent risk of paralysis. Warren becomes paralyzed after the surgery, and sues Dr. Veronica for lack of informed consent. Dr. Veronica introduces uncontested evidence at trial that most doctors do not disclose the risk of paralysis from this kind of surgery to their patients. Dr. Veronica claims that the jury therefore must find for her on the question of breach. How should the judge rule on this argument?

A. The court should accept the argument because custom is dispositive in medical malpractice cases.

B. The court should accept the argument because Dr. Veronica followed a recognized school of thought in medical malpractice cases.

C. The court should reject the argument because evidence of custom is not dispositive in informed consent cases.

D. The court should reject the argument because full information might have deterred Warren from having beneficial treatment.

ANALYSIS. Though evidence of custom is dispositive in medical treatment cases, it is generally not dispositive in informed consent cases. The fact that most doctors do not disclose the risk of paralysis does not answer the question whether it was a breach to fail to disclose the risk to a patient. Instead the question for the jury is whether the paralysis information would be a *material risk* that most patients would want to know. Choices **A** and **B** are wrong because they state that custom is dispositive in informed consent cases. Choice **D** is incorrect because it reflects a paternalistic view of medicine that has been rejected by American courts: It is for the patient to decide on treatment, and a doctor must disclose material risks if this means that the patient with full information may decide against a treatment option that a doctor recommends. Choice **C** correctly explains that evidence of custom is not dispositive in informed consent cases.

> **QUESTION 6. Lend a (Medical) Hand, Take IV.** Same facts as in Question 4, but Dr. Veronica fails to disclose the information to Warren because she reasonably believes Warren would become very depressed upon hearing about his choices, though it would not affect his treatment outcome. Should a jury find that Dr. Veronica breached her duty of informed consent?
>
> A. Yes, because depression is not enough to eliminate a doctor's requirement to disclose all material risks.
> B. Yes, if it is customary to disclose such information to patients.
> C. No, because Dr. Veronica's belief was reasonable.
> D. No, if Warren was unconscious during the surgery.

ANALYSIS. A doctor's duty to disclose material risks is subject to only two exceptions: First, the patient is unconscious in an emergency situation and there is no one to consent on his behalf and second, the patient is very sensitive emotionally, and disclosure would be counterproductive to treatment. Here, the facts tell us that the doctor reasonably believed Warren would become depressed about hearing of the risk, but it was not so severe that it would affect his treatment outcome. On these facts, Dr. Veronica has a duty to disclose all material risks, including the risk of paralysis. That's Choice **A**, the correct choice. Choice **B** is incorrect because custom is not the operative standard in informed consent cases: It is the requirement to disclose all material risks, subject to narrow exceptions. Choice **C** is incorrect because even if Dr. Veronica had a reasonable belief Warren would be depressed, depression is not enough to fall into the exception: The choice must affect treatment. Choice **D** is incorrect because even if Warren was unconscious during surgery, this was not an emergency situation and Dr. Veronica could have disclosed all material risks while Warren was conscious.

B. Negligence per se

1. The general rule

Consider a driver who drives down a residential street at 50 mph. The posted speed limit on the street is 30 mph. The driver sees a pedestrian crossing the street; though the driver slams on her brakes, she cannot stop in time and hits the pedestrian, who sustains serious personal injuries.

If the pedestrian sues the driver for negligence, the pedestrian could try to prove breach using a balancing test (the burden would be driving slower, compared to the probability and severity of harm of driving so fast down a residential street).[9] An alternative, however, is to argue that the driver's breaking of the speed limit proves negligence: It is negligence in and of itself (or *negligence per se*).

This is a somewhat odd way of proving negligence. Rather than rely upon direct proof to the jury of a failure to use reasonable care, the plaintiff relies upon a state legislature (or other government body, such as a city council or Congress) to set a *criminal statute,* which then defines what constitutes reasonable care. Thus, in some circumstances a plaintiff may prove negligence (in a civil torts case) by showing the defendant violated a *criminal* statute.

Under what circumstances can *negligence per se* apply? First, the criminal statute must be silent as to civil liability. If the statute speaks directly of its effect on civil liability, that statement controls over these general rules.[10] Assuming the criminal statute is silent on civil liability, a plaintiff must meet a five-part test in order to be able to use violation of the civil statute as proof of negligence:

1. *A criminal statute, ordinance, or administrative regulation imposes a specific duty upon someone for the protection of others* (for example, a statute imposes a 30 mph speed limit).
2. *The defendant neglects to perform that duty* (for example, the defendant speeds).
3. *Plaintiff is within the class of people whom the statute was designed to protect* (for example, the speeding statute is designed to protect pedestrians and other drivers).
4. *The statute was designed to protect against the type of accident the defendant causes* (for example, the speeding statute is designed to protect against collisions between cars and other cars, people, or property).
5. *Plaintiff's injuries were caused by defendant's violation of the statute, ordinance or regulation* (for example, the pedestrian would not have been injured had the driver not been speeding).[11]

See *Osborne v. McMasters,* 41 N.W. 543 (Minn. 1889); REST. (3D) TORTS: LIABILITY FOR PHYSICAL HARM § 14 (P.F.D. 2005).

---

9. Make sure you understand from the last chapter and the earlier section of this chapter why common sense or custom would not be a good way for the pedestrian to try to prove the driver's breach.
10. For example, a speeding ordinance might say that violation of the ordinance creates a civil cause of action for anyone injured by a speeding driver. In such circumstances *negligence per se* does not apply. Instead, an injured plaintiff sues directly under the statute.
11. The meaning of causation here is the same as actual causation discussed in Chapter 13. Technically, this goes beyond the tortious conduct portion of the prima facie case, but it is often incorporated as part of the *negligence per se* test. We will ignore issues related to this element in this chapter.

In addition, as we will see in the next section, even if plaintiff can meet the five-part test, the defendant still may be found to be not liable for negligence if the defendant's conduct is *excused* (for example, the driver was driving quickly to rush his wife having a heart attack to the hospital). *Tedla v. Ellman*, 19 N.E.2d 987 (N.Y. 1939); REST. (3D) TORTS: LIABILITY FOR PHYSICAL HARM § 14 (P.F.D. 2005).

Questions may arise under any of the five requirements. For example, under the third requirement, courts sometimes used to question whether fellow employees injured on the job would be within the class of those the legislature intended to protect in consumer safety statutes. Some of the most intellectually challenging issues arise under the fourth requirement: That the injury be *of the type* that the statute was designed to prevent.

To understand this requirement, consider the facts of the *Osborne* case and a somewhat off-the-wall variation. In *Osborne*, a state statute required pharmacists to label as "poison" any poisonous items. The pharmacist failed to do so with a bottle of poison, and someone drank the poison, dying from it. The family sued, and the court said that the doctrine of *negligence per se* could apply to prove the pharmacist's negligence. (Review the five elements above to make sure you understand how the family could prove each element.)

Now consider the off-the-wall variation. Imagine the same statute, and the pharmacist's same failure to label the bottle of poison as poison. A person takes the bottle of poison home and leaves it on the counter. Had it been labeled poison, the person would have locked it up so that the children could not have gotten to it. The person knocks the bottle off the counter. The bottle is glass and the person cuts her foot seriously on the glass. She sues for negligence. Could *negligence per se* apply? Let's run through the elements:

- The statute requires the pharmacist to label poison as poison.
- The pharmacist failed to do so.
- The person is a customer of the pharmacy within the class of people protected by the statute.
- *But* the injury was *not the type of injury* that the statute was designed to prevent. The legislature passed a labeling statute to prevent accidental ingestion of poison, *not* to prevent people from getting cut on the foot by the glass bottles in which the unlabeled poison might sit.[12]

One final point about *negligence per se*: though violation of a statute can be used to prove negligence in certain circumstances, a defendant's *compliance*

---

12. The point won't be clear to you until Chapter 13, but the plaintiff could prove the final element, actual causation: But for the failure of the pharmacist to label the bottle of poison as poison, the bottle would have been locked up and the foot injury never would have occurred.

with a statute, standing alone, generally does not prove non-negligence.[13] *See* REST. (3D) TORTS: LIABILITY FOR PHYSICAL HARM § 16 (P.F.D. 2005).

QUESTION 7. Lead Foot. A state statute bars anyone but police officers from bringing weapons to school. James, an eighth-grader, brought his parent's gun to school (he made sure it was not loaded) for show-and-tell. As he was showing the gun to a friend Amy in the hallway, another child bumped into James and he dropped the gun. It landed on Amy's foot, breaking three of her toes. Amy sues James for negligence. May she rely upon *negligence per se*?

A. Yes, because James violated the statute.
B. Yes, because James was careless.
C. No, even though James violated the statute.
D. No, because Amy was not within the class of people protected by the statute.

ANALYSIS. This is a difficult question. Remember that in order to be able to use *negligence per se*, a plaintiff needs to prove all five elements of the *negligence per se* test (and, as we will see in the next section, even if a plaintiff does so, a defendant may still win with a valid excuse). Let's consider the five elements.

- Did the statute impose a duty upon James? Yes, it imposed a duty upon all people besides police officers not to bring a weapon to school.
- Did James violate the statute? Yes, he brought a weapon to school. It should not matter that the weapon was not loaded. A gun is still a weapon.
- Was Amy within the class of people the legislature intended to protect by the statute? Yes, the statute is designed to protect people on school premises (likely the legislature was especially concerned about protecting students).
- Was the statute designed to prevent these types of injuries? No, anti-weapon statutes are designed to prevent individuals from being injured by weapons *being used as weapons*. Here, Amy was hurt because James dropped the weapon and it broke her toe. The same injury could have occurred if James dropped a heavy book. What makes bringing a weapon onto campus dangerous is not its *weight*. For this reason, *negligence per se* will fail, and Amy will have to prove breach some other way.

---

13. As we will see in Chapter 19, federal preemption law may sometimes trump tort law in this regard.

- Was the violation a cause of the injury? Yes. As we will see in Chapter 13, but for James bringing the gun onto campus, the injury would not have happened.

Given this analysis, even though James violated the statute, *negligence per se* is not available because this is not the type of accident the statute was designed to prevent. For this reason, Choice **A** is wrong and Choice **C** is right. Choice **B** is wrong because nothing indicates that James was careless in handling the gun, and general carelessness does not go to the question of *negligence per se*. Amy can still try to prove negligence based upon balancing or some other way, but not through violation of the statute. Choice **D** is wrong because, as noted in the third bullet point above, Amy is a member of the class the statute was designed to protect.

2. Excuses

Consider again a driver who drives down a residential street at 50 mph. The posted speed limit on the street is 30 mph. The driver sees a pedestrian crossing the street; though the driver slams on her brakes, she cannot stop in time and hits the pedestrian, who sustains serious personal injuries. You should see from the analysis in the last section that the plaintiff should have an easy time meeting the five-part test for *negligence per se*.

But suppose that the driver was driving this quickly to get his wife, who was having a heart attack, to the hospital. Even though the driver violated the statute, a jury might conclude that the driver's behavior was nonetheless reasonable given the emergency circumstances. For this reason, a defendant may raise an *excuse* for violating the statute, which the jury can consider in evaluating whether *negligence per se* should apply. (It is the defendant's job to raise the excuse and prove it, not the plaintiff's to disprove that any excuses exist.)

Of course, not just *any* excuse will do. A person driving fast to get to the Dodgers game won't get out from under the coverage of *negligence per se*. Here is how the Third Restatement frames the types of excuses that may apply:

An actor's violation of a statute is excused and not negligence if:

(a) the violation is reasonable in light of the actor's childhood, physical disability, or physical incapacitation;

(b) the actor exercises reasonable care in attempting to comply with the statute;

(c) the actor neither knows nor should know of the factual circumstances that render the statute applicable;

(d) the actor's violation of the statute is due to the confusing way in which the requirements of the statute are presented to the public; or

(e) the actor's compliance would involve a greater risk of physical harm to the actor or to others than noncompliance.

Rest. (3d) Torts: Liability for Physical Harm § 15 (P.F.D. 2005).

The driver taking his wife to the hospital would claim an excuse under § 15(e), and the jury would have to determine whether in fact compliance with the speed limit would have involved a greater risk of harm to others than noncompliance.

The other excuses are pretty commonsensical. Consider these examples. Under section 15(a), a wheelchair-bound person would not be found to have committed *negligence per se* under a statute that requires nondrivers to walk across the street at a crosswalk. Under section 15(b), a person on crutches who starts to cross a street when the light turns green but cannot get completely across the street before the light turns red likely has an excuse against a claim of *negligence per se*. Under section 15(c), consider a driver whose brake light bulb stops working after he starts driving his car, in violation of a statute requiring drivers to have working brake lights. Under section 15(d), imagine a driver who parks in a "no parking" zone that is not clearly marked as such a zone.

QUESTION 8. Take the High Road.   A state statute provides that on roads without sidewalks, a person should walk on the left side of the road (opposite traffic). Maurice is walking down the road in Summerland, a vacation resort. It is Sunday evening, and there is a great deal of traffic leaving town as vacationers are returning back to the city. There is very little traffic on the right side of the road going into Summerland. Maurice decides to walk on the right side of the road, with traffic, because there is much less traffic on that side of the road. Nina is driving on that side of the road into Summerland. She does not see Maurice until she nearly hits him. She swerves to avoid him and hits a tree, suffering serious personal injuries. She sues Maurice for negligence, and tries to prove his negligence using *negligence per se*.

Maurice's strongest argument against liability for *negligence per se* is:

A. He did not violate the statute.
B. He exercised reasonable care while trying to comply with the statute.
C. He did not know the factual circumstances rendering the statute applicable.
D. Compliance with the statute imposed a greater risk of harm than noncompliance.

ANALYSIS.   This case is based upon *Tedla v. Ellman*, 19 N.E.2d 987 (N.Y. 1939). There is no question that Maurice violated the statute by walking with traffic on the right side of the road. For this reason, Choice **A** is incorrect. Choice **B** is incorrect because this isn't a case where a person was trying to comply with the statute but couldn't: If Maurice could not cross the street to get to the left side of the road, then this excuse could apply. Choice **C** is incorrect because Maurice surely knew of the factual circumstances rendering the statute applicable—he knew he was walking on a road without a sidewalk. His best argument is the one presented in Choice **D**: he would say that with all that traffic leaving town, and little on the other side, it was actually safer for him to walk with the traffic rather than against it.

C.   *Res ipsa loquitur*

Another way of proving breach is through the doctrine of *res ipsa loquitur*, which is a Latin expression meaning that "the thing speaks for itself." William Prosser, one of the great Torts scholars of the last century, is famous for saying of the doctrine: "*Loquitur, vere; sed quid in inferno vult dicere,*"[14] which roughly means, "the thing speaks for itself, but what the hell did it say?"

The doctrine can be confusing, but the easiest way to understand it is to begin with one of the classical cases establishing the doctrine. In *Byrne v. Boadle*, 159 Eng. Rep. 299, 300 (1863), defendant was a dealer in flour. Plaintiff was passing along a highway in front of defendant's premises when he was struck and badly hurt by a barrel of flour that was apparently being lowered from defendant's window. Plaintiff sued the defendant for negligence. At trial, several witnesses testified that they saw the barrel fall and hit plaintiff. Plaintiff did not explain how the barrel fell. (Perhaps one of defendant's workers was careless in handling the barrel being delivered to a customer, but plaintiff put on no proof to that effect.) The jury found for the plaintiff, but the defendant argued that the plaintiff put on no evidence of *how* the defendant (or his employees)[15] might have been negligent; the trial court agreed and granted a "nonsuit," reversing the jury's decision and finding for the defendant.

An English appellate court, the Court of Exchequer, reversed, restoring the jury verdict. It was true that plaintiff could not prove negligence in the ordinary way: Because plaintiff did not say how the accident happened and what precaution could have prevented it, he could not argue that it was *common sense* to take a particular precaution, or under a *balancing test* such a precaution was cost-justified, or even that there was a *custom* among wholesalers to take certain precautions when handling dangerous barrels. Nonetheless, Chief Baron Jonathan Frederick Pollock, writing for the Court

---

14. William L. Prosser, *Res Ipsa Loquitur in California*, 37 Cal. L. Rev. 183, 232 n.274 (1949).
15. As we will see in Chapter 17, employers are normally strictly liable for the torts of their employees under the doctrine of *respondeat superior*. For now, treat the employer and his employees as a single entity.

of Exchequer, stated that "[t]here are certain cases of which it may be said res ipsa loquitur, and this seems one of them." The very fact that the barrel fell out of the window provided circumstantial evidence of negligence: The thing speaks for itself.

Though that intuition that there must have been some negligence in *Byrne v. Boadle* seems to make perfect sense, articulating why it is so turns out to be difficult. The way I like to think of it is as follows. Imagine the universe of cases in which people walking down the street minding their own business get hit in the head by heavy barrels falling out of windows. Ask yourself the various scenarios in which such an incident could occur. If it seems that most of the time such a scenario occurs because of the business owner's negligence rather for some other reason, then *res ispsa* should apply. It is hard to think of scenarios in which the falling barrel could occur without the negligence of defendant (or his employees). The doctrine of *res ipsa loquitur* therefore should apply.

Contrast the barrel scenario with a different one. A driver hits a child who is in the street. It is certainly possible that the accident was caused by the driver's negligence. But it is also possible that the accident was caused instead by the negligence of the child, or perhaps through no one's negligence. Unlike the barrel falling out of the window — which itself "says" negligence — an automobile accident doesn't necessarily say that the defendant was negligent, and therefore *res ipsa* does not apply.

Over the years, courts and commentators have proposed various statements of the doctrine. "A number of courts adopt a two-step inquiry: step one asks whether the accident is of a type that usually happens because of negligence, while step two asks whether the 'instrumentality' inflicting the harm was under the 'exclusive control' of the defendant." *See* Rest. (3D) Torts: Liability for Physical Harm § 17, cmt. *b* (P.F.D. 2005). The Restatement more straightforwardly provides this test:

The factfinder may infer that the defendant has been negligent when the accident causing the plaintiff's physical harm is a type of accident that ordinarily happens as a result of the negligence of a class of actors of which the defendant is a relevant member.[16]

Both of these tests assume a basically passive plaintiff: That is, under the facts it is hard to imagine that the plaintiff has done anything negligent to contribute to the injury. (Think of the plaintiff in *Byrne v. Boadle*, who was unlucky enough to be walking in the wrong place at the wrong time.)

---

16. The Restatement criticizes the older test as indeterminate, and argues that "exclusive control" is not an "effective proxy" for the underlying question of which party was probably negligent. It gives the example of a consumer who buys a new car whose brakes fail the next day. The consumer had "exclusive control" of the car at the time of the accident, but arguably res ipsa should apply against the car manufacturer. *Id.*, cmt. b.

QUESTION 9. **Escalating Negligence.**   Jackie is at the Pacifica
International Airport riding up on an escalator to reach the gates. Jackie is
holding on to the handrail when the escalator malfunctions. The handrail
keeps moving, but the stairs stop moving, causing Jackie to lose her balance
and fall, breaking her leg. Jackie sues the airport for negligence, but
presents no proof of why the handrail malfunctioned. The airport
performed all of its own maintenance. The airport argues that the
negligence case cannot go to the jury, because Jackie presented no proof of
breach. How should the court rule on the airport's argument?

A. The court should accept the argument because a plaintiff must show
   how a defendant failed to use ordinary care to avoid a reasonably
   foreseeable risk to the plaintiff.
B. The court should accept the argument because Jackie fell and no one
   pushed her.
C. The court should reject the argument if the jury could believe that this
   kind of escalator malfunction ordinarily does not occur in the absence of
   the negligence of the person in charge of keeping escalators in good
   repair.
D. The court should reject the argument because it is the defendant, not
   the plaintiff, that bears the burden of proof in negligence cases.

ANALYSIS.   This is a difficult question, based upon the facts in the case of
Colmenares Vivas v. Sun Alliance Insurance Co., 807 F.2d 1102 (3d Cir. 1986).
Under the facts of the question, Jackie has presented no evidence as to how
the accident happened or as to what precaution the airport could have taken
to prevent this accident from occurring. So if Jackie is going to succeed in
proving breach, it is going to have to be through *res ipsa loquitur.* The
operative question is whether incidents in which handrails of escalators stop
moving while the stairs keep moving is ordinarily because of the negligence
of the escalator's owner or for some other reason. (Jackie was a passive
plaintiff here, so it doesn't look like she could have done anything to cause
the accident.) This question is a difficult one, one which divided the judges
in the *Colmenares Vivas* case. With this background, let's consider each of
the four choices.

Choice **A** is incorrect because it says that a plaintiff must always show
how an accident happened and what precaution could be taken to have
avoided injury to the plaintiff. The doctrine of *res ipsa* shows that this is an
incorrect statement of the law.

Choice **B** is the easiest one to eliminate. That fact that no one pushed
Jackie says nothing about whether it might be possible to prove negligence
through *res ipsa* or otherwise.

Choice **C** is correct in stating that the court should let the issue go to a jury *if* the jury might determine that these kinds of incidents are the kind that ordinarily do not occur in the absence of negligence.

Choice **D** is incorrect. It is the plaintiff, not the defendant, who bears the burden of proof in negligence cases.

Inference of Negligence: Permissive Inferences and Rebuttable Presumptions. Note the beginning of the Third Restatement's *res ipsa* rule: The factfinder "may infer" negligence upon proof of certain facts. This language means that a jury *may* but *need not* accept the inference of negligence upon proof of the elements of *res ipsa*. We call this a "permissive inference." Considering the facts of the last question, a jury can, *but need not*, find the airport had breached its duty to Jackie if it believes that incidents in which the handrails on escalators stop while the stairs keep moving ordinarily do not occur in the absence of negligence.

In a minority of jurisdictions, proof of the *res ipsa* elements creates a *rebuttable presumption*: If a jury believes that incidents in which handrails on escalators stop while the stairs keep moving ordinarily do not occur in the absence of negligence, and the airport puts on no evidence to rebut the inference that it was negligent (such as proof it used reasonable care in maintaining the escalator), then the jury *must* find that the airport breached.

QUESTION 10. Roll Out the Barrel. David is walking down the street minding his own business when he is hit in the head with a barrel falling out of Tiffany's warehouse. David sues Tiffany for negligence. He puts on no evidence showing how the incident occurred or what precaution Tiffany could have taken to prevent it. Tiffany puts on no evidence in her own case, arguing instead that the jury should not infer negligence. In a jurisdiction applying the rebuttable presumption rule in *res ipsa loquitur* cases:

A. The jury may infer negligence if it believes these kinds of incidents ordinarily do not occur in the absence of the negligence of a person like Tiffany.

B. The jury must infer negligence if it believes these kinds of incidents ordinarily do not occur in the absence of the negligence of a person like Tiffany.

C. The jury cannot infer negligence absent direct proof of how the barrel came to fall out the window.

D. The jury cannot infer negligence because David did not present any evidence of balancing, custom, or common sense.

ANALYSIS. This question tests your knowledge of the meaning of the rebuttable presumption rule (a minority rule for application of *res ipsa*).

Under this rule, if a plaintiff presents facts meeting the inference of *res ipsa*, the jury *must* infer that the defendant was negligent unless the defendant presents evidence rebutting the inference. In this case, the plaintiff put on evidence that raises an inference of negligence under *res ipsa* (the facts are based upon the classic *Byrne v. Boadle* case, the poster child for *res ipsa*). The defendant put on no evidence in rebuttal. Thus, in a rebuttable presumption jurisdiction the jury *must* find negligence on the defendant's part. (In contrast, in the majority permissive inference jurisdictions the jury need not find negligence even if the defendant puts on no rebuttal.) Choice **A** is wrong because it states the "may infer" standard applicable in permissive inference jurisdictions. Choice **B** is correct because it correctly states the "must infer" standard applicable in rebuttable presumption jurisdictions. Choice **C** is incorrect because it states an incorrect rule of law: *Res ipsa* allows an inference of negligence based upon circumstantial, rather than direct, proof of negligence. Choice **D** is incorrect because it too ignores *res ipsa* as a way of proving breach besides the other methods discussed in the last two chapters.

D.   The Closer: Choosing a way to prove breach

We have now seen five ways of proving breach:

- Common sense
- Balancing
- Custom
- *Negligence per se*
- *Res ipsa loquitur*

Obviously, not all five of these methods will work in all cases. We have already seen that common sense only works in a small class of cases where it is obvious that a defendant's conduct falls below what constitutes reasonable care. Custom works only in cases where there is some evidence of an industry custom. *Negligence per se* is a potential means of proving breach only if there is a relevant statute, and *res ipsa loquitur*, like common sense, applies only in a small subset of cases in which the type of harm that occurred is one that ordinarily does not occur absent the negligence of a class in which the defendant is a member.

In other circumstances, there may be more than one way to prove breach. In a case such as that of the tug owner without the working radio, arguments under common sense, balancing, and custom may be combined. In the case involving the child who brings the gun to the classroom and drops it on a classmate's foot, *negligence per se* ultimately may fail, but that doesn't prevent the classmate from trying to prove negligence using balancing. *Res ipsa loquitur* is most useful in cases in which the plaintiff, through civil discovery, cannot learn how an incident causing her injury occurred. But even if she has such information, *res ipsa* might be a cheaper and easier way of proving breach than trying to rely on balancing.

So in the real world (and in Torts classes focused on the real world), it is important for lawyers (and law students) to consider which ways of proving breach make the most sense given the particular facts and circumstances.

QUESTION 11. Distracted Driver.   Orit is driving down the street. With one hand, she is adjusting the radio. With another hand she is holding her cell phone. She crashes into Peter's car. A state statute provides that a driver shall keep at least one of his or her hands on the wheel at all times while operating a motor vehicle. Peter sues Orit for negligence.

Which means of proving breach is likely going to be the least effective?

A. Custom
B. *Negligence* per se
C. Balancing
D. Common sense

ANALYSIS.   Peter has a number of ways of trying to prove breach here. It looks like Orit has violated a state statute by taking both hands off the steering wheel. Other drivers are likely in the class of people that the statute was designed to protect for injuries such as driving collisions. Failure to keep her hands on the wheel may have caused Peter's injuries. For this reason, *negligence per se* looks like a good claim (making Choice **B** wrong). There is also a strong argument under balancing, when one considers the costs of keeping one hand on the wheel while driving compared to the probability of harm multiplied by the severity of harm of not doing so (making Choice **C** incorrect). There's even a common sense argument, too: Everyone knows it is not safe to drive with no hands on the wheel while fiddling with the radio and cell phone (making Choice **D** incorrect). This leaves Choice **A**, custom, the correct answer. There is no industry here, and therefore no industry custom. Custom will not play a role in Peter's case of negligence against Orit.

 Rick's picks

1. Lend a (Customary) Hand   C
2. Sword or Shield?   D

3. Lend a (Medical) Hand	A
4. Lend a (Medical) Hand, Take II	D
5. Lend a (Medical) Hand, Take III	C
6. Lend a (Medical) Hand, Take IV	A
7. Lead Foot	C
8. Take the High Road	D
9. Escalating Negligence	C
10. Roll Out the Barrel	B
11. Distracted Driver	A

10

Affirmative Defenses to Negligence: Contributory Negligence, Comparative Negligence, and Assumption of Risk

CHAPTER OVERVIEW
A. Comparative negligence
    1. The old rule of contributory negligence and its exceptions
    2. The new rule: Comparative negligence
B. Assumption of risk (consent) as an affirmative defense
C. The Closer: The difficulty of comparative responsibility as a weighing of plaintiff's negligence and consent
◈ Rick's picks

A.   Comparative negligence

1. The old rule of contributory negligence and its exceptions

I n the last two chapters we saw how much of the tortious conduct portion of the prima facie case for negligence works. First, we assumed that in most instances a defendant owes a *duty* to plaintiff to avoid creating reasonably foreseeable risks that could injure the defendant. (In the next two chapters, we will explore the concept of duty in greater detail, noting the exceptions and complications to our initial statement of the duty rule.) Second, we discussed the many issues that arise when plaintiff tries to prove *breach*, which we defined generally as follows:

*A defendant **breaches** a duty to a plaintiff when, judged from the perspective of a reasonably prudent person in the defendant's position, the defendant failed to use reasonable care to avoid a reasonably foreseeable risk to the plaintiff.*

If a plaintiff proves both duty and breach by a preponderance of the evidence, the plaintiff has satisfied the tortious conduct portion of the prima facie case for negligence. Then, if the plaintiff also proves actual causation, proximate cause, and damages, plaintiff has made out the prima facie case for the tort of negligence. In this chapter, we discuss *affirmative defenses* that a defendant may raise after a plaintiff has made the prima facie case for negligence.

You will recall that we discussed some of the affirmative defenses applicable to some of the intentional torts, such as self-defense, necessity, and recapture of chattels. These affirmative defenses do *not* apply to the tort of negligence.

The two important affirmative defenses we consider in this chapter are *comparative negligence* and *assumption of risk.* But to understand the status of these affirmative defenses today, we need to go back to the historical treatment of affirmative defenses in a negligence case, beginning with *contributory negligence.*

As the tort of negligence emerged as its own tort (see Chapter 8), courts took the view that a plaintiff's own negligence, referred to as a plaintiff's contributory negligence, generally barred plaintiff's recovery of any damages. *See Butterfield v. Forrester*, 103 Eng. Rep. 926 (K.B. 1809). So, if Arlene is driving carelessly down the street and hits Becky, a pedestrian who crosses the street without looking, Becky would recover nothing. In other words, if *both* a defendant and a plaintiff were negligent and contributed in causing plaintiff's injury, plaintiff would recover nothing because plaintiff's contributory negligence would serve as a *complete defense* to negligence.

A defendant would bear the burden of proving plaintiff's negligence, and the defendant would do so in ways that mirror breach: through common sense, balancing, custom, or *negligence per se* (violation of a statute).[1] For example, Arlene could try to prove Becky's negligence in crossing the street without looking through a common sense argument to the jury, through a balancing argument about the costs and benefits of taking more care before crossing the street, or through Becky's violation of a statute that requires pedestrians to look both ways before they cross the street.

---

1. Given the nature of *res ipsa loquitur*, discussed in the last chapter, it would not make sense for a defendant to prove plaintiff's contributory negligence through *res ipsa loquitur*.

This point is worth emphasizing: *When a defendant tries to prove plaintiff's negligence as an affirmative defense, it proves plaintiff's negligence in a way that is equivalent to the way a plaintiff tries to prove that the defendant breached.*

QUESTION 1. Take the High Road, Take II. A state statute provides that on roads without sidewalks, a person should walk on left side of the road (opposite traffic). Maurice is walking down the road in Summerland, a vacation resort. It is Sunday evening, and there is a great deal of traffic leaving town as vacationers are returning back to the city. There is very little traffic on the right side of the road going into Summerland. Maurice decides to walk on the right side of the road, with traffic, because there is much less traffic on that side of the road. Nina is driving on that side of the road into Summerland. Because she is busy talking on her cell phone and not paying attention to the road, she does not see Maurice until she nearly hits him. She hits Maurice, and he sustains severe personal injuries. Maurice sues Nina for negligence, and Nina raises Maurice's own negligence as an affirmative defense. If Nina successfully proves Maurice's negligence using *negligence per se in a jurisdiction using the traditional contributory negligence rules*:

A. Maurice will recover nothing because of his negligence.
B. Maurice will recover nothing because he was more negligent than Nina.
C. Maurice will recover nothing if he was more negligent than Nina.
D. Maurice and Nina will split Maurice's damages.

ANALYSIS. This is a variation on a question appearing in the last chapter. There, it was *the defendant* that was negligent under *negligence per se*; here it is *the plaintiff.* Under the traditional rules of contributory negligence, a plaintiff's negligence generally barred plaintiff's recovery entirely. It does not matter if the plaintiff is *more negligent* than Nina (so Choices **B** and **C** are incorrect). A finding of contributory negligence *completely barred plaintiff's recovery*, making Choice **D** incorrect. Choice **A** correctly states the old law.

Last Clear Chance and Other Doctrines. The contributory negligence affirmative defense operated harshly: It completely barred recovery for plaintiffs *even when* a defendant was negligent and that negligence was a cause of plaintiff's injury. The defendant's behavior was still wrongful, but the defendant would get off scot-free. (Contrast this with affirmative defenses in intentional torts: A defendant who hits a plaintiff in self-defense arguably did not act wrongfully. And in cases of borderline wrongful conduct, such as stealing someone's food while starving, the law used the necessity defense to require some compensation to the plaintiff.)

For this reason, courts developed certain ameliorative doctrines to deal with the harshness of the rule. For example, under the "last clear chance" doctrine, if both a defendant and plaintiff were negligent, a plaintiff could still recover damages if the jury found that the defendant had the last clear chance to avoid the accident. In one of the more famous applications of this doctrine, an elderly person riding his one-horse wagon fell asleep with his wagon stuck on the railroad tracks. The conductor of the train failed to slow down, assuming the wagon would get out of the way. Unfortunately the train hit the wagon, killing the elderly person. Though both parties were negligent, the court held that the family of the deceased could recover damages for his death because the train conductor had the last clear chance to avoid the accident. *Fuller v. Illinois Central R.R.*, 56 So. 783 (Miss. 1911).

Note that under last clear chance as well, the choice for the jury was all or nothing: Even though defendant and plaintiff were both negligent, the jury either let the plaintiff recover *all* of the damages he suffered or *none* of them.

Courts developed other doctrines as well, sometimes taking into account whether the defendant's conduct was so bad as to amount to "gross negligence." In other words, under the traditional approach, if a defendant's conduct was *much worse* than the plaintiff's the jury sometimes had an option to award plaintiff all of her damages, even upon a finding that the plaintiff was negligent if the defendant's conduct was much worse than the plaintiff's conduct.

QUESTION 2. Take the High Road, Take III. A state statute provides that on roads without sidewalks, a person should walk on the left side of the road (opposite traffic). Maurice is walking down the road in Summerland, a vacation resort. It is Sunday evening, and there is a great deal of traffic leaving town as vacationers are returning back to the city. There is very little traffic on the right side of the road going into Summerland. Maurice decides to walk on the right side of the road, with traffic, because there is much less traffic on that side of the road. He stops to rest, and falls asleep on the side of the road. Nina is driving on that side of the road into Summerland. Because she is busy talking on her cell phone and not paying attention to the road, she does not see Maurice until she nearly hits him. She hits Maurice, and he sustains severe personal injuries. Maurice sues Nina for negligence, and Nina raises Maurice's own negligence as an affirmative defense. If Nina successfully proves Maurice's negligence using *negligence per se in a jurisdiction using the traditional contributory negligence rules*:

A. Maurice will recover nothing because of his negligence.
B. Maurice will recover nothing because of his negligence, unless the jury determines Nina had the last clear chance to avoid the accident.
C. Maurice will recover nothing if he was more negligent than Nina.
D. Maurice and Nina will split Maurice's damages.

ANALYSIS. This is a variation on Question 1. The only difference in facts is that Maurice had fallen asleep on the side of the road a la *Fuller*, making the "last clear chance" argument plausible. Under that doctrine, if both plaintiff and defendant are negligent, the plaintiff recovers all of his damages if the jury finds the defendant had the last clear chance to avoid the accident. Choice **B** accurately conveys this idea, and is more complete than Choice **A**. Choice **C** is incorrect because it is not a comparison as to who was *more* negligent: It is a question whether, assuming both plaintiff and defendant were negligent, who had the last clear chance to avoid the accident. Choice **D** is wrong because traditionally there was no splitting of liability between plaintiffs and defendants in cases of contributory negligence.

2. The new rule: Comparative negligence

In the past 40 years, most, though not all, American jurisdictions have shifted from the all-or-nothing rule of contributory negligence to a rule of *comparative negligence* (sometimes called "comparative responsibility" for reasons that will become clear in Section C of this chapter).[2] Under a rule of comparative negligence, when both a defendant and a plaintiff are negligent, there is sometimes a sharing of liability between the plaintiff and the defendant. Jurisdictions split into two camps:

- In *pure* comparative negligence jurisdictions, plaintiffs and defendants split plaintiff's damages based upon shares of fault or responsibility, whether or not the jury finds the defendant to be more or less at fault than the plaintiff.
- In *impure* comparative negligence jurisdictions, plaintiffs and defendants split plaintiff's damages based upon shares of fault or responsibility, but only *if* the jury finds the defendant to be *more at fault* than the plaintiff: If the plaintiff is found to be equally or more at fault, the plaintiff recovers nothing.

The benefit of a comparative negligence rule compared to a contributory negligence rule is that it eliminates (or, in impure comparative negligence jurisdictions, it *mostly* eliminates) the all-or-nothing nature of liability in a situation where the defendant is a wrongdoer. The sharing of responsibility gives the jury a chance to allocate percentages of fault or responsibility (adding up to 100 percent) to allocate liability between a defendant and a plaintiff.[3]

---

2. As of 2007, the states still using contributory negligence as a complete defense are Alabama, Maryland, North Carolina, and Virginia. The old rule applies in Washington, D.C. as well. *See* VICTOR E. SCHWARTZ, COMPARATIVE NEGLIGENCE 513-518 (2002 & 2007 SUPP.).

3. There may be multiple defendants, and liability may be allocated among defendants and plaintiff together. Some courts compare the plaintiff's share of responsibility against the shares of responsibility of all the defendants together. Other courts compare the plaintiff's share against each individual defendant. Chapter 22 on joint and several liability considers more issues related to multiple tortfeasors.

Because of the nature of the sharing, as jurisdictions moved from contributory negligence to comparative negligence they eliminated a separate role for ameliorative doctrines such as the last clear chance doctrine. If the defendant had the last clear chance to avoid an accident, that fact is *relevant* to how a jury may allocate shares of fault or responsibility, but it does not function to put all the liability on one party or another

---

QUESTION 3. Take the High Road, Take IV.   A state statute provides that on roads without sidewalks, a person should walk on the left side of the road (opposite traffic). Maurice is walking down the road in Summerland, a vacation resort. It is Sunday evening, and there is a great deal of traffic leaving town as vacationers are returning back to the city. There is very little traffic on the right side of the road going into Summerland. Maurice decides to walk on the right side of the road, with traffic, because there is much less traffic on that side of the road. He stops to rest, and falls asleep on the side of the road. Nina is driving on that side of the road into Summerland. Because she is busy talking on her cell phone and not paying attention to the road, she does not see Maurice until she nearly hits him. She hits Maurice, and he sustains severe personal injuries. Maurice sues Nina for negligence, and Nina raises Maurice's own negligence as an affirmative defense. If Nina successfully proves Maurice's negligence using negligence per se *in a jurisdiction using pure comparative negligence rules*:

A. Maurice will recover nothing because of his negligence.
B. Maurice will recover nothing because of his negligence, unless the jury determines Nina had the last clear chance to avoid the accident.
C. Maurice will recover nothing if he was more negligent than Nina.
D. Maurice and Nina will split Maurice's damages.

ANALYSIS.   This is a variation on Question 2. The fact pattern is exactly the same; the only difference is the legal rule. The question shifts from a contributory negligence jurisdiction to a jurisdiction using the rules of pure comparative negligence. In a *pure* comparative negligence system, when both a defendant and a plaintiff are negligent, the jury apportions shares of responsibility or fault between the parties, even if the plaintiff is more at fault than the defendant and even if the defendant had the last clear chance to avoid

---

One other important issue that will have to wait until Chapter 13 on actual causation: Both defendant's negligence and a plaintiff's comparative negligence must be *causally related* to the plaintiff's injury. Thus, a plaintiff who is drunk and stopped properly at a stop sign when rear-ended by a negligently driving defendant can recover the full amount of damages, not reduced for plaintiff's fault in driving drunk, because the plaintiff's negligence was not *causally related* to the plaintiff's injury.

the accident. (In contrast, in an *impure* system, the plaintiff would recover nothing if the jury concluded the plaintiff was equally or more at fault than the defendant.) Choice **A** is incorrect because in a pure comparative negligence system, a plaintiff's negligence does not bar recovery of damages; instead there is a sharing based upon shares of fault or responsibility. Choice **B** is incorrect because in a comparative negligence system, last clear chance is only one factor in the allocation of fault or responsibility and not a total ameliorative doctrine. Choice **C** is incorrect because this is a *pure* comparative negligence system. It would have been the correct answer if this were an *impure* comparative negligence system. Choice **D** is the correct answer. Maurice and Nina will share liability based upon the jury's allocation of fault.

QUESTION 4. Impure Intentions. Mitch and Fred are involved in an automobile accident in which Fred is injured. Fred sues for negligence in a jurisdiction using the impure comparative negligence rules. The jury determines that Fred suffered $100,000 in damages, and that he was 55 percent at fault, compared to 45 percent at fault for Mitch.

How much may Fred recover from Mitch?

A. 0
B. $45,000
C. $55,000
D. $100,000

ANALYSIS. Under a comparative negligence system, a plaintiff's damages are reduced in proportion to his share of fault. In an impure comparative negligence system, however, if a jury finds that the plaintiff is equally or more at fault than the defendant, the plaintiff may not recover anything. In this case, the jury found that Fred, the plaintiff, was more at fault (55 percent) than the defendant, Mitch (45 percent). For this reason, Fred recovers nothing and Choice **A** is correct. Choice **B** would be correct in a *pure* comparative negligence jurisdiction: Fred would be able to recover his $100,000 less an allocation of $55,000 (55 percent of $100,000) representing his share of responsibility, or $45,000 total. Choice **C** is incorrect under any comparative negligence system. Choice **D** is incorrect because in a comparative negligence system, when both the plaintiff and the defendant are found to be partially responsible, a plaintiff may not recover the full amount of her damages; instead the total amount is reduced to account for plaintiff's share of responsibility (or, in an impure jurisdiction, is reduced to a recovery of 0 in those cases in which the plaintiff is more at fault than the defendant).

B.   Assumption of risk (consent) as an affirmative defense

We turn now to one of the most difficult issues in the first-year Torts course: the role of assumption of risk. Part of the problem here is one of terminology. The term "assumption of risk" refers to three different concepts that are somewhat interrelated:

1. *Express Assumption of Risk.* In certain circumstances in which one person might negligently injure another, the parties may enter into an agreement to contract around tort liability. (The provisions in these contracts are sometimes referred to as *exculpatory clauses.*) Thus, if I sign a release before I go skydiving, I cannot sue the skydiving company for injuries caused by the company's negligence if the release is enforceable. Whether or not the release is enforceable is primarily a question of *contract law,* not tort law. The issue turns upon questions of public policy. Courts have generally held that in contracts for basic life necessities (food, shelter, medical care), such clauses are unenforceable as a violation of public policy. *See Tunkl v. Regents of University of California,* 383 P.2d 441 (Cal. 1963). But the skydiving contract is likely to be enforceable.

2. *Primary Implied Assumption of Risk.* Under this doctrine, which we consider more fully in the next chapter, courts for policy reasons sometimes say that a person injured in certain amateur sports and recreation activities may not recover any damages for negligently inflicted injuries occurring during the sport or recreational activity.[4] Doctrinally, courts applying this doctrine say that the defendant had *no duty* to use reasonable care to avoid reasonably foreseeable risks in the sports and recreation context. There is much more to say about this, but it will await the next chapter.

3. *Secondary Implied Assumption of Risk.* Under this doctrine, a plaintiff's decision to voluntarily and knowingly encounter a risk — equivalent to what we termed "consent" in the first part of this book considering affirmative defenses to intentional torts — acts as an *affirmative defense* in a negligence case. This chapter considers how that affirmative defense works in the era of comparative negligence.

Obviously, some fact patterns involving sports and recreation activities could fall under either implied assumption of risk doctrine. Consider one person carelessly injuring another during a game of basketball at the local park. A court could say (under the primary implied assumption of risk

---

4. If the parties signed a contract before engaging in the sporting activity, then questions of express assumption of risk can come into play as well.

doctrine) that the injurer had *no duty* to the other player. Alternatively, a court could say (under the secondary implied assumption of risk doctrine) that the other player "assumed the risk" of injury, raising an *affirmative defense* equivalent to consent. Historically, the choice between these two means of dealing with plaintiffs in sports cases did not matter: Either way, a plaintiff's case was completely barred. Under the first path, plaintiff's claim fails because she cannot make out one of the elements of her prima facie case, duty. Under the second path, plaintiff's claim fails because the defendant may successfully raise an affirmative defense.

But things have gotten more complicated in recent years.

QUESTION 5. Dumb Chicken. Gary, a teenager, is out playing near the railroad tracks with his friends. On a dare, he agrees to stand on the railroad tracks as a train approaches. He decides to stand there until the train stops. Unfortunately, the train conductor, who is not paying attention to the tracks, does not see Gary on the tracks, and the train runs him over, causing Gary to suffer serious personal injuries. Gary sues the train conductor for negligence. What is the strongest argument the conductor may raise against Gary?

A. Express assumption of the risk.
B. Primary implied assumption of the risk.
C. Secondary implied assumption of the risk.
D. Consent.

ANALYSIS. This question is meant simply to get you familiar with the terminology used in these cases. The conductor would not raise express assumption of the risk in this case, because there was no contract between the train conductor (or railroad) and Gary. Without a contract (which could in some circumstances be an express oral agreement), express assumption of risk fails as an affirmative defense. For this reason, Choice **A** fails. Primary implied assumption of risk does not apply because this is not a sports case. For this reason, Choice **B** fails. The strongest argument is Choice **C**, secondary implied assumption of the risk. Arguably Gary has voluntarily and knowingly encountered the risk, a viable affirmative defense. (It is also possible that this would count as a kind of comparative negligence, an issue we consider below.) Choice **D** is incorrect because we do not use the terminology of "consent" in negligence cases, though the concept of consent is similar to that covered by the terminology of secondary implied assumption of the risk.

The Meaning of Secondary Implied Assumption of Risk. As I have noted, the terminology surrounding assumption of risk is pretty confusing. But if you think of secondary implied assumption of risk as equivalent to consent, then the issues that arise become much clearer. The operative question for secondary implied assumption of risk is whether the plaintiff has voluntarily and knowingly encountered a risk. If the encountering of the risk is not voluntary and knowing (for example, a plaintiff falls down a manhole that the city left uncovered and that the plaintiff did not notice), then this affirmative defense is not available.

Of course, this kind of question often presents a factual dispute and a judgment call for the jury. Did the plaintiff really not know what she was getting into? Did the plaintiff have free choice in deciding to encounter the risk? Juries may resolve these issues in different ways.

QUESTION 6. No Good Deed Goes Unpunished.   Jules is walking near the railroad tracks when he sees a dog whose paw is caught in the tracks. Jules works to free the dog from the tracks as a train approaches. Jules does not see or hear the train coming. Unfortunately, the train conductor, who is not paying attention to the tracks, does not see Jules on the tracks, and the train runs him over, causing Jules to suffer serious personal injuries. Jules sues the train conductor for negligence.

What is Jules's strongest argument against the conductor's affirmative defense of secondary implied assumption of the risk?

A. Jules used reasonable care in trying to free the dog.
B. Jules did not know that a train was likely to approach.
C. Jules had no agreement with the conductor (or railroad) exculpating them for their negligence.
D. The railroad had the last clear chance to avoid the accident.

ANALYSIS.   In order to raise secondary implied assumption of risk as an affirmative defense, the conductor will have to prove that Jules voluntarily and knowingly encountered the risk. Relevant to that question of "knowingly" encountering the risk would be the fact that Jules did not know a train was likely to approach. Choice **B** sets forth this correct answer. Choice **A** is incorrect because whether or not Jules acted with reasonable care is a separate question from that of whether or not he voluntarily and knowingly encountered the risk. Choice **C** is wrong because whether or not there was a contract with an exculpatory clause is relevant to the issue of *express* assumption of risk, not secondary implied assumption of risk. Choice **D** is wrong because the "last clear chance" doctrine is relevant to the question of comparative negligence (and used to be very important as an ameliorative doctrine under the old contributory negligence rules). It is not relevant to the secondary implied assumption of risk question.

Implied Assumption of Risk in the Comparative Negligence Era. As jurisdictions moved from the "all or nothing" approach of contributory negligence to the "sharing" approach of comparative negligence based upon relative fault or responsibility, courts had to grapple with the question whether secondary implied assumption of risk still should be treated as a complete defense (thereby negating plaintiff's entire case) or subject to the same kind of sharing.

Most states have abolished secondary implied assumption of risk as a complete defense, holding instead that the facts related to assumption of risk would be folded into the comparative negligence case. *See, e.g., Knight v. Jewett,* 834 P.2d 696 (Cal. 1992). *See also* 1 COMPARATIVE NEGLIGENCE MANUAL §1:23 (3d ed. 1995) ("Depending on the jurisdiction, this may then act as a complete defense to the plaintiff's action in tort, but *more often than not* will result in apportioning liability under comparative negligence rules.") (Emphasis added). *See also id.*, Appendix III (table summarizing the current status of comparative negligence in each state); REST. (3D) TORTS: APPORTIONMENT OF LIABILITY § 3 (abolishing all "ameliorative doctrine" for defining plaintiff's negligence, including assumption of the risk); *but see Ex Parte Barran,* 730 So.2d 203, 206 (Ala. 1998) (continuing to recognize assumption of risk as a complete defense to a negligence case). Some states have gone even further, abolishing *primary* implied assumption of risk as well. *See, e.g., Perez v. McConkey,* 872 S.W.2d 897, 905 (Tenn. 1994).

What do I mean that the issue of secondary assumption of risk is "folded into the comparative negligence case"? I mean that in a case in which a defendant has been negligent and a plaintiff has been negligent and/or has voluntarily and knowingly encountered the risk from the defendant's conduct, the jury will be asked to apportion liability between the plaintiff and the defendant based upon each party's share of responsibility. Because both negligence and consent issues are now involved in the apportionment of liability, many courts refer to the apportionment as one of "comparative responsibility" rather than "comparative fault."

Here is how the Restatement (Third) of Torts: Apportionment of Liability § 8 says that the losses should be apportioned:

> Factors for assigning percentages of responsibility to each person whose legal responsibility has been established include
> (a) the nature of the person's risk-creating conduct, including any awareness or indifference with respect to the risks created by the conduct and any intent with respect to the harm by the conduct; and
> (b) the strength of the causal connection between the person's risk-creating conduct and the harm.

Note that the Restatement approach says to look at fault, consent, and causation. The jury gets to look at each of these factors and come up with some allocation of responsibility (for example, 60 percent for the defendant and 40 percent for the plaintiff) adding up to 100 percent of the responsibility.

QUESTION 7. Dumb Chicken, Take II. Gary, a teenager, is out playing near the railroad tracks with his friends. On a dare, he agrees to stand on the railroad tracks as a train approaches. He decides to stand there until the train stops. Unfortunately, the train conductor, who is not paying attention to the tracks, does not see Gary on the tracks, and the train runs him over, causing Gary to suffer serious personal injuries. Gary sues the train conductor for negligence. Under the modern rules of comparative responsibility, in determining how much the conductor should have to pay for Gary's injuries compared to how much Gary should pay:

A. The jurors should compare the conductor's negligence with Gary's negligence.

B. The jurors should compare the conductor's negligence with Gary's negligence and his awareness and appreciation of the risks.

C. The jurors should assign all the loss to Gary, because he was negligent.

D. The jurors must split liability equally between the conductor and Gary.

ANALYSIS.   Under the modern rules, the jurors will be comparing the defendant's negligence in conducting the train with the plaintiff's negligence and consent (secondary implied assumption of risk) in playing the game of chicken with the train. Choice **A** is incorrect because it is incomplete: It is not just Gary's negligence we look at, but also his consent. Choice **C** is incorrect because it reflects the old contributory negligence rules making contributory negligence or secondary implied assumption of risk a *complete defense* in a negligence action. Choice **D** is incorrect because the jury is to assign percentages of responsibility taking into account considerations of fault, responsibility, and cause. Though jurors *could* decide to split liability 50/50, it is not *required* that jurors do so. Choice **B** states the correct answer, requiring the jurors to compare the conductor's fault with Gary's negligence and consent.

C. The Closer: The difficulty of comparative responsibility as a weighing of plaintiff's negligence and consent

The last section explained that in a case in which a defendant has been negligent and a plaintiff has been negligent and/or has voluntarily and knowingly encountered the risk from the defendant's conduct, the jury will be asked to apportion liability between the plaintiff and the defendant based upon each party's share of responsibility. These shares of responsibility are assigned by the jury as percentages to add up to a total liability of 100 percent.

How is the jury going to do so? It is not self-evident how the comparison is to be made. Consider first how a jury might make an allocation of responsibility when the question involves only one of comparing *fault*: A driver drives drunk down the street who hits pedestrian, who crosses without looking as the "Don't Walk" light flashes. We can see that jurors are likely to award a higher percentage of responsibility to the defendant rather than the plaintiff because defendant's conduct is further from the behavior of reasonable people than the behavior of the plaintiff.

But the comparison becomes more difficult when the comparison must fold in the issue of secondary implied assumption of risk. Suppose that pedestrian crosses the street *knowing* the light is flashing "Don't Walk." Or suppose that the light is red and cars are coming, but the pedestrian believes she can get across before any cars come. The jury is going to have to compare not only each party's *fault*, but also its consent.

Now, you might argue, that's not too hard, because the pedestrian's conduct in crossing at the flashing or red light is not only knowing and voluntary: It is also unreasonable. In other words, some people say that secondary implied assumption of risk is actually a *type* of plaintiff's negligence and therefore there is no problem making the comparison.

I think that argument assumes away the problem. To see why, imagine that the pedestrian crosses the street at the red light, but she does so, though seeing traffic coming, because she sees a toddler somehow separated from his parents about to walk into the street. The behavior in crossing the red light under those circumstances is probably reasonable, meaning that pedestrian was not *at fault* in crossing the street. Still, the pedestrian has voluntarily and knowingly encountered a risk in choosing to cross at the red light while cars are coming. A jury asked to apportion responsibility in a case like this will be asked to compare the driver's negligence in driving drunk with the pedestrian's voluntary and knowing encountering of a risk.

This appears to be an apples-to-oranges kind of comparison. How is the jury to compare the two? On what scale? Courts have not answered the question other than to point to the obvious reality that jurors asked to do so will do so. That is, jurors who are instructed to apportion shares of "responsibility" between driver and pedestrian in this example will somehow come up with two numbers that add up to 100 percent. (Ask yourself what numbers you would assign to driver and pedestrian in this example. If you have a friend also using this book, compare notes. There's a good chance you have numbers that differ significantly from one another.)

Even in cases in which plaintiff's conduct constitutes both a form of negligence and a form of consent, jurors are supposed to take *both* into account in coming up with a fair allocation of responsibility. It is not just about comparing negligence to negligence; it is a global allocation of responsibility.

QUESTION 8. No Good Deed Goes Unpunished, Take II. Jules is walking near the railroad tracks when he sees a dog with its paw caught in the tracks. Jules works to free the dog from the tracks as a train approaches. Jules sees the train coming, and hurries to try to free the dog. Unfortunately, the train conductor, who is not paying attention to the tracks, does not see Jules on the tracks, and the train runs him over, causing Jules to suffer serious personal injuries. Jules sues the train conductor for negligence. Assume that the jury will find that the conductor acted negligently in how he drove the train.

In considering how to allocate shares of responsibility between Jules and the conductor following the Restatement approach:

A. The jury should consider the reasonableness of Jules's behavior in trying to free the dog as the train approached.
B. The jury should consider Jules's awareness of the approaching train and his appreciation of the danger of trying to free the dog in face of the approaching train.
C. The jury should consider both A and B.
D. The jury should consider neither A nor B because the conductor was negligent.

ANALYSIS. Under these facts, there is an argument that Jules did not act reasonably in trying to free the dog as the train approached. There is also an argument that Jules had voluntarily and knowingly chosen to encounter the risk because the facts tell us he knew the train was coming and tried to work to free the dog before the train arrived. Now it might be that some jurors would find Jules's behavior reasonable, but that's beside the point in answering this question. The jurors must consider both the reasonableness of Jules's behavior (noted in Choice **A**) and his consenting behavior (noted in Choice **B**). Choice **C**, combining both of these answers, provides the best choice. Choice **D** is flatly incorrect. Even assuming that the train conductor was negligent, the jury still must engage in the allocation. Recall that comparative responsibility is something that the conductor will raise as an affirmative defense *assuming* the conductor is negligent. Under the modern rules, proof of either Jules's negligence, consent, or both provides a basis for the jury to apportion liability between the two parties based upon shares of responsibility, taking into account the defendant's fault on one hand, with the plaintiff's fault and consent on the other.

 ## Rick's picks

1. Take the High Road, Take II	**A**
2. Take the High Road, Take III	**B**
3. Take the High Road, Take IV	**D**
4. Impure Intentions	**A**
5. Dumb Chicken	**C**
6. No Good Deed Goes Unpunished	**B**
7. Dumb Chicken, Take II	**B**
8. No Good Deed Goes Unpunished, Take II	**C**

11

Basic Duty Rules: Foreseeable Plaintiffs, the Sports Cases, and Risk Creation

CHAPTER OVERVIEW
A. Introduction: The role of duty in a negligence case
B. The foreseeable plaintiff requirement
C. Special rules for amateur sports and recreation cases
D. The risk creation requirement
E. The Closer: Legislating a duty to rescue?
 Rick's picks

A. Introduction: The role of duty in a negligence case

As explained in Chapter 8, the tortious conduct portion of the prima facie case for negligence has two elements:

1. Duty
2. Breach

The plaintiff must prove *both* duty and breach in order to meet the tortious conduct portion of the prima facie case for negligence. As noted in the earlier negligence chapters, duty is generally a policy question for a court, and not a fact question for a jury. The last three chapters focused on the *breach* portion of the prima facie case, making a temporary simplifying assumption about *duty*:

*A defendant has a **duty** (or responsibility) to everyone to avoid creating unreasonable risks of harm to others.*

In this chapter and the next, we delve into the duty rules, relaxing and modifying this earlier assumption. Before doing so, it is worth noting why the law imposes a duty requirement in a negligence case. Why should it not be enough for the plaintiff to prove (in addition to actual cause, proximate cause, and damages) that the defendant failed to use reasonable care to avoid a reasonably foreseeable risk to the plaintiff? As we shall see, the "duty" requirement injects the question of policy into the negligence case. In some cases, even when a defendant has failed to use reasonable care, and because of that failure the plaintiff has been injured, the law concludes that the defendant *for policy reasons* should nonetheless not have to pay any damages to the plaintiff on account of the injury. (As we will see in Chapter 14, proximate cause serves a similar policy purpose not limited — as with duty — to negligence cases.)

The key to understanding the concept of duty is to recognize that it is a (primarily judicial) policy determination, *not* a factual determination. As the drafters of the Third Restatement recently explained:

> A no-duty ruling represents a determination, a purely legal question, that no liability should be imposed on actors in a category of cases. Such a ruling should be explained and justified based on articulated policies or principles that justify exempting these actors from liability or modifying the ordinary duty of care.

Rest. (3d) Torts: Liability for Physical Harm § 7 cmt. *j* (P.F.D. No. 1, 2005).

In this chapter, we consider three limitations on a defendant's responsibility to use reasonable care in relationship to the plaintiff:

1. The plaintiff must be *foreseeable.*
2. The defendant has no duty to use care to avoid the inherent risks *in sports and recreation cases.*
3. The defendant has no duty in the absence of *risk creation* unless there is a *special relationship* between the parties.

QUESTION 1. Half-a-Loaf, Take II. Allan sues Becky for negligence arising out of an automobile accident. Before the case goes to a jury, Becky argues that Allan's suit cannot go forward because he cannot prove to the judge that Becky owed Allan a duty of care. Allan concedes the point, but says he has uncontradicted evidence of breach, that is, of Becky's failure to use reasonable care to avoid a reasonably foreseeable risk to Allan. Therefore, his case should go forward nonetheless. How should the court rule?

> **A.** Accept Allan's argument, letting the case go to the jury for half of Allan's damages.
> **B.** Accept the argument, letting the case go to the jury for half of Allan's damages, except that Allan will get to recover nothing if Becky can prove at least one of her affirmative defenses.
> **C.** Reject the argument because Allan must prove all the elements of his prima facie case in order to recover anything at trial.
> **D.** Reject the argument because duty is a more important element of the negligence tort than breach.

ANALYSIS. This question is a variation on the first question in Chapter 8 and is meant to remind you that in order for a plaintiff to win anything in any tort suit, the plaintiff must prove *each* of the elements of his prima facie case by a preponderance of the evidence. A plaintiff who proves only half of the elements is not entitled to half of the damages. For this reason, Choice **A** is wrong. Choice **B** is wrong for two reasons. First, it is wrong for the reason that Choice **A** is wrong: One cannot get half the damages for proving fewer than all of the elements of the prima facie case. Second, it is wrong because in a negligence case, proof by a defendant of an affirmative defense is not automatic grounds for the plaintiff to get nothing; instead, as we saw in Chapter 10, there is generally a *sharing* of the liability between the plaintiff and the defendant. Choice **C** correctly explains the principle that the plaintiff must prove *each* of the elements of the prima facie case by a preponderance of the evidence in order to prevail in the suit. Choice **D** reaches the right result — the court should reject Allan's argument — but for the wrong reason. Some elements of the prima facie case are not more "important" than others. It is necessary to prove all of the elements of the tort if the plaintiff is going to prevail at trial.

B.   The foreseeable plaintiff requirement

One of the most famous of all American torts cases is *Palsgraf v. Long Island R.R.*, 162 N.E. 99 (N.Y. 1928). In *Palsgraf*, a man was getting on a commuter train at a train station. He was carrying some newspapers, and, unbeknownst to the workers on the train, he had some fireworks wrapped inside the newspapers. The train was about to leave the station, and one of the train workers pushed him onto the train while another worker tried to pull him up as the train was leaving the station. In shoving the man, he dropped the newspapers, causing the fireworks to ignite and creating an explosion. Plaintiff, Palsgraf, was standing on the other end of the platform. The vibrations from the explosion caused some scales at the other end of the platform to fall on Palsgraf, injuring her.

The question before the New York Court of Appeals (New York's highest state court) was whether Palsgraf could recover for the negligence of train operators in shoving the man onto the moving train. Let's take it as a given that if the man was injured as he was pushed on the train, he would have been able to prove that the train operators breached.[1] So the question was not whether the train operator failed to use reasonable care, it was whether Palsgraf could recover from the train operator for the failure to use reasonable care.

Justice Cardozo, writing for a majority of the court, said Palsgraf could not recover because she was not a "foreseeable plaintiff." Justice Cardozo cited a then-famous treatise to the effect that "Proof of negligence in the air . . . will not do." Instead, the defendant must owe a *duty* to the plaintiff, and the only plaintiffs to whom defendants owe such a duty are those who are in the "zone of danger" of defendant's negligence.

According to Justice Cardozo, Palsgraf was beyond the zone of danger created by the train operator's negligence. Recall that the negligent act of the train operator was shoving the man onto the train (without knowing that the man was carrying explosives). Who is in the zone of danger of such negligence? Only the man and those reasonably close to him. The danger of shoving the man onto the train is that he could fall, hitting other people or causing them to have to get out of the way. It is not reasonably foreseeable that the act of shoving the man onto the train could cause injury to someone at the far other end of the platform. For this reason, plaintiff could not recover damages.

In considering how broad or how narrow the zone of danger is, one must look at the nature of the activity that the defendant negligently engages in. A negligent driver endangers all those who are in the potential path of the car. A negligent gasoline trucker endangers even more people than a regular driver, because the explosion could injure people far from any road.

Note how conclusory it can be to speak of duty. Why doesn't Palsgraf get to recover? Because defendant does not owe her a duty. The real question is *why* the court has concluded on policy grounds that the defendant is not responsible for preventing injuries to the plaintiff. In *Palsgraf*, Justice Cardozo was concerned that extending liability to unforeseeable plaintiffs would impose administrative burdens on the courts and stifle people from engaging in everyday activities. With broad liability "[l]ife will have to be made over, and human nature transformed, before prevision so extravagant can be accepted as the norm of conduct, the customary standard to which behavior must conform." 162 N.E. 99, 100 (N.Y. 1928).

Justice Andrews, in dissent, rejected Justice Cardozo's view that one owes a duty only to foreseeable plaintiffs. Why should a negligent defendant be let off the hook simply because he did not foresee who precisely would be

---

1. Likely he would do so using common sense or balancing. See Chapter 8.

injured by his negligence? In Justice Andrews's view: "Every one owes to the world at large the duty of refraining from those acts that may unreasonably threaten the safety of others." Justice Andrews did, however, believe some policy limitations in these cases were in order, and he set forth a very influential view of how *proximate cause* can play that role, an issue we return to in Chapter 14. But Justice Cardozo's view on foreseeable plaintiffs won the day, and his position has been adopted by the Restatement. See REST. (2D) TORTS § 281, cmt. *c.* So we can now restate the duty rule as follows:

> *A defendant has a **duty** (or responsibility) to everyone to avoid creating unreasonable risks of harm to **foreseeable plaintiffs**.*

QUESTION 2. *Palsgraf* Revisited. A man is getting on a commuter train at a train station. He is carrying a box of fireworks clearly marked with large letters stating: CAUTION. FIREWORKS! EXTREMELY FLAMMABLE. EXPLOSIVE! The train is about to leave the station, and one of the train workers pushes him onto the train while another worker tries to pull him up as the train is leaving the station. In shoving the man, he drops the fireworks, causing the fireworks to ignite and creating an explosion. Ms. Palsgraf is standing on the other end of the platform. The vibrations from the explosion caused some scales at the other end of the platform to fall on Palsgraf, injuring her.

Ms. Palsgraf sues the train station for negligence (assume the train station is responsible for the actions of its employees). The train station responds by stating that it owed no duty to Palsgraf. How should the court rule on the duty question?

A. The court should rule that the train station owes no duty to Palsgraf if it concludes that the employees used reasonable care to avoid a reasonably foreseeable risk.

B. The court should rule that the train station owes a duty to Palsgraf because its employees failed to use reasonable care when they shoved the man with fireworks on the train.

C. The court should rule that the question of the train station's duty is a factual one to be decided by the jury.

D. The court should rule that the train station owed a duty to Palsgraf.

ANALYSIS. The difference between the actual facts of the *Palsgraf* case and this hypothetical is that in the actual case, the train station employees did not know and had no reason to know that the man being pushed onto the train was carrying explosives. In this question, the employees either know or should know of the fireworks given the prominent warning on the box being carried by the man boarding the train.

The relevance of that warning to the duty question is to expand the "zone of danger" to more plaintiffs. Though shoving a man carrying newspapers onto a train creates a small zone of danger (confined to the man and the people immediately around him), shoving a man carrying fireworks endangers more people, and creates more foreseeable plaintiffs. Under the facts of the hypothetical, Choice **D** is the correct choice: The court should rule that the defendant owes a duty to the Ms. Palsgraf because she is a foreseeable plaintiff.

Choice **A** is incorrect because it confuses the question of duty with the question of breach: Whether or not the train operator failed to use reasonable care is a breach question, not a duty question. Choice **B** fails for the same reason. Choice **C** misunderstands the nature of the duty inquiry. The court is not deciding *facts* when it considers duty; it is making a *policy choice.*

C. Special rules for amateur sports and recreation cases

Wholly apart from the question whether plaintiff is foreseeable is another duty question that arises in certain sports and recreation cases. It is the question we put off in Chapter 10 related to the "primary implied assumption of risk" doctrine. To briefly recap what we have seen on the assumption of risk question so far: Before the rise of comparative negligence/ comparative responsibility, courts sometimes rejected plaintiffs' negligence cases on grounds that the plaintiff "assumed the risk" of injury by the defendant. Sometimes this finding was a consent-like affirmative defense: The plaintiff lost because she voluntarily and knowingly encountered the risk from the defendant's conduct (this idea is now referred to as "secondary implied assumption of risk"). At other times "assumption of risk" worked as a "no duty" rule: On policy grounds the defendant would be found not to be liable to the plaintiff for injuries in particular settings (this idea is now referred to as "primary implied assumption of risk").[2]

Under the old rules, it did not matter for the parties which assumption of risk doctrine applied: Whether assumption of risk functioned as an affirmative defense (secondary implied) or as a means of defeating an element of the prima facie case (primary implied), plaintiff's claim was completely barred. But note what has happened in the comparative negligence era. As most jurisdictions fold secondary implied assumption of risk into the global comparative negligence allocation of responsibility

---

2. There is also "express assumption of risk," which involves contracting around tort law. But we do not need to revisit that concept in this discussion.

(go back to Chapter 10 if this concept seems fuzzy), the question of the survival of primary implied assumption of risk makes a great deal of difference: The difference between plaintiff recovering something and nothing.

This is a difficult point to understand, so let's begin with a simple hypothetical. Billie Jean and Bobby are playing a game of tennis. Billie Jean carelessly hits the tennis ball into Bobby's eye, causing Bobby to suffer some permanent eye damage. Bobby sues Billie Jean for negligence. If a court decides to treat Bobby's participation in the sport under the secondary implied assumption of risk doctrine, then Bobby's consent will be weighed by the jury to come up with an allocation of responsibility between Billie Jean and Bobby. For example, the jury might say that Billie Jean was 70 percent responsible because of her negligence and Bobby was 30 percent responsible because of his consent-like secondary implied assumption of risk. Accordingly, Bobby's damages would be reduced by 30 percent, representing Bobby's share of responsibility.

Suppose instead that the court decides under the primary implied assumption of risk doctrine that tennis players do not owe a duty of care to other players for risks inherent in the sport of tennis. Under this doctrine, a court could decide that Billie Jean owes *no duty of care* to Bobby, meaning Bobby would recover *absolutely nothing* from Billie Jean because he would not be able to prove his prima facie case.

In short, the choice between primary implied assumption of risk and secondary implied assumption of risk is a choice between a *policy decision made by a judge* globally for particular risks of injuries from particular sports and a factual decision and *judgment call made by a jury* comparing the defendant's negligence with plaintiff's consent-like conduct (and negligence, in appropriate cases). In the former, a finding of assumption of risk *bars plaintiff's case completely*; in the latter, a finding of assumption of risk allows for a *sharing of liability* between the parties.

Jurisdictions have split over whether the primary implied assumption of risk doctrine survives in the comparative negligence era. Most jurisdictions continue to accept the doctrine, meaning that in a number of sports and recreation cases defendants sometimes can escape liability for injuries caused by their negligence.[3]

How does the primary implied assumption of risk doctrine work? Under the doctrine, *a defendant owes no duty to the plaintiff to avoid creating*

---

3. *See, e.g., Duffy v. Midlothian Country Club*, 481 N.E.2d 1037 (Ill. App. 1985) (holding that comparative negligence does not affect express and primary implied assumption of risk); *Yoneda v. Tom*, 133 P.3d 796 (Haw. 2006) (holding that in Hawaii, primary assumption of risk continues to operate as a complete bar to liability, but secondary assumption of risk is simply part of the comparative negligence analysis); *Hopkins v. Medeiros*, 48 Mass. App. Ct. 600, 724 N.E.2d 336 (2000) (holding that in Massachusetts, the defense of secondary assumption of risk has been abolished by statute, although primary assumption of risk remains a viable defense).

unreasonable risks of harm for injuries that are inherent in sports and recreation cases.

To take the tennis example again, a court could decide based upon its general knowledge of the game of tennis that being hit in the eye by a negligently hit ball is an inherent risk of the game. On this basis, all plaintiffs who complain in negligence suits about negligently hit balls will lose on duty grounds. The court does not inquire, and does not let a jury inquire, as to whether this particular plaintiff made a knowing and voluntary choice. It is enough that the plaintiff came to play tennis — indeed, spectators of the game would likely face the same fate: no liability for Billie Jean if she negligently hits a ball that injures a plaintiff in the stands.

As noted in the introduction to this chapter, a "no duty" decision is a policy decision. What policy decision does the primary implied assumption of risk doctrine play? It encourages people to participate in sports and recreation activities without fear of lawsuits. Courts adopting the primary implied assumption of risk doctrine in amateur sports and recreation cases[4] are concerned that allowing these cases to go to the jury on the basis of some allocation of responsibility between the injuring defendant and the injured plaintiff would chill participation in sporting activities.

QUESTION 3. Pee Wee Pigskin Piggy Problem. Michael and Kendra are attending a Super Bowl party at a mutual friend's house. During halftime of the Super Bowl, several guests decide to play an informal game of touch football on an adjoining dirt lot, using a "pee wee" football. Each team has four or five players and includes both women and men; Michael and Kendra are on opposing teams. No rules are explicitly discussed before the game.

Five to ten minutes into the game, Michael runs into Kendra during a play. According to Kendra, at that point she told Michael "not to play so rough or I was going to have to stop playing." On the very next play, Kendra is injured. Michael's team was on defense on that play, and he jumped up in an attempt to intercept a pass. He touched the ball but did not catch it, and in coming down he collided with Kendra, knocking her over. When he landed, he stepped backward onto Kendra's right hand, injuring her hand and little finger. Unfortunately, her little finger had to be amputated because of the injury. Kendra sues Michael for negligence in a jurisdiction that continues to apply the primary implied assumption of risk doctrine.

In determining whether or not the primary implied assumption of risk doctrine should apply to bar Kendra's case:

---

4. Various assumption of risk doctrines, including express assumption of risk, appear to bar most negligence cases arising out of injuries to *professional* athletes as well.

> **A.** The court should consider whether Kendra sustained an injury caused by Michael's negligence that was an inherent risk of playing an informal game of football.
> **B.** The court should consider whether Kendra voluntarily and knowingly consented to the inherent risks of this kind of football game.
> **C.** The court should consider whether Kendra's actions constituted a form of negligence.
> **D.** The court should balance Michael's negligence on the one hand with Kendra's negligence and consent on the other.

ANALYSIS. The call of the question tells you that this question arises in a jurisdiction that continues to recognize the primary implied assumption of risk doctrine. Under this doctrine, a person who injures another through negligence in a sports or recreation context is not liable for injuries that are inherent in that activity. Doctrinally, the court says that in such circumstances the injurer owes no duty to use reasonable care to co-participants or spectators.

In making this determination, the court focuses on the risks inherent in the sport. Whether the particular plaintiff voluntarily and knowingly agreed to participate is irrelevant. For this reason, Choice **B** is wrong. Choice **C** is wrong because the question of Kendra's negligence is one that goes to Michael's affirmative defenses. The primary implied assumption of risk doctrine, however, is one that goes to the plaintiff's prima facie case (particularly to the duty element) and not to affirmative defenses. Choice **D** similarly mistakenly focuses on affirmative defenses, and in fact gives the applicable standard in *secondary implied* assumption of risk cases. Choice **A** sets forth the correct standard: The court should consider whether Kendra was injured due to an inherent risk of this kind of football game.

The facts of this question are based upon the influential California Supreme Court case, *Knight v. Jewett*, 834 P.2d 696 (Cal. 1992). In that case, the majority held that Kendra's case would be barred under the primary implied assumption of risk doctrine, which survived California's transition to comparative negligence (with secondary implied assumption of risk being folded into the comparative responsibility allocation by the jury). A dissenting opinion argued that the question of responsibility should not be decided by the court under a "duty" analysis, and instead the question should be one of secondary implied assumption of risk, with the balancing taking place according to the analysis set forth in Choice **D** above by a jury on a case-by-case basis.[5] Justice Kennard pointed out that this "football game" did not even have

---

5. Justice Kennard's dissenting opinion was actually a bit more complicated than that. For those of you who need or want to know the details, here they are: Justice Kennard concluded that most cases of secondary implied assumption of risk involved an *unreasonable* decision to encounter a known risk. In those cases, an allocation of responsibility between a defendant and plaintiff should be done along the lines set forth in Choice **D** above. However, if plaintiff made a *reasonable* decision to

any established rules, so it would be difficult to uncover the inherent risks of such a game.

QUESTION 4. Pee Wee Pigskin Piggy Problem, Take II.   Same facts as in Question 3, except after Michael collides with Kendra, he lands on top of Bill, who is watching the game from the sidelines while drinking a beer. Bill breaks a toe and sues Michael for negligence.

In determining whether or not the primary implied assumption of risk doctrine should apply to bar Bill's case:

A. The court should consider whether Bill sustained an injury caused by Michael's negligence that was an inherent risk of playing an informal game of football.
B. The court should consider whether Bill voluntarily and knowingly consented to the inherent risks of watching this kind of football game.
C. The court should consider whether Bill was careless in not paying attention to the football game's action.
D. The court should balance Michael's negligence on the one hand with Bill's negligence and consent on the other.

ANALYSIS.   The point of this question is a simple one: Spectators are also subject to the same rules as participants in sporting activities. Every so often you hear a story of a tragedy at a professional sports game, such as a child being killed by an errant puck at a hockey game. *See* Kevin Allen, *Death Rocks Youngster's World and NHL*, USA TODAY, March 22, 2002, http://www. usatoday.com/sports/hockey/stories/2002-03-19-puck-death.htm ("Eighth-grader Brittanie Cecil of West Alexandria, Ohio died Monday night from artery damage after being struck in the forehead by a puck two days earlier. Cecil, a cheerleader and soccer player, is the first fan to be killed at an NHL game by a puck leaving the rink and traveling over the glass, though there have been fan deaths at lower levels of hockey.").

In those jurisdictions accepting the primary implied assumption of risk doctrine, sports participants (and organizers, such as sports teams and sports stadiums) have no duty to prevent injuries that are an inherent part of the sport. As with the last question, and for the same reasons, Choice **A** is the correct choice.

Inherent Risks. As we have set out the primary implied assumption of risk doctrine, a defendant owes no duty to the plaintiff to avoid creating

---

voluntarily and knowingly encounter a risk, then according to Justice Kennard that should serve as a *complete defense* in a negligence action. The majority pointed out Justice Kennard's alternative approach creates a somewhat perverse outcome. Those who act unreasonably in encountering a risk are treated more charitably than those who act reasonably in doing so. Confused yet? If not, you haven't been paying attention.

unreasonable risks of harm for injuries *that are inherent in sports and recreation cases.* The question then becomes how a court determines the inherent risks of the sport. Simply put, the court examines the nature of the sport or recreation activity, and then asks whether taking precautions against injury due to negligence would change the nature of the sport. For example, one could greatly reduce the nature of injuries in football games by prohibiting players from touching one another, but that would greatly change the nature of football. Accordingly, lawsuits based upon injuries caused by negligently done tackling or other touching-related injuries in football games are mostly barred in those jurisdictions accepting the primary implied assumption of risk doctrine.

These rules apply not only to injuries caused by co-participants but also by injuries resulting from precautions taken by sports teams, organizers, and stadiums. In another famous opinion by Justice Cardozo, *Murphy v. Steeplechase Amusement Co.*, 166 N.E. 173 (N.Y. 1929), the plaintiff went to the Coney Island amusement park and took a ride on an attraction called "The Flopper." "It is a moving belt, running upward on an inclined plane, on which passengers sit or stand. Many of them are unable to keep their feet because of the movement of the belt, and are thrown backward or aside." People fell onto a padded floor.

Unsurprisingly, plaintiff fell while on the ride and broke his knee. He sued for negligence and Justice Cardozo, for the court, rejected his argument: "The plaintiff was not seeking a retreat for meditation. Visitors were tumbling about the belt to the merriment of onlookers when he made his choice to join them. . . . The timorous may stay at home."

Importantly, Justice Cardozo distinguished those situations in which the dangers in the sport were "obscure or unobserved," such as exposed wood rather than padding on the ground. The risk of The Flopper was the danger of falling. It would not change the inherent nature of the ride to have adequate padding: People did not go on the ride to see if they could avoid getting splinters or worse from exposed wood. Similarly, protecting hockey game spectators in seats close to the ice rink with a glass wall, or protecting baseball game spectators in seats behind home plate with a mesh fence does not change the nature of the game. But replacing the puck or baseball with a "Nerf" puck or ball certainly would change the nature of the game and is not required.

> **QUESTION 5. Foul!** Andy was attending a baseball game of a minor league team, the Studio City Stars. He had great seats, right behind home plate. Between the seats and home plate was a mesh fence. Saul the slugger is up at bat. He hits a foul ball that crashes into the mesh fence behind home plate. The fence was poorly maintained, and the force of the ball

causes a nail holding a piece of mesh to a wood pole to come out of the wood. The nail hits Andy in the eye, causing serious injuries. Andy sues the Studio City Stars, owner of the stadium, for negligence. The Stars argue to the judge that Andy's claim is barred under the primary implied assumption of risk doctrine (a doctrine the jurisdiction applies).

How should the court rule?

A. The court should agree with the Stars because Andy was injured through negligence as a spectator at a sporting event.
B. The court should agree with the Stars because Andy consented to injury by sitting as a spectator at the sporting event.
C. The court should reject the Stars's argument because being hit with a nail is not an inherent risk of attending a baseball game.
D. The court should reject the Stars's argument because Andy was not negligent.

ANALYSIS. Under the primary implied assumption of risk doctrine, a defendant sports participant or organizer owes no duty to prevent injuries due to the inherent nature of the sport. Had Andy been hit by a baseball at the baseball game, the primary implied assumption of risk doctrine likely would have barred Andy's claim. However, Andy was injured when a fence built to prevent injuries to spectators broke, causing a nail to go flying into Andy's eye. A court is likely to conclude that the risk of being hit with nails coming out of the fence is not an inherent risk of the sport of baseball. Think of it this way: Players on the Stars could play just as vigorously, and spectators can enjoy the game just as much, if the nails holding the mesh from the backstop fence to the wood do so securely. A court therefore is likely to conclude that the Stars owe a duty of care to Andy.

For this reason, Choice **C** is the best answer. Choice **A** is wrong because it is not enough that Andy was injured through negligence at a sporting event. It must be from an *inherent* risk of the activity, and this was not. Choice **B** is wrong because the question asks about *primary* implied assumption of risk, and the issue of consent goes to *secondary* implied assumption of risk, which would be relevant to any affirmative defenses that the Stars may raise. Choice **D** fails for a similar reason: Whether or not Andy is negligent goes to the Stars's affirmative defenses.

Worse Than Negligence? As we have set out in the primary implied assump-tion of risk doctrine, a defendant owes no duty to the plaintiff to avoid creating *unreasonable risks of harm* for injuries that are inherent in sports and recreation cases. What if the defendant's conduct is *worse than negligence?* For example, in Question 3, suppose that Michael was playing while drunk, and he knocked into Kendra with all his force while trying to score a touchdown with the pee wee football?

Some courts have recognized that the primary implied assumption of risk doctrine protects defendants only from *negligence* claims. When the defendant engages in riskier conduct, such as *recklessness* (or, in some jurisdictions, *gross negligence*), the primary implied assumption of risk doctrine does not apply. (Recall from Chapter 6 that recklessness is usually defined along the lines of disregarding a substantial risk of a high probability of injury to others, a standard much worse than negligence.)

Why not? Remember that the primary implied assumption of risk doctrine, like all other duty rules, is a *policy choice*. The policy choice behind the doctrine is one to avoid chilling people from engaging vigorously and completely in sporting events. Careless action in sporting events is inevitable, and surely the threat of liability could cause some people to be overly cautious in how they participate in such activities. But courts are not as concerned about deterring reckless conduct or worse. Indeed, many courts would probably be quite happy if the threat of liability prevented sports participants from engaging in reckless conduct.

Suppose that Michael engages in even worse conduct. He uses the occasion of the football game to punch Kendra in the face. In that circumstance, when the conduct goes outside the bounds of the game (and could constitute a safety violation, if there were a referee), Michael could be liable for *battery*, an intentional tort (see Chapter 3), possibly exposing him to punitive damages (discussed in Chapter 23).

QUESTION 6. Reckless Coach?   Student, a 14-year-old novice on a school swim team, broke her neck during a meet when she executed a practice dive into a shallow racing pool located on school property. She sued the school district, alleging that the injury was caused in part by the failure of her coach, a district employee, to give her any instruction in how to safely dive into a shallow pool. She also sued the coach for failing to adequately supervise her and for insisting that she dive or risk dismissal.

The school district and coach argue that Student's case cannot go forward because they owe Student no duty under the primary implied assumption of risk doctrine. How should the court rule?

A. The court should reject the argument because there is evidence the coach was negligent.

B. The court should reject the argument because the Coach's behavior could be considered reckless.

C. The court should accept the argument because breaking one's neck while diving is an inherent risk of diving.

D. The court should accept the argument because Student voluntarily and knowingly accepted the risk of injury.

ANALYSIS.   This case is based upon *Kahn v. East Side Union High School Dist.*, 75 P.3d 30 (Cal. 2003). This is a difficult question. Let's first reject the clearly wrong answers. Choice **A** is wrong because evidence of the coach's negligence goes to the question of breach, not duty. That is, we are not asking the factual question whether the coach was negligent, but the policy question whether the coach may be let out of liability *assuming he is negligent.* We can also eliminate Choice **D**. The question whether or not Student consented goes to the question of affirmative defenses (under secondary implied assumption of risk) and not to the call of the question, which asks about primary implied assumption of risk.

The harder question is the choice between Choice **B** and Choice **C**. Choice **C** presents the usual application of the primary implied assumption of risk doctrine, and it would be correct *if* there were no evidence of the coach's recklessness. On this record, however, there *is* potential evidence of the coach's recklessness. Making a 14-year-old dive into a shallow pool without any training and threatening to kick Student off the team if she fails to do so could be said to show a substantial disregard of the high probability of danger to Student. As the California Supreme Court ruled in *Kahn*, the question should ultimately be one for the jury. Choice **B** is the correct answer.

D.   The risk creation requirement

To this point, we can state our more complicated duty rule in negligence cases as follows:

> *Putting aside special rules in sports and recreation cases, a defendant has a duty (or responsibility) to avoid* **creating** *unreasonable risks of harm to foreseeable plaintiffs.*

In this section, we focus on the concept of "creating" unreasonable risks. We create risks all the time. Every time I drive down the street I create risks to others. This does not mean that I am negligent every time I drive down the street; it means, however, that I am in the business of risk creation when I drive and I therefore owe a duty to foreseeable plaintiffs along my drive to use reasonable care.

Contrast this situation with an alternative situation. John Monster is on vacation in Hawaii. He is sitting on an isolated beach enjoying the ocean. He looks up and sees a small ship sinking in the ocean and the passengers flailing in the water. Monster knows no one on the boat or in the water. Monster thinks about swimming out to sea or using his cell phone to call for help. "Nah," he says, and he goes back to sipping his piña colada. As we shall see, the law says that Monster is not liable for negligence because he is not engaged in risk creation, even though he could have helped those drowning through the trivial cost of a phone call.

In this section we consider what it means to *create* risk and how the law deals with situations in which defendants are not engaged in risk creation. We will end up with the following general definition of duty in a negligence case:

> *Putting aside special rules in sports and recreation cases (and additional special rules described in the next chapter), a defendant has a duty (or responsibility) to avoid creating unreasonable risks of harm to foreseeable plaintiffs. In the absence of risk creation, a person must use reasonable care only in the presence of a special relationship.*

It might seem like the requirement of risk creation is a tough one to meet, but it is not. In virtually all of the examples considered in this part of the book, the defendants have been involved in risk creation, whether it is driving, walking, piloting a boat, swimming, or just about anything besides sitting and doing nothing. And we do not look at risk creation in a vacuum: It is risk creation *in relation to the plaintiff*. So, if John Monster is on the beach lighting a campfire, he is engaged in risk creation in relation to foreseeable plaintiffs around him who might be injured by the fire. But he is not engaged in risk creation in relation to the plaintiffs who are drowning out at sea.

Risk creation issues come up in the context of when one person has a duty to come to the aid of another in the absence of risk creation. The bottom line is that when it comes to strangers, there is no duty to come to the aid of another. A person can be a moral monster and not make the call to 911, but the common law will not hold that person legally responsible for acting in this way. John Monster can sip his piña colada all day long and watch others drown if he likes.

The situation would be different if Monster had a "special relationship" with those in danger. For example, if the people drowning were Monster's minor children, or his students, or his prisoners (if he were a prison warden), then the law would require that he act. The law imposes these special relationships sparingly, and we will talk more about them in the next chapter.

Both the rule that there is no duty in the absence of risk creation and the exceptions in cases of special relationships are examples of how the law imposes policy preferences through the duty requirement. Although some legal scholars and others have argued for the moral imperative[6] or economic efficiency[7] of imposing a duty to rescue, the law follows a libertarian impulse

---

6. For a modern statement of the position, *see* Steven J. Heyman, *The Duty to Rescue: A Liberal-Communitarian Approach*, in THE COMMUNITARIAN READER: BEYOND THE ESSENTIALS (A. Etzioni et al. eds., Rowman & Littlefield 2004). An early approach appears in James Barr Ames, *Law and Morals*, 22 HARV. L. REV. 97 (1908).
7. For those who are interested, I have argued that it would be economically efficient to impose a duty of easy rescue upon strangers. Richard L. Hasen, *The Efficient Duty to Rescue*, 15 INT'L REV. L. & ECON. 141 (1995).

here:[8] It is that when one does not create risks, there is no corresponding obligation to help a stranger in distress.

QUESTION 7. Going Downhill.   Candy is driving on a mountain road late one winter night. The road is very icy. Through no fault of her own, Candy's car stalls at the bottom of a steep hill. Candy knows that any car coming down the hill will be unable to stop because of the icy conditions. She thinks about going to the top of the hill to warn other drivers of the danger and have them stop in time, but then she decides not to bother. Donald, who is driving on the road comes down the icy hill. Though he is driving carefully, he cannot avoid hitting into Candy's car. Donald suffers personal injuries and sues Candy for negligence. Candy argues she cannot be liable for negligence because she does not owe a duty to Donald. How should the court rule on this argument?

A. The court should reject the argument because Candy was engaged in risk creation.

B. The court should reject the argument because Candy was negligent in failing to warn approaching cars of the risk.

C. The court should accept the argument because Candy was not negligent at the moment her car stalled.

D. The court should accept the argument because Donald was not a foreseeable plaintiff.

ANALYSIS. This hypothetical is based upon *Montgomery v. National Convoy & Trucking Co.*, 195 S.E. 247 (S.C. 1938). When Candy was driving, she was engaged in risk creation. Even though she non-negligently created the risk because she engaged in risk creation by driving the car, she had a duty to foreseeable plaintiffs to take steps to protect them from injury, such as walking to the top of the hill and warning people not to go down the icy road. Choice **A** correctly explains the court should reject Candy's "no duty" argument because she was engaged in risk creation. Choice **B** reaches the right result, but for the wrong reason: Whether or not Candy had a duty to warn others comes from the fact of her risk creation not her later failure to warn (if Choice **B** were correct, then John Monster would have a duty to rescue as well). Choice **C** is incorrect because it is not necessary that Candy be negligent in order for a duty to arise: It is enough that she engaged in risk creation. Choice **D** is wrong because, though Candy owed a duty only to foreseeable plaintiffs, Donald *is* a foreseeable plaintiff because he is in the zone of danger arising out of Candy's negligent failure to warn of the stalled truck.

---

8. For a sustained libertarian defense, see Richard Epstein, *A Theory of Strict Liability*, 2 J. LEGAL. STUD. 151, 198-200 (1973).

> **QUESTION 8. Going Downhill, Take II.** Candy is driving on a mountain road late one winter night. The road is very icy. Through no fault of her own, Candy's car stalls at the bottom of a steep hill. Randy is driving by Candy going up the mountain. Randy knows that any car coming down the hill will be unable to stop because of the icy conditions. Randy drives to the top of the hill and thinks about warning other drivers of the danger, but then he decides not to bother. He passes Donald, coming in the opposite direction and headed for Candy. Randy says nothing about the danger up ahead for Donald. Donald drives down the icy hill. Though he is driving carefully, he cannot avoid hitting into Candy's car. Donald suffers personal injuries and sues Randy for negligence. Randy argues he cannot be liable for negligence because he does not owe a duty to Donald. How should the court rule on this argument?
>
> **A.** The court should reject the argument because Randy was engaged in risk creation in relation to Donald's accident.
>
> **B.** The court should reject the argument because Randy was negligent in failing to warn approaching cars of the risk.
>
> **C.** The court should accept the argument because Randy was not engaged in risk creation in relation to Donald's accident.
>
> **D.** The court should accept the argument because Donald was not a foreseeable plaintiff.

ANALYSIS. In this variation on Question 7 it is a stranger who did not create the risk that ultimately caused Donald's injuries. It is true Randy's driving is a form of risk creation, but Randy's driving had nothing to do with Donald's accident. Randy is just like John Monster in the earlier hypothetical; he could cheaply and easily take steps to prevent or lessen injury. But as a stranger in the absence of a special relationship, he need not do so. Choices **A** and **B** are therefore incorrect. Choice **D** is incorrect because, as in the last question, Donald is a foreseeable plaintiff. Here Choice **C** is correct: Randy owes no duty to Donald to prevent injuries caused by Candy because Randy was not engaged in any risk creation to Donald related to the conditions that caused Donald's accident.

Voluntary Undertakings. Although a stranger in the absence of a special relationship and risk creation has no responsibility to come to the aid of another, once the stranger does so, there is an obligation not to make things worse. So if Donald from the last question is on the side of the road bleeding from his injuries, Sandy, a stranger who had nothing to do with the accident is free to keep driving and not stop to render any aid. But once Sandy decides to stop and render aid, he can be liable if he makes things worse, such as by breaking Donald's ribs in an attempt to give him CPR. The fear of liability against Good Samaritans might induce people like Sandy not to stop; for this reason, states have passed statutes reversing the common law and giving Good Samaritans like Sandy immunity from negligence cases unless their conduct is worse than negligent.

QUESTION 9. Monster Returns. John Monster is driving by the scene of an automobile accident. No one else is around. He comes across Frank, a stranger, who is unconscious by the side of the road. John carefully places Frank in the backseat of his car to drive him to the hospital. John starts to drive away and then, 15 minutes later, changes his mind. He gently returns Frank back to the scene of the accident. Frank is ultimately picked up by an ambulance one hour later. Frank later sues John for negligence, arguing his injuries would not have been as bad had he been taken to the hospital sooner. John argues he cannot be liable because he had no duty to John. How should the court rule?

A. The court should accept John's argument because John did not engage in any risk creation.

B. The court should accept John's argument, if John can prove that no one else drove by during the interim period and John's moving of Frank caused him no additional injuries.

C. The court should reject John's argument because Frank was a foreseeable plaintiff.

D. The court should reject John's argument because of the special relationship between the parties.

ANALYSIS. John initially had no duty to Frank, because they were strangers and John was not involved in any way with risk creation tied to Frank's accident. Once John voluntarily undertook to help, however, John had a duty not to make things worse. Choice **A** is incorrect because it misses this aspect of John's duty. Choice **B** correctly explains the standard: For John not to be liable, he'd have to show that he did not make Frank worse, either by moving him or by making it less likely he'd be discovered by others and rescued. Choice **C** is incorrect because it is not enough that Frank is a foreseeable plaintiff in order for John to have a duty to Frank: There also must be risk creation, a special relationship, or a voluntary undertaking. Choice **D** is plainly incorrect because the facts tell us that the two are strangers, and there are no facts indicating any special relationship.

E.   The Closer: Legislating a duty to rescue?

As we have seen in this chapter, the issue of duty is one of policy, not facts, and application of duty rules is primarily the job of the courts, not juries. Courts make duty determinations through the development of the common law. However, common law developments are subject to be overridden through legislation passed by legislatures. Legislatures, not courts, get the last word.

If legislatures wished to do so, they could overrule duty rules related to foreseeable plaintiffs, the primary implied assumption of risk doctrine, or the duty to rescue. *See, e.g.,* OR. REV. STAT. § 31.620 (2007) (abolishing the implied assumption of the risk doctrine). On the last point, one state, Vermont, has imposed by criminal statute a duty of easy rescue. *See* VT. STAT. tit. 12 § 519 (2008). The statute imposes a fine of up to $100 for someone who fails to render reasonable personal assistance to "another [person who] is exposed to grave physical harm" when such assistance can be "rendered without danger or peril to himself or without assistance with important duties owed to others." It is not clear if the criminal statute also imposes tort liability, even though the law has been on the books since the 1970s. There are very few reported cases under the statute suggesting, thankfully, that there aren't too many John Monsters out there.

QUESTION 10. The Last Word.   The legislature of the state of Pacifica wishes to impose a civil law requiring people to come to the rescue of strangers in trouble when aid can be rendered without much cost and without imposing danger upon the would-be rescuer. Is such a law enforceable?

A. No, because courts alone decide the scope of duties to others.
B. No, because legislatures may impose criminal laws, not change the common law.
C. Yes, if courts agree that legislatures can change the rules.
D. Yes, because legislatures can override the common law's duty rules.

ANALYSIS.   This is a straightforward question to end this difficult chapter. As noted above, courts make duty determinations through the development of the common law. However, legislatures can overrule the common law. For this reason, Choices **A** and **B** are wrong. Legislatures do not need to get permission from courts in order to change the common law. For this reason, Choice **C** is also wrong. Choice **D** correctly explains the interplay between courts and legislatures: When it comes to statutes overruling the common law, legislatures get the last word.

✦ Rick's picks

1.	Half-a-Loaf, Take II	C
2.	*Palsgraf* Revisited	D
3.	Pee Wee Pigskin Piggy Problem	A
4.	Pee Wee Pigskin Piggy Problem, Take II	A
5.	Foul!	C
6.	Reckless Coach?	B
7.	Going Downhill	A
8.	Going Downhill, Take II	C
9.	Monster Returns	B
10.	The Last Word	D

More Duty Rules: Special Relationships, Landowners, and Negligent Infliction of Emotional Distress

CHAPTER OVERVIEW
A. Special relationships imposing affirmative duties
   1. Duty to those in special relationship
   2. Duty to third persons because of special relationship
B. Special rules for landowners
C. Special rules for claims of negligent infliction of emotional distress
D. The Closer: Once more on duty versus breach
⊕ Rick's picks

A. Special relationships imposing affirmative duties

1. Duty to those in special relationship

We ended the last chapter with a summary of the rules related to duty in a negligence case:

*Putting aside special rules in sports and recreation cases (and additional special rules described in this chapter), a defendant has a duty (or responsibility) to avoid creating unreasonable risks of harm to foreseeable plaintiffs. In the absence of risk creation, a person must use reasonable care **only in the presence of a special relationship.***

We turn now to those special relationships referred to at the end of this definition.

The decision whether or not to find a "special relationship" giving rise to a duty to give aid is a *policy decision*, not a factual one. As a matter of policy, courts (or, in some cases, legislatures[1]) decide that some relationships *should* require imposition of a duty to come to the aid of another even in the absence of risk creation. Jurisdictions differ on the question of special relationship; the Third Restatement gives the following non-exhaustive list of the relationships endorsed by the Restatement drafters:

(1) a common carrier with its passengers,

(2) an innkeeper with its guests,

(3) a business or other possessor of land that holds its premises open to the public with those who are lawfully on the premises,

(4) an employer with its employees who are:

    (a) in imminent danger; or

    (b) injured and thereby helpless,

(5) a school with its students,

(6) a landlord with its tenants, and

(7) a custodian with those in its custody, if: a) the custodian is required by law to take custody or voluntarily takes custody of the other; and b) the custodian has a superior ability to protect the other.

REST. (3D) TORTS: LIABILITY FOR PHYSICAL HARM § 40(b) (P.F.D. 2005).

What ties these relationships together, as a matter of policy? Some of the relationships involve power or control: teachers control students, landlords control common areas in apartment buildings,[2] and wardens control inmates. Other relationships seem to be based upon the notion that the person in the special relationship has the better *ability* to prevent injuries than the person in need of assistance, such as the employer-employee situation. Still others arise out of heightened duties traditionally imposed by the common law. For example, under the old common law, common carriers and innkeepers were held to have the "highest duty of care" to their customers.

Still, some of these categories remain controversial. Indiana, for example, does not recognize that employers have a duty to employees, even those who are in imminent danger or injured and thereby helpless, or to business invitees.

---

1. *See* REST. (3D) TORTS: LIABILITY FOR PHYSICAL HARM § 38 (P.F.D. 2005) ("When a statute requires an actor to act for the protection of another, the court may rely on the statute to decide that an affirmative duty exists and its scope.").

2. One of the early cases recognizing this duty of landlords is *Kline v. 1500 Massachusetts Ave. Apartment Corp.*, 439 F.2d 477 (D.C. Cir. 1970). Note that the general statement of the Restatement Third goes further, not limiting the special relationship to common areas.

See Stockberger v. U.S., 332 F.3d 479 (7th Cir. 2003).[3] As the number and type of special relationships expand, the no duty to rescue rule shrinks. Thus, imposition of special relationships stands in tension with the libertarian impulse described in the last chapter behind the no duty to rescue rule.

Finally, an important caveat: The special relationship question is relevant *only* in cases in which the defendant has engaged in no risk creation in relation to the plaintiff. When there is *risk creation* (even if it is non-negligent, as we saw in the last chapter), a duty to use reasonable care arises *regardless of* the special relationship between the parties.

QUESTION 1. Monster Returns.   John Monster is a hotel guest sitting by the pool and enjoying the sunny day. On his way back from the bar with his piña colada, though he was acting carefully, he knocks Fatima, a stranger, into the pool. No one else is out at the pool. Fatima cannot swim. John sits down and enjoys his drink. Fatima suffers serious personal injuries that could have been prevented if John helped Fatima out of the pool or called for help. Fatima sues John for negligence, and John argues to the court that the case cannot go to a jury because he owed no duty to Fatima. How should the court rule?

A. The court should accept John's argument because he was not negligent and therefore he had no duty to rescue a stranger.

B. The court should accept John's argument because he and Fatima did not have a special relationship.

C. The court should reject John's argument even though John was not negligent.

D. The court should reject John's argument because innkeepers have the highest duty of care to hotel guests.

ANALYSIS.   Unlike the John Monster hypothetical in the previous chapter, in this chapter John has engaged in risk creation in relation to the drowning plaintiff. Once a person has engaged in risk creation, even if acting non-negligently, the person must use reasonable care to avoid a reasonably foreseeable risk to the plaintiff. Thus, John cannot sit around sipping his drink letting Fatima drown, unless he wants to face tort liability. Choice **C**

---

3. The Restatement recognizes that the scope of the employer special relationship is limited because most such cases would be out of the tort system and governed by workers' compensation rules. "The circumstances in which this duty might apply are largely limited to a criminal attack on an employee by a third party that occurs at the place of employment, an illness or injury suffered by an employee while at work but not resulting from employment that render the employee helpless and in need of emergency medical care or assistance, and the occasional case that falls through the cracks of workers compensation coverage." REST. (3D) TORTS: LIABILITY FOR PHYSICAL HARM § 40 cmt. *k* (P.F.D. 2005).

correctly explains that the court should reject John's "no duty" argument, even though he was not negligent.

Choice **A** is incorrect because it is *risk creation in relation to the plaintiff*, not a finding of negligence, that creates John's duty to act. Choice **B** (the main distractor here that likely ensnared a number of you) is wrong because the special relationship question is *irrelevant* when the defendant has engaged in risk creation. It would only be relevant in this question if Fatima fell into the pool for reasons unrelated to John's actions. Choice **D** gives a correct statement of the law about the duties of innkeepers to use reasonable care, but John is a hotel guest, not an innkeeper, and therefore the question of his responsibility is unrelated to this rule.

QUESTION 2. Give Me the Keys. Maurice, an employee of Terre Industries, is an insulin-dependent diabetic and known to be such by his coworkers—many of whom, indeed, are medical workers. He had hypoglycemic episodes (episodes in which his blood sugar would fall to dangerously low levels), observed by and known to be such by his coworkers, in which he would exhibit personality changes, becoming hostile, suspicious, unresponsive, agitated—and sometimes denying that he had a medical problem. When his coworkers noticed that he was in one of his hypoglycemic states, they would urge him to eat, or to drink Ensure, a nutritious liquid food substitute. One day, one of his coworkers noticed that Maurice, who was complaining about feeling ill and said that he wanted to go home, was having one of his hypoglycemic episodes, and offered him Ensure, which he drank. This made him feel better but he said he still wanted to go home. His coworkers wanted him to remain at work "until he recovered," but he was adamant about leaving. The coworker who had given him Ensure thought that Maurice was in no condition to be driving, but he did not offer to drive Maurice or try to take away his car keys; nor did he try to contact Maurice's supervisor or wife. Maurice got into his pickup truck and began driving home. He drove very erratically, no doubt because of his hypoglycemia, veering off the road and then back onto it, knocking down traffic signs, and eventually colliding with a tree. His truck burst into flames when it hit the tree, and he suffered serious personal injuries.

Maurice sues Terre Industries (which you should assume is responsible for the actions of its employees) for negligence in failing to drive him home or take his keys away. Terre Industries argues that it owed Maurice no duty. How should the court rule on the argument of Terre Industries?

A. The court should reject the argument, if the jurisdiction has determined that employers have a special relationship with their employees.

B. The court should reject the argument because it would have been very easy for the employer to prevent this injury.
C. The court should accept the argument because no courts recognize a special relationship between employers and employees.
D. The court should accept the argument because there is no evidence the employer was negligent.

ANALYSIS. The facts of this case come from the Seventh Circuit *Stockberger* case discussed above. (In the real case, unfortunately, the employee died after veering off the road and the suit was brought by his widow against his employer, the federal prison in Terre Haute, Indiana.) The employer did not create the risk that led to Maurice's injuries. In the absence of risk creation, the employer would have a duty only if the court recognizes a special relationship between employers and employees. On the question whether such a special relationship exists between employers and employees — a policy question, not a factual one — the courts are split. Choice **A** correctly captures the point that the court should reject Terre Industries' "no duty" argument only *if* the jurisdiction has recognized this special relationship. Choice **C** is incorrect in categorically stating that *no* courts recognize this duty, at least in limited circumstances. Choice **B** is wrong because how easy the rescue might be is relevant to the question of breach, not duty. Choice **D** is wrong for the same reason.

2. Duty to third persons because of special relationship

In the first section of this chapter, we considered cases in which a court might declare that there is a special relationship between two parties that requires one of the parties to come to the aid of the other even in the absence of risk creation. We now consider a slightly different topic: Under what circumstances does a special relationship between two parties require one of those parties to come to the aid of a *third person* who is injured by the other party in the special relationship?

The leading case here is a California Supreme Court case, *Tarasoff v. Regents of the University of California*, 551 P.2d 334 (Cal. 1976). A college student sought counseling from university psychological services. During the counseling, the student said he was thinking of killing his ex-girlfriend. Though the therapist warned the campus police, he did not warn the ex-girlfriend directly. She was killed by the student, and the family sued the university for its therapist's failure to warn. Though the court recognized the confidentiality of the therapist-patient relationship, it said that in narrow circumstances of a threat to an identifiable victim, the benefits of disclosure exceeded the costs of chilling patients from being open and forthright with their therapists.

The duty upon therapists to give what has come to be known as a "*Tarasoff* warning" is the most prominent example of the courts, for policy reasons, imposing a duty upon persons not because of a special relationship between the would-be rescuer *and the victim*, but because of a special relationship between the would-be rescuer *and the injurer*.

To frame the issue a slightly different way, these third person cases ask the question: When does one person have a duty to help another fend off some kind of attack? If John Monster, back on the beach, sees one stranger attacking another stranger, he has no responsibility to act.[4] But the therapist in a *Tarasoff* situation must act. The courts again make this choice as a matter of social policy.

The Third Restatement takes the view that a person has a duty to protect a third person from attacks when there is a special relationship in one of the following categories:

(1) a parent with dependent children,
(2) a custodian with those in its custody,
(3) an employer with employees when the employment facilitates the employee's causing harm to third parties, and
(4) a mental health professional with patients.

REST. (3D) TORTS: LIABILITY FOR PHYSICAL HARM § 41(b) (P.F.D. 2005).

As in the last section, these categories appear to be driven by inequality in power, control, or access to information. A word about each of the categories:

- Stating that a parent has a duty of reasonable care with regard to the action's of the parent's minor children is not the same as saying that parents are strictly liable for the torts (or the negligence) of their children. Instead, parents have a duty of reasonable care in regards to their minor children, subject to an argument that the parent's super-vision of the children did not involve any breach. *See* REST. (3D) TORTS: LIABILITY FOR PHYSICAL HARM § 41, cmt. *d* (P.F.D. 2005).

- The custodian situation is one that arises fairly often in real-world cases: Think of the prison that negligently lets the dangerous prisoner escape and the prisoner commits some act of violence on a third person. While the state does not have a tort responsibility to prevent attacks on others, it does have a responsibility to use reasonable care with those whom the state has already incarcerated.

- The employer duty to third parties probably seems the most obscure. Here, think of a nightclub bouncer who uses too much force, or an

---

4. One of the most notorious examples of such a situation was the brutal murder of Kitty Genovese in New York in 1964, witnessed by 38 people, none of whom called the police as she lay bleeding in the street. *See* A.M. ROSENTHAL, THIRTY-EIGHT WITNESSES: THE KITTY GENOVESE CASE (1964).

employer who knows that an employee has battered customers in the past and is still allowed to interact with customers.
- The mental health duty, based on *Tarasoff*, is quite limited, and does not always require a warning to third persons.[5]

QUESTION 3. Controlling Little Jimmy. Little Jimmy, a 7-year-old, has been getting in a lot of trouble in the neighborhood. He has been found to have tortured some of the neighbor's pets, and to have thrown rocks through neighbor's windows. "Kids will be kids" is what Little Jimmy's dad, Big Jimmy, always likes to say. Little Jimmy has now been accused of throwing a rock at Phyllis, an elderly woman who lives across the street. Phyllis suffered a concussion, and has sued Big Jimmy for negligence. Big Jimmy argues that he owes no duty to Phyllis. How should the court rule?

A. The court should accept the argument because Little Jimmy, not big Jimmy, threw the rock that injured Phyllis.
B. The court should accept the argument because parents can never be liable for the torts of their children.
C. The court should reject the argument because parents have a duty to use reasonable care to protect third persons from attack by their minor children.
D. The court should reject the argument because parents are strictly liable for the torts of their children.

ANALYSIS. In limited circumstances, courts recognize a "special relationship" requiring one person to take reasonable care to prevent the other person in the special relationship from injuring a stranger. One of those circumstances arises in the parent-minor child relationship. A parent is not strictly liable for the torts of his minor child. For this reason, Choice **D** is incorrect. But parents can sometimes be liable, if they fail to reasonably supervise their children. For this reason, Choice **B** is incorrect. Choice **A** is incorrect because the suit against Big Jimmy is for negligence, not battery. (It might be that Little Jimmy is liable for battery, for reasons discussed in Chapter 3.) Choice **C** correctly sets forth the legal standard: parents have a duty to use reasonable care to protect third persons from attack by their minor children.

---

5. "A mental health professional has a duty to use customary care in determining whether a patient poses a risk of harm. Depending on the circumstances, once such a patient is identified, reasonable care may require providing appropriate treatment, warning others of the risks posed by the patient, seeking the patient's agreement to a voluntary commitment, making efforts to commit the patient involuntarily, or taking other steps to ameliorate the risk posed by the patient. In some cases, reasonable care may require a warning to someone other than the potential victim, such as parents, law-enforcement officials, or other appropriate government officials." REST. (3D) TORTS: LIABILITY FOR PHYSICAL HARM § 41 cmt. *g* (P.F.D. 2005).

B. Special rules for landowners

One area in which tort law and property law butt heads is in negligence liability for landowners. (The other area we consider in this book, nuisance law, is considered in Chapter 15.) Suppose I have a party at my house and I invite you to attend. You slip on a banana peel in my kitchen, get a concussion, and sue me for negligence.

If we used our normal duty rules, there would be no question that I would owe you a duty: You are a foreseeable plaintiff (because you are in the zone of danger of any risks I create by holding a party), this is not a sports or recreation case, and I am engaged in risk creation.[6] But because of the longstanding influence of property law ("a man's home is his castle" and all that), courts developed special rules in relation to negligence claims against landowners (and land occupiers — I use the term landowners as a shorthand for both).

The traditional formulation divided potential plaintiffs into three categories, and imposed different duties upon landowners *depending upon the status* of the plaintiff.

Status	Description of Status	Duty
Invitee	person invited onto the land, primarily for business purposes	normal duty rule in negligence cases
Licensee	person on land with landowner's permission, including social guest	duty not to create a trap or allow concealed danger to exist on property
Trespasser	one on land without permission	duty to avoid willful and wanton misconduct

See *Robert Addie & Sons (Collieries) Ltd. v. Dumbreck*, [1929] A.C. 358 (H.L.).

As the chart shows, if you slip on the banana peel as a social guest, you would be out of luck under the traditional "trichotomy approach" to landowners' duties. You, as a social guest, would count as a licensee (not an invitee, even though I *invited you* to my party). If you tripped on a banana peel in my kitchen that was not hidden from you as some kind of trap (sometimes called a "latent" as opposed to "patent" defect), then I would have no duty to warn you of the danger and therefore I could not be liable for any negligence in leaving the banana peel on the floor. You'd have a

---

6. If you are wondering why I did not discuss whether there is a special relationship between us (I'm touched, really!), go back and reread the last section: There is no need to consider special relationship questions except in the *absence* of risk creation.

better chance recovering if you fell into a hole I had been digging on my property that was not visible to someone walking in the area.

If, however, a repairman was in your home to repair your refrigerator and slipped on the same banana peel, he would be owed a duty under the traditional approach. Trespassers, unsurprisingly, get the worst treatment under the traditional approach. No duty is owed to warn trespassers of hidden dangers like the hole on the property. The only requirement is to avoid willful and wanton misconduct.

QUESTION 4. Hidden Danger.   Nancy invites James over to her apartment for a visit. During the visit, James uses the bathroom. James cuts himself on one of the handles on the bathroom faucet, severely injuring the nerves in his right hand. He sues Nancy for negligence. Nancy argues she does not owe James a duty of care in a jurisdiction that uses the traditional approach to landowner/land occupier liability.

How should the court rule?

A. Nancy owes James no duty of care because he is a social guest.
B. Nancy owes a duty of care to James, if the danger from the faucet was not easily seen.
C. Nancy owes the normal negligence duty of care to James because he is a foreseeable plaintiff and she was engaged in risk creation.
D. Nancy owes James a duty only to avoid engaging in willful and wanton misconduct.

ANALYSIS.   Under the traditional approach, James is a social guest, meaning he counts as a licensee. Landowners do not owe a duty of reasonable care to licensees; instead landowners must simply warn of hidden dangers or traps. Choice **A** is wrong because it incorrectly states that *no* duty of care is owed to social guests. Choice **C** is wrong because the normal duty rules do not apply either, even though, if this were outside the context of landowners and occupiers, Nancy would owe James a duty for this reason. Choice **D** applies the "willful and wanton" standard applicable to trespassers, not licensees. Choice **B** correctly explains that Nancy owes a duty of care to James, only if the danger from the faucet came from a hidden danger.

Alleviating the Harshness of the Traditional Trichotomy. The traditional rules for landowner liability can be quite harsh in two respects: First, it seems unfair, at least to those of us living in the modern era, that social guests would not be the beneficiaries of the ordinary duty rules that apply outside the landowner context and within the landowner context for business invitees. Why should the refrigerator repairman be treated better than the invited social guest?

The other harshness appeared in the treatment of a child trespasser. Not all trespassers have bad intentions, or are fully aware of the risks on other people's land. Yet children injured when trespassing, even with the full knowledge of the trespasser, usually would lose any negligence suits because the children could not prove that the landowner engaged in wanton or willful misconduct (unless those terms were somehow mangled to allow negligence claims to go forward, as in *Excelsior Wire Rope Co., Ltd. v. Callan,* (1930) A.C. 404).

Though some jurisdictions continue to stick with the trichotomy, *see, e.g., Corley v. Evans,* 835 So.2d 30 (Miss. 2003), others have made some changes.

Attractive Nuisance. Some jurisdictions adopted the attractive nuisance doctrine allowing some children, who were attracted to an artificial condition on a landowner's land (as opposed to a natural condition, like a stream) and who got injured while trespassing, to recover damages in the event the child was too young to appreciate the dangers posed by the condition on the land. *See* REST. (2D) TORTS § 339.[7] Not all children could recover: A child who is old enough to appreciate the risk would be treated like an adult trespasser and not be owed a duty except in the case of willful or wanton misconduct.

Trichotomy to Dichotomy. Some jurisdictions simply collapsed the trichotomy to a dichotomy, treating invitees and licensees as subject to the normal duty rules, preserving the very limited duty rule for trespassers. *See, e.g., Hudson v. Gaitan,* 675 S.W.2d 699 (Tenn. 1984).

Abandoning the Traditional Approach. Finally, some states simply abandoned the traditional approach, holding that the question whether a landowner owed the plaintiff a duty was one to be decided individually in each case, based upon a full consideration of the public policy issues involved. The leading case here is a California Supreme Court case, *Rowland v. Christian,* 443 P.2d 561 (Cal. 1968), adopting a "kitchen sink" approach to the question of duty. The court held that, ordinarily, one person owes a duty of care to another, subject to exceptions as a matter of policy:

> A departure from this fundamental principle involves a balancing of a number of considerations; the major ones are the foreseeability of harm to the plaintiff, the degree of certainty that the plaintiff suffered injury, the closeness of the connection between the defendant's conduct and the injury suffered, the moral blame attached to the defendant's conduct, the policy of preventing future harm, the extent of the burden to the defendant and consequences to the community of imposing a duty to exercise care with resulting liability for breach, and the availability, cost, and prevalence of insurance for the risk involved.

---

7. The Restatement section also requires proof that the landowner knew or had reason to know the condition is one that would attract children to trespass, and that the utility of the condition to the trespasser is slight compared to the risk to the children involved.

Id. at 564. Obviously, a case like *Rowland* gives courts broad leeway to rework the traditional duty rules, ignoring the categorical approach based upon plaintiff's status on the land.

QUESTION 5. Hidden Danger, Take II.   Nancy invites James over to her apartment for a visit. During the visit, James uses the bathroom. James cuts himself on one of the handles on the bathroom faucet, severely injuring the nerves in his right hand. He sues Nancy for negligence. Nancy argues she does not owe James a duty of care in a jurisdiction that has abandoned the traditional approach to landowner/land occupier liability in favor of the *Rowland* approach.

How should the court rule?

A. Nancy owes James no duty of care because he is a social guest.
B. Nancy owes a duty of care to James, if the danger from the faucet was not easily seen.
C. Nancy owes the normal negligence duty of care to James because he is a foreseeable plaintiff and she was engaged in risk creation, unless there is a compelling policy reason not to impose such a duty.
D. Nancy owes James a duty only to avoid engaging in willful and wanton misconduct.

ANALYSIS.   This case, which tracks Question 4 but asks the question under the *Rowland* approach, is based upon the facts of *Rowland*. In *Rowland*, the fact was that the danger of the faucet was hidden, meaning there would still be a duty to social guests under the traditional approach. But the California Supreme Court used the case to abandon the traditional approach and adopt the modern approach which presumes that there is a duty even from landowners, unless there is a compelling policy reason otherwise. Because *Rowland* abandons the categorical approach Choices **A, B,** and **D** are all incorrect. Choice **C** correctly explains that the normal duty rules apply under *Rowland*, even for social guests, unless there is a compelling policy reason to hold that the defendant does not owe a normal duty to the plaintiff.

QUESTION 6. Cliffhanger.   Jack, a 14-year-old boy, and two of his friends sneak onto Ingrid's property, which has access to a cliff at the beach. Ingrid has posted no trespassing posters all over her property. Jack jumps off the cliff and breaks his back. He sues Ingrid for negligence. Ingrid argues that the case cannot go forward because she owes Jack no duty. The jurisdiction has replaced the traditional approach to landowner liability with the dichotomy approach, and it recognizes the attractive nuisance doctrine of the Restatement (2d) of Torts.

How should the court rule on Ingrid's argument?

A. The court should reject Ingrid's argument, under the attractive nuisance doctrine.

B. The court should reject Ingrid's argument because a duty is owed to trespassers under the dichotomy approach.

C. The court should reject Ingrid's argument because Jack is a foreseeable plaintiff and she was engaged in risk creation, unless there is a compelling policy reason not to impose such a duty.

D. The court should accept Ingrid's argument.

ANALYSIS. Under the dichotomy, both licensees and invitees are treated to the normal duty rules. Trespassers continue to be governed by the willful and wanton misconduct approach. For this reason, Choice **B** is incorrect. Choice **C** is incorrect because it states the *Rowland* approach, which rejects the trichotomy and dichotomy approaches.

So the question comes down to Choice **A** or Choice **D**, and application of the attractive nuisance doctrine. Though the jurisdiction recognizes the doctrine as set forth in the Restatement, it cannot help Jack here. This is a *natural* condition on the land, a cliff, and not an artificial one. Also, arguably a 14-year-old can appreciate the risk of jumping off a cliff into the ocean. The correct answer is Choice **D**. Ingrid should win on her motion to have the case ended on grounds she owes Jack no duty.

C. Special rules for claims of negligent infliction of emotional distress

Chapter 6 considered the tort of intentional infliction of emotional distress (IIED). It explained that courts have been wary about allowing plaintiffs to recover damages for emotional distress for two reasons: First, the lack of a market measure for such damages, and second, the possibility that plaintiffs would lie or exaggerate the amount of their distress in order to recover large damages from a jury. So the law developed the IIED tort, but put important limits on recovery for those suffering emotional distress, particularly bystanders who suffered emotional distress from watching actions inflicted on others.

A parallel development occurred in cases in which a defendant's *negligence* (rather than intentional conduct or recklessness) caused emotional distress to plaintiffs. As in the intentional tort area, emotional distress (such as pain and suffering) could always be recovered in negligence cases as *parasitic to* physical harm. So, if I negligently run over your foot with my car, and you have pain and suffering, you may recover damages for your pain and suffering along with your medical bills and lost wages. But suppose I was driving negligently and barely missed running over your foot. You suffered emotional distress from the "near miss." Traditionally, you could not recover for damages in the absence of any "impact." Courts, fearing the expansion of liability for emotional losses, would say that I had *no duty* to you in relation to emotional injuries or use another policy doctrine (such as proximate cause, discussed in Chapter 14) to reach the same result.

Over time, as with the case of IIED, many courts relaxed the rules barring claims of emotional distress that were not accompanied by a physical impact.[8] So long as you are a foreseeable plaintiff within the "zone of danger" of physical impact, you could recover for emotional distress damages as a claim for negligent infliction of emotional distress (NIED). In other words, if there was a good chance I *could have* run you over but didn't, you could recover for your emotional distress damages. The Third Restatement endorses this modern rule. *See* REST. (3D) TORTS: LIABILITY FOR PHYSICAL AND EMOTIONAL HARM § 46(a) (Tentative Draft 2007) ("An actor whose negligent conduct causes serious emotional disturbance to another is subject to liability to the other if the conduct: (a) places the other in imminent danger of bodily harm and the emotional disturbance results from the danger[.]").

QUESTION 7. Plane Crazy. Rufus is on a short commuter flight. The pilot falls asleep in the cockpit and the plane takes a nosedive. Rufus is very frightened. Fortunately, the pilot wakes up just before the plane crashes into the ground, and he is able to bring the plane to a safe stop. Rufus, however, still has nightmares about those few harrowing moments. He sues the pilot for negligence, and the pilot argues that he cannot be liable for negligence because Rufus suffered no physical injuries.

How should the court rule?

A. In a jurisdiction following the traditional approach to negligent infliction of emotional distress, the court should rule for the pilot.

B. In a jurisdiction following the modern approach, Rufus's case should go forward because Rufus was in the zone of physical danger of the pilot's negligence.

C. In all jurisdictions, Rufus cannot recover because he suffered no physical injury.

D. Both A and B, but not C, are correct.

---

8. According to John J. Kircher, *The Four Faces of Tort Law: Liability for Emotional Harm*, 90 MARQ. L. REV. 789, Appendix C (2007), Florida, Georgia, Indiana, Kansas, Kentucky, and Nevada still use the impact rule.

ANALYSIS.   This is a straightforward question, meant to point out the split between the traditional approach and the modern approach to NIED. Under the traditional approach, Rufus would have to show physical impact to recover, which is not present here. That's Choice **A**. Under the modern approach, Rufus could recover even absent physical impact if he was in the zone of danger of such impact. That's Choice **B**. They are both right, meaning Choice **D** is the best answer. Choice **C** incorrectly states the traditional rule as though it applied in all jurisdictions.

Emotional Distress Particularly Foreseeable, But Some Competing Policy Concerns. As some courts have moved from the traditional to the modern approach to NIED, they have also recognized a small class of cases in which there is no danger of physical impact, but emotional distress is particularly foreseeable from negligence and on policy grounds justifiably recoverable. Consider, for example, a funeral home that mishandles human remains. In such cases, the conduct is highly likely to result in emotional distress to the surviving family members, and concerns about false or exaggerated claims are not as worrisome. On policy grounds, courts are becoming more willing to allow NIED claims in these cases. *See* Rest. (3d) Torts: Liability for Physical and Emotional Harm § 46(b) (Tentative Draft 2007) ("An actor whose negligent conduct causes serious emotional disturbance to another is subject to liability to the other if the conduct: . . . (b) occurs in the course of specified categories of activities, undertakings, or relationships in which negligent conduct is especially likely to cause serious emotional disturbance.").

Even in cases in which emotional distress is particularly foreseeable, courts on other policy grounds sometimes reject such claims. For example, some courts have rejected claims based upon fear of getting a disease or illness after exposure to a chemical or substance, out of fear that there would be too many suits over too long a time period to allow such claims to go forward. In California, for example, emotional distress damages are available for fear of future injury only if the plaintiff can prove she is more likely than not to actually get the disease. *See Potter v. Firestone Tire & Rubber Co.,* 863 P.2d 795 (Cal. 1993). There is a wide variation in how courts deal with NIED cases in situations not involving a plaintiff in the zone of physical danger.

QUESTION 8. Dr. Oops.   Mary goes to Dr. Oops because she is not feeling well. Dr. Oops orders some blood tests. He negligently misinterprets the test results, and tells Mary that she had a sexually transmitted disease. Mary tells her husband Roger, who tests negative for the STD. Because of the test result, Roger believes Mary has been cheating on him. They fight and get a divorce. Mary later discovers that Dr. Oops gave the wrong diagnosis. Mary sues Dr. Oops for negligence. Can Mary's case go forward?

A. No in any jurisdiction, because Mary was not in the zone of physical danger from Dr. Oops's conduct.
B. No in any jurisdiction, unless Dr. Oops personally drew blood from Mary.
C. Yes in some jurisdictions, because emotional distress in such circumstances is particularly foreseeable.
D. Yes in all jurisdictions, because persons are always liable for emotional distress they negligently cause.

ANALYSIS. This question parallels the last one and is meant for you to recognize that jurisdictions handle these kinds of claims differently. Some courts, seeing that emotional distress could be particularly foreseeable from a negligent STD diagnosis, will allow such a claim to go forward. Other courts, worrying about an explosion of emotional distress cases, could hold that the case cannot go forward. Because this is jurisdiction-specific, we can eliminate Choices **A** and **D**. Choice **B** is a bit tricky. Even assuming Dr. Oops personally drew blood from Mary, her emotional distress was not from the needle puncture. He was not negligent in relation to the needle puncture. Instead, his negligence was in *interpreting the test results*. For this reason, even in jurisdictions following the impact rule, this impact would not count. Choice **C** correctly explains that some jurisdictions will allow this case to go forward because emotional distress in these circumstances is particularly foreseeable.

The facts of this case are based upon *Molien v. Kaiser Found. Hosps.*, 616 P.2d 813 (Cal. 1980). In the actual case, the California Supreme Court allowed the *husband* to sue for the negligent diagnosis given to the wife, ruling that he was a *foreseeable plaintiff* of the doctor's negligence.

Bystanders. As we saw in Chapter 6 involving IIED claims by bystanders who witness violence against someone else, courts have struggled with this issue for some time. In the IIED context, both the Second and Third Restatement put sharp limits on recoveries of bystanders. A similar evolution has occurred in the context of NIED.

Initially bystanders could not recover for the emotional distress of witnessing bodily injury inflicted on another unless, in some jurisdictions, the bystanders *themselves* were in the zone of physical danger (imagine brother and sister crossing the street, and the car hits brother and barely misses sister). But most courts have relaxed the rules for bystander recoveries.

The leading case setting forth the relaxed approach is the California Supreme Court's decision in *Dillon v. Legg*, 441 P.2d 912 (Cal. 1968). In *Dillon*, a mother and daughter watched as the mother's other daughter was run over by a car. Under the old rules, the daughter who was not hit could recover for her emotional distress because she was in the zone of physical danger, but the mother, who was still on the sidewalk, could not. The California Supreme Court held that both mother and surviving daughter could recover damages for emotional distress caused by witnessing the incident. The Court set forth a three-part test for when a duty arises in bystander cases:

> (1) Whether plaintiff was located near the scene of the accident as contrasted with one who was a distance away from it. (2) Whether the shock resulted from a direct emotional impact upon plaintiff from the sensory and contemporaneous observance of the accident, as contrasted with learning of the accident from others after its occurrence. (3) Whether plaintiff and the victim were closely related, as contrasted with an absence of any relationship or the presence of only a distant relationship.

Courts have tinkered with and altered the *Dillon* factors over time, giving lots of fodder for lawyers (and law students completing their first-year legal writing assignments). Many questions arose: What if the bystander witnessed the negligent injury on television? What if the bystander heard, rather than saw, defendant negligently inflict the injury? Can non-married cohabitants, including gay couples who cannot marry under state law, recover under these rules?

Courts have not given uniform answers to these questions, but the trend has been to limit recovery to those bystanders suffering serious emotional distress from (1) perceiving the negligently inflicted physical injury at the time it happens and (2) who are close family members of the person suffering the bodily injury. *See* REST. (3D) TORTS: LIABILITY FOR PHYSICAL AND EMOTIONAL HARM § 47 (Tentative Draft 2007).

QUESTION 9. Unequal Bystanders.   Peg and Meg are college roommates and best friends. For years, Meg has been estranged from her mother, Katrina. After talking about it a great deal, Meg agrees to let Peg arrange a meeting with Katrina to try to patch things up. The three meet on a street corner downtown. As Meg is crossing the street, while the others stand on the curb, she is hit by Dan, who is driving carelessly after downing a six-pack of beer at home. Meg is killed in the accident, which was witnessed by both Peg and Katrina. Both of them sue Dan for negligent infliction of emotional distress. Dan argues he does not owe either of the plaintiffs a duty of care in these circumstances. In a majority of jurisdictions, how would the court rule?

A. Peg can recover, if she experienced serious emotional distress.

B. Katrina can recover, if she experienced serious emotional distress.

C. Both Peg and Katrina can recover, if each experienced serious emotional distress.

> **D.** Neither Peg nor Katrina can recover because Dan owes a duty only to those in the zone of physical danger.

ANALYSIS.   This question tests you on the bystander factor of immediate family relationship under the *Dillon* test and similar tests. The mother is an immediate family member; she can recover damages for witnessing the death of her daughter *if* she suffered serious emotional distress. (Because the two were estranged, she might have trouble proving this element.) The best friend and college roommate, however, cannot recover, no matter how serious her emotional distress (and even if it is much more severe than the mother's) because she is not an immediate family member. Because Katrina can recover and Peg cannot, Choice **B** is correct and Choices **A** and **C** are incorrect. Choice **D** is incorrect because most jurisdictions agree with *Dillon* that in some circumstances someone outside the zone of physical danger may recover as a bystander for negligently inflicted emotional distress.

D.   The Closer: Once more on duty versus breach

As Part II of this book comes to a close, it is worth reminding you once again to make sure to separate the questions of duty and breach. If the driver in the last question was not negligent, he may owe a duty of care to the mother, but the driver would not be negligent because there is no breach. The same goes for landowners who are careful but who nonetheless face lawsuits from those injured on their land, and for those in special relationships, such as teachers, who have a duty to make sure the students they are in charge of stay safe but who will not be liable if they act reasonably and the student nonetheless gets hurt.

To put it another way, the breach question is always a *factual question and judgment call* about whether the defendant failed to use reasonable care to avoid a reasonably foreseeable risk to the plaintiff. The duty question, in contrast, is a *legal and policy question* about whether defendants should be required to use reasonable care in particular circumstances. Be sure to keep those questions distinct.

> **QUESTION 10. Pour Me One More.**   Joe the bartender has closed up his bar just after 2 A.M. There is a knock at the door from Ray, who says that his friend, Barney, has just been shot. Ray asks to come in to use the telephone to call 911. Joe refuses to let him in. Eventually someone drives by who allows Ray to use the telephone to call for an ambulance. Unfortunately,

because of the delay, Barney suffers permanent paralysis, which doctors believe they could have prevented had Ray been allowed to call from Joe's phone.

Barney sues Joe for negligence for not allowing Ray to use the phone. What is the strongest argument that Joe can raise against liability for negligence?

A. Joe owed Barney no duty because he did not create the risk that led to Barney's injuries.

B. Joe owed Barney no duty because Barney was not a foreseeable plaintiff.

C. Joe did not breach any duty as measured by a balancing test.

D. Joe did not breach because he customarily does not help strangers.

ANALYSIS. The strongest argument here is one based on duty, not breach. The question is whether Joe, like John Monster in the earlier hypotheticals, must assist in a rescue. Here, he does not have to actually help Barney, but not get in Ray's way in using Joe's phone. Because Joe did not engage in risk creation in relation to Barney's injury, his strongest argument is no duty, making Choice **A** correct. (A California intermediate appellate court, *Soldano v. O'Daniels*, 190 Cal. Rptr. 310, 317 (App. 1983), held that the bartender did have a duty not to get in the way of the rescue, but this is likely not an opinion a majority of courts would accept.) Choice **B** is incorrect because Barney looks like a foreseeable plaintiff. Joe knows if he doesn't let Ray use the phone, Barney could suffer further injury. Choices **C** and **D** are wrong because if there were a duty, there is certainly breach. The cost of using the phone to make a free 911 call is negligible under a balancing test. There is no industry custom that applies here. In sum, this is a question raising serious issues about duty, but only trivial questions about breach.

✸ Rick's picks

1.	Monster Returns	C
2.	Give Me the Keys	A
3.	Controlling Little Jimmy	C
4.	Hidden Danger	B
5.	Hidden Danger, Take II	C
6.	Cliffhanger	D
7.	Plane Crazy	D
8.	Dr. Oops	C
9.	Unequal Bystanders	B
10.	Pour Me One More	A

PART III

Causation

13

Actual Cause: "But for" Causation, Its Complications, and Exceptions

A. Actual causation: The "but for" test

1. The basics

You will recall from Chapter 2 that every tort has the same structure. Speaking generically, the plaintiff must prove:

1. That defendant engaged in the requisite tortious conduct
2. Actual causation
3. Proximate causation
4. Damages

The first two parts of this book focused only on the first of these elements, the requisite tortious conduct for a variety of intentional torts and negligence, along with affirmative defenses for these torts.[1] In this part, we consider elements 2 and 3 of the prima facie case for each tort, *actual causation* and *proximate causation*. As I hope to make clear, actual causation is primarily a *factual question* asking something about the state of the world in relation to the tort. In contrast, proximate causation is the poorly chosen term for a *policy question*, much like the duty question in the negligence case (discussed in Chapters 11 and 12), that has very little to do with the question of cause. This chapter considers actual cause; the next considers proximate cause.

Actual causation, also sometimes referred to as "cause-in-fact" or "factual cause," usually involves resolution of the following issue:

The plaintiff must prove (under the usual preponderance of the evidence standard) that but for defendant's tortious conduct, the plaintiff's injury would not have occurred.

This test asks about cause in a straightforward way: If defendant didn't act in a tortious way, would the injury that plaintiff sues for still have happened? Let's take an easy example to flesh this out. Alice punches Ralph in the nose because he says something insulting. Ralph's nose breaks. Let's assume Ralph can prove the tortious conduct portion of the prima facie case for battery. Can Ralph also prove the actual causation element?

Yes. Imagine that everything else in the world is the same, except Alice did not engage in the tortious conduct. Is it more likely than not that Ralph's nose would be broken? No. We then conclude—wholly in line with common sense—that but for Alice's tortious conduct in punching Ralph in the nose, his injury would not have happened. As with the rest of the prima facie case, proof is by a preponderance of the evidence, the "more likely than not" standard.

Now your first reaction might be that proof of tortious conduct *necessarily* proves causation. That is not the case. Imagine this scenario: A driver is driving drunk down the street, very slowly. A small child runs out into the middle of the street. The driver slams on her brakes, but hits the child nonetheless. The child sustains serious injuries. Experts testify that no matter how quickly the driver would have reacted, there would not have been enough time to stop the car to avoid hitting the child. Under this scenario, though the behavior of driving drunk was tortious for the tort of negligence (whether under a balancing test or through *negligence per se*), the driver's negligence was *not* an actual cause of injury. Again, imagine the world where everything else is the same, except the driver did not engage in the tortious conduct. Would the child have sustained the same injuries?

---

1. Part IV of this book will focus on the requisite tortious conduct and defenses for strict liability torts. Part V will focus on the requisite tortious conduct and defenses for the products liability torts.

Because the answer to that question is "yes," the driver's tortious conduct was not a "but for" cause of the child's injury. The child cannot prove the prima facie case and cannot recover damages from the driver.

Note that there will always be more than one "but for" cause of an accident: Imagine a driver who is driving drunk down the street and fails to see a pedestrian who crosses the street without looking. Both are negligent, and both parties' negligence is a but for cause of injury. If *either one* of them had not acted negligently, the injury would not have occurred.

QUESTION 1. Going Overboard. Clarisse is a passenger on the S.S. Danger, a ship sailing from New York to Florida. Clarisse accidentally falls into the water. The S.S. Danger employees forgot to install life preservers on the ship. Clarisse nearly drowns and suffers serious injuries to her lungs because of how long she is in the water. The ship owners eventually get a lifeboat out to her and pull her out of the water. Experts agree that if she had a life preserver thrown to her she could have avoided the lung damage.

Clarisse sues the S.S. Danger for negligence for its failure to have life preservers on board. Assume Clarisse can prove the tortious conduct portion of the prima facie case for negligence. What will she have to prove in relation to *actual causation*?

A. That she, more likely than not, would not have fallen overboard but for the defendant's negligence.

B. That she certainly would not have fallen overboard but for the defendant's negligence.

C. That she, more likely than not, would not have suffered the lung damage but for the defendant's negligence.

D. That she certainly would not have suffered the lung damage but for the defendant's negligence

---

ANALYSIS. Let's begin with the standard of proof. The plaintiff must prove but for causation by a preponderance of the evidence. There is no need to prove anything with certainty. For that reason, we can eliminate Choice **B** and Choice **D**, which speak in terms of certainty. Next, it is important to connect the "but for" cause to the defendant's tortious conduct. The tortious conduct here is the failure to have the life preservers which caused the lung damage. The defendant did nothing to knock Clarisse into the water in the first place. So Choice **C**, which discusses "but for" cause in terms of the lung damage caused by the failure to have the life preservers, is the correct choice. Choice **A**, speaking in terms of Clarisse being knocked into the water, is incorrect.

2. Evidentiary issues: General and specific causation

Though the "but for" test for actual causation is straightforward and in-tuitive, *answering* the question in particular cases can present difficult factual problems for a jury. How would experts *know*, for example, that the driver would not have been able to avoid hitting the child if the driver had not been drunk? In the real world, the child's lawyer would likely find an expert who would testify to the contrary. The evidentiary issue is this: In many cases we don't know for sure what the world would have looked like if the defendant did not engage in the tortious conduct. It is easy to imagine Ralph's nose without Alice's punch, but in many important torts cases the causation issue is much murkier. Between competing experts in the driver/child example above, the question of causation may turn on which expert comes across as more credible or knowledgeable.

When the alleged negligence involves technical issues — was it a faulty wire or something else that caused a plane's engine to stall during a flight, leading to a crash? — jurors necessarily will rely upon expert testimony regarding causation. That testimony can be in sharp conflict because of the limits of our scientific knowledge.

Causation issues present special evidentiary problems in cases of toxic torts and similar issues in which there is a long period between the tortious conduct and the plaintiff's injury. For example, imagine that a plaintiff lives near defendant's factory, and 20 years later develops cancer. Let's take it as a given that the defendant was negligent 20 years earlier in releasing certain dangerous chemicals into the nearby river. In order for plaintiff to prevail, plaintiff will also need to prove causation, which often breaks down into two questions:

1. *General Causation.* Can defendant's tortious actions lead to *these types* of injuries?
2. *Specific Causation.* Did defendant's tortious conduct *in this case* lead to plaintiff's specific injuries?

Proof of either or both of these elements can be difficult in specific cases. On general causation, it might be that scientists have established a link between defendant's chemicals and one type of cancer. But plaintiff has contracted *a different type* of cancer. Plaintiff's case can fail if the plaintiff cannot prove it is more likely than not that defendant's chemicals caused his cancer, and without proof of general causation, this will be impossible under the "but for" test.

Even if plaintiff can prove general causation — that defendant's chemicals can cause the kind of cancer he has contracted — there still may be a specific causation problem: How do we know that the plaintiff contracted the cancer *because* of exposure to defendant's chemicals, and not for some other reason? For example, suppose that in the plaintiff's town, scientists would predict that there would be 10 cases of a particular type of cancer diagnosed in a five-year period. In this town, however, there were 13 cases. That information, alone, would not be enough for a plaintiff to prove it is more likely than not that *his* cancer was caused by the defendant's chemicals. To put the matter differently, even if we are convinced that there are three "extra" cancers in the area caused by the defendant's chemical dump, none of the plaintiffs can recover anything because none of them can prove that it is more likely than not that exposure to defendant's chemicals caused his injury. The end result is that because of the causation requirement, the defendant may not face liability even for admittedly tortious conduct that almost certainly caused damages to some (unidentified) people in the community.[2]

QUESTION 2. Going Overboard, Take II.   Clarisse is a passenger on the S.S. Danger, a ship sailing from New York to Florida. Clarisse accidentally falls into the water. The S.S. Danger employees forgot to install life preservers on the ship. The ship owners eventually get a lifeboat out to her and pull her out of the water. Clarisse nearly drowned, and suffered serious injuries to her lungs because of how long she was in the water. Clarisse could not swim, and experts disagree over whether she could have avoided the lung damage had a life preserver been thrown to her immediately upon going overboard. Clarisse's expert says the life preserver would have allowed her to avoid her injury. The defendant's expert disagrees.

Clarisse sues the S.S. Danger for negligence for its failure to have life preservers on board. Assume Clarisse can prove the tortious conduct portion of the prima facie case for negligence. Will Clarisse be able to prove actual causation?

A. Yes, but only if the jury concludes it is more likely than not that she would not have suffered the lung damage but for defendant's negligence.

B. Yes, because plaintiff's expert concluded it is more likely than not that she would not have suffered the lung damage but for defendant's negligence.

C. No, because if there are conflicting expert opinions a jury cannot make a conclusion about causation based upon a preponderance of the evidence.

---

2. Given this reality, it is not surprising that plaintiffs' lawyers have found experts who are willing to testify without much scientific proof that a defendant's tortious conduct was an actual cause of plaintiff. Such testimony has led to sharp battles over how reliable an expert's testimony on causation must be before it is admissible for a jury to consider. On the federal level, the modern battle began with the Supreme Court case, *Daubert v. Merrell Dow Pharmaceuticals*, 509 U.S. 579 (1993). The issues raised there are more often discussed in an Evidence class rather than a Torts class, but it is a key case for both of these areas of the law.

> **D.** No, because defendant's expert concluded it is more likely than not that Clarisse would have suffered the lung damage but for defendant's negligence.

ANALYSIS. This is a variation on the first question. In the first question, the experts agreed on the causation issue: Clarisse would not have suffered the lung damage but for the defendant's failure to have the life preservers on board. Now, we are told that the experts are split: Clarisse's expert says life preservers would have made a difference; unsurprisingly, the defense expert says they would not have mattered because Clarisse did not know how to swim. Assuming both experts are allowed to testify on their causation theories (a question left for Evidence law rather than Tort law), resolution of the causation question will be in the hands of the jury. The jury will have to determine, based upon the preponderance of the evidence standard, whether it is more likely than not that Clarisse would not have suffered the lung damage "but for" the defendant's failure to have life preservers.

Choices **B** and **D** are wrong for the same reason. A jury need not credit the expert testimony of either the defendant or the plaintiff if it is opposed by the other side. The jury can make an independent judgment. For similar reasons, Choice **C** is incorrect: The jury can make a conclusion, indeed it will be told to make a conclusion, in the face of conflicting expert evidence on causation. Choice **A** is the correct choice: Clarisse will win the causation point only *if* she can prove by a preponderance of the evidence that the defendant's failure to take the precaution of having the life preservers was a "but for" cause of her injury.

QUESTION 3. Shot in the Dark. Wayne was born with autism. His parents believe that the autism was caused by the measles vaccine given to Wayne as an infant. Wayne's parents sue the vaccine makers on Wayne's behalf alleging that the vaccine is faulty. The vaccine manufacturers demonstrate that every major study of childhood vaccines and autism has concluded that there is no link between the vaccines and autism. Wayne has not found an expert to testify to the contrary. The vaccine manufacturers move to have the case dismissed on grounds Wayne has no proof of causation.

How should the court rule on the manufacturer's motion on actual causation?

A. The court should grant it because there is no proof of general causation.

B. The court should grant it because the benefits of marketing the vaccine exceed the risks.

C. The court should deny it because even if there is no proof of general causation, Wayne might be able to prove specific causation.
D. The court should deny it if marketing the vaccine was in fact tortious.

ANALYSIS. These kinds of cases are real. *See* Gardiner Harris, *Opening Statements in Case on Autism and Vaccinations,* N.Y. Times, June 12, 2007, http://www.nytimes.com/2007/06/12/us/12vaccine.html. (As of this writing, the actual cases are ongoing in a special court, the U.S. Court of Federal Claims, http://www.uscfc.uscourts.gov/docket-omnibus-autism-proceeding.)   Under the fact pattern as I have written it, the defendants have presented evidence that there is no "link" between autism and the vaccine, and the plaintiffs have presented nothing to prove general causation. The absence of a link is an absence of proof of general causation, which will doom Wayne's case. And in the absence of proof of general causation (can the substance cause this type of injury generally?), there can be no proof of specific causation (did the substance cause *this plaintiff's injury?*). Choice **A** states the correct answer. Choice **B** is wrong because it is irrelevant: Whether or not the product would fail some balancing test goes to tortious conduct (under a negligence or products liability theory), not to the question of causation. Choice **C** is wrong because if there is no proof of general causation, there can be no proof of specific causation: In this context, if there is no proof that measles vaccines can cause *anyone's* autism, there's necessarily no proof that the measles vaccine caused *Wayne's* autism. Choice **D** is wrong because proof of tortious conduct does not excuse proof of causation. Both are needed for plaintiff's prima facie case.

3. *Incorporation in* negligence per se *test*

If you have already read Chapter 9, you will recall that one of the five ways of proving breach in a negligence case is through defendant's violation of a statute.[3] To use *negligence per se*, the plaintiff must prove five elements (the defendant's case as an affirmative defense appears in parentheses):

1. *A criminal statute, ordinance, or administrative regulation imposes a specific duty upon someone for the protection of others (or, in the case of plaintiff's negligence, for plaintiff's own protection).*
2. *The defendant (plaintiff) neglects to perform that duty.*
3. *Plaintiff is within the class of people whom the statute was designed to protect.*
4. *The statute was designed to protect against the type of accident the defendant (plaintiff) causes.*

---

3. Plaintiff's negligence in a contributory or comparative negligence case can also be proven through these factors.

5. *Plaintiff's injuries were caused by defendant's (plaintiff's) violation of the statute, ordinance, or regulation.*

The highlighted fifth element of the *negligence per se* test simply incorporates the "but for" test for actual causation. Consider again the example that started this chapter: the drunk driving defendant whose car hits the child. If, as suggested in that initial example, the child would have been hit *regardless* of the defendant's drunken impairment, then the *negligence per se* test would fail to hold the driver liable. The jury would not be able to conclude that but for the driver's violation of an applicable anti-drunk driving statute, the injury would have occurred.

The other point worth making regarding the connection between *negligence per se* and actual causation is that the actual causation issue gets tricky for students when there are problems with the *fourth element* of the *negligence per se* test (the "harm within the risk" element). Consider again the facts of Question 7 from Chapter 9:

> A state statute bars anyone but police officers from bringing weapons to school. James, an eighth-grader, brought his parent's gun to school (he made sure it was not loaded) for show-and-tell. As he was showing the gun to a friend, Amy, in the hallway, he carelessly dropped it, and it landed on Amy's foot, breaking three of her toes. Amy sues James for negligence. May she rely upon *negligence per se*?

As we saw there, the answer to the question was that the *negligence per se* claim would fail, because of the fourth element: Anti-weapon statutes are designed to prevent individuals from being injured by weapons *being used as weapons*. Here, Amy was hurt because James dropped the weapon and it broke her toe. The same injury could have occurred if James dropped a heavy book. What makes bringing a weapon onto campus dangerous is not its *weight*.

The point to recognize here, however, is that Amy *could successfully prove* the fifth element of the *negligence per se* test, actual causation. But for James's violation of the statute, this injury would not have occurred. That is, if James complied with the statute, he never would have brought the gun to school and dropped it on Amy's foot.

For some reason, students often have problems with this explanation. They say: Yes, but he might have dropped a book instead of a gun. Maybe so. But we are asking under a preponderance of the evidence test whether it is more likely than not that *that injury* would have happened *at that time* had James not violated the statute. The answer is no, and therefore Amy would be able to prove actual causation. (Amy still loses because of her failure to prove the fourth element.)

QUESTION 4. ***Negligence Per Se* Train-ing.**   Bob Berry is driving his train through Sugar Notch Borough. The speed limit is 40 mph. Berry is driving at 60 mph. The borough has negligently maintained trees along the train tracks. One of the trees falls at exactly the moment that Berry's train passes, damaging the train. Berry sues Sugar Notch Borough for negligence. The borough concedes it was negligent, but argues that Berry's damages should be reduced for Berry's comparative negligence, which it plans to prove through *negligence per se*. Berry responds by claiming any violation of the statute was not an actual cause of his injury.

How should the court rule on Berry's argument?

A. The court should accept the argument because the accident could just as easily have happened if the train was going at 40 mph.
B. The court should accept the argument because there is no question that Berry violated the statute.
C. The court should accept the argument because Sugar Notch Borough's maintenance of the trees, not Berry's conduct, caused the plaintiff's injury.
D. The court should reject the argument.

ANALYSIS.   This case is based upon *Berry v. Sugar Notch Borough*, 43 A. 240 (Pa. 1899). The speeds were much slower, but the facts are basically the same. Here, plaintiff is arguing that his negligence cannot be used to lessen his damages because his speeding was not an actual cause of the injury. This argument should fail, and Choice **D** is the correct one. This is a case of being in the wrong place at the wrong time. It took the train speeding *to exactly 60 mph* for the train to arrive precisely when the tree is going to fall. Had Berry not been speeding (or had he been speeding *even more*, a point we will return to in the next chapter), this injury would not have happened.[4]

Choice **A** is wrong as a matter of *fact*. Had Berry been going only 40 mph, the tree would have fallen before the train arrived and this injury (the damage caused by the tree falling on top of the train) would not have happened. Choice **B** is wrong because under the *negligence per se* test being used in a comparative negligence context, it is not enough to show that the plaintiff violated the statute. Instead, the defendant must show all five elements are met. Choice **C** is wrong because it incorrectly assumes that there can be only one "but for" cause of an injury. That is not the case. Both defendant's tortious conduct and plaintiff's conduct can be "but for" causes of plaintiff's injury.

---

4. If your intuition is that Berry's speeding should not count against him, it is because there is a *proximate cause problem* (equivalent to the fourth element of the *negligence per se* test), an issue we return to in the next chapter.

4. Special objective causation rule for informed consent cases

In Chapter 9, we considered the special tortious conduct rules in medical informed consent cases: Informed consent rules require (with two exceptions not relevant now) that medical professionals disclose *material* risks to patients of alternative therapies and treatments. What counts as such a risk? "[A]ll risks potentially affecting the decision [whether or not to undergo a certain treatment] must be unmasked." *Canterbury v. Spence*, 464 F.2d 772 (D.C. Cir. 1972). Here, we consider a special actual causation rule that the *Canterbury* court announced.

Let's take a case in which a surgeon fails to disclose a risk of paralysis from back surgery to the patient. The patient has the surgery and becomes paralyzed, suing the doctor for lack of informed consent. The tortious conduct question is whether the failure to disclose a risk of paralysis presents a *material risk*. Let's assume the jury believes that it is. In a normal torts case, we would then ask the actual causation question: Was the failure of the doctor to disclose material risks an *actual cause* of the injury? In other words, if the doctor had disclosed the material risks, would the patient have made a different choice about the surgery and not become paralyzed?

The *Canterbury* court, however, feared that such testimony from the plaintiff would be self-serving (though that's always a danger with all party testimony). So instead the court adopted, and most courts have followed, with the adoption of "an 'objective' test of causation. This means that the plaintiff cannot recover merely by showing that she herself would have refused the injury-causing operation had she been fully informed. She will have to go further and show that a reasonable person would also have refused it." DAN B. DOBBS & PAUL H. HAYDEN, TORTS AND COMPENSATION 411 (5th ed. 2005).[5]

This is an odd test — I am aware of no other area of the law imposing this "objective" test of causation — made even stranger by the fact that the *Canterbury* court allows the plaintiff herself to testify as to what a reasonable person in her position would have done. If this testimony is going to come in through the back door, it makes sense to allow it in the front.

QUESTION 5. Plaintiff Foaming at the Mouth. Pauline comes into the emergency room showing symptoms of infections with rabies. She had recently been bitten by a raccoon in her backyard. She consents to a series of injections, without which she would be likely to develop

---

5. Dobbs and Hayden note that "[s]everal courts have sought a compromise saying that the issue should be judged by the reasonable person standard in light of the plaintiff's personal fears and religious beliefs." *Id.*

rabies and die. The doctor does not tell her that the rabies shots are very painful, and that there is a risk she would not be able to engage in normal activities for a few months because of the intense pain. Pauline has intense pain and sues the doctor for failing to inform her of the risks of such intense pain. In proving her case against the doctor:

A. Pauline must prove that the risk of intense pain was a material one.
B. Pauline must prove that the doctor failed to disclose a risk of treatment.
C. Pauline must prove that a reasonable person in her position would have decided not to undergo the treatment had all the material risks been disclosed.
D. Pauline must prove **A** and **C**, but not **B**.

ANALYSIS.   In order for Pauline to win her suit, she will have to show that the risk of intense pain that the doctor failed to inform her about was a *material* one and, under the objective standard of actual causation applicable only in informed consent cases, that a reasonable person in her position would have decided not to undergo the treatment had all the material risks been disclosed. It is not enough for her to prove that the doctor failed to disclose *a risk* of treatment; only material risks count. Because Choices **A** and **C** are correct and **B** is not, Choice **D** is the best answer.

B.   Exception for independent concurrent causation

Almost all cases get decided under the but for actual causation test, which either works (as when Alice punches Ralph) or doesn't (as when the cancer patient cannot connect up her cancer with defendant's chemicals). But in a rare set of cases, when actual causation under the "but for" test fails, one of three other means of proving causation is potentially employed:

    a. independent concurrent causation
    b. alternative liability
    c. market share liability

Though these are interesting doctrines and consume a fair bit of time in a Torts class, in the real world their application is quite limited. It is usually "but for" causation at issue in the vast majority of torts cases. But now we take up these interesting — if rare — alternatives, beginning with independent concurrent causation.

Figure 13-1 illustrates the problem of independent concurrent causation. Imagine a situation where Person *A* and Person *B* each start a fire negligently

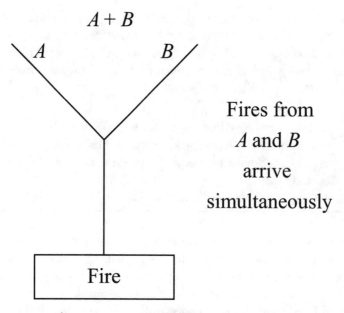

$$A + B$$

A B

Fires from
A and *B*
arrive
simultaneously

Fire

Figure 13-1

and independently of one another. The fire's join and burn down plaintiff's barn. Experts agree that either fire alone would have burned down plaintiff's barn in exactly the same way.[6]

Under the traditional "but for" causation test, if plaintiff sued either *A* or *B*, plaintiff would lose. As to Person *A*, we cannot say that but for Person *A*'s tortious conduct in starting the first fire, the barn would not have burned down. It still would have burned down, thanks to Person *B*'s fire. The same logic would apply to a claim against Person *B*. The upshot of the analysis is that if we apply our usual theory of "but for" causation, the plaintiff loses even though (1) both Person *A* and Person *B* were negligent and (2) either fire alone would have been enough to burn down the barn. The defendants would just be lucky enough that the other fire has come through at exactly the same time.

To deal with this (albeit rare) problem of "independent concurrent causation" (the term should make more sense now), the courts have created a special rule: When there are two independent causes, either one of which would have been enough to cause the same indivisible injury to the plaintiff, both defendants are liable for the damage.[7] *See* REST. (3D) TORTS: LIABILITY FOR PHYSICAL HARM § 27 (P.F.D. No. 1, 2005) ("If multiple acts exist, each of

6. Students are tempted to fight the hypothetical: How do we know either fire would have done the same damage? Taking the facts as a given will help you to focus on the interesting legal issue.
7. More technically, the two are "jointly and severally liable" for the damage, meaning that if only one of the two defendants is found, or can pay, that defendant must pay the entire damage. More on that concept in Chapter 22.

which alone would have been a factual cause under [the usual "but for" test of § 26], each act is regarded as a factual cause of the harm.")[8]

Application of this doctrine is limited. It does not apply:

- when Person A's conduct leads to plaintiff's loss, even if Person B's conduct would have led to the same loss for plaintiff at a later time.
- when Person A's conduct would have been enough to cause plaintiff's injury but Person B's injury would not be (such as if Person A's fire is much larger than Person B's fire, and they join up before burning down the barn). In that circumstance, Person A is an actual cause under the "but for" test, and Person B is not.
- when Person A's conduct causes harm that is divisible from Person B's conduct (as when Person A burns down plaintiff's farm and Person B burns down plaintiff's house). In such circumstances, each defendant is liable for the harm he caused.

QUESTION 6. Twice Burned.   Person A and Person B each start a fire negligently and independently of one another. The fire started by Person A burns down plaintiff's barn. The fire started by Person B comes through five minutes after Person A's fire. Experts agree that if Person A's fire had not burned down plaintiff's barn, the barn would have been burned by the fire started by Person B. Plaintiff sues Person A and Person B for negligence. Person B argues to the court that she cannot be liable because plaintiff cannot prove actual cause. How should the court rule?

A. The court should agree with Person B because two people can never both be actual causes of the same injury.

B. The court should agree with Person B because Person B' actions were not a but for cause of injury and the independent concurrent causation doctrine is inapplicable on these facts.

C. The court should reject Person B's argument because Person B's actions were a but for cause of injury.

D. The court should reject Person B's argument because even though Person B's actions were not a but for cause of injury, a jury could find causation under the independent concurrent causation doctrine.

ANALYSIS.   The following illustration in Figure 13-2 shows the difference between these facts and the facts of the original hypothetical illustrating independent concurrent causation.

---

8. As the Restatement explains, "courts have long imposed liability when a tortfeasor's conduct, while not necessary for the outcome, would have been a factual cause if the other competing cause had not been operating." REST. (3D) TORTS: LIABILITY FOR PHYSICAL HARM § 27 cmt. a (P.F.D. No. 1, 2005).

What if Fire from *A* gets there first?

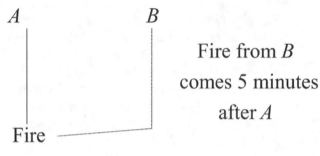

Figure 13-2

Under these facts, the fire started by Person *A* is a but for cause of the injury, and *B*'s fire is not. Though it is true that five minutes *later* the same injury would have happened, we look at causation only at the time of the actual injury. Nor is this a situation of independent concurrent causation. *Focusing on the fire that actually happened*, without Person *A*, the injury would not have occurred. Without Person *B*, the same injury would have occurred. Now there's something unfair or whimsical about the difference between the outcomes in Figures 13-1 and 13-2: After all, in both cases both defendants were negligent and started fires with the potential to burn down plaintiff's barn. But because of serendipity, both Person *A* and Person *B* are liable when the fires hit at the same time, but the person whose fire gets there first is solely liable in these alternative circumstances.

Choice **B** correctly explains that Person *B* wins because plaintiff cannot win under either the but for doctrine or the independent concurrent causation doctrine. Choices **C** and **D** are wrong for the same reason. Choice **A** is wrong because it states an incorrect principle of law: Two persons can both be actual causes of an injury to a plaintiff.

C.   Exception for alternative liability (*Summers v. Tice* rule)

Another rare exception to the but for test goes under the label "alternative liability," and it is a burden shifting doctrine. A California Supreme Court

Alternative liability: *A* or *B*

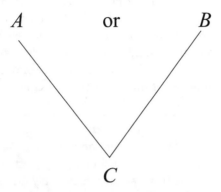

Who shot *C*? *A* or *B*?

Figure 13-3

case, *Summers v. Tice*, 199 P.2d 1 (Cal. 1948), firmly established the doctrine. Two shooters were out hunting with a third shooter, the plaintiff. Both negligently shot in the direction of the plaintiff, but only one of the two hit the plaintiff in the eye, causing an eye injury. The plaintiff did not know which of the two shot the pellet that caused the injury. Because the plaintiff could not prove which defendant shot the injuring shot, plaintiff's claim under "but for" causation would fail for a failure of proof, letting both negligent defendants (one of whom caused the injury) off the hook.

Nor is the independent concurrent causation doctrine applicable. Go back and look at Figure 13-1. We do not have an *A* + *B* situation in the *Summers* case. The two pellets did not join together and cause an eye injury to the plaintiff. Instead, we have an *A* or *B* situation, illustrated in Figure 13-3.

The solution the California Supreme Court conceived was one of *burden shifting*: If the plaintiff can prove that both defendants acted negligently, the burden on actual causation shifts to the defendants, each of whom can try to prove that he was not an actual cause of plaintiff's injury. If neither defendant can *disprove* actual causation, they are *both* liable for the plaintiff's injury (assuming plaintiff can prove the rest of the prima facie case and there are no affirmative defenses).

The Third Restatement states the *Summers* principle more generally:

> When the plaintiff sues all of multiple actors and proves that each engaged in tortious conduct that exposed the plaintiff to a risk of physical harm and that the tortious conduct of one or more of them caused the plaintiff's harm but the plaintiff cannot reasonably be expected to prove which actor

caused the harm, the burden of proof [. . .] on factual causation is shifted to the defendants.

REST. (3D) TORTS: LIABILITY FOR PHYSICAL HARM § 28(b) (P.F.D. No. 1, 2005).

Note the requirement that *all* of the defendants acted tortiously, and the additional requirement that the plaintiff can prove with certainty that it was one of the defendants—and not someone else—who is responsible for plaintiff's injuries. If plaintiff cannot prove even one of these elements, the burden of proof does *not* shift on actual causation.

QUESTION 7. *Summers* Revisited.   Three shooters were out on a hunting trip. Plaintiff was out hunting separately. All three shooters shot in the direction of the plaintiff. Alan and Ben were acting negligently and Carl, because of where he was standing, reasonably did not see that the plaintiff was in his line of fire. Though all three shot in the direction of the plaintiff, only one of the three hit the plaintiff in the eye, causing an eye injury. The plaintiff did not know which of the three shot the pellet that caused the injury. He sues Alan and Carl, but cannot find Ben to sue him. In pretrial motions, the plaintiff argues that the burden of proof should shift to Alan and Carl on the question of actual causation.

How should the court rule?

A. The court should rule that the burden does not shift because plaintiff cannot prove that the shooter who injured him has been brought into the suit.

B. The court should rule that the burden does not shift because not all of the defendants in the suit were negligent.

C. The court should rule that the burden does not shift, for the reasons stated in Choice **A** and Choice **B**.

D. The court should rule that the burden shifts on the question of causation.

ANALYSIS. This is a straightforward question. The plaintiff has two insurmountable problems in his attempt to use burden shifting under these facts. First, one of the defendants, Carl, did not act tortiously. *All* the defendants must be acting tortiously for the *Summers* rule to apply. Second, the plaintiff cannot prove that the wrongdoer is in court. It might have been Ben, who was not sued, who caused the injury. Because of both of these reasons, there will be no burden shifting. Unless plaintiff can prove who caused the injury, plaintiff's case will fail. Choice **C** is the correct choice, and the other choices are wrong for this reason.

D.   The Closer: Market share liability

We close this chapter with an even rarer exception to the "but for" test for actual causation: market share liability. Again, the California Supreme Court led the way in the case of *Sindell v. Abbott Labs*, 607 P.2d 924 (Cal. 1980), though the real credit goes to the law student who wrote a student note that the California Supreme Court relied upon in crafting this novel causation theory.[9]

Here's a basic synopsis of the facts. Plaintiff's mother took an anti-miscarriage drug, DES, while plaintiff was *in utero*. DES can cause the daughters of women who took DES to develop certain types of cancers. Plaintiff in fact contracted one of these cancers. Now, putting aside issues of both general causation (can DES cause these types of cancers?) and specific causation (did DES cause this plaintiff's cancer?), plaintiff had a more fundamental causation problem: She did not know which pharmaceutical manufacturer had made the DES ingested by her mother. This was not plaintiff's fault; it was many years ago. Some of the companies were out of business. So even assuming it was tortious for the manufacturers to market DES, the plaintiff could not use alternative liability because she could not prove that the wrongdoer was necessarily in the court.

Sindell adopted a radical new approach to causation to be applied in very rare circumstances (so rare, in fact, that the doctrine apparently has never been successfully applied by plaintiffs outside the context of DES cases, for reasons that will soon be clear). Under "market share liability," when a number of defendants manufacture an identical (or "fungible" product), and the plaintiff through no fault of her own cannot identify which defendant made the product that caused her injury, if she brings suit against defendants making up a substantial share of the market at the relevant time, she can recover damages from each manufacturer based upon each manufacturer's share of the relevant market. In other words, if a defendant manufactured 30 percent of the DES at the relevant time period, plaintiff could recover 30 percent of her damages from this defendant.

There is a lot of nuance buried in the last paragraph, so it is worth fleshing out a bit that there are four separate requirements for market share liability to apply. A plaintiff must show:

1. All the named defendants are potential tortfeasors;
2. The alleged products of all the tortfeasors share the same properties and are identical;
3. The plaintiff, through no fault of her own, cannot identify which defendant caused the injury; and

---

9. Naomi Sheiner, Comment, *DES and a Proposed Theory of Enterprise Liability*, 46 FORDHAM L. REV. 963 (1978).

   4. Plaintiff brings in as defendants those representing a substantial share
      of the market.

If plaintiff can meet all four requirements, each defendant is liable for
damages representing only its share of the market at the relevant time.[10]
   One of the main reasons market share liability has not extended beyond
the DES cases is the requirement that the products be identical/fungible. Few
products besides prescription drugs manufactured to exacting specifications
are likely to fit into this category.

QUESTION 8. Painting a Sad Picture.   Pam is a child who has suffered
neurological damage because she has ingested lead. The lead came
from paint that had peeled off the wall in her apartment. Her apartment,
which is 100 years old, had been painted with many coats of lead paint over
the years. The paint came from different manufacturers, some out of
business and many impossible to identify. Each formulation of lead paint
contains different amounts of lead. Pam (through her parents) sues the
manufacturers of lead paint that she can find in the area (some are out
of business or bankrupt), arguing that their conduct constituted negligence
and a products defect. She does not know whose paint caused her
injury. The manufacturers argue the case cannot go to a jury because
Pam cannot prove actual causation.

How should the court rule on the manufacturers' argument?

A. The court should reject it because Pam can prove causation under
the independent concurrent causation test.
B. The court should reject it because Pam can shift the burden using
alternative liability.
C. The court should reject it because Pam can prove her case using
market share liability.
D. The court should accept the manufacturers' argument under
existing accepted theories of causation.

ANALYSIS.   This fact pattern is based upon the facts of *Skipworth v. Lead
Industries Association*, 690 A.2d 169 (Pa. 1997). As sympathetic as this

---

10. There are additional complicating issues beyond the scope of this book. For example, how
should courts treat shares of bankrupt manufacturers? What counts as the relevant market? Should a
court allow a defendant to demonstrate in a particular case that it could not have been responsible
for this particular plaintiff's injury? For some court cases considering these issues, see *Hymowitz v.
Eli Lilly & Co.*, 539 N.E.2d 1069 (N.Y. 1989); *McCormack v. Abbott Laboratories*, 617 F.Supp. 1521
(D. Mass. 1985).

plaintiff undoubtedly is, the actual causation element is going to doom Pam's case under existing doctrine. Let's take them one by one:

- *"But for" Causation.* Pam cannot prove but for causation. She cannot point to any defendant and prove that but for this defendant's tortious conduct in marketing the lead paint used some time in the past in her apartment, the injury would not have occurred.
- *Independent Concurrent Causation.* This does not look like an $A + B$ scenario. It is not as though each coat of paint, setting aside the others, would have caused exactly the same injury as Pam actually suffered. Choice **A** is therefore incorrect.
- *Alternative Liability.* Pam cannot prove that the lead paint manufacturer that caused her injury is in court, because some of the manufacturers are out of business or bankrupt. Without such proof, she cannot shift the burden using alternative liability. Choice **B** is incorrect.
- *Market Share Liability.* Unlike DES, lead paint is not an identical/fungible product. We are told that each of the lead paint formulas had different amounts of lead. This is not a situation in which we know that one defendant has caused the injury and others have marketed the identical product to other plaintiffs, allowing for a market share liability approach for all plaintiffs and defendants. We don't know if Pam is suing manufacturers making up a substantial share of the market. For these reasons, even though Pam through no fault of her own cannot prove which defendant's lead paint caused her injury, market share liability cannot work. (That's the conclusion that the Pennsylvania Supreme Court reached in the *Skipworth* case.) For these reasons, Choice **C** is incorrect.

In short, none of the theories of actual causation we have studied would allow Pam's case to go forward; the only way to do so is for the courts to come up with yet another approach to causation (or have the legislature provide a solution independent of the courts). Because all of the existing theories fail, Choice **D** is the correct answer.

 # Rick's picks

1. Going Overboard	C
2. Going Overboard, Take II	A
3. Shot in the Dark	A
4. *Negligence Per Se* Train-ing	D
5. Plaintiff Foaming at the Mouth	D
6. Twice Burned	B
7. *Summers* Revisited	C
8. Painting a Sad Picture	D

14

Proximate Cause: Policy Limitations on the Scope of Liability

A. Proximate causation

1. The basics

Let me remind you again (so that you will say it in your sleep) that every tort has the same structure. Speaking generically, the plaintiff must prove:

1. That defendant engaged in the requisite tortious conduct
2. Actual causation
3. Proximate causation
4. Damages

This part of the book considers the second and third elements. The last chapter explained the actual causation standard. Actual causation is primarily a *factual question* asking something about the state of the world in relation to the tort claimed by the plaintiff against the defendant. As we will see in this chapter, *proximate causation* (sometimes termed *legal cause*), in contrast, is the poorly chosen term for a *policy question*, much like the duty question in the negligence case (discussed in Chapters 11 and 12), that has very little to do with the question of cause. Instead, the question considers the *fairness* or *policy consequences* of holding a defendant liable in tort when the tort occurs in an unusual way.

Before getting into the various proximate cause tests, consider this example. Laurent is running through the airport to catch his plane. Because he is careless, he bumps into Joanne, who is also trying to catch a plane. She falls and hurts her foot. Presumably, no one could raise a good policy argument against Joanne's ability to collect damages for medical bills arising out of Laurent's negligence. He had a duty to use reasonable care (Joanne is a foreseeable plaintiff, this is not a sports or recreation case, and Laurent was engaged in risk creation); he breached that duty when he failed to use reasonable care; and his carelessness was an actual cause (under the "but for" test) of Joanne's foot injury.

But now imagine that instead of causing a foot injury necessitating medical care, the bump was enough to cause Joanne to have to rest a few minutes before she got up, and she missed her plane. Should Laurent be liable for a penalty that Joanne would have to pay to get on the next plane? No matter how you answer that question, note that what *hasn't* changed is duty, breach, or actual causation. Okay, now to make the problem more fantastical, imagine that because of the bump Joanne misses her plane and gets on the next plane, which is struck by lightning. The plane crashes and Joanne suffers serious personal injuries. Again, it should be clear to you that nothing has changed regarding duty, breach, or actual causation: But for Laurent's bump, Joanne never would have gotten on the next plane to be struck by lightning.

Virtually all students, when I pose the lightning hypothetical, want to let Laurent off the hook for Joanne's damages. And it is here that the doctrine of proximate causation comes in. The doctrine allows courts in unusual situations to say for policy reasons that a plaintiff cannot recover damages despite being able to prove the rest of the prima facie case. Duty can function like that as well in a negligence case, but, as we have seen, duty focuses on just a few questions, and duty is not an element for torts besides negligence. Proximate cause in contrast cuts across all torts.

Here is what Justice Andrews said of the function of proximate causation in his famous dissent in *Palsgraf v. Long Island R.R.*, 162 N.E. 99, 103-04 (N.Y. 1928):[1]

---

1. We first discussed *Palsgraf* in Chapter 11 in relation to the "foreseeable plaintiff" duty requirement. In case you are reading this chapter first, here's a brief synopsis of the facts of the case: In *Palsgraf*, a man was getting on a commuter train at a train station. He was carrying some newspapers, and, unbeknownst to the workers on the train, he had some fireworks wrapped inside the newspapers. The train was about to leave the station, and one of the train workers pushed him

A cause, but not the proximate cause. What we do mean by the word "proximate" is, that because of convenience, of public policy, of a rough sense of justice, the law arbitrarily declines to trace a series of events beyond a certain point. This is not logic. It is practical politics. Take our rule as to fires. Sparks from my burning haystack set on fire my house and my neighbor's. I may recover from a negligent railroad. He may not. Yet the wrongful act as directly harmed the one as the other. We may regret that the line was drawn just where it was, but drawn somewhere it had to be.[2]

As the Andrews excerpt makes clear, the term "proximate causation" is about policy, not fact. The term "causation" appears in the term because courts often use words like "remote" to hide (or inartfully explain) their policy choices. Back to the lightning strike downing Joanne's second plane, we might say that there is no proximate causation because the "causal links are too attenuated." But it would be clearer, and fairer, to just say that on policy grounds defendants should not have to pay for such damages. We turn to those policy grounds in the next sections. In the meantime, it is worth noting that the Third Restatement takes the position that the term "proximate causation" is "an especially poor one to describe the idea to which it is connected," preferring instead the term "scope of liability," terminology which more accurately reflects the policy-oriented nature of the term. REST. (3D) TORTS: LIABILITY FOR PHYSICAL HARM, Chapter 6, Special Note on Proximate Cause (P.F.D. No. 1, 2005). The drafters of the Restatement nonetheless include the term "proximate causation" after the term "scope of liability," noting that "[t]he Institute fervently hopes that the Restatement Fourth of Torts will not find this parenthetical necessary." *Id.*

In some ways, proximate cause is the law of the freak accident. Proximate cause comes up as a bona fide dispute in so few cases that Torts casebooks give it more attention that it gets in the real world.

> **QUESTION 1. Lead Foot, Take II.** James, an eighth-grader, brought his parent's gun to school (he made sure it was not loaded) for show-and-tell. As he was showing the gun to a friend, Amy, in the hallway, another child bumped into James and he dropped the gun. It landed on Amy's foot, breaking three of her toes. Amy sues James for negligence. Assume that bringing a gun to school under such circumstances constitutes

---

onto the train while another worker tried to pull him up as the train was leaving the station. After being shoved, the man dropped the newspapers, causing the fireworks to ignite and creating an explosion. Plaintiff, Palsgraf, was standing on the other end of the platform. The vibrations from the explosion caused some scales at the other end of the platform to fall on Palsgraf, injuring her.

2. The particular New York rule as to fires has since been overruled. *See Milwaukee & St. P.R. Co. v. Kellogg*, 94 U.S. 469 (1876).

a failure to use reasonable care. Which is the strongest argument James may make against liability for negligence in this case?

A. James owed no duty to Amy.

B. James did not breach any duty to Amy.

C. James's negligence was not an actual cause of Amy's injury.

D. James's negligence was not a proximate cause of Amy's injury.

ANALYSIS.   This hypothetical, which appeared slightly differently in the *negligence per se* context in Chapter 9 (and more about the connections to *negligence per se* later in this chapter), is meant to drive home the point that in a case like this, proximate cause (and not duty) works to achieve a given policy. There is no question that James owed Amy a duty: Amy is a foreseeable plaintiff, this is not a sports or recreation case, and James was engaged in risk creation. Choice **A** is therefore wrong. Moreover, the facts tell you that James failed to use reasonable care, meaning that he breached his duty to Amy. Choice **B** is therefore wrong. But for James's tortious conduct in bringing the gun to school, this injury never would have happened. Choice **C** is therefore wrong. If we are going to say that James is not liable, it is going to be under proximate cause. Choice **D** is the correct answer. That's not to say it is necessarily a winning argument. It might be that the court holds that he should still be liable for bringing the gun to school. But it is the strongest argument of the four.

2. Directness test

The previous section of this chapter established that proximate causation is a *policy* question, one aimed at identifying cases in which, as Justice Andrews said, "because of convenience, of public policy, of a rough sense of justice, the law arbitrarily declines to trace a series of events beyond a certain point." Two main tests have emerged for proximate causation, the "directness" test and the "foreseeability of type of harm/harm within the risk" test. Both tests appear to be in use in the United States. REST. (3D) TORTS: LIABILITY FOR PHYSICAL HARM § 29, Reporter's note (P.F.D. No. 1, 2005) (stating that "Standard jury instructions on proximate cause in a majority of states include language requiring that the tortious conduct 'in a natural and continuous sequence produces the harm'" but noting that "[a] number of jurisdictions have rejected the 'natural and continuous' language for instructing on proximate cause since the publication of the Restatement Second of Torts.").

Justice Andrews was one of the proponents of the directness test. Under this test, the question is whether the connection between defendant's tortious conduct and plaintiff's injuries were close in time and space. Justice Andrews asked, is there a "natural and continuous sequence — direction connection[?]" He further asked whether the defendant's actions were a "substantial factor" in "producing the result."[3] But this is no mathematical test or factual question; it is an inquiry grounded in policy. There is no bright line to say how close in time and space the connection between defendant's tortious conduct and plaintiff's injuries must be. Under the facts of *Palsgraf*, Justice Andrews would have concluded that there was a close enough connection between the train workers pushing the man onto the train and the scales falling onto the plaintiff at the other end of the platform to allow plaintiff to recover damages from the railroad.

The English courts first endorsed a directness test, *In re Polemis & Furness, Withy & Co.*, [1921] 3 K.B. 560, but then rejected that test in favor of the alternative test for proximate cause, foreseeability of type of harm, in *Overseas Tankship (U.K.) Ltd. v. Morts Dock & Engineering Co., Ltd. (Wagon Mound No. 1)*, [1961] AC 388 (P.C. Aust.).

Both of the cases demonstrate how unusual fact patterns must be in order for there to be a legitimate dispute over proximate cause. In the *Polemis* case, some ship workers negligently dropped a plank into the hold of the ship. What made the action negligent was the possibility that the heavy plank could fall on a person or property, doing damage from the impact. But the dropped plank caused a spark, which ignited some flammable gas in the hold, causing an explosion. The court said that those whose property was damaged by fire could prove proximate cause under the directness test (even though, as we will see in the next section, the case would fail under the alternative proximate cause test). The connection in time and space between the defendant's actions in dropping the plank and the plaintiff's injury from the fire were close enough for liability.

In the *Wagon Mound* case, workers were fixing a damaged ship after an oil spill. The work involved welding, and apparently the workers performed a number of tests to make sure that the oil on the water would not catch on fire from the welding activity. The oil did catch on fire, damaging plaintiff's property. Even though the connection between the negligent spilling of the oil and the damage was close in time and space, the House of Lords rejected its old directness test from *Polemis*, opting instead for the alternative proximate cause test described in the next section.

QUESTION 2. Lead Foot, Take III. James, an eighth-grader, brought his parent's gun to school (he made sure it was not loaded) for show-and-tell. As he was showing the gun to a friend, Amy, in the hallway,

---

3. The Second Restatement picked up this language (*See* Rest. (2d) Torts § 433), leading some courts to follow it and instruct using "substantial factor" language. However, the Third Restatement rejects it. *See* Rest. (3d) Torts: Liability for Physical Harm § 29, cmt. *a* (P.F.D. No. 1, 2005).

another child bumped into James and he dropped the gun. It landed on Amy's foot, breaking three of her toes. Amy sues James for negligence. The jurisdiction uses the directness test for proximate cause, and James argues that Amy should lose her case because she cannot prove proximate cause under the directness test.

A. James should lose on this point because his conduct was close in time and space to Amy's injury.

B. James should lose on this point because his conduct was a foreseeable type of harm stemming from his negligence.

C. James should lose on this point because but for his bringing the gun to school, the injury never would have happened.

D. James should win on this point because the only conclusion under the directness test that a jury could draw is that this injury was indirect.

ANALYSIS. Let's start off by eliminating the clearly wrong answers here. Choice **B** is wrong because it states the alternative (majority) approach to proximate cause, and not the directness test. The facts tell us that this is a jurisdiction using the directness test. Choice **C** is wrong because it sets out the standard for *actual* causation, not *proximate* causation. So this brings us to Choices **A** or **D**. Likely a jury considering whether there is a closeness in time and space between James's negligence and Amy's injury would conclude that there is a close enough connection, but it is not certain. Remember, this is not logic, it is practical politics. With that explanation, Choice **A** is better than Choice **D,** because Choice **D** speaks as though jurors could conclude on these facts only that there is not a direct connection in time and space.

3. Foreseeability of type of harm test/harm within the risk

The main alternative to the directness test for proximate cause is the "foreseeability of type of harm" test. This test asks whether the *type of harm* that occurs was a foreseeable risk of defendant's negligent conduct. Considering *Polemis* again, the question under a foreseeability of type of harm test is whether the *risk of explosion* was a foreseeable kind of risk from carelessly carrying the planks on the ship.[4] Because it was not, the defendant would not be liable for damage under this view of proximate cause. The same result of no liability occurs under the *Wagon Mound* case as well.

Another way of phrasing this same inquiry is to ask whether the conduct is a "harm within the risk" of what makes defendant's conduct negligent.

---

4. To be clear, *harm* (in the form of impact damage from dropping the planks) was still reasonably foreseeable, meaning that plaintiffs would still be able to prove breach from the workers' failure to use reasonable care in carrying the planks. What was not foreseeable was the *type of harm* that actually occurred.

What made the conduct negligent in *Polemis* was the risk that the planks might fall and damage person or property on impact. It was not the risk that dropping the planks would cause a fire and explosion. So *Polemis* is one of the rare cases in which a plaintiff likely could prove proximate causation under the directness test but fail to prove proximate causation under the foreseeability of type of harm test. (In most cases, as noted, plaintiffs who can prove the rest of a prima facie case easily can prove proximate causation under either test.)

The Third Restatement endorses the foreseeability of type of harm/harm within the risk test for proximate causation (which it terms "scope of liability"). "An actor's liability is limited to those physical harms that result from the risks that made the actor's conduct tortious." REST. (3D) TORTS: LIABILITY FOR PHYSICAL HARM § 29 (P.F.D. No. 1, 2005).[5] It is also the test that appears in the fourth element of the test for *negligence per se*, as explained in Chapter 9: *The statute was designed to protect against the type of accident the defendant causes.* (Think of the poison, not labeled as poison by the pharmacist, that cuts the plaintiff's foot when dropped on the floor.)

QUESTION 3. Lead Foot, Take IV. James, an eighth-grader, brought his parent's gun to school (he made sure it was not loaded) for show-and-tell. As he was showing the gun to a friend, Amy, another child bumped into James and he dropped the gun. It landed on Amy's foot, breaking three of her toes. Amy sues James for negligence. The jurisdiction uses the Third Restatement's test for proximate cause, and James argues that Amy should lose her case because she cannot prove proximate cause.

A. James should lose on this point because his conduct was close in time and space to Amy's injury.

B. James should lose on this point because his conduct was a foreseeable type of harm stemming from his negligence.

C. James should lose on this point because but for his bringing the gun to school, the injury never would have happened.

D. James should win on this point because his conduct resulted in an unforeseeable type of harm stemming from his negligence.

ANALYSIS. Again, let's start off by eliminating the clearly wrong answers here. Choice **A** is wrong because it applies the directness test, which is not the harm within the risk test of the Third Restatement. (The Restatement, by the way, refers to the test as the "risk standard.") Choice **C** is wrong because

---

5. *See also* REST. (3D) TORTS: LIABILITY FOR PHYSICAL HARM § 30 ("An actor is not liable for physical harm when the tortious aspect of the actor's conduct was of a type that does not generally increase the risk of that harm.").

it sets out the standard for *actual* causation, not *proximate* causation. So this brings us to Choices **B** or **D**. Choice **D** is the better answer here. The foreseeable danger of bringing a gun to a school is that someone might get shot (or at least pistol-whipped). It is not that the gun would fall on someone's foot and break a toe. One way to see this is to imagine that James was carrying a geometry book rather than a gun. It is not negligent to carry such a book, even though there is a risk it could fall and break someone's toe. The risk of a gun falling and breaking a toe is not a risk that makes the activity negligent.

4. Proximate cause and plaintiff's conduct in negligence and other cases

If you have already read Part II of this book, you know that in negligence cases, proof of a plaintiff's negligence (and, in some circumstances, consent) acts as an affirmative defense that reduces a defendant's liability. (We will see a similar approach to affirmative defenses in some strict liability and products liability torts.) However, in order for a plaintiff's negligence to count as a reduction of liability, it must be both an actual cause (as explained in the last chapter) and a proximate cause of the injury. If it is not, then defendant bears the entire responsibility for the injury.

QUESTION 4. *Negligence Per Se* Train-ing, Take II. Bob Berry is driving his train through Sugar Notch Borough. The speed limit is 40 mph. Berry is driving at 60 mph. The borough has negligently maintained trees along the train tracks. One of the trees falls at exactly the moment that Berry's train passes, damaging the train. Berry sues Sugar Notch Borough for negligence. The borough concedes it was negligent, but argues that Berry's damages should be reduced for Berry's comparative negligence, which it plans to prove through *negligence per se*. Berry responds by claiming any violation of the statute was not a proximate cause of his injury.

How should the court rule on Berry's argument?

A. The court should accept the argument because the accident could just as easily have happened if the train was going 40 mph.
B. The court should accept the argument because there is no question that Berry violated the statute.
C. The court should accept the argument because Sugar Notch Borough's maintenance of the trees, not Berry's conduct, caused the plaintiff's injury.
D. The court should reject the argument.

ANALYSIS. This question, a variation on a question in Chapter 13, is based upon *Berry v. Sugar Notch Borough*, 43 A. 240 (Pa. 1899). The speeds were much slower, but the facts are basically the same. Here, plaintiff is arguing that his negligence cannot be used to lessen his damages because his speeding was not a proximate cause of the injury. It is a good argument: What made the speeding negligent was the risk that the train would be unable to slow down to avoid a collision, not that one would arrive in the wrong place at exactly the wrong time. For this reason, Choice **A** is correct and Choice **D** is incorrect. Choice **B** is wrong because even though Berry violated the statute, that is not enough to prove *negligence per se* against him. Choice **C** is wrong, because more than one party can be an actual cause of an injury, and in any case the question asks about proximate cause, not actual cause.

QUESTION 5. *Negligence Per Se* Train-ing, Take III. Bob Berry is driving his train through Sugar Notch Borough. The speed limit is 40 mph. Berry is driving at 60 mph. The borough has negligently maintained trees along the train tracks. One of the trees fell a few moments before Berry's train arrived, and Berry crashed into the tree, causing the car to derail. Experts agree that if Berry had been driving the speed limit, he likely would have stopped before hitting the tree. Berry sues Sugar Notch Borough for negligence. The borough concedes it was negligent, but argues that Berry's damages should be reduced for Berry's comparative negligence, which it plans to prove through *negligence per se*. Berry responds by claiming any violation of the statute was not a proximate cause of his injury.

How should the court rule on Berry's argument?

A. The court should accept the argument because the accident could just as easily have happened if the train was going at 40 mph.
B. The court should accept the argument because there is no question that Berry violated the statute.
C. The court should accept the argument because Sugar Notch Borough's maintenance of the trees, not Berry's conduct, caused the plaintiff's injury.
D. The court should reject the argument.

ANALYSIS. This question, a variation on the last question, includes this important change in the facts: rather than the tree falling *on* Berry's train, the tree falls *before*, and Berry's train *crashes into it*. The risk of speeding is that you won't be able to stop fast enough to stop collisions, and here that's what happened. The experts agree that if Berry had been going the speed limit, he would have had time to stop. Because the harm that occurred was within the risk of what made the speeding negligent, the court should reject Berry's proximate cause argument. Thus, Choice **D** is correct and Choice **A** is not. Choices **B** and **C** are incorrect for the same reason as in the last question.

B. Intervening and superseding causes

We have seen the two main approaches to proximate cause — the directness test, which looks at closeness in time and space, and the foreseeability of type of harm test. A special proximate cause issue arises when there is the action of a third person or an act of nature that intervenes *between* the time of defendant's tortious conduct and the plaintiff's injury. In some cases, that intervening action lets the defendant out of liability despite his negligent actions. In the language of proximate cause, we could call that intervening action a "superseding cause" that "breaks the chain of causation." But don't be fooled by the causation language: this is still a proximate cause issue judged as a matter of policy.

To see the issue, let's contrast two cases. First, let's go back to the Laurent-Joanne hypo in which Laurent knocks Joanne over at the airport, causing her to miss her plane. Now imagine that the second plane is hijacked by terrorists, and it crashes, leaving Joanne badly injured. Most juries would likely conclude that Laurent should not have to pay for Joanne's injuries, even though he owed Joanne a duty, he was negligent in bumping into her, and his negligence was an actual cause of Joanne's injuries. The lingo that courts would apply here is that the terrorists' actions are a superseding cause breaking the chain of causation. Thus, there would be no liability for Laurent because Joanne cannot prove proximate causation.

Now imagine if the facts are the same, but rather than suing Laurent, Joanne instead sues the security company at the airport that allowed the terrorists to sneak guns onto the plane.[6] Here, most courts would reject the security company's argument that the terrorists' conduct is a superseding cause that breaks the chain of causation.

What's the difference between the two cases? The issue of superseding cause *in both directness and foreseeability of the type of harm jurisdictions* turns on the harm within the risk question. In Laurent's case, it was not a harm within the risk of bumping into someone that it could lead to the type of harm of a terrorist-inflicted injury. In contrast, in the security company's case, it emphatically *was* a type of harm within the risk of inadequately screening passengers for weapons that could lead to the type of harm of a terrorist-inflicted injury.

---

6. We put aside the possibility that various statutory immunities could prevent Joanne from being allowed to sue the security company.

The Restatement sets forth the rule as follows:

> When a force of nature or an independent act is also a factual cause of physical harm, an actor's liability is limited to those harms that result from the risks that made the actor's conduct tortious.

REST. (3D) TORTS: LIABILITY FOR PHYSICAL HARM § 34 (P.F.D. No. 1, 2005).

QUESTION 6. Lead Foot, Take V. James, an eighth-grader, brought his parent's gun to school for show-and-tell. An unknown person stole James's backpack at school, found the gun, and started shooting. One of the bullets hit James's classmate, Amy, in the foot, breaking three of her toes. Amy sues James for negligence. James argues that Amy should lose her case because she cannot prove proximate cause. How should the court rule on this argument?

A. James should lose on this point because his conduct was close in time and space to Amy's injury.

B. James should lose on this point if a jury finds that the risk of someone stealing his gun and injuring someone was one of the risks of bringing a gun to school.

C. James should lose on this point because but for his bringing the gun to school, the injury never would have happened.

D. James should win on this point because the unknown person, not James, shot Amy.

ANALYSIS. This is an intervening cause case, because the unknown person stealing the gun is something that occurred after the negligent conduct of James (bringing the gun to school) and before the plaintiff's injury. The operative question is whether the conduct of this third person is a foreseeable type of harm from bringing the gun to school. Choice **B** correctly explains the standard. James should lose *if* the jury believes that one of the risks of bringing a gun to school is the possibility that someone else might take it and cause injury. Choice **A** is wrong because, even in directness jurisdictions, when it comes to intervening causes, we use a foreseeability of type of harm/ harm within the risk analysis. Choice **C** is wrong because this asks the "but for" actual cause question, not the proximate cause question. Choice **D** is incorrect because the fact that there was a third person involved does not mean that James is let off the hook: If one of the risks that makes one's conduct dangerous is third-party criminal conduct, then proximate cause will not work to relieve the defendant of liability.

One of the most common issues that arise in the superseding cause area concerns third-party criminal conduct, such as attacks at shopping malls, etc. In some jurisdictions, when shopping malls are sued for negligently failing to prevent such attacks, these kinds of questions are considered primarily as one of proximate cause. In other jurisdictions, they raise duty questions: Is the shopping mall responsible for third-party criminal conduct? The scope of such a duty may be dictated by the landowner liability rules discussed in Chapter 12.

Speaking generally, the choice between the use of a duty analysis and a proximate cause analysis is not all that important: What is more important is to recognize that courts in these cases are making a policy decision whether shopping mall owners should be held responsible for criminal activities that take place on their premises. But even if a court holds that there is a duty and that criminal conduct does not constitute a superseding cause that breaks the chain of causation, plaintiffs often face another problem: actual cause. The plaintiff has to prove that the additional security (which the landowner did not provide) would have made a difference on whether or not the attack would have happened.

QUESTION 7. Lights Out.   Cindy owns a shopping mall. It has no security guards and poor lighting in the common areas. One night Alex, an employee of one of the stores, is walking to his car in the mall parking lot. It is about 11 P.M.; Alex is mugged in the parking lot as he is leaving for the night. An unknown assailant steals $200 from Alex and breaks three of his teeth.

Alex sues Cindy for negligence. Which element of the negligence tort is Cindy least likely to contest?

A. Duty
B. Actual cause
C. Proximate cause
D. Damages

ANALYSIS.   Cindy may have a number of good arguments against liability. First, she may argue that she did not owe Alex a duty to prevent third-party criminal attacks. Whether that argument is successful will depend upon the jurisdiction's rules for landowner liability in the commercial context. For this reason, Choice **A** is incorrect. Choice **B** is also incorrect: Alex is going to have to prove that more security and better lighting would have made a difference in his case, something that may be very difficult to prove. Choice **C** is also wrong: Cindy may have a good proximate cause argument that the conduct of the unknown assailant is a "superseding" cause that "breaks the chain of causation." This will again be a policy question for court or jury. The weakest answer is contained in Choice **D**. The facts tell us that the assailant took $200 and broke three of Alex's teeth. You should recognize that as damages, even before you've looked at Part VI of this book.

C.   The economic harm rule

Strictly speaking, we might not consider the economic harm rule a subset of the proximate cause rule (some might consider it a duty rule or a damages rule), but they are closely enough related that it is worth treating the issue here. Under the rule, "a negligence plaintiff who suffers no physical impact to his person or property cannot recover for other losses." Douglas Laycock, Modern American Remedies 116 (3d ed. 2002). The rule functions like proximate causation in that it cuts off some liability on policy grounds.

The easiest way to understand the rule is through an example given in a case written by Judge Friendly, the *Kinsman II* case:

> To anyone familiar with N.Y. traffic there can be no doubt that a foreseeable result of an accident in the Brooklyn Battery Tunnel during rush hour is that thousands of people will be delayed. A driver who negligently caused such an accident would certainly be held accountable to those physically injured in the crash. But we doubt that damages would be recoverable against the negligent driver in favor of truckers or contract carriers who suffered provable losses because of the delay or to the wage earner who was forced to 'clock in' an hour late. And yet it was surely foreseeable that among the many who would be delayed would be truckers and wage earners.

Petition of Kinsman Transport Company (Kinsman II), 388 F.2d 821, 825 n.8 (2d Cir. 1968).

Though the concern here is one of policy (as with proximate cause), the particular policy concern here is different, turning not on the foreseeability of the type of harm (as Judge Friendly admits in the excerpt above). Instead, the fear is one of *crushing liability*. Who among us would be willing to drive on the freeway (and which insurers among us would be willing to insure those drivers), if everyone delayed by an accident could sue the negligent driver for all the economic losses caused by such driving? The law's solution is to tell us under the economic harm rule that we each bear our economic losses, unless there is accompanying property damage or physical injury.

QUESTION 8. Sig-Alert! [7]   Tony is driving with one hand on his cell phone and the other adjusting the radio. He is driving on the freeway and gets into an accident. His car crashes into Joel's car, causing the car

---

7. For the non-Los Angeles readers of this book, a "Sig-Alert" is a non-scheduled freeway lane closure lasting for at least 30 minutes — a dreadful term to hear if you are trying to get home in rush hour. The California Department of Transportation has given it a slightly broader reading. Caltrans FAQ, http://www.dot.ca.gov/hq/paffairs/faq/faq18.htm (last visited July 13, 2008).

extensive damage. A passenger in Joel's car, Bill, injures his back in the crash. Monica is stuck behind this wreck for three hours. All three — Joel, Bill, and Monica — miss work because of Tony's accident.

The three sue Tony for negligence, and Tony argues that the economic harm rule bars their recovery for any damages due to lost work. Which of these plaintiffs cannot recover these damages because of the economic harm rule?

A. Joel
B. Bill
C. Monica
D. They may all recover damages for lost work.

ANALYSIS. Remember, under the economic harm rule damages may be recovered for economic losses only when there is accompanying property damage or physical harm to person. In this case, Joel suffers property damage and Bill suffers physical harm. So they may each recover economic damages in addition to damages for these other losses. Monica, in contrast, suffered *only* economic harm, and for this reason she may not recover her economic losses. For this reason, Choice **C** is correct, and Choices **A**, **B**, and **D** are incorrect.

The economic harm rule is subject to an important exception: It does not apply when the only kind of harm a defendant can inflict upon a plaintiff is economic harm. So if you go to your accountant and the accountant commits malpractice, causing you to pay a substantial tax penalty, the accountant cannot defend herself in a malpractice suit by claiming you are only seeking recovery for economic harm. In this case, the only way that your accountant can harm you is through economic harm, and if we applied the usual rule, accountants would virtually never be liable for accountant malpractice.

QUESTION 9. Malpractice Woes.   Bill, the passenger from Question 8, goes to Dania, an attorney, to sue Tony for negligence arising out of the automobile accident. Dania carelessly forgets to file Bill's negligence case in time, and a court later rules that Bill's case against Tony is barred by the statute of limitations. Bill then sues Dania for attorney malpractice. Dania argues she cannot be liable under the economic harm rule.

How should the court rule on Dania's argument?

A. It should accept the argument because Bill only lost money, without suffering property damage or physical injury, because of Dania's malpractice.

> **B.** It should accept the argument because economic harms are never compensable in tort.
> **C.** It should reject the argument because the only kind of harm Dania could inflict as Bill's lawyer is economic harm.
> **D.** It should reject the argument because the harm originally arose out of an automobile accident.

ANALYSIS. Dania is not a very good lawyer. First she blows the statute of limitations; now she makes a bad legal argument under the economic harm rule. It is true that Dania has not caused any property damage or physical harm to Bill's person, a requirement for the economic harm rule to apply. But this case falls into an exception: The only kind of harm that Dania can inflict on Bill as his lawyer is economic harm. Thus, the economic harm rule does not apply. Choice **C** is the correct choice. Choice **A** is wrong because it fails to account for the exception to the economic harm rule. Choice **B** states an incorrect principle of law: Economic harms are compensable in situations like this and when they are parasitic to property damage or personal injury claims. Choice **D** is wrong because it is irrelevant that the underlying lawsuit arose from an automobile accident. You need to focus on this defendant's wrong to the plaintiff.

D. The Closer: Proximate cause and intentional torts

As noted at the beginning of this chapter, the proximate cause requirement applies to *all* torts, and not just to negligence. But there is a reason that most of the questions in this chapter use negligence rather than the intentional torts covered in Part I of this book. Because proximate cause is a policy question, courts sometimes strike the policy balance different when it comes to intentional torts, at least when there is an intent to cause harm.[8]

The Third Restatement's approach, REST. (3D) TORTS: LIABILITY FOR PHYSICAL HARM § 33 (P.F.D. No. 1, 2005), is a mess. It contains three subparts that are — to say the least — in great tension with one another:

- Part (a) provides that "[a]n actor who intentionally causes physical harm is subject to liability for that harm even if it was unlikely to occur."

---

8. As Part I explains, in some intentional torts (in at least some jurisdictions) a plaintiff need not prove that a defendant intended harm in order to recover damages for an intentional tort.

- Part (b) provides that an actor who intentionally or recklessly causes physical harm "is subject to a broader range of harms for which that actor would be liable if only acting negligently." This part then offers a multi-part balancing test for determining when the scope of liability should limit liability.[9]
- Part (c) provides that notwithstanding the first two parts, defendants in intentional tort cases are not liable for harms "the risk of which was not increased by the actor's intentional or reckless conduct." For this section the Restatement offers the illustration of a plaintiff running away from robbers who gets struck by lightning.

Despite the lack of clarity in the Restatement section, it does appear clear that courts will look less charitably on proximate cause arguments brought by defendants in intentional torts cases, especially when the defendant has intentionally tried to harm the plaintiff. As the Restatement says, the rules should perhaps be bent for a defendant who commits a battery while acting on an unreasonable mistake as to the need for self-defense. Nonetheless, because proximate cause is a policy question (have I mentioned that yet?), courts need not go out of their way to allow intentionally wrongdoing tortfeasors out of liability just because an injury occurs in an unforeseen or unusual way.

QUESTION 10. **Slapstick Tragedy.** Abbott, intending to shoot Costello, aims and misses. The bullet hits a rope above Costello's head, which breaks, causing a sack of bricks to fall on Costello, injuring him seriously. Costello sues Abbott for battery. Abbott concedes that Costello can make out the tortious conduct portion of the prima facie case for battery, but argues that a court should rule his conduct cannot be the proximate cause. How should a jurisdiction following the Restatement rule on Abbott's argument?

A. The court should reject it because Abbott is subject to liability for harm even if it is unlikely to occur.

B. The court should carefully balance factors including the moral culpability of the actor, as reflected in the reasons for and intent in committing the tortious act, the seriousness of harm intended and threatened by those acts, and the degree to which Abbott's conduct deviated from appropriate care.

---

9. "In general, the important factors in determining the scope of liability are the moral culpability of the actor, as reflected in the reasons for and intent in committing the tortious acts, the seriousness of harm intended and threatened by those acts, and the degree to which the actor's conduct deviated from appropriate care."

C. The court should not subject Abbott to liability for battery if it concludes that this was not a harm the risk of which was increased by Abbott's intentional conduct.
D. Any or all of these standards could apply to a court applying the new Restatement approach.

ANALYSIS.   I wrote this question to illustrate the tension within the Restatement approach. The biggest problem with this approach is that it is not clear how the three parts of §33 are meant to interact with each other. Choices **A, B,** and **C** above correspond to the three tests of §33. Choice **D** correctly explains that any or all of these standards could apply under the Restatement in evaluating the scope of Abbott's liability here. My sense is that most courts would reject Abbott's argument, whether under the Restatement or not. Why should a court cut an intentional wrongdoer who was trying to do physical harm to another any slack, simply because the bad action did not happen exactly as planned?

 # Rick's picks

1. Lead Foot, Take II		D
2. Lead Foot, Take III		A
3. Lead Foot, Take IV		D
4. *Negligence Per Se* Train-ing, Take II		A
5. *Negligence Per Se* Train-ing, Take III		D
6. Lead Foot, Take V		B
7. Lights Out		D
8. Sig-Alert!		C
9. Malpractice Woes		C
10. Slapstick Tragedy		D

PART IV

Strict Liability Torts

15

From Traditional Strict Liability to Strict Liability for Abnormally Dangerous Activities

A. Traditional strict liability

1. Why "pockets" of strict liability?

As we saw in Part II, negligence is the usual standard governing lawsuits over injuries arising out of non-intentional conduct.[1] But the law has recognized "pockets" of strict liability for certain non-intentional conduct which allows a plaintiff to recover damages for injuries caused by a defendant without requiring plaintiff to prove the defendant's

---

1. Part I of this book discusses liability for intentional torts.

fault. To make out the prima facie case for one of these pockets of strict liability, it is enough to prove that the defendant engaged in conduct fitting into one of these pockets, and that the defendant's activity was an actual cause and a proximate cause of the plaintiff's injuries.[2] In certain circumstances, defendants may raise affirmative defenses either to defeat plaintiff's claim or to require a sharing of liability between the defendant and the plaintiff.

What explains the emergence of these pockets of strict liability? As we saw in Chapter 7, under both corrective justice and efficiency perspectives, there are strong arguments to be made for both the negligence standard and the strict liability standard. Considering corrective justice, some scholars have taken the view that whoever *causes harm* should compensate for the harm caused regardless of fault. On the other hand, other scholars have taken the view that *proof of fault* is necessary (in addition to proving causation) before a person causing harm to another is morally obligated to pay for the harm. On their face, the corrective justice arguments don't easily lend themselves to the creation of pockets of strict liability, and corrective justice arguments for such pockets are perhaps better left for a course on jurisprudence.

Considering economic analysis, we saw that generally speaking, both strict liability and negligence induce potential injurers to take the efficient level of care. Strict liability has the advantage of being cheaper to administer than negligence cases (because courts do not need to take evidence to determine if a defendant has failed to use reasonable care). Strict liability also causes potential injurers to take into account "activity level effects": Because a defendant in a strict liability system pays all costs of liability, that defendant will consider not only what *level of care* to use but also how much of a risky activity in *which to engage.* On the other hand, some economists have argued that negligence has the advantage of inducing potential victims to take additional care because under a negligence rule there will be some cases (that is, the cases in which a jury finds that a defendant used reasonable care) in which victims are injured but bear their own costs.

From this analysis, some economists have argued that negligence is the preferred rule in situations in which both a potential injurer and potential victim can take steps to minimize the likelihood of accidents (these are situations of *bilateral precaution*). In contrast, in situations in which only the potential injurer is in a position to take care (situations of *unilateral precaution*), strict liability is the preferred rule. As you work your way through this chapter, see if you think the actual development of strict liability pockets matches this distinction between unilateral and bilateral precaution. The distinction seems to work well for abnormally dangerous

---

2. Part III of this book explains the standard for actual causation and proximate causation.

activities, but not necessarily for all pockets of strict liability (such as vicarious liability, discussed in Chapter 17).

The remainder of this chapter focuses not on the question whether or not the pockets of strict liability that developed follow logically from corrective justice or economic approaches to tort law, but rather on the historical development of these pockets of strict liability and the current status of the law.

QUESTION 1. Level with Me. The reference to "activity level effects" in the law and economics debate over the use of negligence versus strict liability for unintentionally caused injuries refers to:

A. The fact that certain activities are abnormally dangerous.

B. The effects of various activities on the social costs of accidents.

C. The idea that a strict liability rule induces potential injurers to consider not only how much care to use but also how much of an activity to engage in.

D. The concept that the law should seek to "level effects" among various dangerous activities.

ANALYSIS. This question asks you to define "activity level effects." It is very easy to answer if you have done the reading early in the chapter, and nearly impossible if you are not familiar with the concept from the economic analysis of tort law. Choice **C** correctly defines activity level effects. A key insight of economic analysis is that negligence law only affects *how much care* an individual chooses to prevent injuries to others. Strict liability, in contrast, induces potential injurers not only to take a cost-justified *level* of care, but also to consider the total *amount* of an activity to engage in. Choices **A**, **B**, and **D** might sound nice to someone unfamiliar with the term "activity level effects," but they do not accurately describe the term.

2. *Rylands v. Fletcher*

One of the earliest and most important English cases in the development of strict liability pockets is *Rylands v. Fletcher*, (1868) L.R. 3 H.L. 330. In *Rylands*, defendants had constructed a reservoir on their land to collect water from rainfall. The water seeped through some underground channels that had been dug in earlier years to remove coal from the defendants' land; the defendants were unaware of these channels. The water escaped from defendants' land and ran onto plaintiff's land and damaged mines he had dug on his land. Various English courts considered whether the defendants should be liable for the damage caused. Ultimately, the House of Lords agreed that the defendants should be liable, regardless of whether they used reasonable care in building and maintaining the reservoir.

The uncertainty about *Rylands* is not about *whether* strict liability applied in the case, but *why* it applied. This issue is important because *Rylands* serves as a precedent (and is still good law in many U.S. jurisdictions), creating a pocket of strict liability. The judges who decided the case offered different views as to why strict liability is appropriate.

Judge Blackburn, writing for the intermediate appellate court, offered what is probably the most accepted test for this strict liability pocket: "the person who for his own purpose brings on his lands and collects and keeps there anything *likely to do mischief if it escapes*, must keep it at his peril, and, if he does not do so, is prima facie answerable for all the damage which is the natural consequence of his escape." *Fletcher v. Rylands*, (1865-66) L.R. 1 Ex. 265 (emphasis added).[3]

Under this reasoning, the defendants collected water on their land; they would be strictly liable because water is "likely to do mischief if it escapes." Contrast that situation with defendants collecting something more innocuous on their land, such as sand, which is not likely to do mischief it is escapes from the defendant's land.

Note the italicized "likely to do mischief" language I have highlighted from the opinion. Here, we see in Judge Blackburn's test the idea (later developed in the cases and the Restatement) that certain dangerous activities should be governed by a strict liability rule. In other words, if the probability of harm from an activity *if there is an accident* is high enough, defendants may be strictly liable even if there is *not* a high probability of an accident.[4]

The alternative formulation of the *Rylands* rule appears in Lord Cairns opinion for the House of Lords in the case. He stated that the defendants should be strictly liable because they put their land to a "non-natural use, for the purpose of introducing into the close that which in its natural condition was not in or upon it."[5] It is not clear precisely how Lord Cairns understood the term "non-natural use." One reading is that the term means an "artificial" use of land. Though some water collects on land naturally when it rains, a reservoir is an artificial structure created on land. Another reading is that the term means an "unreasonable" use of the land. Under this reading, it is unreasonable to collect large amounts of water through a reservoir close to someone else's land. (Of course, if we accept this natural-as-unreasonable

---

3. Judge Blackburn hedged this statement by suggesting that if the escape was due to an "act of God," the defendants might not have been strictly liable. For a recent case holding that *Rylands* would not apply in the context of unusual and unforeseen flooding, *see In re Flood Litigation*, 607 S.E.2d 863 (W. Va. 2004).

4. Lord Cranworth muddied the waters a bit (oops, sorry for that pun!) by endorsing Judge Blackburn's test and paraphrasing it as one imposing strict liability to a "person [who] brings, or accumulates, on his land anything which, if it should escape, *may cause* damage to his neighb[o]r. . . ." *Rylands v. Fletcher*, (1868) L.R. 3 H.L. 330, 340 (emphasis added). The "may cause" language is a much weaker test than the "likely to do mischief" test, and would impose strict liability on a broader set of activities.

5. (1868) L.R. 3 H.L. 330, 339.

understanding of Lord Cairns opinion, the rule approaches one of negligence and not strict liability.)

QUESTION 2. Salty *Rylands*. Big Lake Oil Company owns land with oil wells in Texas. As part of the process of drilling for oil, the Big Lake keeps and stores salt water on its land. Through no fault of Big Lake, the salt water escapes and damages Turner's nearby farmland. Is Big Lake strictly liable for Turner's property damage under the rule of *Rylands v. Fletcher*?

A. Yes, if the jurisdiction applies Judge Cairn's "non-natural use" test.
B. Perhaps, if the jurisdiction applies Judge Cairn's "non-natural use" test.
C. No, because *Rylands* involved fresh water, not salt water.
D. No, under the rule set out by Judge Blackburn in *Rylands*.

ANALYSIS. The facts of this case are based upon *Turner v. Big Lake Oil Co.*, 96 S.W.2d 221 (Tex. 1936). In *Turner*, the Supreme Court of Texas rejected the authority of the *Ryland* case in Texas. It also stated that the storing of water on land in Texas was not a "non-natural" use of the land, understanding that term to mean an "unreasonable" use. Here is what the court said:

> In Texas we have conditions very different from those which obtain in England. A large portion of Texas is an arid or semi-arid region. West of the 98th meridian of longitude, where the rainfall is approximately 30 inches, the rainfall decreases until finally, in the extreme western part of the State, it is only about 10 inches. This land of decreasing rainfall is the great ranch or livestock region of the State, water for which is stored in thousands of ponds, tanks, and lakes on the surface of the ground. The country is almost without streams; and without the storage of water from rainfall in basins constructed for the purpose, or to hold waters pumped from the earth, the great livestock industry of West Texas must perish. No such condition obtains in England. *With us the storage of water is a natural or necessary and common use of the land*, necessarily within the contemplation of the State and its grantees when grants were made, and obviously the rule announced in Rylands v. Fletcher, predicated upon different conditions, can have no application here.

Emphasis added.

The statement from *Turner* shows that under the "non-natural as un-reasonable" interpretation, there would not necessarily be liability under *Rylands*, though under "non-natural as artificial" there could well be liability. For this reason, Choice **B** is correct and Choice **A** is incorrect. Choice **C** is wrong because there is nothing in any of the various rules of *Rylands* that would distinguish between fresh and salt water kept on defendant's land. Choice **D** is wrong because Judge Blackburn set out the "likely to do mischief if it escapes" test, which would seem to apply equally to the fresh water at issue in the *Rylands* case and the salt water at issue in the *Turner* case.

3. Fire

Traditionally, the common law subjected some — but not all — cases involving fires to a strict liability standard. To understand the complex rule, it is useful to separate the fire cases into three types.

1. *Intention to Send Fire onto Plaintiff's Land.* If someone starts a fire with the intention that it spreads to plaintiff's land (such as by throwing a "Molotov cocktail"), that person may be liable for the intentional tort of *trespass to real property*, discussed in Chapter 3. Recall that for trespass, a defendant must intend to enter, or cause something to enter, the plaintiff's land, and such intrusion onto plaintiff's land must occur.
2. *Unintentionally Started Fire that Causes Injury to Plaintiff.* If someone does not try to start a fire, but starts one accidentally (think of the not very bright defendant in the *Vaughan v. Menlove* case, discussed in Chapter 8), causing injury, that person may be liable for *negligence*, discussed in Part II of this book. To recover for negligence, a plaintiff will have to show that the defendant failed to use reasonable care to prevent a reasonably foreseeable injury to the plaintiff.
3. *Intention to Start Fire, But Not for It to Spread to Plaintiff's Land.* If someone tries to start a fire on her own land, but it accidentally spreads to plaintiff's land, causing injury, the common law often subjected the defendant to *strict liability*. That is, even if the defendant was careful in starting the fire, if it spread to the plaintiff's land, causing injury, the defendant would be liable for the injuries caused.

In more modern times, courts have expressed skepticism that strict liability should apply even in cases fitting into category 3, at least for activities such as starting a campfire.[6] Instead, the usual standard is one of *negligence*. Some courts therefore limit strict liability for fire to cases of "controlled burns" on land, such as a "backfire" used to prevent a future wildfire from causing more extensive damage. Cases of controlled burns, however, perhaps are better conceived of as an example of strict liability for "abnormally dangerous" activities, than a rule regarding "fires." *See* REST. (3D) TORTS: LIABILITY FOR PHYSICAL HARM § 20, cmt. *h* (P.F.D. No. 1, 2005).

---

6. *See Koos v. Roth*, 652 P.2d 1255 (Or. 1982); *King v. United States*, 53 F. Supp. 2d 1056 (D. Colo. 1999), *rev'd on other grounds*, 301 F.3d 1270 (10th Cir. 2002).

QUESTION 3. Fired Up. Don lives on a farm in Pacifica, a Western state with a big wildfire problem in the summer and fall months, before the winter rains begin. Because of a drought the past few years, experts have predicted that the upcoming fire season could be the worst one on record.

Don is concerned that his farm could burn down from one of the wildfires. He therefore hires a professional firm with the best experience in the state at managing a controlled burn. In a controlled burn, professionals start small fires to burn away brush, creating a ring of already burned areas to be used to stop a larger wild fire, should one materialize in the future. The firm uses the best available technology in starting the controlled burn. Unfortunately, things go out of control, and the fire accidentally spreads to the neighboring farm, owned by Penelope. The fire causes $10,000 in damage to Penelope's farm.

What is Penelope's strongest tort cause of action against Don (assuming Don is responsible for the action of the firm that he hired)?

A. Trespass to real property.
B. Negligence.
C. Strict liability.
D. No cause of action is likely to be successful.

ANALYSIS. Though strict liability used to be available to plaintiffs for intentionally started fires, that rule has been limited by many courts in recent years to situations of controlled burns. The fact pattern in this question involves a controlled burn, and therefore strict liability looks like a strong case. For this reason, Choice **C** is correct and Choice **D** is incorrect. Choice **A** is wrong because Don did not intend to send fire onto Penelope's land; in fact he was taking all reasonable steps to prevent that from happening. Choice **B** is incorrect because under these facts it looks like Don, as well as the firm he hired, used all reasonable care to prevent the fire from spreading and injuring others.

4. Animals

In certain torts involving animals, the law has long recognized a pocket of strict liability. But strict liability does not apply in all contexts involving animals. Here are the major rules.

Strict Liability for Physical Harm Caused by Intrusion of Livestock or Other Animals upon Another's Land. English common law long accepted the idea that owners of cattle who intrude upon a plaintiff's land are liable for property damage caused by the trespass. The Third Restatement has extended this rule to "livestock or other animals, except for dogs and cats." REST. (3D) TORTS: LIABILITY FOR PHYSICAL HARM § 21 (P.F.D. No. 1, 2005). But the Restatement acknowledges that there is a three-way split of authority among American jurisdictions.

- Some jurisdictions impose strict liability on the livestock owner.
- Some jurisdictions impose strict liability on the livestock owner, but allow the owner to raise as an affirmative defense the plaintiff's failure to "fence out" intruding animals.
- Some jurisdictions impose a negligence standard on the livestock owner.

See id. cmt. *c.* There is an interesting historical debate over whether the rules related to "fencing in" and "fencing out" reflect the relative political power of ranchers and farmers. But in any case, the strict liability rule appears to have general acceptance; the Restatement notes that there is "interesting evidence that American cattle owners regard their own liability as morally sound and accept strict liability in practice even in localities where it is not imposed as a matter of law."[7] *Id.* cmt. *d.*

The Restatement justifies its exception for dogs and cats on grounds of tradition and the fact that "while many dogs and cats may be inclined to intrude onto neighboring property, in doing so they are unlikely to cause substantial harm." *Id.* cmt. *e.*

Strict Liability for Physical Harm Caused by Wild Animals. "Wild" animals are animals "that have not been generally domesticated and that are likely, unless restrained, to cause personal injury." REST. (3D) TORTS: LIABILITY FOR PHYSICAL HARM § 22(b) (P.F.D. No. 1, 2005). Under this definition, it is not enough that the animal be one found in the "wild." It also must be a dangerous kind of animal. Lizards may not be domesticated, but, at least under this definition of "wild animal," lizards would not count, and the owner of a lizard that causes physical harm to another would not be strictly liable for such injuries.

As with the rule for intruding cattle, the strict liability for wild animals rule has a long history in the common law. It also can be justified on the same grounds as "abnormally dangerous" activities discussed later in this chapter: Someone who chooses to keep an alligator as a pet will do so at his peril. Some courts have recognized, however, that strict liability does not apply for injuries caused by wild animals at zoos; people come to the zoo to experience these animals, and in exchange for this benefit, attendees give up the ability to sue in strict liability. *See City and County of Denver v. Kennedy,* 476 P.2d 762 (Colo. Ct. App. 1970); *Cowden v. Bear Country, Inc.,* 382 F. Supp.

---

7. For a fascinating account, see ROBERT ELLICKSON, ORDER WITHOUT LAW: HOW NEIGHBORS SETTLE DISPUTES (2005).

1321 (D.S.D. 1974); *see also* Rest. (3d) Torts: Liability for Physical Harm § 24(a) (P.F.D. No. 1, 2005).

Strict Liability for Physical Harm Caused by Animals Whose Owners Know or Reasonably Should Have Known of Its Dangerous Tendencies. For injuries caused by animals not falling into the first two categories (intruding livestock and other animals, and wild animals), the general standard will be one of negligence. So if Muffy the cat lunges at you and pokes out your eye, Muffy's owner generally will not be liable unless you can prove that the owner failed to use reasonable care with respect to the animal. If, however, Muffy's owner knew or had reason to know of the cat's dangerous propensities, then strict liability applies.

This rule recognizes the benefit that many people enjoy from the companionship of dogs, cats, and other pets. A strict liability rule could overly chill people from keeping pets. For this reason, the law triggers a strict liability rule only when the owner is on notice that the animal is more dangerous than usual.

QUESTION 4. Cow in the Headlights. Cassie is driving down a country road late at night. Despite using all reasonable care, she collides with one of Andrew's cows, which had strayed from Andrew's property and entered the public road. Cassie suffers personal injury and damage to her car. Andrew exercised reasonable care to keep his cows on his property. Will Andrew be strictly liable for injuries caused by his cow?

A. Yes, because the cattle intruded into the road.
B. Yes, because a cow is a wild animal.
C. No, even though the cattle intruded into the road.
D. No, because cattle owners are never strictly liable for intruding cattle.

ANALYSIS. The owner of livestock is liable *to other property owners* for physical harm caused by intruding cattle. The rule does not apply to cattle that enter into public areas and cause damage. Such injuries are governed by a negligence rule. For this reason, Choice **A** is incorrect and Choice **C** is correct. Choice **B** is wrong because cows are not considered wild animals: They are domesticated and not considered to be especially dangerous animals. Choice **D** reaches the right result — no strict liability — but it states an incorrect principle of law: In some circumstances (that is, when intruding cattle enter another's land and cause injury), cattle owners *are* strictly liable for intruding cattle.

An Important Note on Proximate Cause.[8] Not every injury involving an animal covered by the rules above will invoke strict liability: Recall that for

---

8. To fully understand this note, you first will need to understand the concepts in Chapter 14.

each tort, it is necessary that the plaintiff prove actual cause and proximate cause (concepts covered in Part III of this book) as well as tortious conduct and damages. Imagine, for example, that Brenda's lion escapes from her home. The lion walks down main street and steps on some fragile flowers that Tom was selling on a street corner. Brenda would not be strictly liable even though the property damage was caused by Brenda's wild animal: "[i]f the harm the plaintiff incurs is not a product of the risks posed by wild animals, then . . . strict liability . . . does not apply." REST. (3D) TORTS: LIABILITY FOR PHYSICAL HARM § 22, cmt. ƒ (P.F.D. No. 1, 2005). Putting this idea into the terms discussed in Chapter 14, crushing flowers is not a harm within the risk of keeping wild animals.

QUESTION 5. Bear with Me. Tina owns a pet black bear, Coco, which she has trained to be very tame. Tina is very careful to keep Coco safely on her property at all times. Coco nonetheless escapes from Tina's property and begins to wander down Main Street. Sima sees the bear walking down Main Street. She becomes very frightened and has a heart attack. Is Tina strictly liable for Sima's physical harm?

A. Yes, if damage from fright is a harm within the risk of keeping wild animals.

B. Yes, because owners of wild animals are always liable for all damage the animals cause.

C. No, because Tina exercised reasonable care.

D. No, unless Tina reasonably should have known that someone like Sima could become frightened by the bear.

ANALYSIS. To begin with, Tina is keeping a wild animal, and the animal escaped, causing physical harm to Sima. Tina should be strictly liable, then, assuming Sima can prove the rest of the prima facie case. There's an argument here over whether physical harm from fright is a harm within the risk of keeping a wild animal. Choice **A** correctly flags the issue, without resolving it. It is the best answer. Choice **B** is wrong because we know that sometimes owners of wild animals are not liable for damage, as in the example of the lion trampling the flowers. Choice **C** is wrong because whether or not Tina exercised reasonable care is irrelevant to the question whether strict liability applies. Choice **D** is wrong because, like Choice **C**, the answer improperly considers the reasonableness of Tina's conduct, which would be relevant in a negligence case, but not in this strict liability case.

B.   The modern approach: Liability for abnormally dangerous activities

1. The approach of the First and Second Restatements

There's a common, if rough, theme in the traditional pockets of strict liability described above: The cases typically involve defendants doing dangerous things (gathering large quantities of water in a reservoir, intentionally starting fires on land, or keeping wild animals), activities that most people do not ordinarily undertake. Since the 1930s, the Restatement drafters have tried to build upon this insight and create a set of rules to specify which dangerous activities should be subject to a special strict liability standard.

The efforts began with the First Restatement of Torts, which imposed strict liability for "ultrahazardous" activities.[9] It defined such activities as having to meet a two-part test: the activity

> (a) necessarily involves a risk of serious harm to the person, land or chattels of others which cannot be eliminated by the exercise of the utmost care, and
> (b) is not a matter of common usage.

REST. (FIRST) TORTS § 520 (1938).

The Second Restatement replaced the term "ultrahazardous" with "abnormally dangerous," and replaced the two-part test for defining which activities come within the strict liability pocket with six factors to consider:

> (a) existence of a high degree of risk of some harm to the person, land or chattels of others;
> (b) likelihood that the harm that results from it will be great;
> (c) inability to eliminate the risk by the exercise of reasonable care;
> (d) extent to which the activity is not a matter of common usage;
> (e) inappropriateness of the activity to the place where it is carried on; and
> (f) extent to which its value to the community is outweighed by its dangerous attributes.

REST. (2D) TORTS § 520 (1977).

Both Restatement sections have been very influential in American law, solidifying or expanding strict liability for actions such as blasting, handling hazardous materials, fumigating, and other similarly dangerous activities.[10]

---

9. Section 519 of the First Restatement of Torts (1938) provided strict liability, subject to some exceptions, for "one who carries on an ultrahazardous activity . . . although the utmost care is exercised to prevent the harm."

10. Some of the early cases, relying upon the old common law distinction between directly caused injuries, brought under a writ of *trespass*, and indirect injuries, brought under a writ of *case*, imposed strict liability for blasting only when the injury resulted from physical impact of debris (direct, brought under a writ of trespass) and not from injury caused by blasting vibrations (indirect, brought under case). Eventually courts eliminated this distinction, allowing strict liability for injuries

Both tests also focus on both the dangerousness of the activity (and the inability to eliminate the dangers from the activity with reasonable care) and the lack of "common usage."

This common usage prong eliminates activities such as driving automobiles, which could inflict very serious injuries even when operated carefully. The idea seems to be that strict liability should be reserved for activities that either are (1) not engaged in by many people in the community or (2) not engaged in pervasively in the community, such as the transmission of electricity. *See* REST. (3D) TORTS: LIABILITY FOR PHYSICAL HARM § 20, cmt. *j* (P.F.D. No. 1, 2005) (continuing the earlier Restatements' requirement that the activity not be one of "common usage"). One defense of the common usage criterion is that it separates those cases in which there are reciprocal risks of harm (as when we all drive, or enjoy electricity transmitted through our community), for which a negligence rule should apply, with cases of nonreciprocal risks (as when a blaster blows up a building to make way for new construction). Under this argument, strict liability is appropriate in the case of nonreciprocal risks, as a means of compensating those for the extra dangers caused by the activity. *See* George Fletcher, *Fairness and Utility in Tort Theory,* 85 HARV. L. REV. 537 (1972). For reciprocal risks, compensation comes from the enjoyment society as a whole receives from the activity, and therefore a negligence standard is appropriate.

One of the more controversial features of the Second Restatement's approach was factor (f), consideration of the social value of the activity. To critics, the question is not whether the activity should be undertaken because it is socially valuable (as blasting, fumigation, and other dangerous activities), but *who should pay for injuries* caused by these activities. *See Koos v. Roth,* 652 P.2d 1255, 1262 (Or. 1982).

Under the Restatement approach and in the courts, the question whether an activity is "abnormally dangerous" and therefore subject to strict liability is a question for the courts, not for juries.

> **QUESTION 6. And the Rockets Red Glare . . .**   Acme Fireworks Company has the best safety record of all the fireworks companies in the state of Pacifica. As part of its Fourth of July show, Acme sets off a number of fireworks, which are enjoyed by the entire community. Unfortunately, despite using all reasonable care, one of the final rockets set off by Acme veers off course and causes an eye injury to Bugs. Pacifica follows the approach of the Restatement (Second) of Torts to classify which activities count as "abnormally dangerous" activities subject to a strict liability rule.

from blasting whether as a result of physical impact or vibration. *See Spano v. Perini Corp.,* 250 N.E. 2d 31 (N.Y. 1969).

Bugs sues Acme, arguing it is strictly liable for his injuries. In considering whether or not Acme's activities should be subject to strict liability, which factor should the court *not* consider?

A. The inability of Acme to eliminate risk by exercising reasonable care.
B. The extent to which lighting fireworks is a matter of common usage.
C. The social utility of the fireworks to the community.
D. Whether or not Acme has purchased liability insurance.

ANALYSIS.   This question is quite straightforward for anyone familiar with the six factors of the Second Restatement's approach to abnormally dangerous activities. Choices **A**, **B**, and **C** each list factors that are part of the Restatement's test (inability to eliminate the danger through the exercise of reasonable care, common usage, and social utility). Only Choice **D**, whether or not the defendant has insurance, is not a factor listed in the six-part test. So Choice **D** is correct.

By the way, Epstein notes that courts applying the Second Restatement have split over whether or not fireworks count as an abnormally dangerous activity. *See* Richard A. Epstein, Cases and Materials on Torts 667 (9th ed. 2008).

Proximate Cause Again. As with the discussion of animals earlier in this chapter, strict liability for abnormally dangerous activities must satisfy both the actual cause (usually "but for" cause) and proximate cause requirements as well. To understand the rest of this section, you will need to be familiar with the material in Part III of this book.

One of my favorite torts cases is *Madsen v. East Jordan Irrigation Co.*, 125 P.2d 794 (Utah 1942). In *Madsen*, defendant engaged in the abnormally dangerous activity of blasting. The noise from the blasting frightened minks on a nearby mink farm, which caused the nervous mother minks to eat their own young! Even though blasting is an abnormally dangerous activity, the court held that strict liability did not apply. The court discussed the issue in terms of the animal's conduct "breaking the chain of causation" (see Chapter 14), but there is a more straightforward "harm within the risk" analysis that applies here: What makes blasting dangerous is the possibility of flying debris or falling objects from shaking. It is not that the loud noise would cause animals to eat their young. (Indeed, a loud airplane overhead could have had the same effect as the blasting: Excessive noise is not a risk that makes blasting abnormally dangerous.)

QUESTION 7. Gas Explosion.   Jim is an independent gasoline hauler. His tanker truck moves gasoline from the refinery to a number of local gas stations. Jim stops for lunch at a local diner. Crazy Al, the local pyromaniac, sees Jim's truck parked in the diner parking lot. He goes over with a match and a rag, opens the gas tank of the tanker, sticks in the rag, and lights it on fire. The tanker truck explodes, causing severe damage to the diner, owned by Alice.

If Alice sues Jim alleging he is strictly liable for the damage to the diner, what is Jim's strongest argument in response?

A. Transporting gasoline is not an abnormally dangerous activity.
B. Alice cannot prove proximate cause, because Crazy Al's actions break the chain of causation.
C. Jim exercised reasonable care in transporting the gasoline.
D. Jim's transportation of gasoline was not a cause in fact of Alice's injuries.

ANALYSIS. Transporting hazardous materials, as mentioned earlier, is one of the well-accepted types of activities to which a rule of strict liability for abnormally dangerous activities applies. For this reason Choice **A** is incorrect. Choice **C** is incorrect because whether or not Jim exercised reasonable care is not relevant to the question whether or not he should be strictly liable for injuries caused by his transportation of gasoline. Choice **D** is wrong because Jim's transportation of the gasoline is a "but for" cause of Alice's injuries: But for Jim's transportation of the gasoline, the injury to Alice's restaurant would not occur.

Choice **B** is correct: The strongest argument Jim can raise is that Crazy Al's conduct should count as an intervening cause that, under proximate cause doctrines, "breaks the chain of causation." Whether or not a court accepts that argument is not certain (for reasons set forth in Chapter 14), but it is the strongest by far of the four possible arguments listed in the question.

2. The Third Restatement approach: A blast from the past

The recently completed Third Restatement moves away from the six-part test of the Second Restatement, back to something close to the approach of the First Restatement. An activity is now considered abnormally dangerous if:

> (1) the activity creates a foreseeable and highly significant risk of physical harm even when reasonable care is exercised by all actors and
> (2) the activity is not one of common usage.

REST. (3D) TORTS: LIABILITY FOR PHYSICAL HARM § 20(b) (P.F.D. No. 1, 2005). As with the Second Restatement, lack of "common usage" plays an important role, as well as the high dangerousness of the activity. Gone, however, is consideration of the social utility of the activity: "the value that the defendant or others derive from the activity is not a direct factor in determining whether the activity is abnormally dangerous." *Id.* cmt. *k.*

How does one know whether an activity involves a highly significant risk of harm? Thinking in terms of the Hand formula (discussed in detail in Chapter 8), these are cases in which either *P*, the probability of harm, or *L*, the severity of harm if an accident occurs, are high. You might wonder why, in cases in which *P* or *L* are high, a court would not find engaging in the activity to be not only abnormally dangerous, but also negligent. The answer is that for there to be negligence (at least under the Hand formula economic formulation), *P* multiplied by *L* must be higher than the burden of taking a precaution. Operating a nuclear power plant may not be negligent, because the probability of harm is so low, making the product of *P* and *L* low as well; But the activity should be considered abnormally dangerous because *L* alone is extremely high. *See id.* cmt. *g.*

QUESTION 8. And the Rockets Red Glare . . . Take II. Acme Fireworks Company has the best safety record in the state of Pacifica. As part of its Fourth of July show, Acme sets off a number of fireworks, which are enjoyed by the entire community. Unfortunately, despite using all reasonable care, one of the final rockets set off by Acme veers off course and causes an eye injury to Bugs. Pacifica follows the approach of the Restatement (Third) of Torts to classify which activities count as "abnormally dangerous" activities subject to a strict liability rule.

Bugs sues Acme, arguing it is strictly liable for his injuries. In considering whether or not Acme's activities should be subject to strict liability, which factor should the court *not* consider?

A. The inability of Acme to eliminate risk by exercising reasonable care.
B. The extent to which lighting fireworks is a matter of common usage.
C. The social utility of the fireworks to the community.
D. The high likelihood of serious injury if there is an accident.

ANALYSIS. This question is quite straightforward for anyone familiar with the two-part test of the Third Restatement's approach to abnormally dangerous activities. Choices **A**, **B**, and **D** each list factors that are part of the Restatement's test (inability to eliminate the danger through the exercise of reasonable care, common usage, and significant risk of harm). Only Choice **C**, the social utility of the fireworks to the community, is not a factor listed in the Third Restatement (making the Third Restatement's approach on this issue different from the approach of the Second Restatement). So Choice **C** is correct.

C.   The Closer: Abnormally dangerous activities and affirmative defenses

The Second Restatement's approach to affirmative defenses to the abnormally dangerous activity tort was a mess and has been used to torture many first-year law students. In a nutshell, the approach was this: The plaintiff's negligence was *not* an affirmative defense (think of a plaintiff inadvertently wandering into an area in which blasting is taking place), but the plaintiff's consent (called assumption of risk in this context; think of a person who chooses to get close to watch an impending blast) *was* a complete affirmative defense, defeating plaintiff's case completely. Even if the plaintiff's consent was unreasonable, and possibly considered a form of negligence, the consent operated as a complete defense. *See* REST. (2D) TORTS §§ 523, 524 (1977).

The Third Restatement's approach is a bit easier to understand, though at bottom it requires jurors to engage in a somewhat incoherent exercise. The Third Restatement adopts a comparative responsibility approach to strict liability claims. *See* REST. (3D) TORTS: LIABILITY FOR PHYSICAL HARM § 25 (P.F.D. No. 1, 2005). As described in detail in Chapter 10, the comparative responsibility approach requires the jury to allocate percentages of responsibility between the plaintiff and the defendant, adding up to 100 percent. The plaintiff is entitled to damages equal to the percentage of the defendant's responsibility. For example, if the jury finds that the defendant is 70 percent responsible and the plaintiff is 30 percent responsible, and the plaintiff suffered $10,000 in injuries, the defendant would be required to pay $7,000 in damages to the plaintiff.

In a negligence case, the jury compares the defendant's fault with the plaintiff's fault and consent to come up with the allocation of responsibility. As Chapter 10 explains, that is a difficult comparison for juries in some cases: The jury must compare fault with consent. But the problem is even harder in a strict liability case, which, by definition, is not based upon the defendant's fault. So consider this problem. Defendant is a blasting company that is very careful in blasting. Plaintiff sneaks into the blast site because he wants to watch the blast and gets injured. It is unclear how a jury should apportion responsibility between the strictly liable defendant and a plaintiff who has consented and (at least arguably) acted negligently. But regardless of the mental process jurors must go through, they will be expected to pick two numbers that add up to 100 percent of the responsibility.

> **QUESTION 9. Having a Blast!**   Romeo has just met the love of his life, Juliet. He is walking through the park, thinking about his new girlfriend. He is so busy daydreaming that he misses the numerous signs warning that the Shakespeare Blasting Company is doing some blasting in the park

today to build a new duck pond. Romeo walks into the blast zone and suffers an eye injury from flying debris.

Under the applicable rules of civil procedure, Romeo can sue either in his state, which uses the Second Restatement's approach to abnormally dangerous activities, or the state of the Shakespeare Blasting Company, which uses the Third Restatement's approach. Assume Romeo's lawyer believes a jury is likely to find that Romeo acted negligently in failing to see the signs, but that he did not consent. Would it be better for Romeo's lawyer to sue on his behalf in his state or the state of the blasting company?

A. Romeo's state.

B. Shakespeare Blasting Company's state.

C. The result would be the same in either state.

D. We do not have enough information to know which state would be a more advantageous forum for Romeo.

ANALYSIS. Under either jurisdiction, there seems no question that blasting will be considered an abnormally dangerous activity, subjecting the Shakespeare Blasting Company to strict liability. The difference in the two jurisdictions relates to affirmative defenses. Recall that under the Second Restatement, a plaintiff's contributory negligence is *not* a defense to an abnormally dangerous activity tort. (In contrast, plaintiff's assumption of risk/consent acted as a complete defense, but there's no indication that Romeo consented here.) Under the Third Restatement, the plaintiff's negligence must be compared with the defendant's conduct to come up with an allocation of responsibility adding to 100 percent. Given these rules, it would be better for Romeo to sue in his state, which uses the Second Restatement because he would be entitled to a full recovery of his damages and not simply a percentage as under the Third Restatement. For this reason, Choice **A** is correct, and Choices **B**, **C**, and **D** are incorrect.

✸ Rick's picks

1. Level with Me	C
2. Salty *Rylands*	B
3. Fired Up	C
4. Cow in the Headlights	C
5. Bear with Me	A
6. And the Rockets Red Glare . . .	D
7. Gas Explosion	B
8. And the Rockets Red Glare . . . Take II	C
9. Having a Blast!	A

16

Nuisance

CHAPTER OVERVIEW
A. The basics: Nuisance versus trespass to land
B. Private nuisance
C. Public nuisance
D. The Closer: Coming to the nuisance and extrasensitivity
✦ Rick's picks

A. The basics: Nuisance versus trespass to land

We treat nuisance law separately from other traditional strict liability torts because nuisance law is something of an amalgam of strict liability and negligence law, with certain aspects of intentional torts mixed in. *See* REST. (3D) TORTS: LIABILITY FOR PHYSICAL HARM § 20, cmt. *c* (noting how the Second Restatement's treatment of nuisance law sometimes uses a negligence standard and sometimes uses a strict liability standard). Whatever standard applies, the law is something of a mess; Prosser described the law of nuisance as an "impenetrable jungle." RICHARD A. EPSTEIN, TORTS 355 (1999) (quoting William L. Prosser). Mercifully, we will just focus on the basics in this chapter.

As an introductory note, much of what would be governed by nuisance law under the common law is no longer subject to tort law. Local, state, and federal law governs land uses and environmental impacts, removing many of these cases from the courts and placing decisions for incompatible land uses into the hands of regulators, subject to judicial review. This chapter considers only those cases that remain as common law torts in the tort system.

To begin an analysis of nuisance, we need to distinguish a nuisance from trespass to land (discussed in Chapter 3). If I am your neighbor and come by and dump my garbage on your lawn, you certainly would consider that a "nuisance," but your tort suit against me would be for trespass to land. Trespass to land occurs when I intentionally come on to your land or send or direct something onto your land. Nuisance in contrast, is an invasion of the right to enjoy one's land (or for the public to enjoy the use of its land), that doesn't necessarily amount to a trespass. If I keep a cow barn on my property and the stench from it bothers you day and night, you would sue for nuisance, not trespass.

Conduct can also be both a nuisance *and* a trespass. If I dump garbage on your lawn *every day*, then you could sue me for *both* trespass *and* nuisance. *See* Rest. (2d) Torts § 821D, cmt. *e* ("If the interference with the use and enjoyment of the land is a significant one, sufficient in itself to amount to a private nuisance, the fact that it arises out of or is accompanied by a trespass will not prevent recovery for the nuisance, and the action may be maintained upon either basis as the plaintiff elects or both.").

The initial dividing line within nuisance is between a public nuisance and a private nuisance. A private nuisance is "a nontrespassory invasion of another's interest in the private use and enjoyment of land." Rest. (2d) Torts § 821D. A public nuisance, in contrast, "is an unreasonable interference with a right common to the general public." *Id.* § 821B(1).

Nuisance law arises principally out of the clash of land uses between nearby landowners.[1] If nothing that we did on our land affected others, there would be no need for nuisance law. But sometimes what we do on our land creates costs imposed on others, what economists call "negative externalities."[2] In certain circumstances, the law imposes on a landowner a requirement to stop the negative activity through an injunction, to pay for damage caused by the activity, or both. More on nuisance remedies at the end of this chapter.

Which activities count as nuisances? "As a first approximation, the usual suspects cover most of the field: fumes and stench that waft across P's boundary; filth that leaks from a privy onto P's land; smoke that drifts across the border; water that enters a basement; pollution from whatever source; noise and vibration that rattle foundations and jangle nerves; particulate matter released by spraying and painting." Epstein, *supra*, at 356.

QUESTION 1. Annoying Neighbor. Jared and Shana are neighboring landowners who do not get along. Which of the following claims could be brought as a tort suit for trespass to land in addition to a nuisance claim?

---

1. I write of landowners, but other possessors of land interests may bring suit as well.
2. Not all externalities are negative. I might live next to a bakery, and enjoy the smell of the baking bread. That would be a positive externality (though I'd suspect that non-economists would not think of it in such clinical terms).

A. Jared's sewage line backs up and leaks onto Shana's lawn.
B. Jared sends his dog Layla every night onto Shana's lawn to relieve herself.
C. Jared works outside on his model airplanes, sending a strong smell of airplane glue into Shana's kitchen.
D. Jared plays his drums really loudly late at night and early in the morning, waking Shana.

ANALYSIS. While each of these activities may be a "nuisance" to Shana, the question is one of the legal standard of trespass. A trespass to land occurs when one intentionally enters or intentionally sends or directs something onto plaintiff's land. Of these four choices, only Choice **B** involves Jared sending something (in this case his dog) onto Shana's land. Choice **A** is incorrect because, even though the sewage entered Shana's land, Jared had no intention to send the sewage onto Shana's land. (Note that this claim might also be covered under the *Rylands* rule discussed in the last chapter.) Choices **C** and **D** are wrong because nothing tangible entered Shana's land (in one case, an odor and in the other case sound and vibration).

B.   Private nuisance

The Restatement sets forth the basic elements of the private nuisance tort:

> One is subject to liability for a private nuisance if, but only if, his conduct is a legal cause of an invasion of another's interest in the private use and enjoyment of land, and the invasion is either
>
> (a) intentional and unreasonable, or
>
> (b) unintentional and otherwise actionable under the rules controlling liability for negligent or reckless conduct, or for abnormally dangerous conditions or activities.

Rest. (2d) Torts § 822.

Parsing the tortious conduct element of § 822, we see that for all claims of private nuisance, the defendant's conduct must invade plaintiff's interest in plaintiff's private use and enjoyment of land. This requirement is straightforward, falling into the kinds of activities described in the last section—such as odors or smoke wafting onto plaintiff's property—that can interfere with plaintiff's use and enjoyment of land.

In addition, to constitute a private nuisance the defendant's conduct must be either (1) intentional and unreasonable, or (2) unintentional, but otherwise constitutes a tort under the rules for negligence, recklessness, or abnormally dangerous activities. Let's consider each of these in turn.

Intentional and Unreasonable Invasion. Under this option, the defendant's behavior must be *both* intentional and unreasonable. By intentional, the Restatement means that defendant's invasion must be done with the *purpose* of invading plaintiff's use and enjoyment of his land or done with *knowledge* that such an invasion is substantially certain to occur. *Id.* § 825. For example, if Jared plays his drums at night in order to annoy his neighbor Shana, his conduct would meet the intentionality requirement. Jared also could be liable if he does so just because he likes to play at night, knowing that Shana has complained that the drumming has kept her awake. The intentionality requirement here matches intentionality for intentional torts.[3]

QUESTION 2. Airport Insomnia.   Deborah lives near a small regional airport, the Pacifica Municipal Airport (PMA). The planes fly directly over her house morning and night, and the noise keeps her up at night and wakes her up in the morning. Deborah brings suit against PMA alleging that the airport constitutes a nuisance under the "intentional and unreasonable" prong of Restatement § 822. The jurisdiction follows the approach to nuisance of the Restatement (Second) of Torts. (Assume no state or federal law affects Deborah's tort claim.)

PMA concedes that the planes from the airport fly regularly over Deborah's house and acknowledges that Deborah has complained regularly about the noise. But it argues that it cannot be liable for nuisance because it does not intend to interfere with Deborah's use and enjoyment of her land. How should the court rule on PMA's argument?

A. The court should accept the argument because PMA did not act with a malicious intent.

B. The court should accept the argument because PMA did not have the purpose to invade Deborah's interest in her use and enjoyment of her land.

C. The court should reject the argument because under the "intentional and unreasonable" prong, landowners are strictly liable for any interference with others' enjoyment of the use of their land.

D. The court should reject the argument because PMA had knowledge that the noise from the airport was substantially certain to interfere with Deborah's use and enjoyment of her land.

ANALYSIS.   This question probes your understanding of the meaning of intent under Restatement (Second) of Torts § 822(a). The standard is one of *purpose* or *knowledge*. There is no evidence in this fact pattern of PMA's

---

3. See Chapter 3 for more on the intentionality requirement in intentional torts, especially if you are unsure why the second example counts as "intentional" conduct.

purpose to interfere with Deborah's enjoyment of the use of her land. But PMA has *knowledge* that interference is substantially certain to occur; they know, among other reasons, because Deborah has complained about the noise. Choice **D** correctly explains this knowledge standard.

Choice **A** is incorrect because there is no requirement of any malicious intent to sustain an action for private nuisance (though such an intent is certainly sufficient). Choice **B** is incorrect because purpose is not required; knowledge is enough. Choice **C** incorrectly states that a cause of action for private nuisance always creates strict liability for interfering landowners. This is incorrect.

Unreasonable invasion. Under Restatement § 822's first option, it is not enough for plaintiff to prove intention to invade plaintiff's use and enjoyment of his land. Defendant's actions must also be *unreasonable.* For unreasonableness, the Restatement generally uses a type of balancing test, finding unreasonable harm when either "the gravity of the harm outweighs the utility of the" defendant's conduct or "the harm caused by the conduct is serious and the financial burden of compensating for this and similar harm to others would not make the continuation of the conduct not feasible." *Id.* § 826.

Note the difference between the alternative balancing tests. The first balancing test (gravity versus utility) looks like a straightforward application of the Hand formula (discussed in connection with the breach standard for negligence cases in Chapter 8). But the second balancing test seems to recognize instances in which the utility of the action outweighs the gravity but there is still *serious harm* caused by the activities (minor harm is not going to qualify).

Stripping out the hard-to-understand double negative of this Restatement section,[4] the activity could still be considered a nuisance if it was feasible to compensate plaintiff and similarly situated people without imposing a strong financial burden on the defendant. The Restatement gives the example here of operating an airport: The utility of the airport likely exceeds the gravity of the noise and pollution caused to neighbors of the airport.[5] But the Restatement leaves open the possibility of requiring the airport to compensate those — like Deborah in Question 2 — who suffer serious harm from the airport's activities. If compensation would cause the airport to have to shut down, however, there would be no cause of action for private nuisance.

---

4. "[T]he financial burden of compensating for this and similar harm to others would *not* make the continuation of the conduct *not* feasible."
5. Certainly the airport does not operate with the purpose of bothering the neighbors from its noise and vibration. But airport officials have knowledge that such annoyance is substantially certain to occur.

QUESTION 3. Soot City. Lori lives near a cement factory. Each morning, her car is covered with a fine dust emitted from the factory. The factory knows about this problem, as Lori and the neighbors have complained repeatedly about it. Scientists have determined that the dust is not dangerous, but it is a constant annoyance. It would be very expensive to eliminate.

The cement factory is a major employer in the area, and its value is estimated at around $45 million. The local economy is also heavily dependent on taxes from the factory. Experts have estimated that the loss of property value to Lori and other nearby homeowners from the dust is about $185,000. Lori and these other homeowners sue for private nuisance, arguing that the factory's conduct is a nuisance under Restatement (Second) of Torts § 822(a). They want damages for their decline in property values. The factory concedes Lori and the other homeowners can prove intent, but argue that their behavior is not unreasonable.

How should the court respond to this argument?

A. The court should accept the argument because the gain to the cement factory exceeds the loss to Lori and the other homeowners.
B. The court should accept the argument because to allow nuisance claims like Lori's to go forward means shutting down big factories.
C. The court should reject the argument, so long as the court believes the harm to the plaintiffs is serious and the factory can compensate Lori and the other homeowners without facing an insurmountable financial burden.
D. The court should reject the argument because the costs of eliminating the dust are exceeded by the benefits of allowing pollution to go forward.

ANALYSIS. This is a hard question, based loosely on *Boomer v. Atlantic Cement Co.*, 257 N.E. 2d 870 (N.Y. 1970). The factory has conceded intent (based upon knowledge, not purpose), so the question turns on whether the factory's conduct is "unreasonable." There are two tests for unreasonable conduct. The first is a Hand formula–type balancing test. It looks like the kind of activity here would not flunk the Hand formula: The burden of eliminating the dust likely would exceed the benefits of doing so. For this reason, Choice **D** is incorrect. But the second way of proving unreasonable conduct might apply here: If the burden on Lori and the homeowners is serious, a court can require the payment of damages so long as doing so won't bankrupt the cement factory. This answer is correctly spelled out in Choice **C**. Choice **A** is incorrect because even though the factory's conduct likely does not flunk the balancing test, there still may be liability (as described in Choice **C**) under the alternative test for reasonable conduct. Finally, Choice **B** is incorrect because Lori is not seeking to shut the factory down. Instead, she only wants damages for her loss of property value. We will return to this point below.

More on Unreasonableness. If this first prong for private nuisance under the Restatement was not complicated enough, the Second Restatement offers one more alternative definition of unreasonable conduct (which it does not bother to mention in § 822!): "An intentional invasion of another's interest in the use and enjoyment of land is unreasonable if the harm resulting from the invasion is severe and greater than the other should be required to bear without compensation." REST. (2D) TORTS § 829A.

This standard appears to be a *strict liability standard*, despite the use of the term "unreasonable." According to this section, if one landowner's conduct causes a "severe" invasion in another's interest in the enjoyment and use of his land, then such conduct may be considered "unreasonable" even if plaintiff cannot prove unreasonableness under the balancing tests set forth in § 826. Instead, the defendant can be liable if fairness dictates that the plaintiff should be compensated for the severe invasion. *See* REST. (3D) TORTS: LIABILITY FOR PHYSICAL HARM § 20, cmt. *c* (characterizing the Second Restatement standard of § 829A as a strict liability standard).

While it is not clear precisely when compensation is justified under this section, it is clear that the focus is on a limited set of cases in which there is *severe* harm to plaintiff. "Just as there are certain types of conduct that require holding that the invasion is unreasonable (see § 829), so certain types of harm may be so severe as to require a holding of unreasonableness as a matter of law, regardless of the utility of the conduct. This is particularly true if the harm resulting from the invasion is physical in character." REST. (2D) TORTS § 829A, cmt. *b*. The Restatement gives this cryptic example: "A's factory produces severe vibrations that reach B's house 100 feet away. The vibrations shake window panes loose, cause ceilings to fall and produce cracks in the plaster. A's invasion is unreasonable." *Id.* illus. 1.

QUESTION 4. Soot City, Take II. Lori lives near a cement factory. Each morning, her car is covered with a fine dust emitted from the factory. The factory knows about this problem, as Lori has complained repeatedly about it. Scientists have determined that the dust is not dangerous, but it is a constant annoyance. Because of the wind patterns, only Lori has the dust problem.

The cement factory is a major employer in the area, and its value is estimated at around $45 million. The local economy is also heavily dependent on taxes from the factory. Experts have estimated that the loss of property value to Lori is about $1,000. Lori has sued for private nuisance, arguing that the factory's conduct is a nuisance under Restatement (Second) of Torts § 822(a). She wants damages for the decline in her home's property value. She argues the factory's behavior is unreasonable under § 829A, and therefore she need not prove unreasonableness in the ways set forth in § 826.

How should the court respond to this argument?

A. The court should accept the argument because Lori's harm is serious.

B. The court should reject the argument because Lori's harm is not severe.

C. The court should reject the argument, so long as the court believes the harm to the plaintiffs is serious and the factory can compensate Lori and the other homeowners without facing an insurmountable financial burden.

D. The court should reject the argument because the costs of eliminating the dust are exceeded by the benefits of allowing pollution to go forward.

ANALYSIS. This question is straightforward *if* you understand the distinction between the standard set forth in § 826 and § 829A. The important point here is that under § 829A, the plaintiff must face a *severe* interference, like the fallen ceilings from vibration in Illustration 1 described before this question. If you know that, then it is easy to pick Choice **B.** Choices **A, C,** and **D** are incorrect because they state aspects of the alternative standards under § 826, not § 829A. Serious harm is relevant to 826(b).

Unintentional but Otherwise Actionable Nuisances. All of the (complicated) earlier discussion of the Restatement's views of nuisance came under the first prong for "intentional and unreasonable" conduct. We turn now to the second prong, invasions that are "unintentional and otherwise actionable under the rules controlling liability for negligent or reckless conduct, or for abnormally dangerous conditions or activities." § 822(b).

This prong works very differently than the first prong of private nuisance. It is not necessary to prove that the defendant acted with the *purpose* of invading a landowner's interest in the use and enjoyment of her land or with *knowledge* that such invasion is substantially certain to take place. Instead, under the second prong, the nuisance claim simply piggybacks on another cause of action.

To understand the second prong, consider a few variations on this hypothetical. Oscar owns a country home. At the back of his property is a septic system for treating waste. The septic system is close to the back of Elmo's house.

Variation 1: Oscar does not take reasonable care of his septic system, which causes terrible odors to emanate from it and waft into Elmo's kitchen window. Oscar does not know that this is happening. If he is sued for private nuisance by Elmo, Elmo can recover for the nuisance if he can show that the smell invaded his interest in the use and enjoyment of his land, and that, though unintentional, Oscar's conduct in failing to use reasonable care met all the requirements for proof of the tort of negligence (discussed in Chapter 2 of this book).

Variation 2: Oscar takes excellent care of his septic system. Nonetheless, the system breaks, causing terrible odors to emanate from it and waft into Elmo's kitchen window. Oscar does not know that this is happening. If he is sued for private nuisance by Elmo, Elmo cannot recover for nuisance. Even though the smell invaded his interest in the use and enjoyment of his land, Oscar used reasonable care and because Elmo cannot prove all the requirements for proof of the tort of negligence, he cannot prove private nuisance.

Variation 3: Oscar takes excellent care of his septic system. Nonetheless, the system breaks, causing sewage to seep out from the system and flow onto Elmo's land. Oscar does not know that this is happening. If Oscar is sued for private nuisance by Elmo, Elmo can recover for nuisance if he can show that the sewage invaded his interest in the use and enjoyment of his land, and that Oscar's conduct, though reasonable, meets the jurisdiction's requirements for strict liability for abnormally dangerous activities (described in Chapter 15).

These three variations should demonstrate that under the second prong of § 822, liability for private nuisance is derivative of other tort law, coupled with a showing that the defendant has unintentionally interfered with the plaintiff's use and enjoyment of his land.

QUESTION 5. Annoying Neighbor, Take II. Jared and Shana are neighboring landowners. Jared practices the drums late at night, after he gets home from work. The drumming drives Shana crazy, keeping her up at night, but Shana has never tells Jared that the drumming bothers her, and he reasonably believes that his neighbors cannot hear his drumming because of the distance between his house and the homes of his neighbors.

Shana sues Jared for private nuisance in a jurisdiction that follows the Restatement's approach to private nuisance. Can Shana recover damages for Jared's past drumming?

A. No, because Jared did not intentionally invade Shana's interests and his conduct does not constitute negligence or engagement in an abnormally dangerous activity.

B. No, because Jared did not commit a trespass to land.

C. Yes, because the drumming invaded her interest in the use and enjoyment of her land.

D. Yes, because landowners are strictly liable for any invasions of others' interests in the use and enjoyment of land.

ANALYSIS. For private nuisance, there are two prongs, so we need to consider them both. First, Jared's conduct cannot fit into the "intentional and unreasonable" prong. He did not act with the purpose or the knowledge of causing this invasion, so Shana cannot prove the requisite intention. Second, Jared cannot fit into the second prong, because he has committed no other tort. He did not act negligently, because the facts tell us he *reasonably* believed he was not disturbing his neighbors with his drumming, and drumming would not constitute an abnormally dangerous activity under the Restatement (see Chapter 15 for a refresher on this point). Choice **A** correctly states the reason that Shana's case will not be successful.

Choice **B** is incorrect because a plaintiff need not prove a trespass in order to be able to recover for a private nuisance. Choice **C** is wrong because it is not enough that the conduct caused an invasion of plaintiff's use and enjoyment of her land. That is necessary, but it is not sufficient to establish liability for private nuisance. Choice **D** states an incorrect principle of law. As we have seen earlier in this chapter, in limited circumstances private nuisance works like a strict liability principle, but it is not true all the time.

Remedies for Private Nuisance. Part VI of this book discusses issues related to tort remedies, primarily damages, but an important remedies issue arises with respect to nuisance claims that is worth mentioning now.

Ordinarily, if a plaintiff has good proof that the defendant is about to commit a tort, the plaintiff has an opportunity to go to court and seek a court order, called an *injunction*, preventing the defendant from engaging in the activity. (The rules on when injunctions may issue generally is a subject discussed in detail in a Remedies course.) So if Cain knows that Abel is about to build a structure on land that Cain thinks belongs to Cain, not Abel, a court could enjoin Abel from committing the trespass.

In contrast to an injunction, damages are appropriate when there has been some *past harm* to compensate for that past harm. So if Abel has already gone onto Cain's land and cut down some trees, a court might grant damages for the value of the trees already cut down *and* an injunction barring Abel from entering the land again.

These same principles can apply in nuisance cases. If Jared's drumming constitutes a private nuisance to Shana, she could seek damages for the past invasion of her interest in the use and enjoyment of her land and an injunction barring Jared from drumming late at night in the future. But because private nuisance cases involve competing uses, a court could decide that it is fair or equitable for a defendant to pay a plaintiff damage *for past and expected future damages* but deny an injunction to the plaintiff to prevent the activity. Here is how the Restatement puts it: "[F]or the purpose of determining whether the conduct producing the invasion should be enjoined, additional factors must be considered. It may be reasonable to continue an important activity if payment is made for the harm it is causing but unreasonable to initiate or continue it without paying." REST. (2D) TORTS § 822, cmt. *d.*

QUESTION 6. Soot City, Take III. Lori lives near a cement factory. Each morning, her car is covered with a fine dust emitted from the factory. The factory knows about this problem, as Lori and the neighbors have complained repeatedly about it. Scientists have determined that the dust is not dangerous, but it is a constant annoyance.

The cement factory is a major employer in the area, and its value is estimated at around $45 million. The local economy is also heavily dependent on taxes from the factory. Experts have estimated that the loss of property value to Lori and other nearby homeowners from the dust is about $185,000. Lori and these other homeowners sue for private nuisance, arguing that the factory's conduct is a nuisance under Restatement (Second) of Torts § 822(a). They want damages for their decline in property values and they want an injunction barring the factory from further operation unless the dust can be eliminated. Assume Lori and the homeowners can prove that the action of the factory constitutes a nuisance. Are the plaintiffs entitled to damages and/or an injunction?

A. The court should grant damages for past harm and decide if it is reasonable to grant an injunction barring future operation of the factory by balancing all relevant factors.

B. The court should grant an injunction barring future operation of the factory and decide if it is reasonable to grant damages for past harm.

C. Once the court determined the activity constituted a private nuisance, the court must grant damages and an injunction barring future operation of the factory.

D. The plaintiffs are entitled to neither damages nor an injunction because the factory creates more value than the loss to the homeowners.

ANALYSIS. There is no question that Lori and the other homeowners are entitled to damages for past harm — it has been established that the factory's actions constitute a nuisance, and that the plaintiffs have been harmed. The question whether an injunction should be issued closing the factory depends upon a careful balancing of factors. (In *Boomer v. Atlantic Cement Co.*, 257 N.E. 2d 870 (N.Y. 1970), the model for this question, the court granted past and expected future damages to the homeowners but denied their request for an injunction given the importance of the factory to the local economy.) Choice **A** correctly sets forth this standard. Choice **B** has it exactly backward, saying the injunction is a matter of right but that damages are discretionary. Choice **C** is incorrect because it states that the court *must* grant both damages and an injunction upon a finding of private nuisance; the issue of the injunction will be in the discretion of the court. Finally, Choice **D** is wrong because even if the benefits to the factory (and society) exceed the losses to the homeowners, that does not mean that the factory is off the hook in paying for the damages that the factory causes to these homeowners.

C. Public nuisance

The standard for establishing a public nuisance is slightly different from the standard for establishing a private nuisance. As noted above, a public nuisance is "an unreasonable interference with a right common to the general public." REST. (2D) TORTS § 821B(1). To establish that the interference is unreasonable, the Restatement sets forth a non-exhaustive list of alternative bases for finding a public nuisance:

> (a) Whether the conduct involves a significant interference with the public health, the public safety, the public peace, the public comfort or the public convenience, or
> (b) whether the conduct is proscribed by a statute, ordinance or administrative regulation, or
> (c) whether the conduct is of a continuing nature or has produced a permanent or long-lasting effect, and, as the actor knows or has reason to know, has a significant effect upon the public right.

Id. § 821B(2).

Examples here include a defendant keeping a mosquito-infested swamp on his land that allows disease-carrying mosquitoes to infect the local population, overgrowth of trees into public areas that block the public from walking through the areas, and criminal activity, such as gang activity, which deters people from engaging in their ordinary activities.

Note that in each of these examples, it is not necessary that any person suffer an invasion in her interest in the private use of her land. This difference distinguishes public nuisance from private nuisance. It is possible that the same action is *both* a public and private nuisance, as when the mosquitoes come onto a plaintiff's land and invade the plaintiff's interest in the use and enjoyment of her land.

It is also worth noting that statutes or ordinances can define conduct as nuisances that might not have been considered nuisances under the common law. For example, a local ordinance may bar the playing of loud music after 8 P.M. in residential areas, and it might be considered a public nuisance to play music at that hour even if under the common law playing music at that time did not constitute a nuisance.

> **QUESTION 7. Yuck.** Jeff is an amateur taxidermist and animal skin tanner. He conducts these activities in his front yard, which abuts a public square. The activity produces a strong, unpleasant smell. The smell from the activity makes many people sick, and people have stopped coming to the square, causing a decline in business in the area.
>
> If Jeff is sued for creating a public nuisance:
>
> **A.** The court should reject the claim because no one's land interest has been invaded.
> **B.** The court should reject the claim because people have the right to do whatever they want on their own property.
> **C.** The court should consider whether Jeff's conduct significantly interferes with the public's comfort.
> **D.** The court should consider Jeff's conduct a public nuisance only if a statute or ordinance bars such conduct on private property.

ANALYSIS. Jeff's conduct could be a public nuisance, if the court determines that the conduct unreasonably burdens the public's enjoyment of the public square. Choice **A** is incorrect because for *public* (as opposed to *private*) nuisance, it is not necessary to show that anyone's land interest has been invaded. Choice **B** is squarely wrong. If it were right, there would be no need for this chapter. Choice **D** is incorrect because although a statute *may* establish the basis for a public nuisance claim, it is not necessary for such a claim. Choice **C** correctly states the operative standard.

Remedies in Public Nuisance Cases. Before you start suing any of your local neighborhood taxidermists as a "get rich quick" scheme, in suits for public nuisance, in order to recover damages an individual "must have suffered harm of a kind different from that suffered by other members of the public exercising the right common to the general public that was the subject of interference." § 821C(1). So damage suits are few and far between.

More common is a request for an injunction. But members of the general public cannot seek the injunction. Instead,

> In order to maintain a proceeding to enjoin to abate a public nuisance, one must
>> (a) have the right to recover damages, as indicated in Subsection (1), or

(b) have authority as a public official or public agency to represent the state or a political subdivision in the matter, or

(c) have standing to sue as a representative of the general public, as a citizen in a citizen's action or as a member of a class in a class action.

Id. § 821C(2).

QUESTION 8. Yuck, Take II.   Jeff is an amateur taxidermist and animal skin tanner. He conducts these activities in his front yard, which abuts a public square. The activity produces a strong, unpleasant smell. The smell from the activity makes many people sick, and people have stopped coming to the square, causing a decline in business in the area.

Jeff is sued for creating a public nuisance by Kathryn, who wants to recover damages. She is an animal lover, and is heartbroken by his activities, and reminded of them each time she passes by through the smell. Assuming Jeff's conduct constitutes a public nuisance, is Kathryn entitled to damages?

A. No, unless her land interest has been invaded.

B. No, unless the court considers her damage different in kind from that suffered by the general public.

C. Yes, because all members of the public may receive damages for a public nuisance.

D. Yes, if Kathryn is a public official.

ANALYSIS.   Under the Restatement, most people cannot recover damages for public nuisances. A person may do so only if she suffers a damage "different in kind" from that suffered by the general public. It is unclear whether her emotional distress from Jeff's activities could constitute a difference in kind. Choice **B** correctly states this standard. Choice **A** is wrong because land ownership is relevant only for private nuisance. Choice **C** states an incorrect principle of law: Most members of the public *cannot* recover damages for public nuisance. Choice **D** is wrong because a person seeking damages need not be a public official. Being a public official is one of the categories of persons who may seek an *injunction* for a public nuisance, not damages.

D.   The Closer: Coming to the nuisance and extrasensitivity

Affirmative defenses to nuisance claims usually arise in one of two contexts. (1) Plaintiff moves to an area after the defendant has already established activities that could constitute a nuisance; or (2) Plaintiff is more sensitive than others to the defendant's activities (think of Kathryn's reaction to Jeff's taxidermy activities).

The first of these issues is the "coming to the nuisance" problem, which is appropriately considered a consent/assumption of risk type argument. (Jeff to Kathryn: "You did not need to move in next door to me. You noticed the odors from my hobby before you bought your house.") Courts have been reluctant to accept a coming to the nuisance argument as a bar to recovery, but the Restatement takes a middle of the road position on it: "The fact that the plaintiff has acquired or improved his land after a nuisance interfering with it has come into existence is not in itself sufficient to bar his action, but it is a factor to be considered in determining whether the nuisance is actionable." *Id.* § 840D.

The Restatement's position on extrasensitivity is less generous to plaintiffs: There is liability only for significant harm "of a kind that would be suffered by a normal person in the community or by property in normal condition and used for a normal purpose." *Id.* § 821F. As we will see in Chapter 20, this treatment of extrasensitivity in the nuisance context is in contrast with the normal rule of torts, the "thin-skulled" or "eggshell" plaintiff rule, which says that you take the plaintiff as you find her.

> **QUESTION 9. Soot City, Take IV.** Lori moves in next to a cement factory. Each morning, her car is covered with a fine dust emitted from the factory. She also has an unusual high allergy to dust, and has been suffering from allergy problems since she moved in. Lori was warned about the dust by her realtor before she bought her house, and the house's price was lower because of its proximity to the factory. The factory knows about this problem, as Lori has complained repeatedly about it to the factory, which has done nothing. Scientists have determined that the dust is not dangerous to most persons, but it is a constant annoyance.
>
> Lori sues the factory stating that its conduct constitutes a private nuisance. In response, the factory argues (1) Lori cannot recover any damages because she assumed the risk when she bought the house and (2) the court should not consider her allergies in assessing damages, if any. How should the court, following the Second Restatement, rule on these two arguments?
>
> **A.** Lori's coming to the nuisance is a factor the court will consider in determining whether to find this is a private nuisance, and the court will not consider damages for Lori's allergies.
>
> **B.** The court will not consider Lori's coming to the nuisance as a factor in determining whether to find this is a private nuisance; nor will the court consider damages for Lori's allergies.

C. The court will not consider Lori's coming to the nuisance as a factor in determining whether to find this is a private nuisance, but the court will consider damages for Lori's allergies.

D. Lori's coming to the nuisance is a factor the court will consider in determining whether to find this is a private nuisance and the court will consider damages for Lori's allergies.

ANALYSIS.   Coming to the nuisance is a factor the courts will consider in determining whether or not to consider the dust from the factory to be a private nuisance. But the court will not consider extrasensitivitiy of the plaintiff in assessing damages. Choice **A** correctly states these two rules, and Choices **B**, **C**, and **D** incorrectly state at least one of these rules.

 # Rick's picks

1. Annoying Neighbor	B
2. Airport Insomnia	D
3. Soot City	C
4. Soot City, Take II	B
5. Annoying Neighbor, Take II	A
6. Soot City, Take III	A
7. Yuck	C
8. Yuck, Take II	B
9. Soot City, Take IV	A

17

Vicarious Liability

CHAPTER OVERVIEW
A. Introduction: Vicarious liability as strict liability
B. Vicarious liability for employers: *Respondeat superior*
C. Other potential vicarious liability relationships
   1. Independent contractors
   2. Corporate officers and directors
D. The Closer: Should parents be vicariously liable for the torts of their children?
   ✦ Rick's picks

A. Introduction: Vicarious liability as strict liability

Vicarious liability is a doctrine holding one person strictly liable for the tort of another, without regard to fault. So imagine that a Deliverex driver on a delivery route runs over your foot. If the Deliverex driver would be liable in tort (most likely for the tort of negligence), then Deliverex will be liable too, through vicarious liability, regardless of whether Deliverex itself was negligent in training or supervising the driver.

Vicarious liability is not a *tort* like negligence, strict liability for an abnormally dangerous activity, or trespass. Instead, it is a *tort doctrine* imposing strict liability on some persons for the torts committed by others. In order to be vicariously liable for the tort of another, the plaintiff must prove two things:

1. Under the rules of vicarious liability, the defendant may be held vicariously liable for the tort committed by another; and
2. The other has committed a tort.

So if you sue Deliverex, you would have to show not only that Deliverex is liable for the tort of its driver, but also that the driver committed a tort. If, for example, you cannot prove the prima facie case for a tort against the driver, or if Deliverex can raise an affirmative defense that the driver could have raised against you to defeat your claim, then you cannot recover.[1]

You might wonder why you should bother suing Deliverex; after all, if you could prove that the driver committed a tort, you could simply sue the driver. The reason for doing so is financial; often the party against whom the plaintiff seeks to apply vicarious liability has more assets (a so-called deep pocket) than the party committing the tort. Under principles of joint and several liability, discussed in Chapter 22, Deliverex and the driver would both be on the hook for damages to you, and you could collect from either (or both) until you had been compensated for all of your damages. Generally speaking, the employer, rather than the employee, is in the best position to pay damages to injured plaintiffs, making vicarious liability against employers popular.

The remainder of this chapter considers when vicarious liability applies and why it applies. Ordinarily, one person is not liable for the torts of another. Even parents are not vicariously liable for the torts of their minor children, as we will see in Section C below. But because of considerations of fairness and perhaps for economic reasons, the courts — especially in the employment context — have imposed vicarious liability in various contexts.

QUESTION 1. Spill in Aisle 4. An unknown person knocks down a few hundred jars of baby food in the FineFoods supermarket. Many of the jars shatter, making a big, slippery mess on the floor. Latrice, the supermarket manager, closes down the aisle with some orange cones and orders all available stock personnel to clean the mess. Andy, who is not paying attention while shopping in the supermarket, wanders past the orange cones, slips, and breaks his arm. He sues Latrice for negligence and sues FineFoods as well, claiming FineFoods is vicariously liable solely based upon Latrice's negligence.

If the jury finds that Latrice was not negligent in how she handled the cleanup:

A. FineFoods still can be held vicariously liable for Andy's injuries because FineFoods owns the store.

B. FineFoods still can be held vicariously liable for Andy's injuries if the jury concludes that Andy was not at fault.

C. FineFoods cannot be held vicariously liable for Andy's injuries because Andy was also at fault.

---

1. In addition, if the jury allocates 70 percent of responsibility to the driver and 30 percent to you, Deliverex would be responsible for 70 percent of the damages. For more on this principle, see Chapter 10 on comparative responsibility.

> **D.** FineFoods cannot be held vicariously liable for Andy's injuries because Latrice was not negligent.

ANALYSIS. In order to be vicariously liable for another's tort, the other must have actually committed a tort. Here, Andy bases his vicarious liability claim against FineFoods "solely upon Latrice's negligence." The question then asks you about vicarious liability assuming the jury finds that Latrice was *not* negligent. In such a case, FineFoods cannot be vicariously liable. Choice **D** correctly gives this answer. Choice **C** reaches the right result — FineFoods cannot be vicariously liable — but for the wrong reason. If in fact the jury found that both Latrice and Andy were negligent, there would likely be a sharing of responsibility between them, and FineFoods would be jointly and severally liable with Latrice for Latrice's portion of the damages. (See footnote 1.) Choices **A** and **B** are incorrect because they both reach the wrong conclusion: that FineFoods still can be held vicariously liable in these circumstances even if Latrice were not negligent.

B.   Vicarious liability for employers: *Respondeat superior*

As noted in the first part of this chapter, the most common use of vicarious liability in American courts is in the employment context. Generally speaking, under the doctrine of *respondeat superior,* employers are strictly liable for the torts of their employees committed in the course and scope of their employment. That black letter is straightforward; some interesting cases arise over how to tell *when* an employee is acting in the course and scope of employment.

Let's begin with two polar cases. The Deliverex driver who runs over your foot while delivering a package for Deliverex in a Deliverex truck certainly is acting in the course and scope of employment: The activity took place while the driver was engaged in employment-related driving for the employer using employer property. The same driver, who runs over your foot while on a personal errand on a weekend in his own car certainly is *not* acting in the course and scope of employment: The activity took place while the driver was engaged in private activity not for the employer and not using employer property.

Between these polar examples are innumerable variations. For example:

- The driver causes the injury on his way to stop at the local coffee shop between deliveries, needing a caffeine boost to make it through the day.

- The driver causes injury on his way home from work in his Deliverex truck, which Deliverex allows drivers to take home each work night.
- The driver causes injury when he intentionally rams a car in front of him in a "road rage" incident, as the car in front of him was driving too slowly while the driver was trying to make deliveries on time.
- The driver causes injury when he is driving his Deliverex truck between deliveries and intentionally runs over a man he believes to be his wife's lover.

In the first two examples, the driver is not directly doing the business of the employer but has deviated somewhat from that business. The law calls these cases "frolic and detour" cases. In both cases, the deviations could be said to further the employer's interests (caffeine perhaps makes happy and alert drivers, and allowing the Deliverex drivers to take trucks home at the end of the day could be for the administrative convenience of the company, or perhaps to make the drivers happy as well).

In any event, courts generally will find that minor deviations from employment responsibilities are still within the "scope of employment," thereby subjecting the employer to vicarious liability for the torts of its employees. But more "major" deviations from the employee's serving of the employer's interests will take the case out of the realm of the employer's vicarious liability. All courts likely would find in the first example that the coffee break is still within the course and scope of employment. The latter case, involving taking the delivery truck home for the evening, divides courts. *Compare Craig v. Gentry*, 792 S.W.2d 77 (Tenn. Ct. App. 1990) (holding that the driver of an automobile involved in an accident with a motorcycle was acting within the course and scope of her employment, as her attempt to deal with a possible mechanical problem with her vehicle was part and parcel of her journey to make employer's bank deposit, rather than a personal mission of her own), *with Gifford-Hill & Co. v. Moore*, 479 S.W.2d 711 (Tex. Civ. App. 1972) (holding that use of employer's vehicle for the purpose of visiting family for the holidays was a major deviation from the course and scope of employment, and that, therefore, appellant-corporation was not vicariously liable for the collision that occurred during the trip).

QUESTION 2. Costly Cheesecake. Monty is on a business trip out of town. He drives 200 miles to New City. Rather than drive straight to his meeting, Monty drives five miles out of his way to get a slice of his favorite cheesecake from the New City Diner. He walks into the diner and puts down his suitcase. Unfortunately, the suitcase falls over and breaks Jessica's toes.

Jessica sues Monty for negligence and argues that Monty's employer, Corpco, is vicariously liable for Monty's negligence. Corpco concedes

Monty was negligent, but argues it is not vicariously liable because Monty was not acting in the course and scope of employment. How should the court rule on Corpco's argument?

A. The court should accept the argument if it concludes that Monty made a major deviation from his travel in service to his employer.

B. The court should reject the argument if it concludes that Monty made a minor deviation from his travel in service to his employer.

C. Both **A** and **B** are correct.

D. Neither **A** nor **B** are correct, because it is necessary for Jessica to prove not only that Monty was negligent, but that Corpco was negligent as well.

ANALYSIS. Let's begin this one by eliminating the clearly wrong answer, Choice **D**. This answer is incorrect because the entire point of vicarious liability is that the person being held vicariously liable faces *strict liability* upon proof that the other person has committed a tort (without any applicable affirmative defenses). So Jessica need not prove that Corpco was negligent in order for Corpco to be held vicariously liable for Monty's actions. It is enough that Monty was negligent and acting in the course and scope of his employment.

Given that Corpco conceded Monty's negligence, the difficult question here is whether Monty had deviated too much from serving his employer by driving five miles out of the way to get a slice of cheesecake before his meeting. Choices **A** and **B** both are plausible. We could call this a "minor" deviation, in which case vicarious liability for Corpco would apply. Or we could call this a more "major" deviation, in which case vicarious liability would not apply. Choice **C** is the best answer, because it recognizes that this is a close case, which could be resolved either way by the courts.

The first two of the hypotheticals I gave you represented *geographic* deviations from the usual work requirements of the job. The second two are different: Both involve intentional torts that seem only tangentially related to the employment context. Courts used to deal with these cases by asking the question whether the employee's actions were done, at least in part, to serve the interests of the employer. *See* REST. (2D) OF AGENCY § 228(1) (1958). Under such a test, arguably the "road rage" example would be considered within the scope of employment, as the battery by the driver seemed in part motivated by the employee's desire to deliver the packages on time for the employer. The latter example does not seem motivated by serving the employer at all, and likely would not be considered within the scope of employment under a "serve the employer" test.

The courts applying the "serve the employer" test sometimes bent the test to expand vicarious liability for employers. In *Nelson v. American-West*

African Line, 86 F.2d 730 (2d Cir. 1936), Judge Hand (yes, the same judge from the "Hand formula" and *The T.J. Hooper*) held that ship owners could be vicariously liable under this test for a ship employee who woke another employee by beating him and yelling "Get up, you big son of a bitch, and turn to." *Id.* at 731.

More modern courts rejected the "serve the employer" test, replacing it with a test imposing vicarious liability on employers so long as the actions of the employee are not wholly unforeseeable and personal. The leading case here is another Second Circuit case, this one written by the well-respected Judge Friendly, *Ira S. Bushey & Sons, Inc. v. United States*, 398 F.2d 167 (2d Cir. 1968). In that case, a drunken sailor returned to the dry dock after shore leave, and for unexplained reasons he turned a valve on the dry dock, flooding it and injuring a nearby ship. The court held vicarious liability could apply because it was not unforeseeable that one of these employees could get drunk and negligently, or even intentionally, cause some damage.

Judge Friendly explained the limits of the respondeat superior:

> If [the employee] had set fire to the bar where he had been imbibing or had caused an accident on the street while returning to the drydock, the [employer] would not be liable; the activities of the "enterprise" do not reach into areas where the servant does not create risks different from those attendant on the activities of the community in general. We agree with the district judge that if the seaman upon returning to the drydock, recognized the Bushey security guard as his wife's lover and shot him, vicarious liability would not follow; the incident would have related to the seaman's domestic life, not to his seafaring activity, and it would have been the most unlikely happenstance that the confrontation with the paramour occurred on a drydock rather than at the traditional spot.[2]

Citation and internal quotation marks omitted.

Under the test of the *Ira S. Bushey* case, our hypotheticals would come out the same way as under the traditional test, but for a different reason: The road rage example, being somewhat related to work, would subject the employer to vicarious liability; in the second example, the "happenstance" of seeing his wife's lover while on the job and running him over would not create vicarious liability for Deliverex.

Note that under either the traditional test or the newer *Ira S. Bushey* test, it is possible for an employer to be liable for the intentional torts of its employees. To be sure, many cases involving intentional torts by employees will not lead to vicarious liability for the employer; but there is no *per se* rule against vicarious liability for intentional torts.

---

2. Boy, that Judge Friendly knew how to write!

> **QUESTION 3. Bounced Around.** Damien works as a bouncer at the Hot Spot, a local nightclub. One night Phillip arrives outside the Hot Spot with a group of his friends. Phillip is intoxicated and acting obnoxiously, hooting at the women going in and out of the club. Phillip's behavior annoys Damien, who asks Phillip to stop acting in this way, but Phillip ignores him. Damien then punches Phillip in the face, breaking his nose.
>
> Phillip sues the Hot Spot and Damien, claiming that the Hot Spot is vicariously liable for Damien's battery (assume Phillip can prove all the elements of battery against Damien and that Damien can raise no affirmative defenses). Is the Hot Spot vicariously liable for Damien's tort?
>
> **A.** No, because Damien committed an intentional tort.
> **B.** No, because there is no evidence the Hot Spot was negligent in supervising Damien.
> **C.** Yes, because employers are always liable for the torts of their employees.
> **D.** Yes, because such action by a bouncer is not unforeseeable and the battery was not wholly personal.

ANALYSIS. Let's take each of these answers one by one. Choice **A** is incorrect because there is no categorical rule barring employers from being vicariously liable for the intentional torts of their employees. Indeed, the context of a bouncer tortiously injuring a patron is one of the best examples of the kind of case in which an employer may be vicariously liable for the intentional tort of an employee. Choice **B** is incorrect because it includes the wrong legal standard. For vicarious liability to apply, it is not necessary for the employer to act negligently in supervising the employee. Remember, vicarious liability is strict liability.

Choice **C** is wrong because it is an overstatement. As the text before this question makes clear, sometimes employers are strictly liable for the torts of their employees and sometimes they are not. Choice **D** is the correct answer. It is the best choice, incorporating the *Ira S. Bushey* test. Note here how the battery was not wholly personal: Damien slugged Phillip after he was harassing customers of the night club. That's not to say Damien's conduct is excused. It is still a battery, but it is somewhat related to employment and not wholly personal.

Despite the *Ira S. Bushey* test, there are some cases that are undoubtedly work related, but which, for reasons of fairness, courts decline to impose vicarious liability. A recent case in this regard is *Yamaguchi v. Harnsmut*, 130 Cal. Rptr. 2d 706 (App. 2003). Two restaurant workers, Wisan, the head chef, and Noy, a kitchen assistant, did not get along. They had a few run-ins in the kitchen over responsibilities at the restaurant. They never socialized outside of work. One day, at the beginning of the workday, Wisan let Noy into the kitchen to prepare food, and then stabbed Noy in the back as he bent over. Another kitchen employee summoned help from two police officers, and when the officers arrived Wisan threw hot oil at them, wounding one of them. One of the police officers later sued the restaurant owner, arguing the owner was vicariously liable for Wisan's battery.

The court acknowledged that "[a]n employer may ... be vicariously liable for the employee's tort — even if it was malicious, willful, or criminal — if the employee's act was an outgrowth of his employment, inherent in the working environment, typical of or broadly incidental to the employer's business, or, in a general way, foreseeable from his duties." *Id.* at 482 (citations and quotation marks omitted). But the court also held that vicarious liability would not apply when "the conduct is so unusual or startling that it would seem unfair to include the loss resulting from it among other costs of the employer's business." *Id.* (citations and quotation marks omitted). The court remanded the case to the trial court for a trial in which the jury could decide that fairness dictated that the employer should not be liable for Wisan's battery, even though it was connected to the employment relationship and foreseeable given the earlier run-ins between Wisan and Noy.

QUESTION 4. Abuse of Power. Lisa, a 19-year-old pregnant woman, was involved in a minor fall at a movie theater. She went to the Pacifica Hospital emergency room for an examination to make sure there was no problem with her fetus. She was taken into a room to be examined by Bruce, an ultrasound technician employed by the hospital. Bruce refused to let Lisa's boyfriend accompany them into the room. Bruce took ultrasound pictures by placing a gel and probe on Lisa's abdomen. After Bruce determined that there was no damage to the fetus, he asked Lisa is she wanted to know the gender of her fetus. When Lisa said yes, Bruce purported to examine Lisa, but instead he sexually molested her. Lisa later realized that she was molested, and Bruce was prosecuted for criminal assault and sexual battery.

Lisa sued Bruce and Pacifica Hospital, arguing that the hospital is vicariously liable for Bruce's torts. The hospital did not dispute that Bruce committed the torts, but argued that it should not be vicariously liable for Bruce's torts. How should the court rule on this argument?

A. The court should accept the argument because Bruce's conduct was wholly unrelated to his employment.

B. Given the startling nature of Bruce's conduct, the court should allow the jury to decide if on fairness grounds the hospital should not be vicariously liable, even though Bruce's conduct was work related.

C. The court should reject the argument because the incident occurred while Bruce was at work.

D. The court should reject the argument because Lisa was injured at the hospital.

ANALYSIS.   This disturbing question is based upon the divided California Supreme Court opinion in *Lisa M. v. Henry Mayo Newhall Memorial Hospital*, 907 P.2d 358 (Cal. 1995). This is a tough question. Let's eliminate the clearly wrong answers first. Choice **C** is wrong because it is not enough for vicarious liability to apply that an incident occurred at work (again, think of the lover found by happenstance at work). Similarly, Choice **D** is incorrect because the fact that Lisa was injured on hospital grounds also is not enough to create liability for the hospital. The hospital must be found to be either liable itself for its own actions or, as is the case here, alleged to be vicariously liable for a tort of another.

The question comes down to Choices **A** and **B**. In this case Choice **B** is the stronger answer. As with *Yamaguchi*, there are circumstances in which a jury could decide that an employee's action is so unusual or startling that it is not fair to hold the employer vicariously liable for the employee's torts. (A majority of the California Supreme Court indeed granted summary judgment for the hospital on this point, not even requiring the hospital to make the argument to a jury.) Choice **A** is the next best answer, that the conduct is wholly unrelated to work. In fact, the California Supreme Court suggested as such in the *Lisa M.* case. But it is a fiction to say that the conduct is not related to work at all: It was work that gave Bruce the opportunity to engage in this conduct and to have access to the patient. A better understanding of the result in *Lisa M.* is that fairness dictates an exception given the startling nature of Bruce's actions.

C.   Other potential vicarious liability relationships

1. Independent contractors

The last section explained that one of the main issues that arises under *respondeat superior* — the use of vicarious liability against employers — is whether the employee committed the tort while acting in the course and scope of employment. But another question also arises: Is the tortfeasor really an *employee*? If it turns out that the tortfeasor is an *independent contractor* rather than an employee, then vicarious liability ordinarily does not apply.

Independent contractor status is an issue that comes up in a variety of contexts — including issues related to payroll taxes and workers' compensation. What follows here deals with the question only as it relates to vicarious liability, and not necessarily to these other contexts. Generally speaking, an independent contractor is someone (like an employee) paid for a service, such as gardening. To be considered an independent contractor, the person usually must bring his or her own tools or equipment to do the job, and determines how the work is to be done. The more control the employer exerts over the person doing the work, the more likely the court will classify the worker as an employee (for which vicarious liability applies) rather than as an independent contractor (for which it does not).

So one way of holding a person hiring an independent contractor vicariously liable for the contractor's torts is by showing that the hirer has *actual authority* over the work done by the contractor. But that's not the only way. Consider doctors, who perform surgery and undertake other medical activities in hospitals. For most hospitals (unlike the Kaiser system, popular in California and elsewhere), these doctors are independent contractors, not employees. The hospital does not tell the doctor how to do his job, and it is the doctor, not the hospital, that sets the protocol in the operating room.

But hospitals sometimes advertise their services (such as their emergency room services) by talking about how great "the hospital's doctors" are. Here in Los Angeles, Cedars-Sinai Medical Center had an advertising campaign touting the expertise of the "doctors of Cedars Sinai." Such advertising can in fact create vicarious liability when one of these doctors commits a tort. The doctrine here is called *ostensible agency* or *apparent authority*, and it says that vicarious liability applies when the hirer holds the contractor out as an employee or someone under the control of the hirer, and the plaintiff justifiably relied upon that "holding out." So while "doctors of Cedars-Sinai" may be great marketing, it could increase the potential for liability by the hospital.

QUESTION 5. Toe-Away Zone.   Francesca goes to see a surgeon, Dr. No, about a nasty bunion she has on her big toe on her right foot. The doctor says that the best treatment for this bunion is surgery. Francesca agrees to the surgery. The doctor tells Francesca that the surgery will take place at Pacifica Hospital on an outpatient basis. Francesca shows up for the surgery at the hospital. Dr. No has privileges at the hospital, but is not a hospital employee. Dr. No performs the surgery, assisted by a hospital nurse. Unfortunately, Dr. No botches the surgery, and Francesca must have her toe amputated.

There is no question that Dr. No acted negligently. But Dr. No has no assets, thanks to other malpractice claims against the doctor. May

Francesca sue Pacifica Hospital, on grounds that it is vicariously liable for Dr. No's tort?

A. No, because the hospital neither directed Dr. No's actions nor held itself out as Dr. No's employer.

B. No, because torts by independent contractors never create liability.

C. Yes, because the surgery took place at the hospital.

D. Yes, under the ostensible agency doctrine.

ANALYSIS. Dr. No, like most doctors, is not an employee of the hospital. Instead, the doctor is an independent contractor. Torts by independent contractors do not create vicarious liability unless the hirer had actual authority or apparent authority over the contractor. Here, there is no evidence of either actual authority (nothing indicates that the hospital told Dr. No how to perform the surgery), and no evidence of apparent authority (or ostensible agency) either: Unlike the emergency room situation, the patient dealt with the doctor before the hospital, and nothing in the facts tell us that the hospital held itself out as Dr. No's employer or that Francesca justifiably relied upon such holding out. For this reason, Choice **A** is correct.

Choice **B** reaches the right result — no vicarious liability — but for the wrong reason. It is incorrect to say that there can *never* be vicarious liability in an independent contractor situation. Choice **C** is incorrect because the mere fact that the surgery took place at the hospital does not create vicarious liability for the hospital. For the hospital to be liable, either hospital employees would have had to commit the tort or an independent contractor would have had to do so — acting under the actual or apparent authority of the hospital. Choice **D** is wrong because, as explained above, there are no facts here supporting application of the ostensible agency doctrine in this case.

2. Corporate officers and directors

When a corporation acts as an employer, the vicarious liability rules for the torts of its employees are the same as if the employer were a natural person. (Indeed, in the examples given in earlier sections of this Chapter, including those involving Deliverex and Pacifica Hospital, it is virtually inconceivable that these employers would be anything but owned in the form of a corporation.) But corporations are also liable for the torts of their *officers and directors*, when those torts are done within the scope of corporate business. Similar issues arise as in the "scope of employment" cases, discussed above. Torts that are wholly personal to the officer and director are not included within the corporation's vicarious liability.

It is not necessary that the corporate board approved (or later ratified) the action of the officer or director for vicarious liability to apply. When there is such approval or ratification, then the corporation could be liable itself for the actions, and not just vicariously liable. This distinction could matter if, for example, a plaintiff seeks punitive damages from a corporation. In some states, corporations are not vicariously liable for punitive damages and must be shown to have approved or ratified the action of the officer or director.[3] *Compare Potomac Leasing Co. v. Bulger*, 531 So.2d 307, 311 (Ala. 1998), *with Abston v. Kelley Bros. Contractors, Inc.*, 990 F. Supp. 1392 (S.D. Ala. 1998).

QUESTION 6. CEO DUI. Gordon Gekko is CEO of RaiderCorp. He leaves the company Christmas party in his car, highly intoxicated. He is driving to his country home for the weekend. Unsurprisingly, Gekko crashes his car, causing injury to Bud. Gekko has recently gone bankrupt thanks to some bad business deals, and Bud wishes to hold RaiderCorp vicariously liable for Gekko's tort. Can Bud do so?

A. No, if Gekko's conduct was no more than negligent.

B. No, because Gekko's driving home was part of his personal life, unconnected to the corporation.

C. Yes, because corporations are always liable for the torts of their officers and directors.

D. Yes, because RaiderCorp supplied the alcohol.

ANALYSIS. Corporations are vicariously liable for the torts of their officers and directors so long as the actions of those officers and directors are done within the scope of corporate business. Here, it does not appear that there is a business connection; rather, Gekko was engaged in the wholly personal act of driving to his country home for the weekend. Choice **B** correctly states this principle and explains why RaiderCorp is not vicariously liable for Gekko's actions in this case.

Choice **A** is incorrect because whether or not Gekko's conduct was worse than negligence is irrelevant to the vicarious liability question here — Gekko's actions were wholly personal. Choice **C** is wrong because it overstates the law: Corporations are *sometimes*, not *always*, liable for the torts of their officers and directors. Choice **D** is wrong because RaiderCorp's decision to supply alcohol to an intoxicated Gekko might be grounds for RaiderCorp's *independent liability* for negligence or some other tort (though most states have statutes preventing imposition of liability in such circumstances). But whether or not RaiderCorp is independently liable for some tortious conduct is irrelevant to the call of the question, which asks only about Raidercorp's *vicarious* liability for *Gekko*'s actions.

---

3. Chapter 23 considers punitive damages issues in detail.

D. The Closer: Should parents be vicariously liable for the torts of their children?

My sense is that the core vicarious liability application — holding employers strictly liable for the torts of their employees — is popular because the public believes that employers should accept as a cost of doing business damages inflicted by their employees acting tortiously within the scope of employment. But the law has a different treatment for parents whose children commit torts. Contrary to what many students seem to think before entering law school, parents are not vicariously liable for the torts of their minor children. We do not accept it as a "cost of having children" that parents must pay for the damage caused by their children. Instead, for a parent to be liable for a child's torts, an injured plaintiff must prove that the parent was himself or herself *negligent* in failing to supervise the child.

Why the difference in treatment? After all, both corporations and parents benefit from the actions of those in their charge. I believe the answer for the different treatment is twofold. First, having children is much more common than owning a business. Analogous to the "common usage" exception to the abnormally dangerous strict liability tort, the exclusion of children is perhaps justified on grounds that it would be unfair to require so many people to be subject to strict liability for everyday torts. Second, as we saw in Chapter 8, tort law treats minor children more generously for negligence purposes, encouraging children to experiment with taking risks as they mature. Just as a reasonable person standard might chill children from taking risks, a vicarious liability obligation on parents could cause parents to over-supervise their children, and also limit the maturation process for children.

These are just my thoughts on the different treatment. What are yours?

> **QUESTION 7. Cat Out of the Bag.** Donald thought he had a model child, Manny, a 10-year-old who always does what he is told and is helpful to others. Manny has never been in trouble at school or elsewhere. Donald has no clue that Manny is a troublemaker. So Donald is surprised when the police knock at his door and tell him that they've caught Manny on videotape capturing and torturing to death many of the neighborhood's cats.
>
> Patricia, who owns one of the cats tortured to death by Manny, sues Manny for conversion, negligence, and intentional infliction of emotional distress. She also sues Donald, arguing Donald is strictly liable for Manny's torts. Donald argues he is not strictly liable for Manny's torts. How should the court rule?

A. Donald is strictly liable because parents are vicariously liable for all the torts of their children.
B. Donald is strictly liable for negligence, but not intentional torts, committed by his minor child through strict liability.
C. Donald is not strictly liable for Manny's torts, unless he actually knew about Manny's propensity to cause injury.
D. Donald is not strictly liable for Manny's torts, even if he actually knew about Manny's propensity to cause injury.

ANALYSIS. As noted above, parents are not vicariously liable for the torts of their minor children. Though parents could be liable in appropriate cases for *negligent supervision* of children, that claim is not the same as vicarious liability. Choices **A** and **B** therefore both misstate the applicable law. It does not matter *which torts* are involved; parents are not vicariously liable for their children's torts.

So the answer here comes down to Choices **C** and **D**. It might be tempting for you to choose Choice **C** because in fact a parent can be liable for a child's tort if the parent knows that the child is dangerous and needs supervision, and then the parent fails to provide that supervision. But that liability is in *negligence*, not through vicarious liability. Choice **D** is a better answer here because in terms of *strict liability*, it does not matter what Donald knows about Manny's dangerous propensities.

Rick's picks

1. Spill in Aisle 4	D
2. Costly Cheesecake	C
3. Bounced Around	D
4. Abuse of Power	B
5. Toe-Away Zone	A
6. CEO DUI	B
7. Cat Out of the Bag	D

PART V

Products Liability

The Prima Facie Case for Products Liability Torts

A. Introduction: Products liability history from contract to tort

Products liability is a very large and important area in tort law, so much so that students interested in the topic should take a separate course in it; there's simply no time in a typical first-year Torts course to get into the details, history, jurisdictional splits, and interesting theoretical issues. This book cannot cover all the details either. So this chapter focuses on the modern approach to products liability lawsuits raising personal injury claims (rather than property damage or other kinds of damages) in tort. It focuses primarily on the approach of the Restatement (Third) of Torts: Products Liability. This chapter does not cover breach of warranty claims, which are *contract* claims, except to mention the relationship between tort and contract law in this area. The next chapter considers affirmative defenses to personal injury suits arising from product injuries, including the important question of federal preemption. But bear in mind that these two chapters just skim the surface of the topic.

Before turning to modern products liability law, I provide a very brief overview of the development of the law in this area, which is useful in understanding the background to the drafting of the very influential Restatement provisions.[1] The development of products liability law dates to the nineteenth century and the consequences of the Industrial Revolution.

The first English products suits were brought in contract, for breach of a warranty (or promise) over a product. Situating the actions in contract had two important consequences. First, only those in a direct contractual relationship (the term used here is "in privity") could bring suit. With middlemen selling goods even then, there would often be no contractual relationship between the manufacturer of a product and the consumer. Moreover, third persons (who did not purchase the product) were not in privity and could not sue for injuries caused by defective products; they could not claim coverage as third-party beneficiaries. In *Winterbottom v. Wright*, 10 M. & W. 109, 152 E.R. 402 (Ex. 1842), for example, the court refused to allow a postal employee injured by a defective coach sold to his employer to recover for personal injuries.

Second, contract law meant that the extent of the seller's liability could be limited in contract and set by the terms of the contract. Early contract law recognized some default promises (called "implied warranties"), but these promises were limited. Epstein reports that "[i]n early times, these implied warranties, regardless of the form of action used, seemed to require P to prove D's conceit or concealment."[2]

Courts gradually softened the harshness of the *Winterbottom* rule by creating exceptions for inherently dangerous products (such as poisons), defectively constructed products, and dangerous products known to be defective by the seller. In *MacPherson v. Buick*, 111 N.E. 1050 (N.Y. 1916), Justice Cardozo wrote an influential opinion that collapsed the distinction between inherently dangerous products and other products, leading to a situation where by the middle of the twentieth century anyone injured by a defective product could bring suit in tort, regardless of the privity of contract question.[3]

---

1. This introduction draws from the account in RICHARD A. EPSTEIN, TORTS ch. 15 (1999).
2. Epstein, *supra* n. 1, at 384.
3. *See Henningsen v. Bloomfield Motors, Inc.*, 161 A.2d 69 (N.J. 1960).

Once the courts determined that products liability would sound in tort, rather than contract, for personal injuries,[4] the question then became whether the laws would be governed by the usual negligence rule for non-intentional torts or treated as a pocket of strict liability. Different jurisdictions reached different conclusions on this question. California Supreme Court Justice Traynor wrote an important concurring opinion in *Escola v. Coca Cola Bottling Co.*, 150 P.2d 436 (Cal. 1944), arguing in favor of a strict liability approach on grounds that manufacturers were the cheapest cost avoiders, that manufacturers rather than consumers were in a position to reduce the risks of injury (the situation of "unilateral precaution"), and that manufacturers could pass on the costs of paying damage judgments to the public as a "cost of doing business" (loss spreading). The California Supreme Court later endorsed Justice Traynor's concurrence,[5] but in more recent years, as we will see, that court and others moved away from strict liability and toward negligence in most products liability cases.

> **QUESTION 1. Training on Traynor.** Which was *not* a rationale offered by Justice Traynor in the *Escola* case in support of a strict liability standard in the case of personal injury caused by defective products?
>
> **A.** Loss spreading.
> **B.** Manufacturers are cheapest cost avoiders.
> **C.** A negligence standard causes manufacturers to overinvest in safety.
> **D.** Product injuries are unilateral precaution situations.

ANALYSIS. This question is a reward for those of you who managed to read through the history set forth in the last pages and stay awake. If you were paying attention, you will see that three of the rationales, loss spreading, cheapest cost avoider, and unilateral precaution are all mentioned in the text. For this reason, Choices **A**, **B**, and **D** are incorrect. Choice **C** is the correct choice because Justice Traynor did not suggest that the problem with the negligence standard was that it caused manufacturers to be *too careful.* To the contrary, for the other reasons given, Justice Traynor wanted to use a strict liability standard to induce manufacturers to invest *more*, rather than less, in safety improvements.

---

4. For property damage and other business losses, the Uniform Commercial Code allows for limitations on remedies and warranties unless they are unconscionable. *See* U.C.C. § 2-719(3). But this is a question for a Contracts or Sales class, and is not covered in this book.
5. *Greenman v. Yuba Power Products, Inc.*, 377 P.2d 897 (Cal. 1963).

B.   Modern products liability law for personal injury

1. Introduction: Three classes of defects

The cornerstone of modern products liability law is the distinction between three kinds of products defects:

1. *Manufacturing Defect* (also known as a "construction defect"): The product is manufactured not to the manufacturer's own specifications. Think of a car windshield that the manufacturer's specifications say should be 1.5 cm thick, but is manufactured at only 1.2 cm thick.

2. *Design Defect*: The product is manufactured to the manufacturer's own specifications, but the plaintiff is complaining that there is something about the design that is defective. Think of a car windshield that the manufacturer's specifications say should be 1.5 cm thick. In fact it is that thick, but plaintiff argues that the windshield should have been 1.7 cm thick so as to have prevented plaintiff's injury.

3. *Warning Defect* (also known as "failure to warn"): The product is manufactured to the manufacturer's own specifications, but the plaintiff is complaining that the manufacturer failed to give adequate instructions or warnings about the dangers of the product. Think of a car windshield that the manufacturer's specifications say should be 1.5 cm thick. It is in fact that thick, but plaintiff claims that the manufacturer should have warned that with glass of this thickness, a baseball hit from a nearby park could break the windshield and cause personal injury.

As products liability law developed, it has developed different rules for each of these types of defects. In addition some jurisdictions apply certain special rules to products such as foodstuffs, blood, and prescription drugs. Section B.7 below considers the special rules for prescription drugs. Other rules will have to wait for a special products liability course.

The influential § 402A of the Restatement (Second) of Torts did not distinguish among these three types of defects in its black letter. It just provided, opaquely, that there would be liability for products "in a defective condition unreasonably dangerous" that cause injury. The language caused courts to go through many contortions to figure out exactly what standard applied, especially given an intricate and somewhat contradictory set of comments following the black letter.

The Restatement (Third) of Torts: Products Liability, completed in 1998, brought much greater clarity to the field, expressly defining the three types of defects separately, and providing rules for each. The new Restatement sections remain somewhat controversial, but at least they are understandable, which is more than could be said for the Second Restatement. The remainder of the Restatement references in this chapter and the next refer to the current Third Restatement, not the Second.

QUESTION 2. Chasing the Hickie. Paul works as a pressman at a printing press. While he is running a printing job, he notices a blemish on the pages of the book he was printing. The blemish was caused by a small piece of dirt, or "hickie," on the press. Rather than shut down the press (which would have taken three hours to restart), Paul does a very dangerous procedure known in the printing business as "chasing the hickie," which involves climbing up near the spinning printing press and very lightly applying a piece of plastic to scrape the hickie off the press. Unfortunately, during this procedure Paul's hand gets trapped and eventually has to be amputated. Paul later claims in his lawsuit that the press was defective because it did not contain a hand-guard to prevent users from "chasing the hickie."

What kind of defect is Paul claiming when he argues the product was defective because it lacked a hand-guard?

A. Manufacturing defect.
B. Design defect.
C. Warning defect.
D. All of the above.

ANALYSIS. This hypothetical is based upon *Micallef v. Miehle Co.*, 39 N.Y.2d 376 (1976). (We will be returning to this example throughout this chapter and the next.) Paul is arguing that the product could have been designed in a better way, that is, with a hand-guard. That's a design defect claim. Therefore, Choice **B** is correct. Choice **A** is incorrect, because Paul is not alleging that the manufacturer's own specifications included a hand-guard that the manufacturer failed to include. Choice **C** is wrong because he is not stating that the product should have contained a warning not to chase the hickie. Choice **D** is wrong because choices **A** and **C** are wrong.

2. The prima facie case

The Prima Facie Case for Products Liability Torts. Before turning to the three classes of defects, I can now set out the generic prima facie case for the products liability tort. Generally speaking, a person injured by a product can sue anyone in the manufacturing and distribution chain for the product (including the manufacturer, distributor and retailer).[6] The plaintiff must prove the following prima facie case:[7]

1. Defendant manufactured, distributed or sold *a defective product.*
2. The defect in the product was an *actual cause* of plaintiff's injury.
3. The defect in the product was a *proximate cause* of plaintiff's injury.
4. Plaintiff suffered *damages.*

See REST. (3D) TORTS: PRODUCTS LIABILITY § 1 (1998).

The remainder of this chapter considers what it means for a defendant to be liable for manufacturing, distributing, or selling a defective product. You should already be familiar with the actual cause and proximate cause requirements from Part III of this book (if not, you won't be able to tackle the next question). Part VI discusses damages.

QUESTION 3. Just Cause. Motorco has manufactured an automobile with brakes that are prone to failing every third time a driver presses down on the pedal. Pauline buys a car from a Motorco dealer and drives it off the lot. The first time she uses her brakes, she stops at a red light. She stops completely and normally. Dante, driving a sports car, rams into Pauline's car, destroying the car and inflicting serious personal injuries to Pauline.

If Pauline sues Motorco under products liability law for her injuries, a court should rule:

A. Pauline's case fails because her car was not defective.
B. Pauline's case fails because the defect in the car was not an actual cause of her injuries.
C. Pauline's case fails because Dante's actions were an intervening cause of injury that broke the chain of causation.
D. Pauline's case fails because she suffered no damages.

ANALYSIS.   This question asks you to identify the aspect of the prima facie case that will prevent Pauline from being able to sue Motorco successfully (whether or not she has a good case against Dante is a separate question). We haven't yet gotten into the details of what a defect is, but don't leave your common sense at the door: A car whose brakes fail every third time must be defective. So Choice **A** is incorrect. Choice **B** is the correct answer, something that should be familiar to you from Part III of this book. Even though the car was defective, that defect had absolutely nothing to do with

---

6. Other aspects of products liability law not covered here set forth how liability is allocated among the defendants.
7. Under the *Barker* test discussed below under design defect, the prima facie case is different because the law provides for burden shifting.

this injury. Pauline was stopped normally at a red light when the injury happened; the problem with the brakes was not a "but for" cause of the injury. Choice **C** is incorrect, because Dante's actions could not be an "intervening cause." As we know from Part III, in intervening cause cases, the defendant's actions must be an actual cause, and then a third party's actions intervene so that on policy grounds the court says it is not fair to hold the defendant liable for plaintiff's injuries. Here, because the defendant's actions were not an actual cause of injury, there is no intervening cause issue. Choice **D** is the easiest answer to eliminate as incorrect; the facts tell us flatly that Pauline suffered property damage and personal injuries.

3. Manufacturing defects: Strict liability

Recall that a product contains a *manufacturing defect* (also known as a "construction defect") when it is manufactured not to the manufacturer's own specifications. Both case law and the Restatement agree that manufacturing defects are subject to a *strict liability standard.*[8] REST. (3D) TORTS: PRODUCTS LIABILITY § 2(a) (1998) (product contains a manufacturing defect "when the product departs from its intended design *even though all possible care was exercised* in the preparation and marketing of the product" (emphasis added)).

So, to expand on an example given earlier, suppose Pablo is injured in an automobile accident in which a rock falls from a cliff on the side of the road and hits his car windshield. The windshield shatters, causing glass to go into Pablo's right eye, blinding him in that eye. Pablo's lawyer investigates the accident and discovers that the windshield glass was 1.2 cm thick, when the manufacturer's own specifications for the glass say it should be 1.5 cm thick. On these facts, Pablo can prove that the windshield was defective because it deviated from the manufacturer's intended design; and it does not matter if the manufacturer can prove that it used the best technology to prevent errors of this type and that there was nothing negligent about the manufacture of the glass.

Of course, proving a manufacturing defect alone does not guarantee that Pablo will win the case. He will also have to prove *actual cause*: he must prove by a preponderance of the evidence that the same injury would not have happened had the glass been manufactured as intended, at 1.5 cm thick. If the same injury would have happened, then the defect was not a cause of

---

8. *See Soufflas v. Zimmer, Inc.*, 474 F. Supp. 2d 737 (E.D. Pa. 2007). One exception is Virginia. "Virginia has not adopted strict products liability in tort, but an action for breach of implied warranty of merchantability provides the substantial equivalent. Virginia case law repeatedly has expressed the concept of reasonable safety. *See, e.g., Featherall v. Firestone Tire & Rubber Co.*, 252 S.E.2d 358 (Va. 1979); *Turner v. Manning, Maxwell & Moore, Inc.*, 217 S.E.2d 863 (Va. 1975))." REST. (3D) TORTS: PRODUCTS LIABILITY § 2.

the injury. (Pablo will also have to prove proximate cause and damages, and his claim is subject to any affirmative defenses that the manufacturer could raise.)

Why subject manufacturers to strict liability (rather than negligence) for manufacturing defects? Among the reasons given in the Third Restatement are: "encourag[ing manufacturers'] greater investment in product safety," "discourag[ing consumers'] consumption of defective products by causing the purchase price of products to reflect, more than would a rule of negligence, the cost of defects," "reduc[ing] transaction costs involved in litigating" plaintiff's case, and "allowing deserving plaintiffs to succeed notwithstanding what would otherwise be difficult or insuperable problems of proof." REST. (3D) TORTS: PRODUCTS LIABILITY § 2 cmt. *a* (1998).

QUESTION 4. Popping Pop. Sodaco makes the popular Orange Fizz soda. It manufactures the soda in a state-of-the-art facility. Even using the best available technology, however, one out of every 1 million cans of Orange Fizz will not seal as Sodaco intends. These cans may explode, causing potential injury to the consumer of the soda. Layla was unlucky enough to buy one of the poorly sealed cans of Orange Fizz. It explodes, cutting her hand, and causing a serious tendon injury. Layla sues Sodaco under products liability law claiming a manufacturing defect.

Sodaco concedes that the can that injured Layla deviated from its own specifications. What is Sodaco's strongest argument, if proven, that the product does not contain a manufacturing defect?

A. Other soda manufacturers have a higher rate of producing cans that explode.
B. There is no better technology to prevent the creation of exploding cans.
C. Sodaco's facility is "state-of-the-art."
D. None of these arguments will defeat Layla's claim.

ANALYSIS. Once Layla can show that the product deviates from Sodaco's own specifications, she can establish a manufacturing defect. It does not matter that Sodaco was not negligent, or used the best available technology. This is what we mean when we say that the law imposes strict liability for a manufacturing defect. Choices **A**, **B**, and **C** are therefore all incorrect. Choice **D** is correct.

4. Design defects: The negligence-like approach of the Restatement, and the res ipsa exception

In contrast with the widespread acceptance of a strict liability standard for manufacturing defect claims, there has been much more debate and disagreement over the proper standard for addressing design defect claims. Recall that for a design defect claim, the product is manufactured to the manufacturer's own specifications, but the plaintiff is complaining that there is something about the design that is defective. I begin here with the Third Restatement's approach to design defects, and then discuss some alternative approaches.

The basic approach of the Restatement to design defect claims is negligence-like. I say "negligence-like" rather than negligence to emphasize that this claim is not being brought as a straightforward negligence claim subject to the detailed rules discussed in Part II of this book. Instead, the claim is one brought as a products liability tort, but the applicable products liability standard incorporates a Hand formula-type balancing test in measuring product defect.

Under the Restatement, a product has a defect in design:

> when the foreseeable risks of harm posed by the product could have been reduced or avoided by the adoption of a reasonable alternative design by the seller or other distributor, or a predecessor in the commercial chain of distribution, and the omission of the alternative design renders the product not reasonably safe.

REST. (3D) TORTS: PRODUCTS LIABILITY § 2(b) (1998).

Note the balancing required here, much like balancing in a negligence case. Note also the requirement that the plaintiff point to a *reasonable alternative design*. It is not enough for the plaintiff to point to the general design of a product and call that design "defective" or "unsafe." Instead, the plaintiff must identify the specific design features that could have been changed, and prove that the defendant's decision not to use the alternative design was unreasonable under a balancing test. Unlike prior law in some jurisdictions, the fact that a danger is "open and obvious" does not defeat a design defect claim brought by a plaintiff, though it is one factor that courts can consider. *See id.* illus. 3.

Again, to expand on an example given earlier, suppose Pablo is injured in an automobile accident in which a rock falls from a cliff on the side of the road and hits his car windshield. The windshield shatters, causing glass to go into Pablo's right eye, blinding him in that eye. Pablo's lawyer investigates the accident and discovers that the windshield glass was 1.5 cm thick, meeting the manufacturer's own specifications.[9] Pablo could raise a design defect claim under the Restatement if he can prove that, had the glass been manufactured to a thickness of 1.7 cm, the additional costs of making the glass thicker would have been outweighed by the accident savings from the use of the thicker glass.

---

9. So there is no manufacturing defect.

In judging the reasonableness of the design, the jury must consider the question at the time of the manufacturing or distribution of the product. If a product is put on the market in 2000, reasonableness is judged from the year 2000. If technology advances in 2009 make possible a safe and cheap plastic windshield that was not possible to make in 2000, the new technology would not retroactively make the design from the year 2000 defective.

In addition to proving defect, the plaintiff has to show that the defendant's failure to adopt a reasonable alternative design was an *actual cause* of the plaintiff's injury. Pablo must prove by a preponderance of the evidence that the same injury would not have happened had the glass been manufactured as he suggests, at 1.7 cm thick. If the same injury would have happened, then the defect was not a cause of the injury. (Pablo will also have to prove proximate cause and damages, and his claim is subject to any affirmative defenses that the manufacturer could raise.)

Why a negligence-like standard rather than a strict liability standard as used for manufacturing defects? According to the Restatement, unlike manufacturing defects, in which the standard is set by the manufacturer itself, for design (and warning) defects "[s]ome sort of independent assessment of advantages and disadvantages, to which some attach the label 'risk-utility balancing,' is necessary." "The emphasis is on creating incentives for manufacturers to achieve optimal levels of safety in designing and marketing products. Society does not benefit from products that are excessively safe — for example, automobiles designed with maximum speeds of 20 miles per hour — any more than it benefits from products that are too risky." REST. (3D) TORTS: PRODUCTS LIABILITY § 2, cmt. *a* (1998).[10]

QUESTION 5. Chasing the Hickie, Take II.   Paul works as a pressman at a printing press. While he is running a printing job, he notices a blemish on the pages of the book he was printing. The blemish was caused by a small piece of dirt, or "hickie," on the press. Rather than shut down the press (which would have taken three hours to restart), Paul does a very dangerous procedure known in the printing business as "chasing the hickie," which involves climbing up near the spinning printing press and very lightly applying a piece of plastic to scrape the hickie off the press. Unfortunately, during this procedure Paul's hand gets trapped and eventually has to be amputated. Paul later claims in his lawsuit that the

---

10. The Restatement also says that "manufacturers may persuasively ask to be judged by a normative behavior standard to which it is reasonably possible for manufacturers to conform." *Id.* If that is the case, then it is hard to see how the Restatement drafters can justify strict liability for manufacturing defects in cases in which the manufacturer has used reasonable care, and has still manufactured a product that deviates from its own specifications. I, for one, am not satisfied that the Restatement drafters have adequately explained the different role of blameworthiness for design defect and manufacturing defect cases.

press was defective because it did not contain a hand-guard to prevent users from "chasing the hickie."

In determining whether the product contains a design defect under the Restatement (Third) of Torts: Products Liability, which factor should not be considered by the court?

A. Designs for hand-guards that were technologically feasible beginning ten years after manufacture and distribution of the product.
B. The number of accidents that would be prevented by the hand-guard.
C. The cost of adding the hand-guard to the product.
D. The fact that the danger of chasing the hickie is open and obvious.

ANALYSIS. In considering whether a product has a design defect under the Third Restatement, the factfinder must engage in a cost-benefit analysis of "reasonable alternative design," comparing the injuries likely to occur with and without the hand-guard to the additional costs of the hand-guard. For this reason, Choices **B** and **C** are incorrect. Moreover, although the fact that a danger is "open and obvious" does not defeat a design defect claim under the Restatement, it is a relevant question. For this reason, Choice **D** is incorrect. Choice **A**, the correct answer, lists a factor that should *not* be considered in assessing design defect: alternative designs that were not technologically feasible at the time of manufacture and distribution.

Narrow Exception for "Manifestly Unreasonable Design." You may sometimes hear news reports about products liability suits brought against tobacco or gun manufacturers, claiming that the products have a "defective design." The Third Restatement rejects the idea that these kinds of suits can go forward, because these products have some social utility and there is no reasonable alternative design. (Just to be clear, if there were a "safer" cigarette or gun with the same general properties, that kind of suit could go forward under the Restatement; we are talking instead about a claim that *all* cigarettes or guns are defective products.) The general approach of the Restatement is to recognize that many products are dangerous, but they are not also *defective*—even if there is no way to make the products safer—if the products also have some social utility.

The Restatement does, however, recognize a very narrow class of products that "have low social utility and a high degree of danger [so that] liability should attach even absent proof of a reasonable alternative design." REST. (3D) TORTS: PRODUCTS LIABILITY § 2, cmt. *e* (1998). But the only example the Restatement can come up with is a toy exploding cigar that can cause major fires. "The utility of the exploding cigar is so low and the risk of injury is so high as to warrant a conclusion that the cigar is defective and should not have been marketed at all." *Id.* illus. 5.

QUESTION 6. **Bye-Bye, BB?** Trenton was playing with a BB gun that his parents bought him for Christmas. He was doing some target practice in his backyard, but the gun misfires, causing a serious injury to Trenton's ear. Trenton sues the BB gun's manufacturer, BBCo, claiming the gun has a "manifestly unreasonable design" under the Restatement (Third) of Torts: Products Liability.

What is BBCo's strongest argument to defeat Trenton's claim that the BB gun has a "manifestly unreasonable design"?

A. Toy guns that shoot hard pellets have social utility for those who enjoy shooting them.
B. Trenton's own negligence contributed to his injury.
C. This is the safest BB gun on the market today.
D. The cost of replacing BB gun pellets with softer pellets would be too high.

ANALYSIS. To claim a "manifestly unreasonable design," Trenton would have to prove that the BB gun has such low social utility and a high degree of danger that liability should attach even absent proof of a reasonable alternative design. For BBCo to defeat this argument, it should argue that the design of the BB gun is not unreasonable in that the ability to shoot hard pellets is what gives the gun its social utility. Choice **A** is therefore correct. Choice **B** is wrong because the question of Trenton's own negligence is relevant to affirmative defenses, not to design defect. Choice **C** is wrong because the safety of the gun compared to other guns on the market goes to reasonable alternative designs for the BB gun, and not to the question whether all BB guns are manifestly unreasonable to market. Choice **D** is wrong because it too goes to the question of "reasonable alternative design."

Res Ipsa Loquitur *and Products Liability.* You will recall from Chapter 9 that one way that plaintiffs in a rare set of cases may prove negligence is through the doctrine of *res ipsa loquitur.* Roughly speaking, under that doctrine a plaintiff need not provide direct proof of defendant's negligence, but can ask the jury to *infer* that the defendant was negligent by the very fact that an accident occurred in a particular way. In the classic example, a plaintiff walking down the street gets hit in the head with a barrel full of flour that falls out of defendant's window.

The Restatement recognizes a similar "inference of defect" in limited circumstances. Under the Third Restatement, § 3, a jury may infer that the product had a defect without proof of a specific defect when the incident that harmed the plaintiff "was of a kind that ordinarily occurs as the result of a product defect" and it "was not, in the particular case, solely the result of causes other than product defect existing at the time of sale or distribution."

To understand this section, contrast two car accidents. In the first, a car is involved in a 2 mph collision and bursts into flames. In the second, a car is involved in a 60 mph collision and bursts into flames. Under the Restatement's § 3, a jury might be allowed to infer product defect in the first example absent proof of a specific manufacturing defect or design flaw in the product. It is enough to know that cars do not ordinarily explode in 2 mph collisions. In the second example, this section likely would not come into play, because cars may explode in 60 mph collisions.

Precisely where the dividing line is on cases getting the *res ipsa* presumption is hard to say (collisions at 20 mph? or 30? or 40?), but the general principle is clear: In those rare cases where the facts cry out "defect," a jury is allowed to infer defect under the Restatement.

Res ipsa for products liability is especially useful in two kinds of cases. First, sometimes a product is destroyed as plaintiff is injured, making proof of a manufacturing defect difficult, if not impossible. Second, using *res ipsa* in appropriate cases will be cheaper than proving a design defect because the plaintiff need not hire an expert and put on potentially complex testimony about "reasonable alternative designs."

QUESTION 7. Plane Crazy. Sandy is an amateur pilot. She buys her first plane, a brand new airplane from PlaneCo. Her takeoff goes fine, but after about ten minutes of flying, the left wing of the plane falls off. Sandy parachutes to safety, but breaks a leg when landing on the ground. The plane is destroyed on impact.

Sandy sues PlaneCo for her injuries claiming the product is defective under the Restatement (Third), but she concedes that because the plane is destroyed she cannot prove that the plane had a manufacturing defect. PlaneCo therefore argues Sandy's products liability suit must fail. How can Sandy try to defeat PlaneCo's argument?

A. Through Restatement § 3's *res ipsa* inference.
B. Through proof that there was a reasonable alternative design for the plane which would not have caused the wing to fall off.
C. Through the methods set forth in Choice A or Choice B.
D. Through neither Choice A nor Choice B; Sandy will lose her products liability suit because she cannot prove defect.

ANALYSIS. The facts tell us that Sandy cannot prove a manufacturing defect because the plane was destroyed. That does not prevent her from trying to rely upon the Restatement's *res ipsa* provisions. A wing falling off a brand new plane seems like the kind of thing that ordinarily does not occur in the absence of some defect (either manufacturing or design defect) in the product. Sandy's alternative, which likely is going to be more expensive for her, is to hire an expert to try to prove that the plane had a design flaw: She has to show that there is a reasonable alternative design that would have prevented the wing from falling off. Because Sandy could try the methods in either Choice **A** or Choice **B**, the correct answer is Choice **C**, giving the option of proving defect either way. Choice **D**, which says Sandy is going to lose because she cannot prove a product defect, is incorrect.

5. Design defects: The consumer expectations test and other strict liability type approaches

Love it or hate it, the Third Restatement's approach to design defect has the virtue of coherence: We can at least understand how the Restatement test works and how it relates to the debate over negligence versus strict liability for products liability claims. Unfortunately, that clarity is lacking not only (as mentioned above) in the Second Restatement's § 402A approach to products liability, but also in the products liability law of many states. Some states have used a negligence approach; others a strict liability approach. The terminology is confusing, so that in some states what is labeled "strict products liability" is not really a strict liability approach at all. In some jurisdictions a product is not defective if it contains an "open and obvious" (or "patent") defect, even if there is a reasonable alternative design.[11] In New Jersey at one point (but no longer),[12] whether or not a product had a design defect was judged not at the time of sale or distribution, but at the time of *trial*, thereby importing a strict liability standard in through the back door by holding manufacturers to a standard they could not necessarily have met when they first sold the product.

California's approach to design defect claims, if not typical, is interesting and worth a look. In the state, plaintiffs can seek to prove a products liability suit in two ways:

Risk-Utility Test with Burden Shifting. If a plaintiff injured by a product points to a design feature of the product that was the *actual cause* of plaintiff's injury (think of the 1.5 cm thick glass that could have been designed at 1.7 cm and saved Pablo from injury), then the burden shifts to the defendant to prove that the design of the product as used was reasonable, and that the alternative design favored by the plaintiff was not cost justified.[13] This is akin to the negligence-like Third Restatement's approach to design defect, except for the burden-shifting aspect, which obviously favors plaintiffs in close cases.

---

11. *See Griffin v. Summit Specialties*, 622 So.2d 1299 (Ala. 1993) (applying Georgia law); *McCollum v. Grove Mfg. Co.*, 293 S.E.2d 632, 635 (N.C. Ct. App. 1982).
12. *Beshada v. Johns-Manville Prods. Corp.*, 447 A.2d 539 (N.J. 1982), limited in *Feldman v. Lederle Labs.*, 479 A.2d 374, 388 (N.J. 1984) and *Fischer v. Johns-Manville Corp.*, 512 A.2d 466 (N.J. 1986).
13. *Barker v. Lull Eng'g Co.*, 573 P.2d 443 (Cal. 1978).

Consumer Expectations Test. An alternative means of proving a defective design in California is under the "consumer expectations test," which finds a product defective when it fails to perform as safely as an ordinary consumer would expect, regardless of the costs and benefits of an alternative design. When first in place in California, and as is still true in some other jurisdictions,[14] the consumer expectations test had some teeth and functioned like a strict liability test. It did not matter if there was no reasonable alternative design for the product; if it failed to be as safe as an ordinary consumer would expect, then the product would be considered defective.

In recent years, however, the California Supreme Court severely limited the consumer expectations test, so that it now looks like the "*res ipsa*" version of defect in the Third Restatement's § 3. In *Soule v. General Motors Corp.*, 882 P.2d 298 (Cal. 1994), the California Supreme Court said that consumers usually have "no idea" about how safe a product should be, and that the consumer expectations test was reserved for rare situations such as the following:

> For example, the ordinary consumers of modern automobiles may and do expect that such vehicles will be designed so as not to explode while idling at stoplights, experience sudden steering or brake failure as they leave the dealership, or roll over and catch fire in two-mile-per-hour collisions. If the plaintiff in a product liability action proved that a vehicle's design produced such a result, the jury could find forthwith that the car failed to perform as safely as its ordinary consumers would expect, and was therefore defective.

Id. at 308 n.3. Given the rarity of vehicles exploding at stoplights or rolling over and catching fire in 2 mph collisions, it is now clear that the consumer expectations test of California law is all but dead except in *res ipsa*-type circumstances.

QUESTION 8. Cracked Windshield, California Style. Pablo is injured in an automobile accident in which a rock falls from a cliff on the side of the road and hits his car windshield. The windshield shatters, causing glass to go into Pablo's right eye, blinding him in that eye. Pablo presents evidence that the windshield was designed and manufactured to be 1.5 cm thick, and that a windshield 1.7 cm thick would have prevented the accident.

Which is the most accurate statement regarding Pablo's design defect claim brought in a California court?

---

14. *See Potter v. Chicago Pneumatic Tool Co.*, 694 A.2d 1319 (Conn. 1997).

> **A.** Pablo will be able to prove defect if he can show that the windshield failed to perform as safely as he expected.
> **B.** Pablo must prove that the 1.7 cm thicker windshield was cost-justified under a risk-utility balancing test.
> **C.** If Pablo and the manufacturer put on no further evidence, Pablo will succeed in proving that the windshield had a design defect.
> **D.** Pablo must prove the product was in a defective condition unreasonably dangerous.

ANALYSIS. This is a tough question. Let's take each possible answer one by one. Choice **A** is an incorrect answer following the *Soule* case. In California today, the consumer expectations test is limited to those circumstances in which a product has a catastrophic failure of design, such as exploding in a 2 mph collision. Here, the consumer expectations test won't work because Pablo and other consumers generally have "no idea" how safely a windshield should perform when hit by a rock.

Choice **B** is incorrect for a different reason. This would be the right choice if this case were governed by § 2(b) of the Third Restatement. But in California, once the plaintiff has put forward evidence of actual causation (which Pablo did according to the facts of this question), the burden *shifts* to the defendant to prove there is no defect under a risk-utility balancing test. So Choice **B** is wrong because it says that *Pablo* must prove defect. In fact, *the manufacturer* must prove *no defect.* If the manufacturer puts on no evidence, Pablo wins because of the burden shifting. That's why Choice **C** is the correct choice. Choice **D** is the easy one to eliminate; it states not the California standard, but the standard of the Second Restatement's § 402A.

6. Warning defects: A negligence-like approach

That last set of materials on design defect is tough going. Take a break.

(Humming.)

Okay, welcome back. You will be happy to hear that the law on failure to give adequate instructions or warnings ("warning defects," for short) is much more straightforward. Putting aside a few outlier cases that may no longer be good law, the rule is a negligence-like standard for warning defects. The Third Restatement provides that a product has a warning defect:

> when the foreseeable risks of harm posed by the product could have been reduced or avoided by the provision of reasonable instructions or warnings by the seller or other distributor, or a predecessor in the commercial chain of distribution, and the omission of the instructions or warnings renders the product not reasonably safe.

REST. (3D) TORTS: PRODUCTS LIABILITY § 2(c) (1998).

As with the Third Restatement's approach to design defect, we see here a balancing test that weighs the risks and benefits of additional or different warnings or instructions. Now, at first glance, it might seem that adding additional warnings is virtually costless: An extra page of a product insert or more words on the product itself will not add much to the cost of the product. The problem with this logic is that in the area of warnings "more" does not necessarily equal "better." Because of the problems of information overload, lack of consumer attention, and other issues, a few prominent warnings on a product may be much more effective in reducing injury than a more comprehensive, but harder to read and understand, set of warnings.

In addition to pointing to an alternative warning or set of instructions, plaintiffs raising failure to warn claims will have to prove *actual causation*. In the real world, this can be a difficult hurdle for plaintiffs in many cases. The jury would have to believe that, had the defendant given a different or better set of warnings or instructions, the plaintiff would have made a different decision about whether or how to use the product, and this decision more likely than not would have prevented the injury from taking place.

One other question that arises under warning defect claims is whether the manufacturer does enough by warning an intermediary (such as a doctor or employer) rather than the ultimate consumer or user of the product. I address this point in section B.7 below.

> **QUESTION 9. Chasing the Hickie, Take III.** Paul works as a pressman at a printing press. While he is running a printing job, he notices a blemish on the pages of the book he was printing. The blemish was caused by a small piece of dirt, or "hickie," on the press. Rather than shut down the press (which would have taken three hours to restart), Paul does a very dangerous procedure known in the printing business as "chasing the hickie," which involves climbing up near the spinning printing press and very lightly applying a piece of plastic to scrape the hickie off the press. Unfortunately, during this procedure Paul's hand gets trapped and eventually has to be amputated. A hand-guard would have prevented users from "chasing the hickie." Paul admits that the instructions for the printing press warned of "serious injury or death" from chasing the hickie.
>
> What is Paul's best products liability cause of action in a jurisdiction that applies the Third Restatement's approach to products liability?
>
> A. Manufacturing defect.
> B. Design defect.
> C. Warning defect.
> D. Choices B and C, but not A.

ANALYSIS.   Again, the only way to answer a question like this is to take the choices one by one. It does not look like Paul has a viable manufacturing defect claim. There is no evidence here that the printing press deviated from the manufacturer's own specifications. So Choice **A** is wrong and Choice **D**, which says Choice **A** is wrong, looks promising. Choice **B** says this might be a design defect claim, and that's right: If Paul can point to a reasonable alternative design (that is, if the hand-guard is a cost-justified precaution that should have been taken), then he can prove that the product is defective in design. This still leaves Choice **D** in contention, but Choice **D** is wrong because Choice **C** is also wrong: There is no viable warning claim. Paul read the warning of serious injury or death occasioned by chasing the hickie. Though in theory he could come up with an even stronger warning, it will be hard to argue that a stronger warning would have caused him not to chase the hickie, given that he did so after being warned of serious injury or death. Choice **B** is the best choice.

Allergies. If you have ever looked closely at a package of plain M&Ms, you would have noticed the package warns that it may contain traces of peanuts. For most of us, that warning is irrelevant. But for those with severe peanut allergies, that warning is exceedingly important: People with such allergies run the risk of anaphylactic shock, and even death, from peanut exposure.

The black letter of the Restatement does not speak about allergies, only about "reasonable instructions or warnings," but the Restatement comments take the position that "a warning is required when the harm-causing ingredient is one to which a substantial number of persons are allergic. . . . The more severe the harm, the more justified is a conclusion that the number of persons at risk need not be large to be considered 'substantial' so as to require a warning." REST. (3D) TORTS: PRODUCTS LIABILITY § 2, cmt. *k* (1998). Given the number of people with peanut allergies, and the likelihood that people would not necessarily expect traces of peanuts to be in *plain* chocolate candy, it makes sense that this warning appears on the package of plain M&Ms. Of course, as with the case of warnings generally, there is no need to warn of an obvious risk. A package of peanuts, for example, need not contain a warning that the product contains peanuts.

QUESTION 10. If the Glove Fits . . .   John is a hospital orderly. Each day he puts on about 50 pairs of disposable latex gloves to do his work. The gloves come in a box containing 200 pairs of gloves. In each box, in small letters, there is a warning that reads: "Warning: Contains latex. If redness or other symptoms arise, discontinue use." The warnings do not say that latex allergies can emerge unexpectedly among people who have been asymptomatic, that the more the exposure the greater the risk of developing the allergy, and that for some people latex exposure can result in a serious health condition, even death. Thousands of workers have developed latex allergies in the last decade from exposure to latex gloves.

If John develops a serious latex allergy and sues the glove manufacturer for failure to provide an adequate warning under the Third Restatement,

A. John will necessarily lose because the box did contain a warning about latex dangers.
B. John will lose because there is no requirement to warn of allergies that do not affect most people.
C. John may be able to prove a warning defect, on grounds the warning actually given was inadequate.
D. John may be able to prove a warning defect, but only if the product had no reasonable alternative design.

ANALYSIS. Just because a product contains a warning, that does not preclude the possibility that the warning is inadequate. Here, it looks like a substantial number of people have developed allergies, and there is a decent argument that an understated warning (of redness, etc.) in small letters is not adequate. Choice **A** is incorrect because giving "a warning" may not be enough; one must give a reasonable warning, which mentions some of the more serious effects and what to do about it. Choice **B** is wrong because the Restatement says a warning needs to be given in the case of allergies when a "substantial" number of people are affected; given that the allergy can cause serious problems, even death, the number of people affected need not be substantial for the warning to have to be given. Choice **D** is wrong because the reasonable alternative design question goes to whether or not the product has a *design* defect, a separate tort from the *warning* defect claim at issue here. Choice **C** correctly states the idea that John can win, if he proves the warning was inadequate.

7. The special case of prescription drugs and medical devices (including the learned intermediary doctrine)

Section 6 of the Third Restatement singles out prescription drugs and medical devices (but not over-the-counter medications, such as regular strength ibuprofen) for special treatment.[15]

---

15. The Second Restatement's § 402A, cmt. *k*, contained special rules for "unavoidably unsafe products," products which included, but were not limited to, prescription drugs and medical devices. Comment *k* was very influential, and the jurisprudence that evolved around the term "unavoidably unsafe products" is both extensive and contradictory.

Manufacturing Defects. The rules for manufacturing defects are the same: Strict liability applies. Rᴇsᴛ. (3ᴅ) Tᴏʀᴛs: Pʀᴏᴅᴜᴄᴛs Lɪᴀʙɪʟɪᴛʏ § 6(b)(1).

Design Defects. Design defect claims against prescription drug or medical device manufacturers[16] are much harder to win than normal design defect claims under the Third Restatement § 2(b). Like § 2(b), the prescription drug design defect test uses a balancing test; but under that balancing test, a product is defective only when the foreseeable risks of the design of the product exceed the foreseeable benefits for *all* patients.

To make this clear, consider the drug thalidomide, which was an anti-nausea drug given to pregnant women. The drug causes severe birth defects, and it should not be handled by women of child-bearing age. A defective drug? Not under the Restatement. It turns out that thalidomide is an effective drug for some cancer patients. Because the benefits of the drug exceed the risks for "any class of patients," a person injured by thalidomide may not bring a design defect claim under the Restatement. The person may sue for a warning defect claim in appropriate circumstances, as we will see below.

QUESTION 11. Ask Your Doctor About . . . Heart Attacks. Pharmco sells Relievex, an anti-inflammatory prescription drug marketed for treating arthritis. Tests indicate that the drug is no more effective than over-the-counter ibuprofen for arthritis. But Relievex doubles a person's risk of heart attack compared to ibuprofen.

Jane takes Relievex for a year and has a heart attack. She sues Pharmco for marketing a defectively designed product under the Third Restatement. Will Jane be able to prove the product has a defective design?

A. Yes, if she can show that the product's risk exceeded the benefits for patients like Jane.
B. Yes, if she can show that the products risks exceeded the benefits for all classes of patients using the drug.
C. No, because the product is effective in reducing the effects of arthritis.
D. No, if the product contained a warning of its dangers.

ANALYSIS. Under the Restatement's approach for prescription drugs and medical devices, a product has a design defect only if its risks exceed its benefits for all classes of patients. The test is all classes of patients, and not just patients like the plaintiff. For this reason, Choice **A** is wrong and

---

16. It is even harder to bring a claim against a retailer or distributor of prescription drugs and medical devices. Other than for a manufacturing defect, for which strict liability applies, the retailer or distributor may be liable for a design or warning defect only if the seller or distributor "fails to exercise reasonable care and such failure causes harm to persons." Rᴇsᴛ. (3ᴅ) Tᴏʀᴛs: Pʀᴏᴅᴜᴄᴛs Lɪᴀʙɪʟɪᴛʏ § 6(e)(2) (1998).

Choice **B** is right. Choice **C** is wrong because the product is no more effective than another drug in alleviating the effects of arthritis, but it has greater risks. Choice **D** is incorrect because a warning of dangers does not defeat an argument that a product has a defective design.

Warning Defects and the Learned Intermediary Rule. The Third Restatement's approach to warnings and instructions for prescription drugs is basically the same as the approach for warnings and instructions generally: The warning must be a reasonable one judged under a balancing test. The big issue that arises in the prescription drug context is the question of *to whom* the warning is to be given. Generally, prescription drug manufacturers take the position that it should be enough to give an adequate warning to the treating physician or other health care provider. They say that warning the "learned intermediary" of the dangers should be enough. Some courts have accepted this learned intermediary doctrine.

The Restatement takes a middle position, stating that a reasonable warning to the health care provider (such as a warning not to allow pregnant women to come into contact with thalidomide) often discharges the manufacturer's responsibility to warn. However, the Restatement also provides that warnings or instructions also need to be given to patients "when the manufacturer knows or has reason to know that health-care providers will not be in a position to reduce the risk of harm in accordance with the instructions or warnings." REST. (3D) TORTS: PRODUCTS LIABILITY § 6(d)(2) (1998). A good example is birth control pills; some courts have held that manufacturers must warn of risks directly to consumers. *See MacDonald v. Ortho Pharmaceutical Corp.*, 475 N.E.2d 65 (Mass. 1985).

QUESTION 12. Relievex, Take II.   Pharmco sells Relievex, an anti-inflammatory prescription drug marketed for treating arthritis. At the time the product is marketed, reasonable testing by Pharmco indicates that it is more effective than ibuprofen in alleviating pain from arthritis. Moreover, the tests do not reveal any adverse side effects of the drug.

Jane takes Relievex for a year and has a heart attack. Additional testing by Pharmco reveals that the drug is no more effective than over-the-counter ibuprofen for arthritis. But Relievex doubles a person's risk of heart attack compared to ibuprofen. Pharmco has taken Relievex off the market. Jane sues Pharmco for failing to warn of the extra risk of heart attack in a jurisdiction following the Third Restatement. Will she be able to prove a warning defect?

A. Yes, because Pharmco failed to warn of the risk of heart attack, a serious health problem.
B. Yes, because the foreseeable risks of harm exceeded the products benefits for all classes of users.

> **C.** No, because a manufacturer needs to warn only of foreseeable risks
>   of harm at the time of manufacturing and sale, and the risk of
>   heart attack was not known or reasonably knowable at the time.
> **D.** No, because not all users of the product would have a heart attack.

ANALYSIS. For both prescription drugs and other products, the Restatement requires a reasonable warning based upon what was known or reasonably knowable at the time of marketing and distribution. Here, the facts tell us that Pharmco did reasonable testing, and the risk of heart attack was not known. For this reason, Jane's case will fail on warning grounds. Choice **C** correctly explains this point and Choice **A** is incorrect for the same reason. Choice **B** is wrong because that is the test for *design* defect of prescription drugs and medical devices, not warning defect. Choice **D** is easily eliminated as a wrong answer because that is not the standard for when a warning must be given of the dangers of a product.

C. The Closer: Should products liability return to contract law?

Products liability law has been controversial. Some conservatives have argued that products liability lawsuits are part of a torts "crisis" that makes it difficult for manufacturers to get reasonable insurance, raising the costs of products and forcing some manufacturers out of business. Liberals tend to see these concerns as exaggerated, and dispute the idea that products liability rules are responsible for any economic problems.

Among the conservative proposals to deal with products liability law is to return some of the law to contract law, at least to a limited extent. For example, in return for a discount on a product, a consumer could agree to forego recovery for noneconomic damages (such as pain and suffering, discussed in Chapter 20) in the event he is injured by the product. *See* Richard A. Epstein, Cases and Materials on Torts 841 (9th ed. 2008) (suggesting contractual defenses in products liability actions but noting that both the Restatement and the Uniform Commercial Code reject the possibility of contracting around products liability law in the case of personal injuries).

Opponents of such plans (including yours truly) believe that consumers lack the ability to make rational calculations when it comes to deciding whether the benefits of a discount would outweigh the cost of a low probability catastrophic event. An extensive psychological literature shows rationality problems in these and related areas. *See* Cass Sunstein, Worst Case Scenarios (2007). To Epstein, this approach is too paternalistic; freedom of contract should rule the day.

What do you think?

QUESTION 13. Bloody Margarita. Richard buys a blender from Bladeco. Like other blenders, the blade of the blender operates even when the top of the blender is off so that users can add ingredients while blending. Richard makes strawberry margaritas, and in the process of doing so, some of the strawberries get stuck on the blade. Richard puts a fork into the blender to try to dislodge them, but his hand slips and is cut by the whirling blade. Richard sues Bladeco, claiming that the product has a defective design because its top can come off while the blender is in use. In response, Bladeco points to the sales contract, which states that Bladeco's liability is limited to the repair or replacement of the blender, at Bladeco's option. It says it cannot be liable for Richard's injuries. How should the court respond to Bladeco's argument?

A. The court should accept it if Richard read the provision before the injury.
B. The court should accept it if the provision was displayed prominently, even if Richard did not read it.
C. The court should reject it because such limitations are unenforceable.
D. The court should reject it because his claim is for design defect, not a warning defect.

ANALYSIS. The purpose of this question is to get you to distinguish contractual limitations on liability from warning claims. Despite the urging of some scholars to the contrary, the law is clear: Contractual limitations on liability for personal injury arising out of product defects are unenforceable. Choice **C** is correct. Choices **A** and **B** are incorrect because the clause's unenforceability does not depend upon whether or not Richard agreed to it or read it. Choice **D** is incorrect because it does not matter what the nature of Richard's products liability claim is: So long as the claim is one for personal injury, the contractual limitation is unenforceable.

✵ Rick's picks

1. Training on Traynor	C
2. Chasing the Hickie	B
3. Just Cause	B
4. Popping Pop	D
5. Chasing the Hickie, Take II	A

6. Bye-Bye, BB?	A
7. Plane Crazy	C
8. Cracked Windshield, California Style	C
9. Chasing the Hickie, Take III	B
10. If the Glove Fits . . .	C
11. Ask Your Doctor About . . . Heart Attacks	B
12. Relievex, Take II	C
13. Bloody Margarita	C

19

Products Liability Torts Defenses, Including Preemption

CHAPTER OVERVIEW
A. Introduction: The traditional approach: Contributory negligence, assumption of risk, "open and obvious" dangers, and product misuse
B. The modern approach: Comparative responsibility
C. Federal preemption of state products liability law
D. The Closer: The Third Restatement, design and warning defects, and "unreasonable misuse" of products
⬥ Rick's picks

A. Introduction: The traditional approach: Contributory negligence, assumption of risk, "open and obvious" dangers, and product misuse

A brief recap: As we saw in the last chapter, products liability law has gone through an evolution from the nineteenth to twenty-first centuries. In the beginning, products suits were quite limited, with many barred by the privity of contract requirement. Courts eventually relaxed the privity requirement, allowing most people injured by products to sue for products defects. Those suits began as negligence suits, but some courts, including some influenced by a particular reading of the Second Restatement's § 402A, adopted a strict liability standard for judging such suits. The strict liability standard has stuck for cases alleging manufacturing defects, but many courts, and now the Third Restatement, have adopted a negligence-like balancing approach for design defect and warning defect claims.

During the evolution of products liability law, particularly as courts abandoned the privity requirement, some courts developed affirmative defenses or similarly functioning doctrines that made it difficult for plaintiffs to recover for product-related injuries. In addition to the usual contributory negligence and assumption of risk defenses, which functioned to completely bar a plaintiff's negligence claim,[1] the following other doctrines also often played a role in the early products liability cases.

Open and Obvious Danger/Patent Danger. In *Campo v. Scofield*, 95 N.E.2d 802 (N.Y. 1950), plaintiff was working in the fields with an "onion topping" machine designed to trim onions, when his hands got caught in the machine and became badly injured. He sued, alleging the product was defective, but the court rejected the argument, noting that there was no allegation in the complaint that the danger of the machine was hidden:

> The cases establish that the manufacturer of a machine or any other article, dangerous because of the way in which it functions, and patently so, owes to those who use it a duty merely to make it free from latent defects and concealed dangers. Accordingly, if a remote user sues a manufacturer of an article for injuries suffered, he must allege and prove the existence of a latent defect or a danger not known to plaintiff or other users.

Id. at 803. Though the rule is phrased in terms of the manufacturer's "duty," we may conceive of the same point as an argument that products with obvious danger are not "defective," or that a person who uses a product with such open and obvious dangers consents or "assumes the risk" of such injury. Regardless of the characterization, in many courts plaintiffs injured by obviously dangerous products were out of luck in their products liability suit.

Today, most courts have rejected the open and obvious danger rule, seeing the obviousness of the product's danger as only one factor among many to be considered in a design defect case. *See Micallef v. Miehle Co.*, 39 N.Y.2d 376 (1976) (the "chasing the hickie" case described in the last chapter; New York's highest court rejected *Campos* in *Micallef*); *but see* RICHARD A. EPSTEIN, TORTS 409 (1999) (noting that the "open and obvious rule is still followed in some jurisdictions").

Product Misuse. Early on in the development of products liability law, some courts took the position that the plaintiff's case could not succeed if the plaintiff misused the product in some way. To some extent, this is an argument about plaintiff's negligence or assumption of risk. But some of the cases went further, holding that a manufacturer has no "duty" to design a product to prevent injury from a misuse of the product, or that a product

---

1. See Chapter 10 for a detailed explanation of how these defenses worked historically.

not designed to prevent injuries from misuse is not "defective." At its extreme, some courts ruled that manufacturers could not be liable for designing cars that do not hold up well in car crashes, on grounds that automobiles are designed for transportation, and not to be crashed into one another! Consider *Evans v. General Motors Corp.*, 359 F.2d 822 (7th Cir. 1966, applying Indiana law):

> The intended purpose of an automobile does not include its participation in collisions with other objects, despite the manufacturer's ability to foresee the possibility that such collisions may occur. As defendant argues, the defendant also knows that its automobiles may be driven into bodies of water, but it is not suggested that defendant has a duty to equip them with pontoons.

Id. at 825.

Courts have abandoned this strict reading of products liability law,[2] though the concept of misuse has not been eliminated from modern law. Indeed, we shall see that the issue of misuse is not only relevant in the comparative responsibility allocation discussed in the next section; the Third Restatement (as described in section D of this chapter) has revived the idea for "unreasonable" misuses of a product.

QUESTION 1. Chasing the Hickie, Take IV. Paul works as a pressman at a printing press. While he is running a printing job, he notices a blemish on the pages of the book he was printing. The blemish was caused by a small piece of dirt, or "hickie," on the press. Rather than shut down the press (which would have taken three hours to restart), though Paul knew it was very dangerous, he performs a procedure known in the printing business as "chasing the hickie," which involves climbing up near the spinning printing press and very lightly applying a piece of plastic to scrape the hickie off the press. Unfortunately, during this procedure Paul's hand gets trapped and eventually has to be amputated. Paul later claims in his lawsuit that the press was defective because it did not contain a hand-guard to prevent users from "chasing the hickie."

Under the traditional products liability rules, which argument may the manufacturer raise to defeat liability?

A. The product is not defective because the danger from the product is open and obvious.

B. Paul cannot recover because he misused the product.

C. Paul cannot recover because he assumed the risk of injury.

D. The manufacturer could raise each of these arguments.

---

2. The Seventh Circuit overruled *Evans* in *Huff v. White Motor Corp.*, 565 F.2d 104 (7th Cir. 1977).

ANALYSIS. This question is meant to be easy, and designed to get you to see how many kinds of arguments products liability defendants could raise under the traditional rules. First, Paul saw that the machine was dangerous and lacked a hand-guard. The danger was open and obvious, as mentioned in Choice **A**. Second, the printing press was designed for printing, not designed for people to climb on the printing press to remove blemishes, as suggested in Choice **B**. Third, Paul knew he was doing a dangerous procedure, suggesting he voluntarily and knowingly encountered the risk, as noted in Choice **C**. Because each of these choices raises a plausible argument for the manufacturer, the correct answer is Choice **D**, all of the above choices.

B. The modern approach: Comparative responsibility

As the last example demonstrates, products liability defendants had a number of weapons in their arsenal to defeat products liability claims even for the marketing of obviously dangerous products. As products liability law tilted in a more plaintiff-friendly direction, however, many courts backed away from some of the tougher doctrines, including those related to open and obvious dangers and foreseeable misuses.

The Second Restatement, § 402A cmt. *n*, went even further in the new direction, taking the position that contributory negligence in the form of plaintiff's "failure to discover the defect in the product, or to guard against the possibility of its existence" was not a defense. However, it affirmed that assumption of risk remained a complete defense.

The Third Restatement in turn backed away from the Second Restatement's treatment of affirmative defenses, adopting instead a rule of *comparative responsibility* analogous to the rules adopted in many states in negligence cases. REST. (3D) TORTS: PRODUCTS LIABILITY § 17 (1998). Chapter 10 covers this ground in much greater detail in the context of a negligence case (and you need to know that material to make sense of what follows), but here's a brief synopsis: In situations in which a defendant has been found to have marketed or sold a defective product that injures the plaintiff and a plaintiff has been negligent and/or has voluntarily and knowingly encountered the risk from the defendant's conduct, the jury will be asked to apportion liability between the plaintiff and the defendant based upon each party's *share of responsibility*.

Thus, consider again — with a twist this time — a hypothetical from last chapter. Suppose Pablo is injured in an automobile accident in which a rock falls from a cliff on the side of the road and hits his car windshield. The windshield shatters, causing glass to go into Pablo's right eye, blinding him in that eye. Pablo's lawyer investigates the accident and discovers that the windshield glass was 1.2 cm thick, when the manufacturer's own specifications for the glass say it should be 1.5 cm thick. The manufacturer investigates and determines that Pablo took his car on the road past a sign that warned: "Danger: Falling Rocks. Enter at your own risk."

If the jury finds that the product was defective (which it should, under the rules for manufacturing defects as described in the last chapter) *and* that Pablo's conduct in driving through the area despite the sign constituted a kind of negligence and/or a kind of consent/assumption of the risk, the jury must *apportion responsibility* between the manufacturer and Pablo in percentages equaling 100 percent. For example, the jury might hold the manufacturer 70 percent responsible and Pablo 30 percent responsible, allowing Pablo to recover 70 percent of his damages.

How is the jury to make the apportionment of responsibility? The Third Restatement points to the "generally applicable rules apportioning responsibility." REST. (3D) TORTS: PRODUCTS LIABILITY § 17(b) (1998). Those generally applicable rules appear in the RESTATEMENT (THIRD) OF TORTS: APPORTIONMENT OF LIABILITY § 8:

> Factors for assigning percentages of responsibility to each person whose legal responsibility has been established include
>
> (a) the nature of the person's risk-creating conduct, including any awareness or indifference with respect to the risks created by the conduct and any intent with respect to the harm created by the conduct; and
>
> (b) the strength of the causal connection between the person's risk-creating conduct and the harm.

As noted at the end of Chapter 10, there is something of a logical difficulty in some of the negligence cases comparing a defendant's negligence on the one hand with plaintiff's negligence and consent on the other. It is something like comparing apples to oranges: What is the scale of fault measured against consent?

That same problem arises in design and warning defect cases under the Third Restatement, because each of these defect standards uses a negligence-like test in evaluating defect. But the apples-to-oranges problem is even more pronounced in a case involving a *manufacturing defect*, as in the latest iteration of the Pablo hypothetical above. Recall that manufacturing defect claims are strict liability, so for purposes of liability it does not matter whether or not the manufacturer used reasonable care or not to try to prevent the defect from occurring.

But under the Restatement's approach, the jury would still be told to apportion liability. Suppose that the manufacturer puts on evidence that it had an excellent quality control program in place, and that this thinner window still made it through the process. That evidence might lead a jury to assign a smaller share of responsibility to the manufacturer compared to Pablo, even though manufacturing defect claims are strict liability torts.

In sum, the problem that arises with some products liability tort affirmative defenses is analogous to the problem that arises in modern negligence cases and even in strict liability claims for abnormally dangerous activities: The jury will be told to compare things that are not easily comparable and to come up with an allocation based upon the jurors' views of what is a fair allocation of responsibility. No doubt, conscientious jurors will do their best to come up with a number, and jurors easily can pick two percentages that sum to 100 percent. But behind the "black box" of the jury, there may be some pretty interesting types of incommensurable comparisons going on, if only subconsciously.

QUESTION 2. Chasing the Hickie, Take V. Paul works as a pressman at a printing press. While he is running a printing job, he notices a blemish on the pages of the book he was printing. The blemish was caused by a small piece of dirt, or "hickie," on the press. Rather than shut down the press (which would have taken three hours to restart), though Paul knew it was very dangerous, he performs a procedure known in the printing business as "chasing the hickie," which involves climbing up near the spinning printing press and very lightly applying a piece of plastic to scrape the hickie off the press. Unfortunately, during this procedure Paul's hand gets trapped and eventually has to be amputated. Paul later claims in his lawsuit that the press was defective because it did not contain a hand-guard to prevent users from "chasing the hickie." The manufacturer contends Paul was negligent and assumed the risk when he tried to chase the hickie.

Assume the jury finds (1) that the product had a design defect because it lacked a hand-guard and (2) that Paul assumed the risk of injury. What should be the result for Paul in the trial court in a jurisdiction following the Third Restatement?

A. Paul should recover nothing because the danger from the product is open and obvious.
B. The jury will apportion responsibility between the manufacturer and Paul, allowing Paul to recover a share of his damages based upon the manufacturer's share of responsibility.
C. Paul should recover all of his damages because contributory negligence is no defense in a products liability action.
D. Paul should recover nothing, even though contributory negligence is no defense in a products liability action because he also assumed the risk of injury when he undertook a procedure he knows to be dangerous.

ANALYSIS. The answer here depends upon an understanding of how the rules of the Third Restatement work. Under those rules, there are no separate doctrines or defenses of open and obvious dangers, contributory negligence, or assumption of the risk. Instead, the jury must undertake a look at all of the conduct of both parties (including the sale of a defective product, and plaintiff's potential negligence and consent), to arrive at a global allocation of responsibility between the two parties. This will be expressed in terms of percentages that will add up to 100 percent. Choice **B**, the correct answer, states the job that the jury faces.

Choice **A** is wrong because the global allocation of responsibility does not contain all-or-nothing rules like the old rule barring plaintiff's case completely for "open and obvious" dangers. Choices **C** and **D** are wrong because they state rules that come from the approach of the *Second* Restatement's § 402A cmt. *n*, allowing assumption of risk to serve as a complete defense for products liability defendants but not allowing contri-butory negligence in cases of a plaintiff failing to discover a product defect.

It is worth noting here the contrast between the outcomes in this question and in Question 1 from this chapter. Under the old rules, in a case like *Micallef*, the plaintiff was likely to recover nothing, even if it would be cheap and easy for the manufacturer of the printing press to add a hand-guard. Under the modern rules, as expressed in the Third Restatement, the plaintiff stands a chance of recovering *something* from the defendant in a case in which it would be cheap and easy for the manufacturer to add a hand-guard. Now it is not clear *how much* a plaintiff in a case like this would get: Any negligence of the plaintiff, consent, and deliberate decision to act in the face of what really is an open and obvious danger are going to be factored in by the jury in coming up with the appropriate allocation of responsibility. But this sharing of responsibility, rather than the all-or-nothing rule of the Restatement, means that more plaintiffs will recover *some* damages from products liability defendants.

C. Federal preemption of state products liability law

One of the most important—and difficult—current issues in products liability law concerns the extent to which federal law "preempts" state products liability lawsuits. The defendant in a products liability suit may raise federal preemption as an affirmative defense; if it succeeds, the defense operates as a complete bar to the plaintiff's case.

The issue of preemption arises because of a provision in Article VI of the U.S. Constitution known as the "Supremacy Clause" providing that federal law is the "supreme Law of the Land" trumping state law, including state tort law. So if Congress passed a statute barring any or all aspects of state tort law, that law would trump state tort law (assuming the courts agreed that Congress had the power to pass such a law in the first place — but that's a topic for a Constitutional Law course). In such a circumstance, we would say that Congress (or the statute) has preempted state tort law.

That's the simple part. The difficult part is understanding *when* it is that Congress has passed a statute that preempts state tort law. Speaking very roughly, preemption can be either *express* or *implied*. Express preemption occurs when Congress expressly states in a statute that it intends the federal law to bar state law, including state tort actions. Analysis of express preemption is more complicated than its sounds because there are often conflicting reasonable statutory interpretation arguments on both sides over whether Congress's language demonstrates express preemption.[3]

Aside from express preemption, Congress may *impliedly* preempt state tort law actions as well.

> Even in the absence of express preemptive language . . . federal law can preempt state law by implication in two other ways. First, Congress implicitly may indicate an intent to occupy an entire field to the exclusion of state law. Second, even if Congress has not occupied the field, state law is nevertheless pre-empted to the extent it actually conflicts with federal law, that is, when compliance with both state and federal law is impossible, or when the state law stands as an obstacle to the accomplishment and execution of the full purposes and objectives of Congress. And, whether through field or conflict preemption, state laws can be pre-empted by federal regulations as well as by federal statutes.

Good v. Altria Group, 501 F.3d 29 (1st Cir. 2007), *cert granted*, 128 S. Ct. 1119 (Mem.) (2008) (citations and internal quotations omitted).

Buried within the implied preemption test are three separate potential grounds for finding preemption:

1. Congress intended to occupy the entire field to the exclusion of state law.
2. State law actually conflicts with federal law because compliance with both laws is impossible.
3. State law actually conflicts with federal law because state law stands as an obstacle to the accomplishment of congressional purposes.

Though the courts sometimes say that there is a presumption against preemption,[4] the Supreme Court in more recent years has been willing to find implied preemption in a number of cases. In *Geier*, for example, the Court held that a federal automobile safety statute preempted a design defect claim based upon an automobile's failure to have airbags. In *Cipollone*

---

3. *See Geier v. American Honda Motor Co.*, 529 U.S. 861 (2000) (holding that Congress did not expressly preempt state law tort claims for failure to equip an automobile with air bags).
4. *See Medtronic, Inc. v. Lohr*, 518 U.S. 470, 485 (1996).

v. Liggett Group, Inc., 505 U.S. 504 (1992), the Court held that some of plaintiff's failure to warn claims against cigarette manufacturers were expressly barred by federal cigarette laws.

Though the *Lohr* case held that a federal law regarding FDA approval of medical devices did not preempt a state products liability claim for a pacemaker on design and warning claims, the Court last term distinguished *Lohr* and held that another provision of the same federal statute barred a products liability claim against the manufacturer of a catheter used to perform a heart proce-dure.[5] It remains unclear exactly how far the Court is going to change preemption law generally, as there were important differences in the premarket approval processes at issue in these two cases. In any event, the Supreme Court is hearing two more preemption cases in the October 2008 term, one raising the question whether "the Federal Cigarette Labeling and Advertising Act preempts state law deceptive practice claims in connection with the advertising of cigarettes as 'light' or containing 'lower tar and nicotine'"[6] and the other raising the question whether "federal law preempts state torts claims imposing liability on drug labeling that the FDA had previously approved."[7] In the meantime, the FDA has issued a "preamble" to a rule stating a strong view that its labeling decisions preempt state tort claims.[8]

As should be obvious from this brief overview of preemption doctrine, the issues raised are quite complicated and hotly debated at the highest levels of our court system. You should at least be aware that some major classes of products liability cases face the prospect of being removed from the state tort law system by virtue of federal court interpretation of congressional statutes regulating drugs, medical devices, cigarettes, and other products.

> **QUESTION 3. Expressly Implied.** Federal law imposes detailed labeling requirements on pesticides. It says nothing about the effect of the labeling law on state law. Carlos is injured when he inhales fumes from an ant spray that he used in his kitchen. He claims that the spray's label did not give him a clear enough warning about the need for adequate ventilation when using the product. The manufacturer of the product argues that Carlos's claim is preempted by federal law.

---

5. *Riegel v. Medtronic, Inc.*, 128 S. Ct. 999 (2008).

6. *Altria Group v. Good, cert granted*, 128 S. Ct. 1119 (2008).

7. *Wyeth v. Levine, cert granted*, 128 S. Ct. 1118 (2008).

8. 71 Fed. Reg. 3922 (Jan. 24, 2006). The June 2008 update to the Franklin, Rabin, and Green casebook reports that "[a] significant number of federal district court and state court cases — new ones every day — have been confronting this issue and splitting on the matter." MARC A. FRANKLIN, ROBERT L. RABIN & MICHAEL D. GREEN, TORT LAW AND ALTERNATIVES 32 (Supp. 2008). It is also possible that the new Obama administration will reverse FDA policy on this question.

Which type of preemption defense may the manufacturer reasonably raise against Carlos?

A. Express preemption.
B. Implied preemption.
C. Both express and implied preemption.
D. Neither express nor implied preemption.

ANALYSIS. The difference between express and implied preemption claims turns on whether the federal statute or regulation *explicitly* states something about the effects of the federal statute on the operation of state law. In this fact pattern, the facts tell us that federal law imposes a detailed labeling scheme for pesticides, but it says nothing about whether Congress intended the law to preempt state tort law. In such circumstances, the manufacturer cannot reasonably raise an express preemption argument against Carlos. For this reason, Choices **A** and **C** are incorrect.

The next question is about the possibility of raising an implied preemption claim. An implied preemption claim may be raised in three circumstances: when Congress intended to occupy the field, when compliance with both federal and state law is impossible, and when state law would serve as an impediment to Congress's statutory purpose. Here, given that Congress has imposed "extensive" labeling requirements, it seems reasonable for the manufacturer to raise implied preemption under either the first or third types of implied preemption listed. Because implied preemption is a reasonable argument to make (though not necessarily a winner), Choice **B** is correct and Choice **D** is incorrect.

Of course, this is a relatively simple question about an exceedingly complex topic. For a taste of the complexity, in a case involving an action under the Federal Insecticide, Fungicide, and Rodenticide Act (FIFRA), 7 U.S.C. §§ 136 et seq., *see Bates v. Dow Agrosciences LLC*, 544 U.S. 431 (2005).

D.   The Closer: The Third Restatement, design and warning defects, and "unreasonable misuse" of products

As sections A and B of this chapter explained, the Third Restatement rejected the old all-or-nothing rules about affirmative defenses, replacing them instead with a regime of *comparative responsibility*. The upshot of this change is that plaintiff's negligence, consent or other misconduct in relation to a product generally counts as a factor in the allocation of responsibility between defendant and plaintiff, but it does not serve to defeat plaintiff's case entirely.

The Restatement does contain one exception to this point, however, and it is an exception that could serve to be important within the class of misuse cases. According to the Restatement (Third) of Torts: Products Liability § 2 cmt. *p*, product manufacturers and drafters have no responsibility to design against or warn about "unreasonable" misuses of a product.[9] The result of a conclusion by a court (not a jury) that the plaintiff has engaged in an unreasonable misuse of a product is that the plaintiff recovers *nothing*; there is no allocation of responsibility between the seller and plaintiff because a conclusion that there is no defect means that the plaintiff cannot prove at least one element of the prima facie case against the seller.

What constitutes an unreasonable misuse? The Restatement gives the example of a person who climbs on the top bar of a wooden chair to reach the top shelf of a bookcase. "The . . . chair is not defectively designed. [Plaintiff]'s misuse of the product is so unreasonable that the risks it entails need not be designed against."[10]

The result in this hypothetical is not objectionable, but the broader rule arguably is. It is hard to imagine any jury assigning any responsibility to a seller who fails to design a chair so that someone can stand on the top part of it to reach tall objects. A consumer's decision to use a chair in this manner is both unreasonable and unforeseeable.

But consider a more difficult case. Alan is a teenager who gets high drinking Cleartussin cough suppressant. He suffers serious abdominal injuries from drinking too much of the over-the-counter medication. The manufacturer of Cleartussin knows that teenagers have been abusing the product. There is a relatively inexpensive substitute formula that the manufacturer can use that will keep Cleartussin just as effective as a cough suppressant, but lack any ingredients allowing anyone to get high from drinking it. But the manufacturer chooses not to change the formula.

Under the Restatement's rule, Alan stands to recover nothing if he sues the manufacturer of Cleartussin claiming a design defect. A court would likely rule that drinking cough suppressant is an unreasonable misuse of the product. In my view, that's a bad result. Unlike the chair hypo from the Restatement, Alan's conduct is *foreseeable*. If there are cost-justified steps that a manufacturer could take to eliminate foreseeable misuses of the product, the manufacturer should have to take those steps.

That's not to say that Alan should be able to recover *all* of his damages. To the contrary, in any allocation of responsibility between Alan and the

---

9. *See* REST. (3D) TORTS: PRODUCTS LIABILITY § 2, cmt. *p* ("the post sale-conduct of a user may be so unreasonable, unusual, and costly to avoid that a seller has no duty to design or warn against them. When a court so concludes, the product is not defective . . . ").
10. *Id.* illus. 20.

manufacturer, many jurors will be tempted to put a great deal of responsibility on Alan's shoulders. But at least Alan gets to make his claim to the jury, and a manufacturer such as the maker of Cleartussin would have an incentive to take cost-justified measures to prevent foreseeable misuses of the product.

QUESTION 4. A Bottle of Trouble.   Jenny, a six-year-old girl, is playing "house" with her friend Samantha. During their "coffee break," Jenny took out some baby oil from the bathroom and poured it into toy cups Jenny had in her room. As Jenny and Samantha pretend to drink their "coffee," Jenny's dog runs into the room, startling the girls. Jenny gasps, and in the process she aspirates baby oil in her lungs. Unfortunately, Jenny has now suffered serious lung damage.

Jenny sues the manufacturer of the baby oil, arguing that its failure to have a child-proof cap constituted a design defect. The case is brought in a jurisdiction that has adopted the Restatement (Third) of Torts: Products Liability. If the manufacturer argues that the product does not contain a design defect:

A. The court should accept the argument if it concludes that Jenny's conduct constituted an unreasonable misuse of the product.
B. The court should accept the argument because the danger of baby oil is open and obvious.
C. The court should accept the argument if it concludes that Jenny's conduct constitutes negligence.
D. The court should accept the argument because coffee breaks are an adult activity.

ANALYSIS.   This is a difficult question, and the best way to answer the question is to consider each answer in turn. Choice **A** turns out to be the correct answer: Under the Third Restatement, a product does not contain a design or warning defect if the plaintiff has engaged in an unreasonable misuse of the product. Here, a jury would have to determine if a six-year-old's use of baby oil as part of pretend play constitutes an unreasonable misuse of a product.

Choice **B** is incorrect for two reasons. First, the Restatement has rejected the open and obvious nature of a product as a means for defeating a products liability claim. Second, it is not clear to me that aspiration of baby oil is an open and obvious danger of baby oil. Few people actually know how dangerous aspirated baby oil can be. Choice **C** is incorrect because whether or not Jenny's conduct constitutes negligence goes to the question of affirmative defense, not to the question of whether or not the product has a defect. True, whether Jenny made an unreasonable misuse of a project would be relevant to the comparative responsibility allocation too. But the question asks about design defect, and Jenny's negligence may or may not be related to an unreasonable misuse of the project.

Finally, Choice **D** is the easiest answer to eliminate from the list. Adult activity rules are applicable to children, and could indeed arise in this case. But Jenny was not having a "coffee break" (likely not considered an "adult activity" in any event; she was playing house). More importantly, whether or not Jenny engaged in an adult activity does not answer the question whether or not the product is defective.

 # Rick's picks

1. Chasing the Hickie, Take IV   D
2. Chasing the Hickie, Take V   B
3. Expressly Implied   B
4. A Bottle of Trouble   A

Damages

20

Compensatory Damages

CHAPTER OVERVIEW
A. **Introduction: The usual requirement to prove plaintiff's damages**
B. **Tort damages: Compensation and deterrence**
C. **Economic and noneconomic damages**
D. **Special rules for wrongful death and related claims**
E. **The Closer: The thin-skulled plaintiff rule and the contrast with proximate cause rules**
◈ **Rick's picks**

A. Introduction: The usual requirement to prove plaintiff's damages

Tort remedies are an important part of real-world tort law practice; but remedies issues usually get raised at the end of the Torts course (and appear here at the end of this book), sometimes getting short shrift as professors rush to complete material before finals. That's a shame; remedies issues are not only interesting, but they are the "bottom line" that your future clients care about, much more so than the debate between Justices Andrews and Cardozo over proximate cause and duty.[1]

The final four chapters of this book consider Torts remedies issues. This chapter focuses on the basics of tort damages. The next chapter adds in complications related to offsetting benefits, collateral sources, and mitigation. Chapter 22 considers the issues of multiple tortfeasors, and the rules related to joint and several liability. Finally, Chapter 23 considers the important question of punitive damages.

Let's begin by recalling the prima facie case for all torts, as first noted in Chapter 2.

---

1. I teach a separate course in Remedies, and I've written about Remedies in Richard L. Hasen, Remedies: Examples and Explanations (2007). Some of the material in this part of the book is drawn from the Remedies book.

The plaintiff must prove:

1. That defendant engaged in the requisite tortious conduct
2. Actual causation
3. Proximate causation
4. **Damages**

Before going forward, it is worth noting a few exceptions to the idea that the plaintiff must prove damages.

Plaintiff Seeks an Injunction, Rather than Damages. If I know that someone is going to come onto my land to cut down my trees, I can seek a court order, called an injunction, barring the person from doing so. I don't have to wait for the trees to be cut down before I seek relief.

Injunctions prevent future harm (or the future bad effects of past harm) as opposed to damages, which compensate for past (or expected future) harm. The circumstances in which a plaintiff is entitled to an injunction rather than damages are discussed in detail in a Remedies course.[2]

Plaintiff Seeks Nominal Damages. Occasionally, a plaintiff seeks only nominal damages (such as the sum of $1). As we saw in Chapter 3, plaintiffs in trespass to land cases sometimes seek nominal damages as a way of resolving a land dispute. In this context, damages don't serve their usual function of compensating plaintiffs; instead they serve the *declaratory* function of stating the rights and obligations of parties in conflict.

Presumed Damages. This book does not cover the tort of *defamation*, which is usually covered in an Advanced Torts or First Amendment course. Defamation is a tort defined as "the act of harming the reputation of another by making a false statement to a third person." BLACK'S LAW DICTIONARY 448 (8th ed. 2004). Given the difficult administrative and evidentiary burdens of proving damage to reputation, courts sometimes relax the usual damages rules in defamation cases, allowing plaintiffs to recover "presumed damages," a sum set by the jury without actual proof of the extent of injury. For more details, *see* HASEN, *supra*, 45-46.

Putting aside these exceptions, the usual rule is that the plaintiff must prove damages with reasonable certainty in order to prove the last element of the plaintiff's prima facie case. Without proof of damages (or one of the exceptions above), plaintiff loses her case.

When the plaintiff proves damages, the plaintiff gets a sum of money to compensate for the losses inflicted by the defendant. In this way, damages serve as a *substitute* for the thing that was lost. Sometimes money serves as a better substitute than at other times. If I steal your television, a sum of money to buy a television set of the same quality seems like an adequate substitute. Money seems less adequate if I stole and destroyed your wedding album, or if I broke

---

2. *See also* HASEN, *supra*, ch. 7. In some circumstances, a plaintiff can also seek to recover defendant's gains in restitution rather than damages. That too is beyond the scope of a normal Torts course, and therefore, this book. For more information, *see id.* ch. 11.

your leg. Some things are not easily replaceable on the market, and in those circumstances money as substitutionary relief can seem incomplete, even hollow. We explore these issues further in the next sections of this chapter.

QUESTION 1. $1 Grass. Jared and Hank are neighbors who do not get along. Every afternoon, Hank runs onto Jared's lawn and yells nasty things into his house. Jared is upset, so he sues Hank for trespass to land, seeking $1 for the trampling of his grass. Hank responds by stating that Jared cannot prove his prima facie case for trespass to land because he has not suffered any damages.

How should the court rule on Hank's argument?

A. The court should accept Hank's argument because plaintiffs must always prove damages as part of the prima facie case.

B. The court should reject Hank's argument because Hank was acting intentionally.

C. The court should reject Hank's argument because plaintiffs never need to prove damages as part of the prima facie case.

D. The court should reject Hank's argument because Jared could seek nominal damages as a means of declaring the rights between the two parties.

ANALYSIS. Generally speaking, plaintiffs must prove damages as part of the prima facie case for all torts. However, as noted in the text, this rule is subject to some exceptions, such as when a plaintiff seeks nominal damages. For this reason, Choices **A** (plaintiffs must always prove damages) and **C** (plaintiffs never need to prove damages) are both incorrect. Choice **B** is wrong because whether or not Hank was acting intentionally is irrelevant to Hank's argument. That is, even if Hank concedes he has acted intentionally in entering Jared's land, he is claiming that Jared's failure to prove damages should doom his case. Choice **D** is the best answer: For certain kinds of cases, such as trespass to land, a person can seek nominal damages as a means of declaring the rights between the parties. Jared wants to use damages as a way of telling Hank to keep off his land. If Hank continues to do so after the case, Jared might seek an injunction or punitive damages for later violations.

B.   Tort damages: Compensation and deterrence

Generally speaking, the law recognizes the primary function of damages to be *compensation* — hence the name "compensatory damages."[3] To compensate

---

3. Punitive damages, discussed in Chapter 23, serve other functions besides compensation.

means "to make satisfactory payment or reparation to; recompense or reimburse." AMERICAN HERITAGE DICTIONARY OF THE ENGLISH LANGUAGE 376 (4th ed. 2000). The idea that damages should serve a compensatory function traces back far in history, even to Aristotle's *Nicomachean Ethics*.[4] The idea is to put the plaintiff back in the *rightful position*, that is, the position that the plaintiff would have been in but for the defendant's wrong.[5]

For most tort cases, the general tort measure compares the position of the plaintiff after the defendant's wrong with the *status quo ante* (that is, the position that the plaintiff was in before the wrong, in relation to the defendant).[6] It might be useful to picture this idea graphically. So imagine that I steal $100 from your wallet, and you sue me for conversion. See figure 20-1 below.

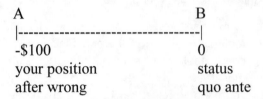

Figure 20-1

Your position after the wrong is position A; you are at -$100. Before I stole the wallet you were at position B, the status quo ante. The purpose of compensatory damages is to move you from position A back to position B. Putting aside a lot of complications (including things like the costs of litigation and attorneys' fees, not to mention interest to compensate you for the amount of time when you did not have access to the $100[7]), you would be compensated if the court awarded you damages equal to B − A. 0 − -$100 = $100.[8] Again, ignoring the complications, giving you $100 in damages puts you in the same position you would have been in but for the wrong. Giving you only $50 would undercompensate you; giving you $200 would overcompensate you.

Of course, in the real world, computing damages is a lot harder than in the stolen $100 example. Imagine a terrible car accident, which causes permanent disability for the plaintiff. Past medical expenses will be relatively straightforward to measure. But what about future expected medical expenses

---

4. For more, *see* Ernest J. Weinrib, *Corrective Justice in a Nutshell*, 52 U. TORONTO L.J. 349 (2002).

5. *See* HASEN, *supra*, at 5 (citing Professor Douglas Laycock for coining the phrase).

6. The major exception to this conception involves fraud (and related misrepresentation) cases, an area not covered in most first-year Torts courses. For those kinds of torts, damages conceptually could look like contracts damages, measuring the difference between what was (fraudulently) promised and what was received. Traditionally, courts did not allow plaintiffs to recover such "benefit of the bargain" damages in tort, leaving plaintiffs to sue for breach of contract instead. But that has changed somewhat in recent years in some jurisdictions. For more on this point, *see* HASEN, *supra*, ch. 5.2. Other torts involve no promises, so there is no possibility of measuring damages from a "promised position."

7. Generally speaking, attorneys' fees are not recoverable in tort cases and interest sometimes is recoverable. *See* HASEN, *supra*, Chapters 2.5.1, 17.3.

8. Don't forget that two negatives turn into a positive!

for a person expected to live with a serious disability for many years? Past lost wages also may be straightforward to measure, but what about future expected lost wages, if the plaintiff is now too disabled to work? What wages would the plaintiff have earned in ten years? And, raising a question of *present value*, how much should the jury award the plaintiff now for damages that won't accrue for ten years?

And these are the *easy* questions because there at least is a medical expenses market and a job market to use as a baseline in attempting to come up with a reasonable approximation of damages. We haven't even considered how to measure the pain and suffering that can accompany a disabling injury. What amount of money accurately represents point A on our chart and will the payment of that amount really restore the plaintiff to the status quo ante, or point B? We return to consider these issues in the next section.

QUESTION 2. Damage Defining.   Generally speaking, compensatory damages in tort law measure:

A. The difference between what the defendant promised plaintiff and what the plaintiff received.
B. The difference between the plaintiff's position before and after the defendant's wrong.
C. The amount it would take to deter defendant from engaging in wrongful activity.
D. The amount necessary to declare to the world that the defendant invaded the plaintiff's rights.

ANALYSIS.   This is a straightforward question about the usual measure of tort damages, which is the difference in the plaintiff's position before and after the defendant's wrong, as correctly stated in Choice **B**. Choice **A** is incorrect because that is the proper measure of *contract* damages and, in some limited circumstances, the tort measure in fraud (and related misrepresentation) cases. See footnote 6 above. Though tort damages may serve a deterring function, compensation — and not deterrence — is the usual measure of damages. Choice **C** is not the usual measure of tort damages; the deterrence point is discussed in the text immediately below this question. Choice **D** is wrong; as noted earlier in the chapter, though in rare circumstances plaintiffs will seek nominal damages to serve a declaratory function, the usual purpose of tort damages is compensatory, not declaratory.

Tort Damages and the Law-and-Economics Approach. For economists,[9] the compensatory function is one of two important functions of tort damages. Compensation to plaintiffs is important not for reasons of corrective justice

---

9. Chapter 7 explained the Kaldor-Hicks efficiency criterion applied by law and economics scholars. You might want to review that explanation before reading the next few paragraphs.

(not a primary concern for economists) but because without it, potential tort victims would overinvest in items to protect themselves from injury rather than put their resources toward a productive use.

From the economic perspective, damages also serve an important function for tort defendants as well. The possibility of a damage award should deter defendants from engaging in activities likely to result in such awards. Damages therefore serve as a *price*, and so long as taking a precaution is cheaper than an expected damages award, the rational potential torts defendant will opt for the precaution over the expected damages award. To take a concrete example, suppose a given precaution that will lessen the risk of automobile accidents costs $600. Suppose that the chance of being in an accident and having to pay a tort judgment of $10,000 if the precaution is not taken is 10 percent. In such circumstances, the defendant takes the precaution, because $600 is less than the $1,000 in expected accident costs (10 percent of $10,000).

The example shows that the economic model is sensitive to errors in calculating the costs of precautions and expected accident costs. It is also sensitive to errors in the judicial system. That is, suppose that because of problems of proof faced by plaintiffs, only half of plaintiffs who should recover damages from defendants who have injured them are able to do so. In that circumstance, expected accident costs are cut in half, to $500. The rational risk-neutral defendant does not take a $600 precaution to avoid $500 in expected accident costs. (Of course, the opposite could occur as well. If the tort system sometimes held defendants liable in tort even when they took cost justified precautions, potential tort defendants could *overinvest* in precautions to avoid high expected accident costs.)

In Chapter 23, we will return to this idea of tort damages as setting prices for potential tort defendants; some economists have suggested that punitive damages can serve to compensate for the underdeterrence of the tort system. For now, it is enough to note that from the economic perspective, damages can serve a deterrence function for potential defendants as well as a compensatory function for injured plaintiffs.

QUESTION 3. Economically Speaking.   With which statement about tort damages is a law-and-economics scholar likely to agree?

A. Tort damages serve a deterrence function, inducing potential injurers to take a cost-justified level of precautions.
B. Defendants have a moral obligation to pay tort damages so as to restore plaintiffs to their rightful position.
C. Tort damages have no effect on the precautions take by potential injurers.
D. The deterrence function of tort law does not vary with errors in assessing tort damages.

ANALYSIS. The easiest statement to eliminate is Choice **B**. As we saw in earlier chapters, economists care about Kaldor-Hicks efficiency, not about moral issues surrounding tort law. Considering the remaining three choices is more difficult. Choice **A**, the correct answer, explains one of the primary functions of tort law recognized by economists: deterrence of potential injurers. If the system works right, then the prospect of paying tort damages should induce potential injurers to take cost-justified precautions. For this same reason, Choice **C** is wrong; tort damages *do* matter to potential injurers.

Though tort damages can have a deterrence function in theory, the system does not always work right in practice: Errors in assessing tort damages may create problems of overdeterrence or underdeterrence. For this reason, Choice **D** is incorrect.

C. Economic and noneconomic damages

We can break damages into two categories: *Economic damages*, which are damages for which there is an economic market, such as lost wages, property damage, and medical expenses; and *noneconomic damages*, which are damages plaintiffs may claim for items with no functioning economic market, such as pain, suffering, and emotional distress.[10] When I say that there is "no functioning economic market," I mean that we cannot put a price on these costs because money cannot buy a "replacement" or substitute for emotional distress.

Economic Damages. Though economic damages are easier to compute than noneconomic damages, problems sometimes arise with the computation of economic damages. I have already mentioned one problem: For future expected economic damages (most importantly, future lost wages and medical expenses), jurors need to make an educated guess about these figures into the future, and then discount the amount awarded today to *present value.*

Another problem occurs, as in the wedding album example, when objective market measures of value are *much lower than a plaintiff's subjective valuation.* If I run over your pet, the cost of a replacement pet is likely to be much lower than the amount you would have to be paid to voluntarily give up your pet. For most property losses, emotional distress damages are unavailable. See Chapter 12 (discussing limits on recovery of such damages through a negligent infliction of emotional distress claim).

---

10. Despite the use of the term "economic," the term has nothing to do with the law and economics analysis discussed in the last section of the chapter. For economists, both economic and noneconomic damages are real damages that the tort system should be designed to minimize along with precaution costs.

Still another problem arises with *certain used goods*, such as automobiles. The law usually measures damages based upon the resale value of the item that has been destroyed. In the case of a car, however, that resale value is likely to be lower than the cost of purchasing a similar quality car. Why? Economist George Akerlof described a "lemon" effect that makes the market for such goods poorly functioning.[11] It is difficult to judge the quality of these goods, and uncertainty about whether the good is of high quality or is a poor-quality "lemon" pervades the market. Buyers offer lower prices for these goods to take into account the uncertainty, and the lower price means that *fewer sellers with high quality goods would choose to sell.* As such, higher quality goods are driven from the market, leaving an abundance of "lemons." So a buyer would have to pay more to get the same quality automobile that she lost.[12]

But, putting aside these problems, a jury will determine market value based upon the cost of the item in a competitive open market at the time of the wrong, or sometimes the cost to repair the item at the time of the wrong — whichever measure turns out to be less expensive for the defendant.

QUESTION 4. TV Turnoff. Carrie negligently starts a fire burning down Samir's house. Among the items lost was Samir's television set. The television was six years old, and purchased six years ago at a cost of $1,000. In most jurisdictions, to how much in damages is Samir entitled for the loss of the television?

A. $1,000.
B. The value of $1,000 from six years ago in today's dollars.
C. The market value of the six-year-old television at the time it was destroyed.
D. The cost to buy a television of similar quality today.

ANALYSIS. Generally speaking, for destroyed goods the value is the market value at the time the item was destroyed. Choice **C** correctly states this answer. Because of the lemons problem, discussed earlier in the text, that amount might not be enough to buy a television of similar quality today (though if the price of quality televisions has decreased, perhaps it will be). For this reason, Choices **A**, **B**, and **D** are each incorrect. Choice **B** seems to confuse the concept of present value, which is not implicated in this case. Present value issues arise only when one is paying damages *now* for a loss that will be incurred in the future (such as medical expenses ten years from now).

---

11. *See* George Akerlof, *The Market for Lemons*, 84 Q.J. Econ. 488 (1970).
12. Recognizing this problem, a few courts have allowed a more generous damage measure based upon replacement cost less depreciation for household goods and apparel. *See* Hasen, *supra*, at 23-24.

Noneconomic Damages. Let's begin with what should be an obvious point: Even though noneconomic damages involve losses for which there is no functioning market, they still have great value to people—most people who suffer serious pain because of a defendant's tort likely would not have accepted the pain for any amount of money offered by the defendant before the tort.

Because of the lack of a functioning market, noneconomic damage awards tend to be all over the place. Some juries will award much higher amounts on the same facts than other juries. One technique that plaintiffs' lawyers sometimes use to get jurors to give higher awards for pain and suffering is to make a "per diem" argument, asking for a certain amount of damages per day. Suppose you ask for $10 per hour, 16 hours a day, 7 days a week, 52 weeks per year, for 40 years for a serious debilitating injury. Compensating someone $10 per hour for great pain does not seem like much, but that amount, as aggregated, adds up to $2.3 million (assuming we do not discount any of the future pain to present value). Some courts allow per diem arguments, but others do not, viewing them as prejudicial.[13]

Both courts and legislative bodies have responded to the variance (and sometimes very high amount) of tort awards for noneconomic damages. Courts sometimes will reduce an award that the court views as "shocking the conscience" or under some other standard. That kind of review allows judges to impose more uniformity on jury verdicts in similar cases. Appellate courts naturally can perform this uniformity function better than individual trial judges. When a judge reduces the award, it generally comes in the form of an option for the plaintiff. Either the plaintiff accepts the new, lower award (called a "remittitur"), or the plaintiff can choose a new trial on the damages question only. There's no guarantee, however, that the judge won't order remittitur after a second trial as well.

Legislative bodies have also reacted to noneconomic damages by imposing caps in certain circumstances. In California, for example, plaintiffs who are injured by a health care provider may recover no more than $250,000 in noneconomic damages;[14] there are no limits on economic damages recoverable from health care providers.

Caps on noneconomic damages have been a popular element of defendant-oriented tort reform proposals. The insurance industry in particular has claimed that caps on noneconomic damages are necessary to keep liability insurance rates—particularly medical malpractice insurance rates—in a reasonable range. Plaintiffs' lawyers have argued that such caps are unnecessary, that any insurance crisis is artificially manufactured, and that such limits tend

---

13. *See Botta v. Brunner*, 138 A.2d 713 (N.J. 1958).
14. CAL. CIV. CODE § 3333.2 (West 1997). California voters also enacted a measure changing the rules for joint and several liability for noneconomic damages. See Chapter 22.

to penalize the most severely injured people by undercompensating them. The empirical debate is beyond what we can cover here.

QUESTION 5. Easing the Pain?   Charlie is injured in an automobile accident caused by Shira, a drunk driver. Charlie sues Shira for negligence. Charlie is able to work, but he has constant neck pain as a result of the accident. Shira agrees she was negligent and that she needs to pay for damages to Charlie's car, but she argues that she need not pay any damages for Charlie's neck pain because there is no way to measure those damages accurately.

How should a court respond to Shira's argument?

A. The court should accept the argument because tort plaintiffs can recover only economic damages.
B. The court should accept the argument unless Charlie puts into evidence the market value of neck pain.
C. The court should reject the argument because pain and suffering damages have a ready market value.
D. The court should reject the argument even though pain and suffering damages do not have a ready market value.

ANALYSIS.   Just because there is no market for pain and suffering (or emotional distress), that doesn't mean that such damages are noncompensable. Courts can, and do, allow an award for such noneconomic damages, though they police high awards that shock the conscience. Choice **D** correctly states (and Choice **C** incorrectly contradicts) the principle that pain and suffering damages are compensable even though they do not have a ready market value. Choices **A** and **B** simply misstate the law: Plaintiffs may recover noneconomic damages and can do so without proof of any market value.

Conscious Pain and Suffering versus Loss of the Value of Life. One interesting issue that has come up in the courts is whether plaintiffs who are so injured mentally that they cannot experience pain should be allowed to recover for the "loss of enjoyment of life" as a kind of noneconomic damage. The argument in favor of allowing such damages is that they are compensating for an objective loss, like the loss of a limb.

The leading case on this question is *McDougald v. Garber*, 536 N.E.2d 372 (N.Y. 1989). The court there said that such damages could not be recoverable as a separate element of noneconomic damages, and that there had to be proof that a plaintiff is capable of experiencing pain and/or emotion before an award of noneconomic damages could be allowed. The court concluded that so long as there was some proof of cognitive awareness, it was not necessary for plaintiff's lawyers to prove the extent to which the plaintiff could experience pain.

The dissenters argued that the result was paradoxical because it meant that the more severe the injury to plaintiff, the less the defendant had to pay. The majority responded, however, that the purpose of damages is compensation, not punishment, and this argument of the paradox appealed to a desire to punish the defendant.

QUESTION 6. No Pain, No Money?   Pam was injured in a terrible automobile accident, which left her "brain dead." Her family has kept her on life support, at great expense, but she has no functioning mental capacity. The defendant who caused the accident argues that it need not pay any damages, because the plaintiff is incapable of experiencing pain.

How should a court respond to the defendant's argument?

A. The court should accept it, ruling that Pam can recover no damages for her injuries.

B. The court should accept it in part, ruling that Pam can recover no noneconomic damages.

C. The court should accept it in part, ruling that Pam can recover no economic damages.

D. The court should reject it.

ANALYSIS.   To answer this question, you first must need to know the difference between economic and noneconomic damages. In this case, economic damages would include the medical expenses to take care of Pam. The noneconomic damages would be any pain and suffering — though in this case she is not capable of experiencing any. The rule from *McDougald* bars noneconomic damages when a plaintiff is incapable of experiencing pain or emotional distress, and that would seem to apply in this case.

Given all of this, Pam should be able to recover for her medical expenses (economic damages) but not any pain and suffering (noneconomic damages). Choice **B** correctly gives this choice, and it therefore follows that Choices **A**, **C**, and **D** are incorrect.

D.   Special rules for wrongful death and related claims

Torts that result in death raise some of the most difficult valuation questions: of course, there is no sum of money most of us would accept in exchange for giving up our lives. Wrongful death and related claims, however, have been subject to special limitations thanks to the history of the tort as it developed in England.

Briefly,[15] in 1808 a judge in England rejected a husband's claim for damages when the defendant's wrongful conduct caused the death of the husband's wife, holding that the common law did not allow for such damages. *Baker v. Bolton* (1808) 170 Eng. Rep. 1033 (K.B.). The English Parliament overruled *Baker* in 1846, but the statute doing so set forth limits on who could recover for wrongful death and the kind of damages allowed. The parliamentary decision upset any further evolution of the common law, which meant that the extent of plaintiffs' recovery in the case of wrongful death depended upon how the legislative body defined the scope of recovery.

Baker was accepted as precedent in many parts of the United States. Even today, in many states the ability of a family to recover damages for a loved one's wrongful death depends upon, and is limited by, the state's wrongful death statutes. Statutes differ by state. For example, in Kansas heirs may recover for financial losses, but spouses face a cap of $250,000 on "non-pecuniary" (or noneconomic) damages. Children cannot recover damages for loss of a parent. *See* KAN. STAT. ANN. § 60-1903(a) (2004): *Howell v. Calvert*, 1 P.3d 310, 316 (Kan. 2000). In contrast, in New Jersey family members may recover only for pecuniary losses, N.J. STAT. ANN. § 2A:31-5 (2000), which the New Jersey Supreme Court has defined to include "the contributions, reduced to monetary terms, which the decedent might reasonably have been expected to make to his or her survivors," as well as "the hospital, medical and funeral expenses incurred for the deceased." *Smith v. Whitaker*, 734 A.2d 243, 248 (N.J. 1999). Punitive damages are not available for wrongful death actions in New Jersey. *Id.*

Given these limitations, and of course the economic damages for future lost medical expenses that are saved when a person is killed, it is no exaggeration to say that many wrongful death verdicts will be smaller than the damages awarded by a jury in the case of a serious, but non-fatal, injury.

> **QUESTION 7. Understanding Wrongful Death Claims.** Sally is killed while walking across the street. Nanette, who is driving negligently, runs her over. Sally is survived by her 8-year-old son, Thomas. Thomas sues Nanette for wrongful death, claiming pecuniary and nonpecuniary damages. Assuming Thomas can prove that Nanette was negligent, may he recover damages from her?

---

15. For a very readable summary of the development of the law of wrongful death and related areas, *see* RICHARD A. EPSTEIN, CASES AND MATERIALS ON TORTS 902-909 (9th ed. 2008).

> **A.** He may recover pecuniary damages, but not nonpecuniary damages.
> **B.** He may recover nonpecuniary damages, but not pecuniary damages.
> **C.** He may recover no damages.
> **D.** He may be able to recover some damages, but it depends upon the jurisdiction in which he sues.

ANALYSIS. The purpose of this question is to drive home a single point: The ability of persons to recover for the wrongful death of a loved one is a creature of state law, usually state statues, and the statutes differ from state to state. Choice **D** correctly explains this choice. The other choices may each be true in particular jurisdictions and incorrect in others. But without more knowledge about which jurisdiction the suit arises in, you cannot answer the question with any more information.

Related Tort Actions. Two related torts actions also are available in some circumstances arising out of the death of a loved one.

- *Survival Actions.* In some states, surviving family members may recover damages for any pain and suffering that a tort victim suffered before his death. These damages are important not only in their own right, but also because in some states even a nominal award of damages for this pain and suffering may serve as a hook for the recovery of punitive damages as well.[16]
- *Loss of Consortium Actions.* These claims compensate surviving family members for the emotional distress that results from the injury or death of a loved one. In England, such claims are barred.[17] In the United States, the rules on loss of consortium differ from state to state. Earlier cases tended to show a distinct gender bias, limiting recovery to husbands and fathers, and disallowing recovery by wives, mothers and children. The gender bias has now disappeared, but today only a minority of states recognize a parent's right to recover loss of consortium for the death or injury of the parent's child, or the right of a child to recover for loss of consortium upon the death or injury of the child's parent. For more, *see* HASEN, *supra,* at 45. So far as I am aware, in no states can close friends (even non-married cohabitants) recover for loss of consortium, survival, or wrongful death.

> **QUESTION 8. Like Husband and Wife.** Ken and Barbie lived together for many years. Though they had a typical married couple relationship, they were never married. One day, Barbie was killed in an unfortunate

---

16. For more details, *see* HASEN, *supra,* at 43.
17. *See* EPSTEIN, *supra,* at 907.

plastic melting accident caused by G.I. Joe. Ken sues Joe for wrongful death, loss of consortium, and for a survival action. Joe argues that Ken's case cannot go forward. Who is right?

A. Joe is right; Ken is not entitled to bring any of these actions.
B. Joe is partially right; Ken can bring only the loss of consortium claim forward, because he is not Barbie's legal spouse.
C. Ken is right; if Joe would have been liable to Barbie, he will be liable to Ken.
D. We don't know who is right; Ken may be able to recover on some or all of these claims, but it depends upon the jurisdiction in which he sues.

ANALYSIS. As we have seen, the rules on wrongful death and the two related causes of action are strict, thanks to an accident of history. The ability to recover is generally limited both in terms of *who* can recover as well as in terms of *the types of damages* that may be recovered. Although the rules differ from state to state, the states agree that non-family members, even those living as unmarried cohabitants, cannot recover for wrongful death, loss of consortium, or survival. So Choice **A** is correct, and Choice **B, C**, and **D** are incorrect.

E. The Closer: The thin-skulled plaintiff rule and the contrast with proximate cause rules

You may recall the facts of *Vosburg v. Putney*, 50 N.W. 403 (Wis. 1891), from your Torts class or from Chapter 3: In *Vosburg*, an 11-year-old and a 14-year-old sat across from each other in a classroom. The first bell had rung, but the teacher had not yet begun class. The 11-year-old moved his foot across the aisle and kicked the 14-year-old in the shin. Unfortunately, the 14-year-old had a prior infection in his leg, and the kick caused the infection to spread, leading to permanent loss of use of the leg.

We first looked at *Vosburg* to understand the general principles of intent for battery and other intentional torts. Even though the jury found that at the time the 11-year-old kicked the 14-year-old he did not intend to cause harm, the Wisconsin Supreme Court held that the 11-year-old still could be liable for battery.

Here, we look at a different principle from *Vosburg*, which generally goes under the name of the "thin-skulled" or "eggshell" plaintiff rule. Under this rule, you take the plaintiff as you find him. If you are unlucky enough to knock Humpty Dumpty, rather than a sturdier figure, off the wall, you are going to pay for the damages you cause.

The defendant in *Vosburg* could definitely claim that the extent of plaintiff's harm was unforeseeable. But that did not save him from being responsible for the full extent of the plaintiff's damages. Tort law does make a few narrow exceptions to this rule. For example, under the tort of intentional infliction of emotional distress (discussed in Chapter 6), a defendant is not liable for emotional distress intentionally inflicted on an extra-sensitive individual, unless the defendant knows of the extra-sensitivity. *See* REST. (3D) TORTS: LIABILITY FOR PHYSICAL AND EMOTIONAL HARM § 45 cmt. *i*, ("[t]here is no liability for mental harm suffered by an unusually vulnerable plaintiff, unless the defendant knew of the plaintiff's special vulnerability"); *see also* REST. (2D) TORTS § 46 cmt. *f*; and see Chapter 6 above.

QUESTION 9. Locked Up. John and Tammy worked in the same office. One day, as a practical joke, John locked Tammy in the supply closet for an hour. Tammy had been kidnapped as a child and kept locked in a basement for three months. Since then, she always had a fear of confined spaces. John did not know any of this. Tammy had a nervous breakdown after being locked in the closed, and is currently in a mental institution.

Tammy sues John for false imprisonment and intentional infliction of emotional distress. Assume Tammy can prove the tortious conduct portion of the prima facie case for each tort. Can Tammy recover for the full extent of her emotional distress damages from John?

A. Yes, as to both claims.
B. Yes, as to the false imprisonment claim; no as to the IIED claim.
C. Yes, as to the IIED claim; no as to the false imprisonment claim.
D. No, as to either claim because the extent of her injuries were not foreseeable.

ANALYSIS. The general rule that applies in tort is the thin-skulled plaintiff rule. You take the plaintiff as you find him and must pay all damages even if the extent of the harm is not foreseeable. For the tort of IIED, however, this rule is subject to an exception for extra-sensitive individuals, unless the person committing the tort knows of the extra-sensitivity. Here, John did not know of Tammy's extra-sensitivity, so she cannot recover emotional distress damages under IIED. But it appears she can recover those same damages as part of her claim for false imprisonment. John must take Tammy as he finds her, and he finds her particularly susceptible to emotional distress resulting from being confined against her will. Choice **B** correctly states the rule, and for this reason Choices **A**, **C**, and **D** are all incorrect.

Contrast with Proximate Cause Rules. You should recall from Chapter 14 that one of the major tests for proximate causation is the "foreseeability of type of harm" test. This test asks whether the *type of harm* that occurred was a foreseeable risk of defendant's negligent conduct. In the famous *Polemis* case,[18] some ship workers negligently dropped a plank into the hold of the ship. What made the action negligent was the possibility that the heavy plank could fall on a person or property, doing damage from the impact. But the plank caused a spark, which ignited some flammable gas in the hold, causing an explosion. The *Polemis* court held that the ship owners were liable for their employees' tort, because there was a *direct connection* between the employees' action and plaintiff's property damage. In later cases, however, the English courts overturned *Polemis*, ruling that there could be no liability when the type of harm that occurs is not foreseeable. Here, the *risk of explosion* was not a foreseeable kind of risk from carelessly carrying the planks on the ship.

So note the contrast between the thin-skulled plaintiff rule for damages and the foreseeability of type of harm test for proximate cause. The law (at least in many jurisdictions) says that it is not fair to hold defendants liable when they act negligently and foreseeably cause harm, if the *type of harm* caused is unforeseeable. Yet under the thin-skulled plaintiff rule, it is perfectly fair to hold defendants liable when they act negligently (or otherwise tortiously) and foreseeably cause harm, even if *the extent of harm* caused is unforeseeable. I have yet to see an explanation adequately reconciling these two aspects of modern tort law.

QUESTION 10. Explosive Hypothetical. Ian, the school janitor, leaves a five-pound can of a highly explosive chemical solvent on the teacher's desk in a kindergarten classroom. Timmy, a kindergartner, knocks it over the next day when he is playing before class starts. It hits Timmy in the toe. For most children, this would not have been a serious problem. But Timmy was born with a bone density problem, and the impact of the can causes serious damage, leading to the amputation of the toe.

Assume it would not have been negligent for Ian to leave a five-pound bucket of water on the teacher's desk. Assume further the jurisdiction follows the foreseeability of type of harm test for proximate cause. Timmy sues Ian for negligence. May he recover damages for the loss of the use of his toe?

A. No, because the extent of harm was unforeseeable.
B. No, because the type of harm was unforeseeable.
C. Yes, under the thin-skulled plaintiff rule.
D. Yes, because Ian acted negligently.

---

18. *In Re Polemis & Furness, Withy & Co.*, [1921] 3 K.B. 560.

ANALYSIS.   This is a very tough question. At first, you might be temped to pick Choice **C** because on these facts it should not matter that the extent of the harm was unforeseeable; Ian must take Timmy as he finds him. (For this reason, Choice **A** is definitely wrong as an incorrect statement of the law.) The problem with Choice **C** is that it presupposes that the only issue in the case is damages. But note the other facts and points in the question. You are told to assume that leaving a five-pound bucket of water would not have been negligent, meaning that it was the explosive property of the substance, and not the act of leaving something innocuous on the table, that made the actions of Ian negligent. You are also told that the jurisdiction uses the foreseeability of type of harm test for proximate cause. These assumptions are therefore begging you to consider the proximate cause problem. The problem is that the type of harm is not foreseeable, which means that Timmy will lose on proximate cause grounds in a foreseeability of type of harm jurisdiction like this one. Choice **B** therefore states the correct answer. Finally, Choice **D** is wrong because the fact that Ian acted negligently does not resolve the rest of the prima facie case.

 # Rick's picks

1. $1 Grass	**D**
2. Damage Defining	**B**
3. Economically Speaking	**A**
4. TV Turnoff	**C**
5. Easing the Pain?	**D**
6. No Pain, No Money?	**B**
7. Understanding Wrongful Death Claims	**D**
8. Like Husband and Wife	**A**
9. Locked Up	**B**
10. Explosive Hypothetical	**B**

21

Mitigation, Offsetting Benefits, and Collateral Sources

CHAPTER OVERVIEW
A. Introduction: Complications in the computation of tort damages
B. Mitigation
C. Offsetting benefits
D. The collateral source rule
E. The Closer: The line between mitigation and plaintiff's negligence
🧭 Rick's picks

A. Introduction: Complications in the computation of tort damages

H ere's a brief summary of some of the major points about damages that were covered in the last chapter.

1. With a few narrow exceptions (such as injunctions, presumed damages in defamation, and nominal damages in a small set of cases), plaintiffs must prove damages as part of the prima facie case in tort.
2. Damages are aimed at putting plaintiff in the rightful position; that is, the position but for the defendant's wrong. In tort law, this generally means comparing the position of the plaintiff before and after the defendant wronged the plaintiff.
3. A primary purpose of tort law, as recognized by corrective justice theorists, is *compensation* of injured plaintiffs. The rightful position standard recognizes this compensatory function of tort law. To

economists, the primary purpose of damages is to induce potential injurers to take efficient precautions against injury.

4. In putting plaintiff in the rightful position, courts generally use market value, which is typically measured as the cost to replace or repair, whichever is cheaper.

5. Tort damages for personal injury are difficult to measure because there is no market value for pain and suffering/emotional distress (sometimes referred to by the term "noneconomic damages"). Courts and legislatures have tried various proposals to lower such damages or to achieve uniformity across similar cases. Some of these measures are controversial.

6. Wrongful death and related claims raise special problems in tort law. Thanks to a quirk of English common law, the question of who may recover and for what kinds of damages is usually spelled out in state statutes.

7. A well accepted principle of tort damages is the "thin-skull" or "eggshell" plaintiff rule: You take the plaintiff as you find him. This rule that the foreseeability of the extent of plaintiff's harm is irrelevant stands in contrast to one of the leading proximate cause tests, stating that a defendant is not liable for damages resulting from unforeseeable *types* of harms.

On top of these seven principles, there are other important damages principles applicable in torts cases:

1. Damages must be proven with *reasonable certainty*. Courts (or juries) cannot simply speculate on damages. Especially for economic damages for which there is a market measure, the plaintiff must provide some proof of damages.

2. To compensate for damages that will be incurred in the future, courts often will require jurors to *discount awards to present value*. The details of how to do this are beyond the scope of a Torts course, but the general principle is that the court should award a plaintiff a sum now that, if invested in safe investments, will yield the right amount at the time the expense would be incurred. For example, suppose that the jury believes that ten years from now, a torts plaintiff will have annual medical expenses of $10,000. The jury should award a smaller sum now that, when invested with interest, will yield $10,000 in ten years. Assumptions about costs and interest rates in the future can affect the calculation of damages.

3. To compensate plaintiffs for the delay in having a case heard by a jury and the delay in collecting damages after judgment, states sometimes allow *prejudgment interest* and often allow *postjudgment interest* on damage awards.

4. Tort plaintiffs typically cannot recover *attorneys' fees* from losing defendants. However, many tort plaintiffs' attorneys agree to work on a contingency, recovering a percentage of plaintiff's damage award if plaintiff wins, and nothing if plaintiff loses. This contingency fee arrangement means that many weaker plaintiffs' claims never make it to trial.

The remainder of this chapter considers three other important torts damages issues: mitigation, offsetting benefits, and collateral sources.

QUESTION 1. Damaging Details.   Which statement about tort damages is not correct?

A. The general role of tort damages is to put the plaintiff in the rightful position; that is, the position the plaintiff would have been in but for defendant's wrong.
B. In order to ensure that torts plaintiffs are fully put in the rightful position, winning tort plaintiffs always may recover interest and attorneys' fees from defendants.
C. Tort damages must be proven with reasonable certainty.
D. Awards for losses to be incurred in the future should be reduced to present value.

ANALYSIS.   This is a straightforward question if you read the material immediately preceding the question. Choices **A**, **C**, and **D** each make correct statements about damages rules in tort law. Choice **B** is incorrect — and remember, you were looking for the "incorrect" answer this time. It is true that plaintiffs sometimes may be able to recover interest (postjudgment interest is more common than prejudgment interest), but winning torts plaintiffs generally *cannot* recover attorneys' fees. In light of this fact, plaintiffs typically agree to a contingency fee arrangement with their attorneys, paying nothing to the attorneys but giving the attorneys a percentage of the damages in the event of a successful torts suit.

B.   Mitigation

In assessing damages, the law treats plaintiffs as though they took reasonable steps to avoid further loss — whether or not they actually did so. This "mitigation" or "avoidable consequences" rule helps defendants minimize the amount of damages they must pay, and when it is misunderstood or misapplied by plaintiffs, it can lead to damage awards that leave plaintiffs in a position worse than the "rightful position."

To take a simple example, suppose Alice negligently knocks Bea over on the street. Bea gets some cuts and scrapes on her leg. Rather than take care of the cuts and scrapes by applying an antibiotic ointment, Bea does nothing. Bea develops a stubborn infection, and the leg eventually is amputated to prevent the infection from killing her.

At first glance, Bea might look no different from the thin-skulled plaintiff in *Vosburg*, the schoolboy kicking case. There, the plaintiff sought medical attention, and he still lost the use of his leg. The court allowed plaintiff to recover the full extent of the damages.

In the Alice-Bea hypothetical, however, the additional harm could have been prevented by Bea, but it wasn't. In that situation a court would say that Bea could recover only for losses that were *unavoidable*. Bea should have promptly gone to the doctor but did not.

To give a numerical example, suppose that a jury would value Bea's loss of a leg (and accompanying noneconomic damages) at $500,000. To put her back in the position after the wrong, she would need a payment of $500,000.[1] If the jury believes, however, that it is more likely than not that Bea could have avoided the loss of the leg through reasonable steps in mitigation, and that if she would have mitigated her damages, she would have suffered $1,000 in damages, Bea could recover only $1,000, not $500,000. As you can see from this example, a failure to mitigate can be very costly for plaintiffs!

Though it is sometimes said that plaintiffs have a "duty to mitigate," this terminology is confusing. Bea cannot be sued by Alice if Bea fails to take reasonable steps to mitigate her injuries. But because the law of damages requires the jury to treat Bea as though she mitigated when the defendant raises the issue, Bea has every incentive to mitigate.

QUESTION 2. Door Buster. Deana and Perry are neighbors who do not get along. One day, after Perry is playing his music too loudly, Deana busts down Perry's front door and yells at him to shut off the music. The damage to Perry's front door is $1,000. Perry does not fix his front door for many weeks. One night, unknown criminals come through Perry's broken front door and steal his $2,000 flatscreen television set.

Perry sues Deana for trespass to real property and seeks damages of $3,000. Assume Perry can prove the prima facie case for trespass against Deana, who has no affirmative defenses.

How much may Perry recover in damages from Deana?

A. $1,000
B. $2,000
C. $3,000
D. Nothing, because Perry failed to fix the door in a timely way.

---

1. Here we are ignoring the fact discussed in the last chapter that, for noneconomic damages, it is somewhat of a fiction to talk about damages putting the plaintiff back in the position he was in before the defendant's wrong.

ANALYSIS. This question concerns mitigation. Let's begin with the easier part of the question, the damage for the door. Deana broke Perry's door, causing $1,000 in damage. You are told to assume Perry could prove the prima facie case and that Deana has no viable affirmative defenses to raise. At the very least, then, Perry will be able to claim $1,000 in damages, meaning that Choice **D** is wrong: A failure to mitigate doesn't mean that a plaintiff forfeits a right to *all* damages, only to damages that were *avoidable*.

So the next question is whether Perry can recover for the theft as well. Under principles of mitigation, he should not. Just like Bea, who failed to get prompt medical attention, Perry piled on his damages by waiting weeks to repair a broken front door. The reasonable step in mitigation would have been to fix the door in a timely way. (Had the theft occurred the same night as Deana's trespass, then likely mitigation would not have been a problem.) Perry cannot recover any damages for the television, meaning Choice **A** is correct, and Choices **B** and **C** are incorrect.

Reasonable Steps in Mitigation. The idea that the law expects plaintiffs to mitigate damages is not an absolute principle. A plaintiff need only take *reasonable* steps in mitigation. A good example of this principle is found in *McGinley v. United States*, 329 F. Supp. 62 (E.D. Pa. 1971). There, the court held that plaintiff, who had already undergone surgical procedures to alleviate pain from a herniated disc in his back, could collect future lost wages for his back injury. The court rejected the defendant's argument that the damages should have been reduced because plaintiff refused to undergo additional surgery to help his back problem, which defendant alleged could have allowed plaintiff to work.

The court held that plaintiff need not have mitigated by having further surgery, which had only a 60 percent to 70 percent chance of being successful and could in fact have worsened his condition:

> It is, of course, settled law that if injuries may be cured or alleviated by a simple and safe surgical operation, then refusal to submit thereto should be considered in mitigation of damages. This is not true, however, where the operation is a serious one, or one attended by grave risk of death or failure. A plaintiff has a duty to submit to reasonable medical treatment and the test of reasonableness is to be determined by triers of fact.

Id. at 66 (citations omitted).

One very interesting mitigation question that can arise in tort cases is a failure to mitigate damages because of religious convictions, such as when an injured plaintiff fails to take a blood transfusion for religious reasons. These cases put the tort rule on mitigation directly in conflict with the U.S. Constitution's First Amendment, which provides for the "free exercise" of religion. Putting aside the religion issue, failure to undergo a life-saving blood transfusion will be viewed by most juries as an unreasonable choice, and the jury would likely find that the injured party should have mitigated.

But the freedom of religion issue complicates matters a great deal. If a jury would hold that the failure of a religious person to mitigate as a matter of religious conviction was unreasonable, perhaps that is tantamount to deciding that the injured party's religious convictions are unreasonable. Perhaps unsurprisingly, courts have split over how to deal with the mitigation question in these circumstances.[2] Perhaps religious persons in such circumstances should be viewed under the "thin-skulled" plaintiff rule: You take the plaintiff as you find him.

QUESTION 3. The Honest Truth.   Felice negligently runs over Gerry's foot with her car. Gerry is in a great deal of pain, but he decides not to go to the hospital emergency room because he "doesn't believe in doctors." This is an honest belief of Gerry's; he hasn't been to a doctor since he was a child. Because Gerry did not get prompt medical care, he now has a permanent limp. Experts agree that if he would have gone for prompt medical care, he could have been completely cured of any aftereffects of the accident.

In awarding Gerry damages arising out of the automobile accident, Felice should have to pay:

A. No damages because Gerry failed to mitigate.
B. Damages for permanent, not temporary, injuries.
C. Damages equal to that which Gerry would have incurred had he sought prompt medical attention.
D. All of Gerry's damages, including damages for his permanent limp.

ANALYSIS.   In this case, Gerry failed to mitigate, not out of any religious conviction, but because he honestly did not believe in doctors. An honest belief is not the same as a reasonable belief, however, and it is hard to imagine a jury reaching any conclusion other than that Gerry failed to take reasonable steps in mitigation. The consequences of such a conclusion is not that Gerry forfeits all damages (so Choice **A** is wrong), but that the jury must treat him as though he took reasonable steps in mitigation. Choice **C** sets forth this correct standard, and choices **B** and **D** set forth incorrect standards.

---

2. *Compare Munn v. Algee,* 924 F.2d 568 (5th Cir. 1991) (explaining that religious views are irrelevant to the mitigation question), *with Rozewicz v. New York City Health and Hosps. Corp.,* 656 N.Y.S. 2d 593 (N.Y. Sup. Ct. 1997) (no issue of mitigation and no assumption of risk defense if refusal was based on sincere religious belief) *and Williams v. Bright,* 658 N.Y.S.2d 910 (N.Y. App. Div. 1997) (no mitigation problem if injured party acted as a "reasonable believer").

C. Offsetting benefits

Mitigation issues arise when a plaintiff can take steps to avoid further loss but fails to do so. The issue of *offsetting benefits* arises when a plaintiff actually takes steps to avoid loss. In such a case, those steps taken to avoid loss must be taken into account in computing plaintiff's damages, so as to prevent the plaintiff from obtaining a double recovery.

Consider this example. John works in a factory on an assembly line earning $15 per hour, 40 hours per week. He is injured by Stan, who breaks his arm badly in a barroom fight. Stan is liable for battery, and must pay John damages. Because of the injury, John cannot work at all for one month, and he cannot do his normal job for an additional six months, because it requires the use of both arms. The factory offers John alternate employment for the six months at a job which does not require the use of his broken arm at the rate of $10 per hour. John is capable of doing this job.

As to the first month when John was incapable of working at all, there's no requirement of mitigation. He should be entitled to his wages of $15 per hour, 40 hours per week, for one month, plus interest if allowed by state law.

As to the six-month period after that:

a. *If John Chooses Not to Work.* John will be treated as if he took a reasonable step in mitigation, which would include taking the $10 per hour job. For the six months, then, John would be entitled to the difference in wages, $5 per hour, for 40 hours per week, for six months. He is not entitled to wages at the full $15 hours per week. This result follows from the mitigation principles set forth in the last section of this chapter.

b. *If John Chooses to Take the Alternative Employment.* For the six months, John would again be entitled to the difference in wages, $5 per hour, for 40 hours per week, for six months. He is not entitled to wages at the full $15 per hour, because then he would make more money having been injured ($10 per hour for working, plus $15 per hour in damages) than had he not been injured ($15 per hour from working). The $10 per hour that John would receive is an *offsetting benefit.*

Given that John's damages would be the same whether or not John takes the alternative job, why would he bother taking the alternative job? Because if he does so, he will also earn the $10 per hour for the alternative job, which he will not be able to recover as damages.

Finally, suppose his employer or another employer offered him $15 (or more) for the alternative work. In that case, John would have no damages from lost wages for the six-month period. He would still be entitled to damages for the first month, when he could not work at all, along with medical bills and any noneconomic pain and suffering damages.

QUESTION 4. **The Great American Novel.** Fred worked as a server at the local diner, earning minimum wage plus tips. He was hit by a car while crossing the street. The driver of the car, Wilma, was negligent. Fred is paralyzed and cannot work as a server any longer.

After the accident, Fred writes his first novel. It is very successful, earning him royalties of $1 million. Fred sues Wilma for negligence, and one element of damages he claims is his lost wages from his job as a server. Is Fred entitled to these damages?

A. No, because negligence victims may recover only noneconomic damages.

B. No, if Fred could not have had time to write this book while working as a server.

C. Yes, because negligence victims may recover both economic and noneconomic damages.

D. Yes, because Fred's decision to write a novel was not a reasonable step in mitigation.

ANALYSIS. This is a difficult question. Let's begin by eliminating the one clearly wrong answer, Choice **A**. It states an incorrect principle of law: Negligence victims in fact may recover both economic and noneconomic damages. Choice **C** states that principle correctly, but it is not as good a choice as Choice **B**, which correctly explains that the royalties from the book sales can be considered an offsetting benefit (which would swamp any lost wages) *if* not being able to work anymore freed up Fred's time to be able to write the book. (In contrast, if Fred can show he could have written the book even while working full time, a jury may decide not to consider Fred's book writing activities as an offsetting benefit of the accident.) Choice **D** is wrong because even if writing a book might be considered an unreasonable step in mitigation (how many novels are successful financially, after all?), the question is not about whether Fred should have mitigated. The question is whether he has an offsetting benefit that needs to be credited against his claimed damages.

D. The collateral source rule

One topic that gets mostly ignored in many Torts classes is the role of insurance. Insurance is generally available both to protect individuals against losses to themselves of various kinds (so-called first party insurance, such as health insurance) and against damage judgments resulting from torts committed against others (so-called third party or liability insurance). Liability insurance coverage generally is not available for intentionally wrongful conduct.

The presence or absence of insurance plays a major role in tort litigation. Plaintiffs' attorneys, working on a contingency, usually won't take a case unless they are convinced that the defendant can pay a judgment if the plaintiff succeeds on the merits. Whether defendant has liability insurance is often the deciding factor. Insurance also shapes who gets sued, especially given the rules on joint and several liability discussed in the next chapter.

Here, we consider the collateral source rule, an insurance issue that arises in the context of the damages issues discussed in this chapter. Suppose Ken drives his car down the street and crashes into Lola's fence. The crash causes $1,000 in property damage. Lola makes a claim with her insurance company. The company applies Lola's $250 deductible to her claim, sending her a check for $750 to pay for repairing the fence. Lola then sues Ken for negligence, and the jury agrees that Ken was negligent.

If we apply the principles of offsetting benefits from the last section of this chapter, Lola should be entitled to only $250 in damages from Ken. She received the $750 check from her insurance company *as a benefit* that she would not have received but for Ken's wrong. If she received $250 from Ken and $750 from her insurance company, she'd be put back in the rightful position: She would have $1,000, fully compensating her for her property damage. In contrast, if we allow Lola to recover $1,000 from Ken, Lola would be made better off than if there had been no accident: After the accident she is down $1,000. If she receives $750 from her insurance company and another $1,000 from Ken, she would be up $750 (the first $1,000 brings her back to the rightful position, and the next $750 is a new benefit).

The law allows Lola to get this extra benefit. Under the *collateral source rule*, insurance and certain government benefits that are wholly independent of the tortfeasor[3] do not get deducted from plaintiff's award of damages. Why? The most persuasive answer is that the rule encourages people to purchase insurance. There are going to be a number of cases in which an injured person won't have a defendant to sue, or the defendant will have no assets to pay for damages. The collateral source rule encourages potential tort

---

3. This idea of damages being wholly independent of the tortfeasor is sometimes stretched. For example, in *Mozlof v. United States*, 6 F.3d 461 (7th Cir. 1993), the plaintiff was a veteran who was injured at a Veterans Administration hospital due to a VA employee's negligence. As a veteran, he was entitled to free legal care that he needed as a result of the VA's earlier negligence. The Seventh Circuit held that the value of the medical care should not be deducted from his damage awards: "just because both recoveries come from the *defendant*, however, does not necessarily mean they are coming from the same *source*. 'The source of funds may be determined to be collateral or independent, even though the [tortfeasor] supplies such funds. . . . Application of the collateral source rule depends less upon the source of funds than upon the character of the benefits received.' Thus, in order to determine whether the collateral source rule is applicable, courts look to the nature of the payment and the reason the payment is made rather than simply looking at whether the defendant is paying twice." *Id.* at 465 (citations omitted).

victims to purchase insurance. There is also a potential fairness argument. If we limited Lola to recovering only $250, it means that *Ken*, rather than *Lola*, would get the benefit of the insurance Lola paid.

The collateral source rule does not *inevitably* lead to a double recovery. For example, if Ken ran over Lola rather than Lola's fence, and Lola sought damages from personal injuries she sustained, she might be able to recover damages for her medical expenses as well as have her medical expenses paid by her private insurer (a collateral source). But her contract with the medical insurance company could contain (and many do contain) a *subrogation clause*, requiring that any payments Lola receives to compensate her for medical expenses must first go to pay back the insurer for its costs in taking care of Lola.

QUESTION 5. Adding It Up.   Miguel is injured in an automobile accident caused by Nancy. He receives $10,000 worth of medical care paid for by his health insurer. Miguel paid $500 premium for the medical coverage during the relevant time period. He misses six weeks of work, failing to earn $15,000 in salary. The jury awards Miguel $25,000 in economic damages and $6,000 in noneconomic damages for his pain and suffering.

In a jurisdiction that applies the collateral source rule, how much should the judge deduct from Miguel's award for the medical care paid by his health insurer?

A. 0
B. $9,500
C. $10,000
D. $25,000

ANALYSIS.   In a jurisdiction that applies the collateral source rule, nothing is to be deducted from the award, even if it means that Miguel will get a double recovery. For this reason, Choice **A** is correct, and Choices **B**, **C**, and **D** are incorrect.

QUESTION 6. Adding It Up, Take II.   Miguel is injured in an automobile accident caused by Nancy. He receives $10,000 worth of medical care paid for by his health insurer. Miguel paid $500 premium for the medical coverage during the relevant time period. He misses six weeks of work, failing to earn $15,000 in salary. The jury awards Miguel $25,000 in economic damages and $6,000 in noneconomic damages for his pain and suffering.

In a jurisdiction that has repealed the collateral source rule, how much should the judge deduct from Miguel's award for the medical care paid by his health insurer?

A. 0

B. $9,500

C. $10,000

D. $25,000

ANALYSIS. In a jurisdiction that has repealed the collateral source rule, we treat the insurance benefits as an offsetting benefit. Here, Miguel received a payment of $10,000 from the insurance company, a benefit which he would not have received but for the accident, but to be entitled to the benefits he had to pay a $500 premium. Thus, the judge should deduct the full extent of the insurance benefit, $9,500 ($10,000 payment less the $500 premium). Subtracting that premium is tricky. That's why Choice **B** is correct and Choice **C** is wrong. Choices **A** and **D** are easily eliminated as wrong answers.

E. The Closer: The line between mitigation and plaintiff's negligence

Sometimes the line between issues of mitigation and issues of plaintiff's negligence are unclear. Consider the question of a plaintiff's failure to wear a seat belt when injured in an accident caused by a negligent defendant.

If we treat the failure to wear a seat belt as a type of plaintiff's negligence, then in most jurisdictions (as we saw in Chapter 10) the plaintiff's damages would be reduced by the percentage of responsibility that the jury allocates to the plaintiff. For example, if the jury finds that the plaintiff was 30 percent at fault, plaintiff would recover only 70 percent of the damages that the jury awarded.

In contrast, if we treat the failure to wear a seat belt as a mitigation question, then plaintiff's damages are limited in a different way. Suppose the plaintiff suffers serious personal injuries caused by going through the windshield in the car collision. The jury finds that the plaintiff would have had only a few bumps and bruises had he been wearing a seat belt. If failure to wear a seat belt equals a failure to mitigate damages, then the plaintiff recovers damages *as if* he had mitigated, meaning damages only for the few bumps and bruises.

In short, there's a lot at stake in whether the courts characterize something as a kind of plaintiff's negligence or as a failure to mitigate. The issue has divided the courts and state legislatures.[4]

---

4. *See Derheim v. N. Fiorito Co.*, 492 P.2d 1030 (Wash. 1972); *Spier v. Barker*, 323 N.E.2d 164 (N.Y. 1974); N.Y. Veh. & Traf. Law § 1229-c(8).

One court noted the chronological oddity of treating the failure to wear a seat belt as a mitigation issue:

> We concede that the opportunity to mitigate damages prior to the occurrence of an accident does not ordinarily arise, and that the chronological distinction, on which the concept of mitigation damages rests, is justified in most cases. However, in our opinion, the seat belt affords the automobile occupant an unusual and ordinarily unavailable means by which he or she may minimize her damages *prior* to the accident.[5]

This justification seems to be less about whether an action that must be taken *before* an accident can be considered part of a failure to mitigate damages and more about the extent of the negligence of a plaintiff who fails to wear a seat belt. In other words, if anything, the rule announced by the court is justified less by logic than by a desire on the part of the court to give a punishment against people who fail to wear a seat belt or an extra incentive for people to wear seat belts.

QUESTION 7. Heads Up. Phillip is riding on his motorcycle on a highway without a helmet. Denise makes an illegal lane change, crashing into Phillip. Phillip is knocked off the motorcycle, and sustains a serious brain injury. Experts agree that Phillip would not have suffered the brain injury if he would have been wearing his helmet.

Phillip sues Denise for negligence. Assume the jury will find that Denise was negligent. What is the legal relevance of Phillip's failure to wear a helmet?

A. The court will treat it as a form of plaintiff's negligence and reduce Phillip's recovery under the state's comparative negligence rules.

B. The court will treat it as a failure to mitigate, allowing Phillip to recover only for those injuries that would have been caused had Phillip worn a helmet.

C. Depending upon the jurisdiction, the court may treat Phillip's actions as either a form of negligence or a failure to mitigate.

D. Phillip's failure to wear a helmet prevents Phillip from proving the tortious conduct portion of his prima facie case for negligence.

ANALYSIS. The helmet issue is parallel to the seat belt issue. Unsurprisingly, courts are similarly split over whether to treat the helmet issue as a form of plaintiff's negligence or as a failure to mitigate.[6] Chronologically, it appears that the issue relates to plaintiff's negligence rather than to a step

---

5. *Spier*, 323 N.E.2d at 168.
6. For a variety of approaches, *see* Michael J. Weber, Annotation, *Motorcyclist's Failure to Wear Helmet or Other Protective Equipment as Affecting Recovery for Personal Injury or Death*, 85 A.L.R. 4th 365 (1991 & Supps.).

taken to prevent further injuries after defendant's tortious conduct. But following the logic of the seat belt cases, some courts have found this to be a mitigation issue. For this reason, Choice **C** is correct, and a stronger answer than Choice **A** (true in some jurisdictions) or Choice **B** (true in some other jurisdictions). Choice **D** is wrong because neither the comparative negligence issue nor the mitigation of damages issue would defeat Phillip's prima facie case for negligence.

 # Rick's picks

1. Damaging Details	**B**
2. Door Buster	**A**
3. The Honest Truth	**C**
4. The Great American Novel	**B**
5. Adding It Up	**A**
6. Adding It Up, Take II	**B**
7. Heads Up	**C**

22

Joint and Several Liability

CHAPTER OVERVIEW
A. Introduction: Traditional joint and several liability principles
B. Legislative and judicial changes to traditional principles
C. Sharing among tortfeasors: Contribution, indemnity, and partial equitable indemnity
D. The Closer: Insolvent defendants and modern joint and several liability principles
✦ Rick's picks

A. Introduction: Traditional joint and several liability principles

As much as I could in this book so far, I have avoided fact patterns involving multiple defendants.[1] My reason for doing so is that multiple defendant scenarios raise additional complications. It is now time to address those complications.

Let's begin with a simple scenario. Defendant 1 ("*D1*," for short, for the rest of this chapter) is teaching Defendant 2 ("*D2*") how to shoot a gun. They are both holding the gun and it accidentally goes off, injuring *P*, the plaintiff. Suppose *P* sues *D1* and *D2* for injuries related to the gunshot wound. The jury finds both *D1* and *D2* negligent and that plaintiff was injured in the amount of $10,000. In this circumstance, under the traditional rules, "joint and several liability" applies because *D1* and *D2* have acted together to cause a single, indivisible injury to the plaintiff.

Joint and several liability means that *P* (now called the "judgment creditor" since she's won her verdict) can seek to recover her $10,000 in damages from *D1*, *D2*, or a combination of the two defendants (now called

---

1. I could not avoid multiple defendants in the discussion of actual causation (cases involving independent concurrent causation, alternative liability, and market share liability) in Chapter 13 and in the discussion of vicarious liability in Chapter 17. I return to these issues below.

the "judgment debtors"), until she has received the full $10,000 amount. If *D1* is rich (a so-called deep pocket) and *D2* is poor, *P* rationally may decide to collect all of her damages against *D1*.[2] *P* cannot get more than $10,000 from the defendants as a whole.

Note also the requirement that the defendants committed a *single, indivisible injury*. In our first example, that was the case because there was a single gunshot which resulted from both defendants' actions. A single indivisible injury also could result from two defendants acting separately. For example, suppose *D1* is shooting negligently and *D2* negligently fails to make sure that there are no people in the area in which *D1* is shooting. If *D1*'s shot hits *P*, *D1* and *D2* still both acted tortiously to cause a single indivisible injury to *P*, and they are both jointly and severally liable. This is also true if *D1* negligently shoots in the course and scope of employment, and *D2* is *D1*'s employer. In that case too, *D1* and *D2* would be jointly and severally liable for *P*'s injuries, with *D2*'s liability stemming from the vicarious liability rules discussed in Chapter 17.[3]

But there would not be joint and several liability among joint tortfeasors when the tortfeasors cause separate, apportionable injuries. If *D1* shoots *P* in the leg, and *D2* shoots her in the arm, joint and several liability does not apply unless *D1* and *D2* were acting in concert. *P* has suffered multiple injuries — not a single, indivisible injury. *D1* will be liable for *P*'s leg injury and *D2* will be liable for *P*'s arm injury. The terminology used is that *D1* and *D2* are each "severally" liable for the injuries each one caused.

Traditionally, joint and several liability did not apply in negligence cases when plaintiff was at fault or was found to have assumed the risk (in the secondary implied sense[4]). In such a case, the plaintiff's conduct barred any recovery because it served as a complete defense to plaintiff's negligence case against the defendants.

As you should see, joint and several liability is a good rule for plaintiffs because it gives them the option to collect their damages from whichever defendant can pay, regardless of the relative fault between or among the defendants. It holds both defendants equally responsible to pay even if one defendant was more blameworthy than the other. For these reasons, joint and several liability has been the target of legislative and judicial reform, as discussed in the next section.

---

2. Section C of this chapter addresses the question whether someone in *D1*'s position can then seek some of the money paid to P from *D2*.

3. Similarly, in the situations of independent concurrent causation and alternative liability discussed in Chapter 13, *D1* and *D2* are jointly and severally liable for P's injuries (unless, in the alternative liability situation, one of the defendants proves more likely than not that he was *not* a cause of P's injuries).

4. See Chapter 10 for an explanation of the various types of assumption of risk arguments.

QUESTION 1. Joint and Several Liability Basics. *D1* and *D2* both drive negligently, injuring a pedestrian, *P*. The jury, in a jurisdiction applying traditional joint and several liability rules, finds both defendants negligent and concludes that *P* suffered $10,000 in damages. After trial *P* collects $4,000 from *D1*. How much is *P* entitled to recover from *D2*?

A. 0
B. $5,000
C. $6,000
D. $10,000

ANALYSIS.   Under traditional joint and several liability principles, *P* can collect up to the full amount from any or all of the defendants who caused a single, indivisible injury, until plaintiff has been paid the full amount of her damages. If *P* has received $4,000 so far out of a total judgment of $10,000, she may obtain $6,000 more from any of the other defendants in combination. This is true even if it means that one defendant pays more than another. For this reason, Choice **C** is correct, and Choices **A**, **B**, and **D** are incorrect.

QUESTION 2. Joint and Several Liability Basics, Take II. *D1* and *D2* both drive negligently, injuring a pedestrian, *P*. The jury, in a jurisdiction applying traditional joint and several liability rules, finds both defendants negligent and concludes that *P* suffered a $5,000 eye injury caused by *D1* and a $5,000 foot injury caused by *D2*, for a total of $10,000 in damages. After trial *P* collects $4,000 from *D1*. How much is *P* entitled to recover from *D2*?

A. 0
B. $5,000
C. $6,000
D. $10,000

ANALYSIS.   Even in a jurisdiction that applies traditional joint and several liability rules, joint and several liability does not apply in this case, because *D1* and *D2* inflicted separate, divisible injuries. In such circumstances, *D1* and *D2* are each severally liable for the injuries each caused. *D2* caused $5,000 in damages, and therefore *P* can obtain $5,000 from *D2*. Choice **B** is correct for this reason. It is true that if *P* collects no more money from *D1*, plaintiff will be $1,000 short of the rightful position. But that is not a problem that falls on *D2*, thanks to the fact that the injuries are divisible. Choices **A**, **C**, and **D** are all incorrect.

> **QUESTION 3. Joint and Several Liability Basics, Take III.** *D1* and *D2* both drive negligently, injuring a pedestrian, *P*, who was negligently not looking when she crossed the street. The jury, in a jurisdiction applying traditional joint and several liability rules, finds both defendants negligent and *P* negligent as well and concludes that *P* suffered $10,000 in damages. How much may *P* collect from *D1*?
>
> **A.** 0
> **B.** $5,000
> **C.** $6,000
> **D.** $10,000

ANALYSIS. Even when defendants act tortiously causing single, indivisible injuries, under the traditional rules a plaintiff's own negligence bars any chance for plaintiff to recover damages. *P* therefore can collect nothing from *D1* (and nothing from *D2*). Choice **A** is the correct choice, and Choices **B**, **C**, and **D** are incorrect.

B. Legislative and judicial changes to traditional principles

The rethinking of joint and several liability began with the move toward comparative negligence and then toward comparative responsibility in other non-intentional torts. Once courts were willing to assign percentages of responsibility to multiple defendants, then the pull of joint and several liability seemed less compelling to some.

Imagine a situation such as that described in Question 3. Let's say that *D1* was driving drunk, and *D2* and *P* were also negligent, but not as blameworthy as *D1*. You could see a jury assigning percentages of responsibility along the following lines:

$$D1 - 60\%$$
$$D2 - 10\%$$
$$P - 30\%$$

Under the traditional rules, as we have seen, *P* would recover nothing because *P*'s negligence would bar all recovery. Under the new approach to comparative negligence, however, *P* may recover damages except for *P*'s 30 percent share of injury. The joint and several liability question is whether *D1* and *D2* should be jointly and severally liable for the 70 percent of *P*'s damages that *P* is not responsible for, or whether the old joint and several liability rules should be jettisoned and replaced with several liability only or something else.

Courts and legislative bodies have adopted one of three approaches to the question:[5]

1. *Joint and Several Liability Continues to Apply as to Defendants' Collective Share of Responsibility.* Under this approach, P could go after *D1* alone, *D2* alone, or both defendants in combination to recover up to 70 percent of plaintiff's damages. In certain situations, as under the traditional joint and several liability rules, it means that a deep pocket defendant whose fault is less than that of other defendants (*D2* in this example) could end up paying the lion's share of the damages. But some courts have justified retention of joint and several liability in the comparative negligence era on fairness grounds:

   > [T]he mere fact that it may be possible to assign some percentage figure to the relative culpability of one negligent defendant as compared to another does not in any way suggest that each defendant's negligence is not a proximate cause of the entire indivisible injury....
   >
   > Moreover, even when a plaintiff is partially at fault for his own injury, a plaintiff's culpability is not equivalent to that of a defendant. In this setting, a plaintiff's negligence relates only to a failure to use due care for his own protection, while a defendant's negligence relates to a lack of due care for the safety of others.

   American Motorcycle Association v. Superior Court, 578 P.2d 899, 905-06 (Cal. 1978).

2. *Several Liability Only Applies.* The polar alternative to the rule described above is to abolish joint and several liability in comparative negligence cases. (The rule generally continues to operate in situations in which joint liability is imposed without regard to allocation of responsibility, such as vicarious liability.) Using the example from above, *D1* would be responsible to pay 60 percent of *P*'s damages, and *D2* would be responsible to pay 10 percent of *P*'s damages. If *P* is unable to get *D1* to pay the damages owed, the loss will fall on *P*, not *D2*.

   Some state legislatures have adopted this rule by statute. *See, e.g.,* Colo. Rev. Stat. § 13-21-111.5 (2008). Other state abolitions of the rule have come from the courts. *See, e.g., McIntyre v. Balentine*, 833 S.W.2d 52, 58 (Tenn. 1992).

   Regardless of the usual state's rules on joint and several liability, several liability only applies to "market share liability" cases under *Sindell* in those jurisdictions accepting the market share theory.[6]

---

5. The Restatement punts on the question: "If the independent tortious conduct of two or more persons is a legal cause of an indivisible injury, the law of the applicable jurisdiction determines whether those persons are jointly and severally liable, severally liable, or liable under some hybrid of joint and several and several liability." Rest. (3d) Torts: Apportionment of Liability § 17 (2000).
6. See Chapter 13.

3. *Partial Abolition of Joint and Several Liability.* Some states have crafted compromises to partially end joint and several liability in the comparative responsibility era. In California, for example, voters passed a ballot proposition establishing several liability only for the award of noneconomic damages. *See* CAL. CIV. CODE § 1431.2 (2008). In New Jersey, the legislature passed a statute allowing joint and several liability to apply only when the defendants' collective share of liability exceeds 60 percent. *See* N.J. STAT. 2A:15-5.3 (2008).

Epstein reports that as of 2008 "15 jurisdictions have pure joint and several liability; 15 have several liability only; 7 states allow for reallocation of losses from insolvent to solvent defendants; and 10 states have complex regimes that typically allow for only several liability of noneconomic damages and joint and several liability of economic damages." RICHARD A. EPSTEIN, CASES AND MATERIALS ON TORTS 420 (9th ed. 2008).

QUESTION 4. Joint and Several Liability Basics, Take IV. *D1* and *D2* both drive negligently, injuring a pedestrian, *P,* who was negligently not looking when she crossed the street. The jury, in a jurisdiction that has retained joint and several liability and uses a rule of pure comparative negligence, finds both defendants negligent and *P* negligent as well and concludes that *P* suffered $10,000 in damages. It determines that *D1* is 60 percent at fault, *D2* is 10 percent at fault, and *P* is 30 percent at fault. *P* has collected $4,000 from *D1.* How much is *P* entitled to recover from *D2?*

A. 0
B. $1,000
C. $3,000
D. $6,000

ANALYSIS. In jurisdictions that have retained joint and several liability rules and use pure comparative negligence, the defendants are jointly and severally liable for the defendants' collective share of responsibility, in this case, 70 percent or $7,000. *D1* has paid *P* $4,000, meaning that plaintiff is now in a position to recover an additional $3,000 from *D1, D2* or a combination of the two of them. Choice **C** is therefore the correct answer, and Choices **A, B,** and **D** are incorrect.

QUESTION 5. Joint and Several Liability Basics, Take V. *D1* and *D2* both drive negligently, injuring a pedestrian, *P,* who was negligently not looking when she crossed the street. The jury, in a jurisdiction that has abolished joint and several liability and adopted several liability only, finds both defendants negligent and *P* negligent as well and concludes that *P* suffered $10,000 in damages. It determines that *D1* is 60 percent at fault, *D2* is 10 percent at fault, and *P* is 30 percent at fault. *P* has collected $4,000 from *D1*. How much is *P* entitled to recover from *D2*?

A. 0
B. $1,000
C. $3,000
D. $6,000

ANALYSIS.   In jurisdictions that have abolished joint and several liability and replaced it with several liability only, the defendants are each liable only for damages equal to their own share of responsibility. *D2* is 10 percent responsible for *P*'s $10,000 in damages. The most that *P* can get from *D2* is $1,000. Choice **B** is therefore correct and Choices **A**, **C**, and **D** are incorrect. If P collects no more than $4,000 from *D1*, the additional $2,000 of damages owed to *D1* by *P* will be borne by P.

QUESTION 6. Advanced Joint and Several Liability Issues.   *D1* and *D2* both drive negligently, injuring a pedestrian, *P*, who was negligently not looking when she crossed the street. The jury, in a jurisdiction that has retained joint and several liability for economic damages and abolished joint and several liability for noneconomic damages, finds both defendants negligent and *P* negligent as well and concludes that *P* suffered $10,000 in damages, half of which were economic damages and half of which were noneconomic damages. It determines that *D1* is 60 percent at fault, *D2* is 10 percent at fault, and *P* is 30 percent at fault. *P* has collected nothing from *D1*. How much is *P* entitled to recover from *D2*?

A. 0
B. $3,500
C. $4,000
D. $5,000

ANALYSIS.   Now the math gets harder. The easiest way to approach this problem is to break it up into two parts, the economic losses and the noneconomic losses, considering each separately.

Beginning with the economic losses, *P* suffered $5,000 in economic losses. *D1* and *D2* are jointly and severally liable for 70 percent of those damages, or $3,500.

For the noneconomic losses, *P* suffered $5,000 in noneconomic losses. *D2* is severally liable for these damages, and is 10 percent responsible, for additional damages of $500.

Thus, the total that *D2* may be responsible for is $4,000. For this reason, Choice **C** is correct, and Choices **A**, **B**, and **D** are incorrect.

C. Sharing among tortfeasors: Contribution, indemnity, and partial equitable indemnity

The material covered so far in this chapter considered the issue of multiple defendants from the perspective of the plaintiff. We now consider the issue from the perspective of a paying defendant in a joint and several liability jurisdiction. Consider, for example, *D2* from the last example, who is 10 percent at fault and who pays 70 percent of *P*'s damages. What recourse does the paying defendant have against other defendants?

Traditionally, defendants who have paid plaintiffs have had a difficult time obtaining reimbursement for those payments from other defendants. Courts in limited circumstances allowed a paying defendant to sue for *contribution*, which if successful would allow for a *pro rata* sharing of liability among the defendants. In a *pro rata* system, each defendant bears an equal share of the amount paid. With two defendants, each pays half, with three defendants, each pays a third, and so on. In order to recover for contribution, a defendant would have to show that the other defendant was primarily responsible, or meet some other stringent standard. In other limited circumstances, a paying defendant could seek *indemnification*, which if successful would require the non-paying defendant to reimburse the paying defendant for *all* the funds that have been paid. Indemnification too was subject to a strict standard requiring the paying defendant to show he was much less culpable than the non-paying defendant, and the line between when an indemnity rule applied and when a contribution rule applied was not clear under the common law. *See* RICHARD A. EPSTEIN, TORTS 235-236 (1999).

QUESTION 7. Advanced Joint and Several Liability Issues, Take II.
D1, *D2*, and *D3* each drive negligently, injuring a pedestrian, *P*, who was negligently not looking when she crossed the street. *P* sues *D1* and *D2*; she cannot find *D3*. The jury, in a jurisdiction applying traditional joint and several liability rules, finds both defendants and *D3* negligent and *P* negligent as well and concludes that *P* suffered $9,000 in damages. *D1* pays $9,000 to *P*. *D1* then sues *D2* for indemni-fication in a jurisdiction that uses the traditional rules for indemnification. The court agrees *D1* is entitled to indemnification. How much must *D2* pay *D1*?

A. 0
B. $3,000
C. $4,500
D. $9,000

ANALYSIS. Under the traditional rules, indemnification was difficult to get, but when it was available, the results are quite good for paying defendants: all the payments shift from the paying defendant to the non-paying defendant. Thus, under these rules *D2* would have to pay *D1* the full $9,000. (In contrast, if traditional contribution applied, the defendants would share *pro rata*, meaning *D2* would have to pay *D1* only $3,000 [with three wrongdoers, the amount is divided into thirds].)

Choice **D** is therefore correct, and Choices **A**, **B**, and **C** are incorrect.

Partial Equitable Indemnification. Just as the shift to comparative negligence and comparative responsibility caused many jurisdictions to rework the rules for joint and several liability, the shift also caused many jurisdictions to change their rules regarding contribution and indemnity. A number of states adopted *partial equitable indemnification,* which allows paying defendants to obtain a portion of the amounts paid based upon the relative responsibility of the defendants.[7]

For example, let's return to these numbers:

$$D1 — 60\%$$
$$D2 — 10\%$$
$$P — 30\%$$
$$\text{Damages} — \$10,000$$

Suppose that *D1* paid $7,000 to *P*. *D1* could then seek partial equitable indemnification and they would share their responsibility proportionally. If you compare their relative shares of responsibility, it is 60:10 or 6:1 or 6/7:1/7 (these are all equivalent). *D1* therefore is responsible for 6/7 of $7,000, or $6,000, and *D1* is responsible for 1/7 of $7,000, or $1,000. *D2* therefore would have to pay $1,000 to *D1*.

As you should see, under partial equitable indemnification, there is no longer sharing *pro rata* (as under the old contribution rules) or a complete shifting of damages (as under the old indemnification rules). Instead, it is relative percentages of responsibility that determine the sharing of damages among multiple defendants.

---

7. For example, see *American Motorcycle Association v. Superior Court,* 578 P.2d 899, 912 (Cal. 1978).

> **QUESTION 8. Advanced Joint and Several Liability Issues, Take III.**
> *D1* and *D2* each drive negligently, injuring a pedestrian, *P,* who was
> negligently not looking when she crossed the street. The jury, in a
> jurisdiction applying joint and several liability rules and pure comparative
> negligence, finds both defendants negligent and *P* negligent as well
> and concludes that *P* suffered $10,000 in damages. The jury further assigns
> shares of responsibility as follows: *D1,* 50 percent; *D2,* 30 percent; *P,* 20
> percent.
>
> *D1* pays $8,000 to *P. D1* then sues *D2* for partial equitable indemnification
> in a jurisdiction that has moved to this rule for multiple defendant cases.
> How much must *D2* pay *D1?*
>
> **A.** 0
> **B.** $2,400
> **C.** $3,000
> **D.** $8,000

ANALYSIS. Under partial equitable indemnity, each of the defendants
must pay damages in proportion to their relative share of responsibility. *D1*
must bear 50/80 (5/8) of the damages not attributable to *P,* and *D2* must
bear 30/80 (3/8) of the damages paid by *D1. D2* is responsible for 3/8 of the
$8,000 paid by *D1* (*not* 3/8 of all of *P's* damages). Because *D2* must pay
$3,000, Choice **C** is correct and Choices **A, B,** and **D** are incorrect.

Settlement Under Partial Equitable Indemnification. As if these rules were
not complicated enough, the situation gets even more complicated when one
of the defendants settles with the other plaintiff.

Consider this example. Before trial, *P* settles with *D1* for $3,000 in a
settlement that a court believes was in good faith (that is, an honest attempt
between the parties to reach a fair settlement).

The case against *D2* goes to the jury and the jury allocates responsibility
as follows:[8]

$$D1 - 60\%$$
$$D2 - 10\%$$
$$P - 30\%$$
$$\text{Damages} - \$10,000$$

The settlement will insulate any action by *D2* against *D1.* How much will
D2 have to pay *P*? The courts have generally adopted two approaches:

1. *The* Pro Tanto *Rule.* Under this approach, if *P* makes a settlement
   with one defendant in good faith, the remaining defendants are

---

8. Assume the state rules allow the jury to allocate fault to a party not before the court.

responsible for plaintiff's damages, less a credit for the settlement.[9] So using our example, *D2* would be responsible for the 70 percent of the plaintiff's damages owed by all wrongdoing defendant, in this case $7,000, less a $3,000 credit for the amount *D1* paid in settlement. Thus, *D2*, held to be only 10 percent at fault, ends up with liability of $4,000. Unsurprisingly, critics say this rule is unfair and will encourage culpable parties to settle for less than their fair share of responsibility.

2. *The Proportionate Share Approach*. Under this approach, a plaintiff's settlement with a defendant "diminishes the claim that the injured party has against the other tortfeasors by the amount of the equitable share of the obligation of the released tortfeasor."[10] Using our same example, *D1*'s payment of $3,000 would extinguish *D2*'s obligation to pay *D1*'s 60 percent share of damages. *D2* would owe plaintiff $1,000, or his own 10 percent. That approach means that *P*, rather than *D2*, ends up bearing the risk of a low settlement with *D1*.

QUESTION 9. Advanced Joint and Several Liability Issues, Take IV.
D1 and *D2* each drive negligently, injuring a pedestrian, *P*, who was negligently not looking when she crossed the street. Before trial, *D1* and *P* enter into a good faith settlement for $2,000. The jury, in a jurisdiction applying joint and several liability rules and comparative negligence, finds both defendants negligent and *P* negligent as well and concludes that *P* suffered $10,000 in damages. The jury further assigns shares of responsibility as follows: *D1*, 50 percent; *D2*, 30 percent; *P*, 20 percent.

How much must *D2* pay *D1* in a jurisdiction adopting the *pro tanto* approach to settlements?

A. 0
B. $3,000
C. $6,000
D. $8,000

ANALYSIS. Under the *pro tanto* approach, the remaining defendants are responsible for all defendants' share of responsibility, less any credit for money paid in settlement. In this case, *D1* and *D2* have been found responsible for 80 percent of the $10,000 in damage. *D2* therefore is

---

9. For a court adopting this approach, see *American Motorcycle Association v. Superior Court*, 578 P.2d 899, 912 (Cal. 1978).
10. *McDermott, Inc. v. AmClyde and River Don Castings, Ltd.*, 511 U.S. 202, 209 (1994) (quoting REST. (2D) TORTS § 866A).

responsible for paying $8,000, less a credit for the $2,000 paid by *D1*.[11] *D2* therefore must pay $6,000, making Choice **C** correct, and Choices **A**, **B**, and **D** incorrect.

D. The Closer: Insolvent defendants and modern joint and several liability principles

Plunging ever further into the darkness, we consider one final complication: what happens when one of the defendants is bankrupt? Thus, to use our long-running example, *P* sues *D1* and *D2* for negligence. The case goes to the jury and the jury allocates responsibility as follows:

> *D1* — 60%
> *D2* — 10%
> *P* — 30%
> Damages — $10,000

D1 has no assets. How much should *D2* pay? There are a number of ways of dealing with this question, including the possibility of retaining the usual joint and several liability rule (meaning *D2* would be liable for 70 percent of the damages, or $7,000) or moving to a several only rule in the case of insolvent defendants (meaning *D2* would be liable for 10 percent of the damages, or $1,000).

The California Supreme Court, however, suggested a different approach in *Evangelatos v. Superior Court*, 753 P.2d 585, 590 (Cal. 1998): "[I]f one or more tortfeasors prove to be insolvent and are not able to bear their fair share of the loss, the shortfall created by the insolvency should be apportioned equitably among the remaining culpable parties — both defendants and plaintiffs."

In our hypothetical, this leads to some scary math. So how much does *D2* owe?

Step 1: *D2* is liable for *D2*'s own share of the damages. In this case, that is $1,000 (or 10 percent of the total).

Step 2: *D2* and *P* share *D1*'s $6,000 share of responsibility based upon *the relative culpability* of *D2* and *P*. Recall that *D2* is 10 percent at fault and *P* is 30 percent at fault. That means that they share the liability on a 10:30, or 1:3, or 1/4:3/4 basis. Doing the math, that gives *D2* another $1,500 (1/4 of *D1*'s $6,000 share).

---

11. Under the alternative proportionate share approach, *D2* would have had to pay only *D2*'s own share, 30 percent of $10,000, or $3,000.

Step 3: Add the results from the first two parts. *D2* is liable for $1,000 + $1,500, or a total of $2,500.

QUESTION 10. Ridiculously Hard Joint and Several Liability Question. *D1* and *D2* each drive negligently, injuring a pedestrian, *P*, who was negligently not looking when she crossed the street. The jury, in a jurisdiction applying joint and several liability rules, the *Evangelatos* approach to insolvent defendants, and comparative negligence, finds both defendants negligent and *P* negligent as well and concludes that *P* suffered $10,000 in damages. The jury further assigns shares of responsibility as follows: *D1*, 50 percent; *D2*, 30 percent; *P*, 20 percent.

D1 is bankrupt. How much is *P* entitled to recover from *D2*?

A. 0
B. $3,000
C. $6,000
D. $8,000

ANALYSIS.   Let's do the math.

Step 1: *D2* must pay *D2*'s 30 percent share of responsibility, or $3,000.

Step 2: *D2* and *P* share *D1*'s $5,000 of responsibility on a 3:2 basis. A 3:2 sharing is the same as 3/5 is the same as 60 percent/40 percent. *D2* therefore must pay 60 percent of *D1*'s $5,000, or another $3,000.

Step 3: *D2*'s total liability under the *Evangelatos* rule is $6,000. Choice **C** is correct and Choices **A, B,** and **D** are incorrect.

Aren't you glad this chapter is over?

 Rick's picks

23

Punitive Damages and Their Constitutional Limitations

CHAPTER OVERVIEW

A. Introduction: The purposes of punitive damages
B. Conduct meriting an award of punitive damages
C. Setting and reviewing the amount of punitive damages
D. Constitutional limits on the amount of punitive damages
E. The Closer: Considering defendant's wealth in punitive damages cases
✦ Rick's picks

A. Introduction: The purposes of punitive damages

The damages discussed up to this point in the book have been *compensatory damages*. With rare exceptions (mentioned early in Chapter 20), a plaintiff must prove he has been damaged in order to meet the last element of the prima facie case for all torts.

Punitive damages are different. They are available only in a subset of torts cases.[1] Their primary aim is punishment of the defendant, not compensation of the plaintiff. Many states require plaintiffs to meet a higher standard of proof (beyond the usual preponderance of the evidence standard) before punitive damages may be awarded. And in recent years the Supreme Court has read the U.S. Constitution to place limits on the amounts of such awards. This chapter considers all of these issues in relation to punitive damages, beginning with a closer look at the purposes of punitive damages.

---

1. A recent study found that juries awarded punitive damages in fewer than 5 percent of cases that ended with a plaintiff's win. Theodore Eisenberg et al., *Judges, Juries, and Punitive Damages: Empirical Analyses Using the Civil Justice Survey of State Courts*, 3 J. EMPIRICAL LEGAL STUD. 263, 268-69 (2006).

Punitive damages are damages awarded in addition to compensatory damages that are aimed at *punishing and making an example out of the defendant.*[2] To put it another way, a primary purpose of punitive damages is *deterrence,* both specific deterrence (discouraging the defendant in this lawsuit from engaging in bad behavior again) and general deterrence (discouraging other potential defendants from engaging in similar bad behavior). Indeed, punitive damages are sometimes referred to as *exemplary* damages because they make an example out of the defendant.

Why is additional deterrence necessary? That is, why don't compensatory damages adequately serve a deterrent function? As you may remember from Chapter 20, the economic approach to tort law provides the answer. Compensatory damages serve as a *price* for engaging in tortious behavior, and so long as taking a precaution is cheaper than an expected damages award, the rational potential torts defendant will opt for the precaution over the expected damages award. To take a concrete example, suppose that a given precaution will lessen the risk of automobile accidents costs $600. Suppose that the chance of being in an accident and having to pay a tort judgment of $10,000 if the precaution is not taken is 10 percent. In such circumstances, the defendant takes the precaution, because $600 is less than the $1,000 in expected accident costs (10 percent of $10,000).

The example shows that the economic model is sensitive to errors in calculating the costs of precautions and expected accident costs. It is also sensitive to errors in the judicial system. That is, suppose that because of problems of proof faced by plaintiffs, only half of plaintiffs who should recover damages from defendants who have injured them are able to do so. In that circumstance, expected accident costs are cut in half, to $500. The rational, risk-neutral defendant does not take a $600 precaution to avoid $500 in expected accident costs.

The possibility of punitive damages alters this calculus for rational defendants. Imagine now that the defendant faces not only a prospect of paying $10,000 in compensatory damages, but also $50,000 in punitive damages if found liable. A rational defendant will take a $600 precaution to avoid paying $6,000 (assuming the law is perfectly enforced), or even $3,000 (assuming only half of the defendants who should pay, will pay). In other

---

2. Many states require that a jury must first find the plaintiff entitled to compensatory damages before a plaintiff is entitled to punitive damages. Nominal damages may qualify in some jurisdictions. *See* Richard C. Tinney, Annotation, *Sufficiency of Showing Actual Damages to Support Award of Punitive Damages — Modern Cases,* 40 A.L.R. 4th 11 §§ 6-9 (1985 & 2005 Supp.) (collecting cases on both sides of issue); *but see* N.J. STAT. ANN. 2A:15-5.13c (nominal damages cannot support the award of punitive damages). Plaintiffs sometimes seek nominal damages as a hook to get punitive damages.

words, punitive damages change the calculations of potential defendants so that potential defendants take cost-justified precautions.

The possibility of punitive damages affects the incentives of plaintiffs as well as defendants. Many torts plaintiffs do not pay their lawyers by the hour for their services. Instead many plaintiffs' lawyers agree to work for a contingency fee, collecting attorneys' fees *as a percentage* of any recovery that the plaintiff receives from the defendant. As should be obvious from the example above, the possibility of recovering punitive damages will make torts cases more attractive for plaintiffs' lawyers, meaning that plaintiffs are more likely to find lawyers to take their cases. Indeed, in some cases the compensatory damages would be too small to attract a competent plaintiffs' lawyer; only the possibility of punitive damages makes some torts cases economically viable.

In most states punitive awards go to entirely to the plaintiff (and usually his lawyer).[3] Punitive damages therefore serve a compensatory function as well, and in some cases, the damages can *overcompensate* the plaintiff, putting the plaintiff in a *better position* than she would have been in but for the wrong. For example, suppose that in the automobile accident above, a $10,000 damage award would put the plaintiff exactly in the status quo ante position.[4] An award of an additional $50,000 will put the plaintiff in a better position (being $50,000 richer, less attorneys' fees) than if the defendant did not commit the tort.

Because punitive damages can be overcompensatory, they have been the target of the conservative "tort reform" movement. Typically, those opposing large punitive damage awards focus on cases in which it appears that plaintiff's conduct contributed significantly to her injury or in which defendant's conduct does not appear so reprehensible.[5] In addition, for reasons discussed below, juries often award large amounts as punitive damages aimed at punishing and deterring wealthy wrongdoers. The press focuses on those initial awards, and less attention is paid when trial or appellate courts slash those awards to a fraction of the original amount.

---

3. In a few states, the state takes a portion of the punitive award. *See, e.g.,* OR. REV. STAT. 31.735 (2008) (requiring 60 percent of punitive damage award to go to state, not plaintiff).

4. This is much more likely when the damage is something with a ready market substitute, such as a new car, as opposed to something without a ready market substitute, such as an award for pain and suffering from a personal injury.

5. A good example is a case involving a woman who suffered burns after spilling McDonald's coffee bought at a drive-thru window. Though the plaintiff is often used as a poster child for the tort reform movement, the facts of the case suggest the injury plaintiff suffered was serious (leading to a week in the hospital and numerous skin grafts) and that "in the past decade McDonald's had received at least 700 reports of coffee burns ranging from mild to third degree, and had settled claims arising from scalding injuries for more than $500,000." Andrea Gerlin, *A Matter of Degree: How a Jury Decided That a Coffee Spill Is Worth $2.9 Million*, WALL ST. J., Sept. 1, 1994, at A1.

QUESTION 1. A Far From Punishing Question. Which statement about the purpose of punitive damages is not correct?

A. Punitive damages serve both general deterrence and specific deterrence purposes.
B. Punitive damages aim to put the plaintiff in the position she would have been in but for defendant's wrong.
C. Punitive damages serve a secondary compensatory function.
D. Punitive damages increase the chances that a plaintiffs' lawyer will take a torts case with a contingency fee.

ANALYSIS. This is an easy question to get the ball rolling. Punitive damages serve numerous functions. Their main purpose is to punish and deter. Punitive damages may deter both a defendant in the torts case from committing another wrong (specific deterrence) and other similarly situated potential defendants from committing similar wrongs (general deterrence). For this reason, Choice **A** is incorrect. Though punitive damages aim to punish and deter, most of the proceeds of a punitive damage award usually go to the plaintiff. Thus, punitive damages also serve a compensatory function. For this reason, Choice **C** is incorrect. Some of that money also goes to plaintiffs' lawyers working on contingency fees who take a percentage of the plaintiffs' recovery. The total additional amount at stake in cases with punitive awards adds incentives to plaintiffs' lawyers to take such cases on a contingency. Thus, Choice **D** is incorrect.

The right answer here is Choice **B**. Though punitive damages may serve a compensatory function, their primary purpose is not to put the plaintiff in the position he would have been in but for the wrong; instead, the primary purpose is punishing and deterring wrongdoers.

B. Conduct meriting an award of punitive damages

With all the benefits of punitive damages described in the last section, perhaps they should be available in every case as a way of making up for the fact that a number of torts lawsuits that should be successful are not successful because of procedural barriers or other problems. But doing so creates some problems. Consider the case of Carla, who is engaged in the abnormally dangerous activity of dynamite blasting. Carla uses all reasonable care to avoid causing any damage while demolishing a building, but flying debris still busts the window on David's car. Blasting is a strict liability tort, so Carla will be liable even though she is not at fault.[6]

Economic theory suggests we might want to allow punitive damages against Carla for the same reason we might want them in other torts cases: to create additional incentives for people like Carla not to injure others. But Carla likely is already using a high level of care to avoid paying damages in a strict liability system. Creating additional incentives for Carla to take care might lead to *overdeterrence*— she might be too careful and not engage in the risky but useful activity of blasting.

In addition, there are justice problems with holding Carla liable for punitive damages. If she has done nothing wrong, corrective justice might support still requiring her to *compensate* David (an issue discussed in Chapter 15). But even if the law says Carla should compensate David, why should we also make an example out of Carla and punish her when all agree she has done nothing wrong?

For these reasons, courts have placed certain limits on the ability of plaintiffs to recover punitive damages.

Burden of Proof. One of those limits relates to the burden of proof. Recall that the usual burden of proof in torts cases is the "preponderance of the evidence" standard: A plaintiff must prove each element of the prima facie case under this "more likely than not" test. Defendants similarly prove their affirmative defenses under the same standard. When it comes to punitive damages, however, many states require a higher standard of proof. In California, for example, plaintiffs must prove the conduct allowing for the award of punitive damages under a "clear and convincing evidence" standard, CAL. CIV. CODE § 3294 (2008), a standard greater than preponderance of the evidence standard but not as tough as criminal law's beyond a reasonable doubt standard. A heightened standard makes sense when one considers that the purpose of punitive damages, like a purpose of the criminal law, is punishment of the defendant.

Conduct. The conduct that merits the award of punitive damages must be quite bad. Though states use different language to express this idea (such as "malice" (TEX. CIV. PRAC. & REM. CODE § 41.001(7)) or acting with an "evil mind" (*Linthicum v. Nationwide Life Ins. Co.*, 723 P.2d 675, 679 (Ariz. 1986)), one general point is that the conduct must be *worse than negligence*.

How much worse? It depends upon the jurisdiction. Certainly all states allow punitive damages when a defendant has been proven to have an intent to harm a plaintiff. The harder cases are those in which the defendant acts with something like recklessness, ignoring a substantial probability of serious harm to others. Many states allow such reckless conduct to support punitive damages, but the rules are state-specific. California's standard, for example, requires proof of "oppression, fraud, or malice, express or implied."

---

6. See Chapter 15 for the details on strict liability for abnormally dangerous activities.

Cal. Civ. Code § 3294 (2008). Reckless disregard of others' safety is a kind of "implied malice."[7]

One key point is that in determining if the conduct is bad enough to support an award of punitive damages, you should focus *not* on the cause of action, but upon the conduct. For example, the fact that the tort against Carla for blasting is a strict liability tort does not prevent an award against her if, for example, she acted recklessly by not taking any steps to minimize injury from blasting.

QUESTION 2. Driving While Under the Influence of a Cell Phone.
Kira is driving down the street while speaking on her cell phone. She's having a deep discussion about Kantian virtues when she accidentally runs over Larry's foot. Larry sues Kira for negligence. May Kira be liable for punitive damages in a state that follows California's approach to punitive damages?

A. Yes, if Larry can prove all the elements of the tort of negligence by a preponderance of the evidence.

B. Yes, if Larry can prove all the elements of the tort of negligence by clear and convincing evidence.

C. No, because a defendant may not be liable for punitive damages if sued only for negligence.

D. No, unless the jury finds Kira's conduct to rise to the level of implied malice.

ANALYSIS. The question whether a defendant may be liable for punitive damages is separate and apart from the name of the cause of action. In California, in order to be liable for punitive damages a plaintiff is going to have to prove by clear and convincing evidence that the defendant engaged in conduct showing fraud, oppression, or malice, express or implied. Implied malice is a kind of reckless disregard of the safety of others. So in this case, it will not be enough for Larry to prove the elements of negligence by a preponderance of the evidence, or even to prove them under a higher standard (which is not required). For this reason, Choices **A** and **B** are incorrect. We focus on the *conduct*, not the name of the tort. Thus a defendant may be liable for punitive damages if sued for negligence, if the plaintiff can prove the requisite bad conduct under the applicable punitive damages standard. For this reason, Choice **C** is incorrect. Choice **D** is the correct choice; it explains that Kira may be liable if Larry can prove her conduct rises to the level of implied malice.

---

7. *See Grimshaw v. Ford Motor Co.*, 119 Cal. App. 3d 757, 808-09 (1981).

QUESTION 3. Driving While Under the Influence of a Cell Phone, Take II.   Kira is driving down the street while speaking on her cell phone. She's having a deep discussion about Kantian virtues when she accidentally runs over Larry's foot. Larry sues Kira for negligence. The jury agrees that Larry has proven the prima facie case for negligence. What else must Larry prove in order to be entitled to punitive damages in a state that follows California's approach to punitive damages?

A. That Kira's conduct constituted implied malice by a preponderance of the evidence.
B. That Kira's conduct constituted implied malice by clear and convincing evidence.
C. That Kira failed to use reasonable care to avoid a reasonably foreseeable risk to the plaintiff by clear and convincing evidence.
D. That Kira deserves to be punished.

ANALYSIS.   Under the California standard, in order to recover for punitive damages a plaintiff must prove fraud, oppression, or malice (express or implied) by clear and convincing evidence. For this reason Choice **B** is the correct choice. Choice **A**, which misses the clear and convincing evidence point, is not as strong of an answer. Similarly, Choice **C** hits the correct clear and convincing evidence standard but applies it to the wrong question — Choice **C** gives the standard for breach in a negligence case, not the standard for the award of punitive damages. Choice **D** is not wrong in the abstract, but it is not as good an answer as Choice **B**, which correctly explains how California decides whether or not Kira should be punished.

C.   Setting and reviewing the amount of punitive damages

Much of the controversy surrounding punitive damages concerns not *whether* punitive damages should be awarded (some tort cases involve some really reprehensible conduct), but about the *amount* of those damages. The determination of that amount goes through three phases after it has been established that the plaintiff is entitled to punitive damages:

1. *Initial Determination.* The trier of fact (usually a jury, but sometimes a judge) chooses an amount based upon the applicable state standard for doing so, and generally without knowledge of other punitive damage awards in other cases.

2. *State Law Limits on the Amount of Punitive Damages.* Depending on state law, a trial judge (if a jury has selected the amount of damages) typically reviews the amount, in comparison with awards in similar cases. Appellate courts then typically review the amount of large punitive damage awards on appeal. Besides judicial review of amounts, some state legislatures limit the amounts of awards by statute.

3. *Judicial Review Under Federal Constitutional Standards.* Thanks to a series of recent Supreme Court cases (discussed in the next section of this chapter), courts must review all punitive damage awards to make sure that they comply with federal constitutional standards.

In this section, we consider the first and second phases; in the next section, we consider the federal constitutional standards.

The Initial Determination. Each state sets its own rules for the trier of fact to set the initial amount of punitive damages. Consider these rules from New Jersey:

> If the trier of fact determines that punitive damages should be awarded, the trier of fact shall then determine the amount of those damages. In making that determination, the trier of fact shall consider all relevant evidence, including, but not limited to, the following:
>
> (1) All relevant evidence relating to the factors [used to determine whether punitive damages are to be awarded[8]];
> (2) The profitability of the misconduct to the defendant;
> (3) When the misconduct was terminated; and
> (4) The financial condition of the defendant.

N.J. STAT. ANN. § 2A:15-5.12c.

When faced with instructions such as these, a jury could well choose a very high amount for punitive damages. This is true in part because a jury considering the "financial condition of the defendant" is going to pick a large amount to punish a wealthy defendant. After all, a $100,000 punitive damage award would feel differently as punishment to you compared to how it would feel for a very wealthy person such as Bill Gates. Moreover, the awards are going to be high in some cases because of the very conduct involved. "The purposes of the award—the deterrence of egregious misconduct and

---

8. The factors include the following:

> (1) The likelihood, at the relevant time, that serious harm would arise from the defendant's conduct;
> (2) The defendant's awareness o[r] reckless disregard of the likelihood that the serious harm at issue would arise from the defendant's conduct;
> (3) The conduct of the defendant upon learning that its initial conduct would likely cause harm; and
> (4) The duration of the conduct or any concealment of it by the defendant.

N.J. STAT. ANN. § 2A:15-5.12b.

the punishment of the offender — when mixed with a finding that the defendant is malicious, can readily inflame an otherwise-dispassionate jury." *Lockley v. State of New Jersey Dep't of Corrections*, 828 A.2d 869, 878 (N.J. 2003).

QUESTION 4. Barroom Fan-atic.   Pablo is sitting in a bar, talking to his friends. He is wearing a jersey of his favorite football team. Dante, who hates that football team, walks up to Pablo, whom he has never met, and punches him in the jaw. The punch was hard, breaking Pablo's jaw and knocking out three of his teeth. Pablo suffered $5,000 in medical bills, and has had a lot of pain as a result of the broken jaw and dental implant surgery. A jury determines that Dante has committed a battery and that his conduct merits the award of punitive damages. The jurisdiction follows New Jersey's law on punitive damages.

Under New Jersey law, which factor may the jury not consider in setting the amount of punitive damages?

A. The reprehensibility of Dante's conduct.

B. Dante's financial condition.

C. Dante's awareness of the likelihood that serious harm would result from his actions.

D. The jury can consider all of these factors.

ANALYSIS.   This is an easy question if you have reviewed the New Jersey statute. It lists specific factors that may be considered and adds that all relevant evidence may be considered. All three of the factors listed in Choices **A**, **B**, and **C** appear either in the statute itself or in the statute (incorporated by reference) setting out the standard for awarding punitive damages in the first place. For this reason, Choice **D** is the correct answer.

I know this question is easy, but I've asked it for a reason that will become clear later in this chapter. So keep your answer in mind for later.

State Law Limitations. To deal with problems of large and variable verdicts, many states either cap the amount of punitive damages or provide for courts to lower the amount of punitive damages in certain circumstances. In New Jersey, for example, the maximum amount of punitive damages that may be assessed against a defendant is "five times the liability of that defendant for compensatory damages or $350,000, whichever is greater." N.J. STAT. ANN. § 2A:15-5.14b. In other states, the reviews are more fluid, with judges given discretion to compare like cases and to reduce punitive damage awards that "shock the conscience" or some other similar verbal formulation. The Supreme Court recently reviewed a $2.5 billion punitive damage award (on top of $500 million in compensatory damages) arising out of the

Exxon Valdez oil spill. Sitting as a common law court considering the propriety of a punitive damages award under federal admiralty law, the Supreme Court held that the punitive award had to be limited to a 1:1 ratio of punitive to compensatory damages. *Exxon Shipping Co. v. Baker*, 128 S. Ct. 2605, 2633 (2008). The opinion is likely to be influential, though its reach is far from clear — technically speaking, this was the Supreme Court deciding a case in admiralty, and its ruling is not binding on state courts reviewing the amount of punitive damages under state law.

The Court in *Exxon Shipping* limited the scope of its holding, explaining that the 1:1 ratio applies to "this particular type of case." *Id.* at 2632. It is not clear if cases involving wrongs motivated by the hope of financial gain, or those leading to more serious personal injuries, would be subject to a different ratio. Despite the limiting language, the fact that the Supreme Court of the United States put its stamp of approval on a 1:1 ratio in such a high-profile case could well lead state courts to follow *Exxon Shipping Co.* in review of punitive damage award amounts under state law.

The instinct of the Supreme Court in the *Exxon Shipping Co.* case to put some limit on punitive damages mirrors the treatment of the issue in many states. According to one recent count, "five states either prohibit punitive damages or severely restrict their use. Statutory caps in at least some form exist in half the states. Limits tied to the amount of actual or economic damages exist in 14 states." Joseph Sanders, *Punitive Damages in Consumer Actions*, 8 J. Tex. Consumer L. 22 (Fall 2004) (footnotes omitted).

QUESTION 5. Barroom Fan-atic, Take II. Pablo is sitting in a bar, talking to his friends. He is wearing a jersey of his favorite football team. Dante, who hates that football team, walks up to Pablo, whom he has never met, and punches him in the jaw. The punch was hard, breaking Pablo's jaw and knocking out three of his teeth. Pablo suffered $5,000 in medical bills, and has had a lot of pain as a result of the broken jaw and dental implant surgery. A jury determines that Dante has committed a battery and that his conduct merits the award of punitive damages. It awards $10,000 in compensatory damages and $100,000 in punitive damages. The jurisdiction follows New Jersey's law on punitive damages.

Dante argues the award is excessive under state law. How should the court rule on Dante's argument?

A. Dante wins because the amount of punitive damages exceeds $50,000.
B. Dante wins because punitive damages must be authorized by statute.
C. Dante loses because the amount of punitive damages is under $350,000.
D. Dante loses because the jury awarded compensatory damages for emotional distress, which has no market value.

ANALYSIS. This question requires a close look at the New Jersey statute. It provides that punitive damages are limited to five times the amount of actual damages *or* $350,000, whichever is *greater*. Here, the punitive damages are more than five times the actual damages of $10,000, but at $50,000 they are still under $350,000. For this reason, Dante's argument will fail. Choice **A** is incorrect and Choice **C** is correct. Choice **B** is incorrect because punitive damages in New Jersey are authorized by statute. Choice **D** is incorrect because there is no rule in New Jersey that punitive damages are unlimited in cases in which a jury awards compensatory damages for emotional distress; to the contrary, the law provides for a cap on punitive damages, as described above.

D. Constitutional limits on the amount of punitive damages

As noted in the last section, when it comes to the *amount* of punitive damages, triers of fact initially set the amount of a punitive damage award. The second phase comes with judicial review of an award, either under a standard set by the courts or one set by state statutes. But in some states, there is no judicial review of the amount of awards, or the review is rather deferential to the judgment of the trier of facts.

For this reason, defendants on the wrong end of a large punitive damages award tried for years to get the Supreme Court to read into the U.S. Constitution a federal constitutional limitation (binding in all courts in all states) on the amount of punitive damages. (The Court's recent *Exxon Shipping Co.* case, discussed in the last section, is a case under the federal common law and not binding on states under their own state laws.)

The Supreme Court began its examination of the constitutionality of large punitive damage awards in 1989, when it rejected the idea that the Constitution's Eighth Amendment, prohibiting excessive fines, served as a limit on punitive damage awards. *Browning-Ferris Industries, Inc. v. Kelco Disposal Inc.*, 492 U.S. 257 (1989). But two years later, in *Pacific Mutual Life Insurance Co. v. Haslip*, 499 U.S. 1 (1991), the Court first suggested that a high punitive damage award could violate substantive due process.[9] The Court talked about punitive damages that "run wild" and said that an award

---

9. For those of you who have not yet taken a Constitutional Law course, you should know that the U.S. Constitution provides in the Fourteenth Amendment that no state may deprive any person of life, liberty, or property "without due process of law." The meaning of this "Due Process Clause" consumes quite a bit of time in the typical Constitutional Law course, and one of the major questions is whether the clause guarantees only fair *procedures* (so-called procedural due process) or also fair *outcomes* (so-called substantive due process).

of punitive damages that was four times the amount of compensatory damages was "close to the line" of constitutional excessiveness. The Court next refused to overturn a punitive award with a 500:1 ratio of punitive to compensatory damages (*TXO Production Corp. v. Alliance Resources Corp.*, 509 U.S. 443 (1993)), leading some to wonder whether the Court was serious about reining in the amount of large punitive damage awards.

The breakthrough for defendants came in the 1996 case, *BMW v. Gore*, 517 U.S. 559 (1996). In that case, Dr. Gore purchased a $40,000 BMW sports sedan in Alabama. After driving it around for nine months, he took it to "Slick Finish" to make the car look "snazzier." Mr. Slick (I'm not making this up) informed Gore that his car had been repainted by the dealership before Gore purchased it. It turns out that the car had suffered some damage from acid rain before it arrived at the dealership. BMW's policy was to repaint cars with minor damage, without disclosing the practice. In Alabama, the non-disclosure counted as a fraud, though in some other states it did not.

The jury determined that Gore's compensatory damages were $4,000, based upon expert testimony that the repainting reduced the value of the car by about 10 percent. It then assessed $4 million (!) in punitive damages, finding the non-disclosure policy to be "gross, oppressive or malicious fraud." The Alabama Supreme Court reduced the award to $2 million, on grounds that similar acts by BMW that occurred in other jurisdictions should not be the basis for punishment in Alabama courts. BMW further appealed to the U.S. Supreme Court, which struck down the award on substantive due process grounds. The *BMW v. Gore* opinion was quite tentative, suggesting three "guideposts" for courts to consider in determining whether the amount of punitive damages was constitutionally excessive:

(1) *The Degree of Reprehensibility of the Conduct*: The more reprehensible the conduct, the higher the punitive award should be.
(2) *The Ratio of Punitive Damages to Actual Damages*: The higher the ratio, the more constitutionally suspect is the punitive award.
(3) *Sanctions for Comparable Misconduct*: If civil or criminal penalties for similar conduct are low, then a punitive award should be low as well because those penalties signal that the state does not consider the conduct to be too blameworthy.

The first factor of course seems relevant in any discussion of the proper amount of punitive damages: certainly BMW should not be punished as harshly as someone who intentionally causes physical injury to another person. The ratio factor is somewhat less defensible; the court did not explain why ratio should matter so much, and it issued some caveats related to the use of the ratio. First, the comparison is between punitive damages and the amount of actual *and potential* damages that a defendant could have caused had he not been stopped from acting. Moreover, the court suggested there was no "simple mathematical formula" to determine the constitutionality of a punitive damage award. (Keep this language in mind.) The court gave the example of "a particularly egregious act [that] has resulted in only a small amount of economic damages" which would justify a high ratio. It also noted that a higher ratio "may be justified in cases where the injury is hard to detect or the monetary value of noneconomic harm might have been difficult to determine."

The last factor, sanctions for comparable misconduct, sends a somewhat perverse message. Punitive damages may be *most useful* when the state does not have other civil or criminal sanctions in place to deter bad conduct.

Four justices (Chief Justice Rehnquist, the liberal Justice Ginsburg, and the conservative Justices Thomas and Scalia) dissented, stating that the amount of punitive damages should be determined by state law, and not federalized in this way. After *BMW v. Gore*, courts began to review awards of punitive damages for constitutional excessiveness. In states without great limits on punitive awards, the case had the potential for greater impact than in those states that already conducted some kind of excessiveness review. But because *BMW* imposed a squishy multifactor "guideposts" test, it was not certain whether the opinion would lead to great changes in the law.

Then along came *State Farm v. Campbell*, 538 U.S. 408 (2003). In *Campbell*, two drivers sued a third driver, Campbell, for negligent driving leading to personal injuries and wrongful death. Campbell had an insurance policy with State Farm. The two drivers offered to settle for Campbell's policy limits — $25,000 each. State Farm's own investigation showed that Campbell was completely at fault.

Under applicable insurance law, State Farm had the obligation not to put its interest over that of the insured. The only reasonable conclusion on the facts as read most favorably to the plaintiff was that State Farm should have settled this case for the policy limits. With liability clear for its insured and the injured parties ready to settle for the policy limits (having sustained serious injuries), the insurer's job was to settle. If the case was not settled, then Campbell would have been on the hook personally for any of the damages over the limit. Rather than settle, State Farm fought the claims. It put false facts in the file (including falsely alleging that one of the other drivers had a pregnant girlfriend), and there was evidence that its handling of the case was part of a nationwide practice of rejecting good offers to settle.

The tort case against Campbell went to trial. The jury found Campbell 100 percent liable, and ordered damages in the amount of $185,000. State Farm refused to pay the extra $135,000 and told Campbell to start putting his assets up for sale. Eventually, State Farm agreed to pay the entire damage award, but by then Campbell had sued State Farm for bad faith (fraud) and intentional infliction of emotional distress.[10] In Campbell's bad faith claim

---

10. To settle his claim with the other two drivers, he assigned 90 percent of his bad faith claim against State Farm to the other two drivers.

against State Farm, the jury found Campbell suffered $2.6 million in compensatory damages (primarily for emotional distress, an amount the trial court reduced to $1 million) and an additional $145 million in punitive damages.

Here is how the Supreme Court in *Campbell* changed the *BMW* guideposts related to constitutional review of the amount of these awards in striking down the $145 million punitive award.

(1) *The Court has limited what evidence may be considered for purposes of judging reprehensibility.* The majority said that State Farm's conduct "merits no praise," quite an understatement if one accepts the plaintiff's view of the conduct. More importantly, the Court said that in judging reprehensibility for purposes of the amount of punitive damages, a jury may consider only similar conduct that has a *close nexus* to the kind of bad conduct at issue in the case itself. So defendants will be able to exclude much evidence of a pattern of similar bad conduct.

(2) *The Court has begun using mathematical formulas to limit the ratio of punitive and compensatory damages.* Though the *Campbell* Court said that there are "no rigid benchmarks," it suggested that it would be the rare case where damages could exceed a 9:1 ratio of punitive damages to actual and potential compensatory damages: "Single-digit multipliers are more likely to comport with due process, while still achieving the State's goals of deterrence and retribution, than awards with ratios in the range of 500 to 1 or, in this case, 145 to 1."[11] Indeed, in cases like this one with "substantial" compensatory awards (recall the $1 million in damages plaintiff was awarded for emotional distress), "then a lesser ratio, perhaps only equal to compensatory damages, can reach the outermost limit of the due process guarantee."[12]

(3) *The wealth of the defendant cannot be used as a reason to increase the award of punitive damages.* This is perhaps the biggest and most important change coming from *Campbell*. "The wealth of a defendant cannot justify an otherwise unconstitutional punitive damage award."[13] While absence of wealth might be a reason to *lower* the amount of damages, the presence of wealth cannot be a reason to raise the amount.[14]

---

11. 538 U.S. 408, 410 (2003).
12. *Id.* at 425.
13. *Id.* at 427.
14. On remand in *Campbell* the Utah Supreme Court reduced the punitive award to $9 million. *Campbell v. State Farm Mutual Insurance Co.*, 98 P.3d 409 (2004). Not coincidentally, that created a 9:1 ratio between punitive damages and compensatory damages. The U.S. Supreme Court declined to hear the case a second time.

The most recent Supreme Court case, but certainly not the last, has created added confusion about constitutional standards. In *Philip Morris USA v. Williams*, 549 U.S. 346 1057 (2007), the Court held on a 5-4 vote (with the two newest Justices in the majority) that a jury cannot consider the defendant's similar conduct toward other in-state residents for purposes of punishing the defendant through punitive damages. But the Court added that a jury could consider that similar conduct for purposes of determining reprehensibility (which in turn is a factor to consider when juries determine the amount of punitive damages). The dissenters thought this distinction "elus[ive]" (Justice Stevens) and the opinion's logic "inexplicable" (Justice Ginsburg). Perhaps the Court will clarify things when it reconsiders this case on remand in the October 2008 term, 2008 WL 791949, but I would not bet on it.

QUESTION 6. Barroom Fan-atic, Take III. Pablo is sitting in a bar, talking to his friends. He is wearing a jersey of his favorite football team. Dante, who hates that football team, walks up to Pablo, whom he has never met, and punches him in the jaw. The punch was hard, breaking Pablo's jaw and knocking out three of his teeth. Pablo suffered $5,000 in medical bills, and has had a lot of pain as a result of the broken jaw and dental implant surgery. A jury determines that Dante has committed a battery and that his conduct merits the award of punitive damages. It awards $10,000 in compensatory damages and $100,000 in punitive damages. The jurisdiction follows New Jersey's law on punitive damages.

Dante argues the award is excessive under the due process clause of the U.S. Constitution. How should the court rule on Dante's argument?

A. The court should accept the argument because the ratio exceeds a single digit multiplier.
B. The court should accept the argument because punitive damages can never exceed the amount of actual and potential compensatory damages.
C. The court should reject the argument because this is a state law claim brought in state court.
D. The court should reject the argument because Dante caused physical harm.

ANALYSIS. This question presents a tough choice between Choice **A** and Choice **D**. Let's first eliminate the other possibilities. Choice **B** is wrong because the Supreme Court has never stated that a 1:1 ratio is constitutionally required in all cases — even if it suggested in *Campbell* that the ratio is an appropriate ratio in cases involving substantial punitive damages.

Choice **C** is clearly wrong. Even for state law claims in state courts, federal constitutional limitations on the amounts of punitive damages apply. That's what it means in the Constitution when it declares the supremacy of federal law.

So now we come down to Choices **A** and **D**. Choice **A**, the correct choice, is a stronger answer. The Court has said that a single digit multiplier (meaning a ratio of no more than 9:1[15]) is ordinarily the upper limit allowed in tort cases. This limit exceeds the single-digit multiplier. And though this may be a "particularly egregious act" under *BMW*, it is not one that led to very small economic damages. The fact that Dante's conduct resulted in physical harm *should* be considered in the ratio, but it alone does not appear to be a reason to exceed the single digit multiplier.

QUESTION 7. Barroom Fan-atic, Take IV. Pablo is sitting in a bar, talking to his friends. He is wearing a jersey of his favorite football team. Dante, who hates that football team, walks up to Pablo, whom he has never met, and punches him in the jaw. The punch was hard, breaking Pablo's jaw and knocking out three of his teeth. Pablo suffered $5,000 in medical bills, and has had a lot of pain as a result of the broken jaw and dental implant surgery.

During the trial, Pablo's lawyer introduces evidence that Dante had slugged at least four other people at the same bar in the last year who were wearing the same football jersey as Pablo.

A jury determines that Dante has committed a battery and that his conduct merits the award of punitive damages. It awards $10,000 in compensatory damages and $100,000 in punitive damages. The jurisdiction follows New Jersey's law on punitive damages.

Dante argues it was prejudicial to admit the evidence on the other bar incidents in considering the amount of the punitive damages award. How should the court rule on this argument?

A. The court should accept the argument because a jury may not punish a defendant for bad conduct directed at others.
B. The court should reject the argument because evidence of similar conduct towards others is relevant in assessing Dante's reprehensibility.
C. Both Choice A and Choice B are correct.
D. Neither Choice A nor Choice B are correct.

---

15. Even if we use a ratio of 9.999 to 1, this 10:1 ratio cannot be called a single digit multiplier.

ANALYSIS.   If you find this question confusing, good! It means you have been paying attention. Choices **A** and **B** are, at the least, in tension with one another. But in the recent *Philip Morris* case, the Supreme Court made both of these statements. For this reason, Choice **C** is the best answer and Choice **D** is wrong. Likely the tension between these two will be resolved by having courts instruct juries on these two contradictory points, and then just assume that the jury, being totally befuddled, will ignore the instruction.

E.   The Closer: Considering defendant's wealth in punitive damages cases

For the closer, I want to focus a bit more on the statement in *Campbell* about taking wealth into account in considering the amount of punitive damages. Recall the Supreme Court said there that "[t]he wealth of a defendant cannot justify an otherwise unconstitutional punitive damage award."

Arguably, this is the most indefensible part of the *Campbell* test. Note the New Jersey factors for the award of punitive damages listed earlier in this chapter. Of course, the New Jersey courts (like the courts in many other states) consider the wealth of the defendant to be a relevant factor in assessing the amount of the award, for the reasons discussed above in relation to wealthy people such as Bill Gates: It takes a lot more money to deter a rich person (or corporate management) than a poor person. How this factor is supposed to square with the deterrent purpose of punitive damages is yet to be explained.

Some lower courts have simply ignored the statement and found a way around it. Consider *Mathias v. Accor Economy Lodging, Inc.*, 347 F.3d 672 (7th Cir. 2003). Defendant ran a hotel that was infested with bedbugs. Though hotel guests complained about the bedbugs, the hotel did nothing serious to correct the problem and misrepresented its rooms as clean. Bedbug bites are uncomfortable and unsightly, though not life-threatening. A group of hotel guests sued the hotel in tort for fraud and other torts. A jury awarded $5,000 in compensatory damages and $186,000 in punitive damages. The defendant was quite wealthy.

In an opinion written by the influential Judge Richard A. Posner, the Seventh Circuit upheld the punitive award against a challenge that it was unconstitutionally high. The ratio of the award was quite high, 37.2:1, but the court held it did not violate the rules of *Campbell*, arguing it fit into an exception for cases involving egregious facts but low compensatory damages: "The defendant's behavior was outrageous but the compensable harm done was slight and at the same time difficult to quantify because a large element of it was emotional. And the defendant may well have profited from its misconduct because by concealing the infestation it was able to keep renting rooms."[16] Perhaps most interesting about *Mathias* is what Judge Posner said about the wealth of the defendant issue:

> Finally, if the total stakes in the case were capped at $50,000 . . . , the plaintiffs might well have had difficulty financing this lawsuit. It is here that the defendant's aggregate net worth of $1.6 billion becomes relevant. A defendant's wealth is not a sufficient basis for awarding punitive damages. *Campbell; BMW* (concurring opinion); *Zazú Designs v. L'Oreal, S.A.,* 979 F.2d 499, 508-09 (7th Cir. 1992). That would be discriminatory and would violate the rule of law . . . by making punishment depend on status rather than conduct. Where wealth in the sense of resources enters is in enabling the defendant to mount an extremely aggressive defense against suits such as this and by doing so to make litigating against it very costly, which in turn may make it difficult for the plaintiffs to find a lawyer willing to handle their case, involving as it does only modest stakes, for the usual 33-40 percent contingent fee.
>
> In other words, the defendant is investing in developing a reputation intended to deter plaintiffs. It is difficult otherwise to explain the great stubbornness with which it has defended this case, making a host of frivolous evidentiary arguments despite the very modest stakes even when the punitive damages awarded by the jury are included.

Id.

One of my former students has written a law review note arguing, I think correctly, that *Mathias* is in fact inconsistent with *Campbell* in considering the wealth of the defendant. It seems that Judge Posner is trying to get defendant's wealth information into the case through the back door. My student further argues that *Mathias* is right and that *Campbell* is wrong on the role of the wealth of the defendant in punitive damages cases. Leila C. Orr, Note, *Making a Case for Wealth-Calibrated Punitive Damages,* 37 Loy. L.A. L. Rev. 1739 (2004).

Following *Campbell's* pronouncement about the role of wealth in assessing the amount of punitive damages, it is not clear that jury instruc-tions such as those used in New Jersey (allowing the jury to consider the wealth of the defendant) remain constitutional.

QUESTION 8. Barroom Fan-atic, Take V.   Pablo is sitting in a bar, talking to his friends. He is wearing a jersey of his favorite football team. Dante, who hates that football team, walks up to Pablo, whom he has never met, and punches him in the jaw. The punch was hard, breaking Pablo's jaw and knocking out three of his teeth. Pablo suffered $5,000 in medical

---

16. 347 F.3d 672, 677 (7th Cir. 2003).

bills, and has had a lot of pain as a result of the broken jaw and dental implant surgery.

During the trial, Pablo's lawyer introduces evidence that Dante owns his own home and a fancy sports car.

A jury determines that Dante has committed a battery and that his conduct merits the award of punitive damages. It awards $10,000 in compensatory damages and $100,000 in punitive damages. The jurisdiction follows New Jersey's law on punitive damages.

Dante argues it was prejudicial to admit the evidence of his assets and he argues that the award of punitive damages is too high. How should the court rule on these arguments?

A. The court should order a new trial on the amount of punitive damages because wealth is never admissible in determining the amount of punitive damages.

B. The court should order a new trial on the amount of damages and require that the jurors hear about both Dante and Pablo's wealth.

C. The court should reject the argument that the wealth evidence was inadmissible, but independently examine the amount of the punitive damage award without using Dante's wealth to justify an otherwise unconstitutional award.

D. The court should reject both of Dante's arguments because if an award of punitive damages is going to deter, wealth should be the primary factor considered in setting the amount of punitive damages.

ANALYSIS. The Supreme Court in *Campbell* did not announce a per se rule barring evidence of wealth from entering into the punitive damages phase of a trial. For this reason, Choice **A** is wrong. Nor did the Court say that the wealth of the *plaintiff* was somehow relevant. Thus, Choice **B** is wrong. Instead, the Court stated that the wealth of the defendant cannot justify an otherwise unconstitutional award. Choice **C** best expresses this idea. Choice **D** would make sense if we were talking solely about state law, but the Court in *Campbell* undercut this argument by limiting the role that wealth may play in setting punitive awards.

 Rick's picks

3. Driving While Under the Influence of a Cell Phone, Take II   **B**
4. Barroom Fan-atic   **D**
5. Barroom Fan-atic, Take II   **C**
6. Barroom Fan-atic, Take III   **A**
7. Barroom Fan-atic, Take IV   **C**
8. Barroom Fan-atic, Take V   **C**

24

Closing Closers

These questions are the multiple-choice questions most similar to those likely to appear on a Torts final exam. They introduce an element that is not present in the multiple-choice questions in the earlier chapters: issue spotting. You may not know whether the question requires knowledge of something like the rules of actual cause or something related to affirmative defenses. It could be both. Fortunately, you need not approach the issue-spotting question completely in a vacuum as you must do on an essay exam. Often, there are clues to the issues at play in the various answers set out after the question.

At this point, you may want to quickly return to Chapter 1, which gives some of my hints for tackling multiple-choice questions. I have also placed the answers at the end of this chapter, rather than after each question, so that you can better resist the temptation to peek at the right answer.

Good luck!

QUESTION 1. **Alpo Nightmare.** Over the years, firefighters in Pacifica County develop a tradition of "hazing," playing cruel, often degrading, practical jokes on new firefighters. The fire chief has banned such conduct because it has led to a number of lawsuits against the county. Jim begins working at Pacifica Firehouse #1 and is greeted by friendly veterans of the station. Jim thanks the other firefighters for his warm welcome and expresses relief to them that during his first day on the job he has not been the victim of any hazing. At the end of the day, the firefighters sit down for a hamburger dinner. Unbeknownst to Jim, Charley, the veteran on kitchen duty that day, had made Jim's hamburger out of dog food. Jim takes a bite of the hamburger and immediately tastes there is something wrong with it. He spits it out, causing uproarious laughter among the firefighters at the station. Charley yells out: "It's dog food you fool! Welcome to the Firehouse #1!" Jim runs to the bathroom and vomits. He quits his job and has been seeing a therapist over his nightmares since the incident.

Jim sues Charley in tort. Which tort is Jim least likely to succeed in proving against Charley?

A. Assault
B. Battery
C. Intentional infliction of emotional distress
D. Negligence

Questions 2 and 3 are based upon the following facts:

Acme blasting company is called in to blast its way into a bank vault, which has been accidentally locked with people inside and little air left in the vault. A crowd develops and Acme and bank officials have them moved a reasonably safe distance away. Despite Acme's reasonable efforts to control the crowd, Billy, a 10-year-old child, sneaks through because he thinks it would be cool to watch the blast. The blast occurs, opening the vault but seriously injuring Billy.

QUESTION 2. It's a Blast.   What is Billy's strongest cause of action against Acme?

A. Negligence
B. Battery
C. Strict liability for abnormally dangerous activities
D. Products liability

QUESTION 3. It's a Blast, Take II.   Assume for purposes of this question only that Billy sues Acme for strict liability for abnormally dangerous activities in a jurisdiction that follows the Restatement (Third) of Torts approach to the tort. Assume further that Billy can make out the prima facie case for this tort. What is the legal relevance, if any, of the fact that Billy intentionally got close to the blast because he thought it would be cool to be so close?

A. If characterized as an assumption of the risk, it will bar his recovery.
B. If characterized as a form of contributory negligence, it will not have an effect on his recovery.
C. Both Choice A and Choice B are correct.
D. Neither Choice A nor Choice B is correct.

QUESTION 4. Lucky Strike.   Dan likes playing with matches. He goes out into the forest and begins to play with matches, despite being warned by park rangers and numerous signs that, because of a recent drought, the fire danger is extremely high and no flames should be lit while in the forest.

One of the matches lit by Dan causes a fire that spreads to nearby private property owned by Pat. Five minutes before Dan's fire reaches Pat's home, another fire, started by lightning, burns down Pat's home. Experts agree that Dan's fire would have burned down Pat's home had it not been burned down first by the lightening fire.

Pat sues Dan for negligence, claiming the value of her home as damages. Will Pat's claim be successful?

A. Yes, because Pat is a foreseeable plaintiff, Dan engaged in risk creation, and he failed to use reasonable care to avoid a reasonably foreseeable risk to Pat.

B. Yes, because the type of harm that occurred was a foreseeable type of harm.

C. Yes, because Pat suffered damages.

D. No, even if the facts in Choices **A**, **B**, and **C** are correct.

QUESTION 5. Spontaneous Combustion.   Veronica buys a brand new AcmeMotors Thunder from a new car dealership. As she leaves the dealership, the car explodes. Veronica suffers serious personal injuries. The car is completely destroyed and it cannot be examined by experts to pinpoint a cause.

Veronica sues AcmeMotors under the state's products liability law. Can her claim succeed without any direct proof of a design defect in the car?

A. Yes, if the jurisdiction uses a consumer expectations test for proving that a product is defective.

B. Yes, if the jurisdiction has adopted the Restatement (Third) of Torts: Products Liability.

C. Both Choice **A** and Choice **B** are correct.

D. Neither Choice **A** nor Choice **B** is correct.

Questions 6 and 7 are based upon the following facts:

Ralph is driving on a quiet residential street, paying attention while driving, but driving at 35 mph. The posted speed limit is 25 mph. Sally is an 8-year-old girl playing catch with a friend on the sidewalk. The ball gets away from Sally and she runs in the street after it, without looking. Ralph hits Sally, breaking her leg. A state statute makes it a criminal infraction to drive above the posted speed limit.

QUESTION 6. Per Se? Pourquoi?   Assume for purposes of this question only that experts agree that Sally would have suffered exactly the same injury had Ralph been driving 25 mph. Is Ralph liable for negligence under the *negligence per se* test?

A. Yes, because Sally is within the class of people the statute was designed to protect.

B. Yes, because driving slower was a cost-justified precaution under the Hand formula.

C. No, because Ralph's statutory violation was not an actual cause of the injury.

D. No, because Sally's injury was not the type of injury the statute was designed to prevent.

QUESTION 7. Affirming the Defense. Assume for purposes of this question only that Sally proves Ralph was negligent using *negligence per se.* Ralph raises as an affirmative defense Sally's own negligence. How should the jury determine whether or not Sally was negligent?

A. By considering whether or not Sally violated the statute.

B. By considering whether Sally acted reasonably, given her age, experience, maturity, and intelligence.

C. By considering whether Sally acted as a reasonably prudent person.

D. The jury should not consider Sally's negligence because Sally is a minor.

QUESTION 8. Per Se? Pourquoi?, Take II. Ralph is driving on a quiet residential street. The posted speed limit is 25 mph. He is driving 24 mph. Sally is an 8-year-old girl playing catch with a friend on the sidewalk. The ball gets away from Sally and she runs in the street after it, without looking. Ralph hits Sally, breaking her leg. Sally sues Ralph for negligence.

Ralph's compliance with the statutory speed limit is:

A. Some evidence of the standard of care.

B. Conclusive of the standard of care.

C. Irrelevant to the standard of care.

D. Some evidence of industry custom.

QUESTION 9. Another Nightmare Question. Barry has a problem with sleepwalking and taking other actions in his sleep, such as eating and driving. People have suggested to him that he see a doctor to take medication which would prevent these actions, but he has not done so.

One night, Barry has another sleepwalking episode. In his dream, he imagines he is being chased by enemy spies. He dreams he is trying to escape from them and prevent his capture. In actuality, Barry gets in his car and starts driving. He sees Dave on his front lawn. As part of his dream, he imagines that Dave is one of the enemy spies. Barry drives onto Dave's lawn, knocking down Dave's fence and injuring Dave.

Dave wants to sue Barry in tort. Which is Dave's strongest cause of action?

A. Battery
B. Trespass to real property
C. Negligence
D. Choice **A** or **B**, but not **C**.

QUESTION 10. Slice of the Pie.   Gerald works as a baker employed at Jules Pie Shop, Inc. One day, as Gerald was working in the kitchen, Sal, a driver from one of the shop's suppliers, brought in some fresh fruits for the pies. Gerald was using a large knife to cut dough, and he carelessly dropped the knife on Sal's foot. It severed some tendons, resulting in a permanent partial disability for Sal.

Sal sues Jules Pie Shop, Inc. and Gerald for negligence. Sal's sole theory against the shop is vicarious liability. The jury agrees that Gerald was negligent, and finds Gerald and the shop liable for $100,000 in damages. So far, the shop has paid Sal $45,000 and Gerald has paid nothing. The jurisdiction uses the traditional rules for joint and several liability.

How much more, if anything, may Sal collect against Jules Pie Shop, Inc.?

A. 0
B. $5,000
C. $55,000
D. It depends upon the percentage of damages attributable to noneconomic harm.

QUESTION 11. Bouldered Over.   Jane is a school bus driver who is transporting 48 children on a field trip. While driving, Jane suddenly and without warning comes across a large boulder in the road. Jane deliberately drives into Michael's fence on the side of the road to avoid a certain collision with the boulder. Jane's action knocks down the fence, allowing Michael's farm animals to escape. Michael's attempt to recover damages in his suit for trespass to land will

A. Succeed, because Jane failed to use reasonable care to avoid a reasonably foreseeable risk to a foreseeable plaintiff.
B. Succeed, because Jane must take plaintiff as she finds him.
C. Fail, if Jane can prove public necessity.
D. Fail, because of Jane's defense of others.

Questions 12 and 13 are based upon the following facts:

Phil sues Harry for negligence arising out of an accident in which Harry, driving drunk, ran over Phil's foot. The jury found that Harry was negligent and awarded Phil damages of $10,000. At the end of the trial, in open court and in front of dozens of people, Harry walked over to Phil and deliberately spit in his eye. Phil was angry about the spitting incident, but suffered no physical harm or serious emotional damage.

QUESTION 12. Spit Spat.   Phil sues Harry for battery. Will Phil succeed?

A. Yes, if Phil saw the spit coming before it reached his eye.

B. Yes, whether or not Phil saw the spit coming before it reached his eye.

C. No, whether or not Phil saw the spit coming before it reached his eye because Phil suffered no damages.

D. No, whether or not Phil saw the spit coming before it reached his eye because Harry did not have intent to harm.

QUESTION 13. Spit Spat, Take II.   Assume for purposes of this question only that Phil successfully sues Harry for battery. The jury awards $1 in compensatory damages and $1,000 in punitive damages. Harry raises a constitutional challenge to the amount of punitive damages. Will Harry's challenge succeed?

A. Yes, because punitive damages can never exceed a single digit ratio with compensatory damages.

B. Yes, because a 1:1 ratio between punitive and compensatory is appropriate in cases with substantial compensatory damages.

C. No, if the court concludes this is an appropriate kind of case to exceed a single digit ratio between punitive and compensatory damages.

D. No, because Harry's conduct was reprehensible.

QUESTION 14. Bottle Battle.   A state statute requires pharmacists to label all prescriptions that are poisonous when ingested as poison. Ron, of Ron's pharmacy, sold Mona a liquid medication to be applied to her feet to eliminate bunion problems. The medication is poisonous if swallowed, but Ron failed to label it as poison and Mona did not know it was poison.

Mona went home and placed the medication on the counter of her bathroom sink. If it had been labeled as poison, Mona would have followed her usual procedure of putting the bottle in a locked medicine cabinet so as to keep it away from her children.

Mona was brushing her hair and knocked the medication off of her counter. The glass from the medication shattered as the bottle hit her foot. The glass cut her and gave her a nasty infection. The infection was not caused or exacerbated by the medication in the bottle.

Mona sues Ron for negligence, claiming *negligence per se* in his violation of the state labeling statue. Can Mona win her case using *negligence per se*?

A. No, because Ron's mislabeling was not an actual cause of Mona's injury.

B. No, because Ron's mislabeling was not a proximate cause of Mona's injury.

C. No, because Mona's procedure of locking up the bottle of poisonous medications does not rise to the level of industry custom.

D. Yes.

QUESTION 15. Under the Knife. Dr. Diana is a general surgeon. She agrees to remove Peter's gallbladder, which has been causing Peter a great deal of pain. Though Dr. Diana told Peter that there are always risks with surgery, she did not tell Peter specifically of a 2 percent risk of infection as a complication of surgery.

Unfortunately for Peter, he develops an infection as a result of the surgery, and he is hospitalized with sepsis for more than a month. He sues Dr. Diana for failing to give him the opportunity for informed consent. Which argument by Dr. Diana, if proven, would be least helpful to Dr. Diana in defeating Peter's claim?

A. Most doctors do not disclose the risk of infection from surgery.

B. Most people know that the risk of infection is common.

C. Even if Dr. Diana disclosed the specific risk of infection, a reasonable person in Peter's position still would have chosen to have the surgery.

D. Dr. Diana's general disclosure about the risks of surgery included within it disclosure of the risks of developing an infection.

Answers

1. (A) Alpo Nightmare. Choice **A** is the correct answer. The facts tell us that Jim had no idea that Charley had put dog food into his food until he had taken his first bite. Thus, Jim was not put in any imminent apprehension he was going to suffer an offensive contact before that offensive contact actually happened. In the absence of such apprehension, he cannot prove at least one of the elements of the tort of assault.

Choices **B**, **C**, and **D** are all wrong because Jim has a reasonably good chance of proving the prima facie case for each of these causes of action, and there do not appear to be any strong affirmative defenses.

On battery, there is no question Charley acted by preparing the hamburger and serving it to Jim. It was an intentional action. A jury could well conclude that Charley intended Jim to suffer an offensive contact by serving him the dog food-laced hamburger at dinner time which Charley expected Jim would bite into. Offensive contact resulted when Jim took the bite. Though Charley could argue that this was consensual because Jim knew some hazing could occur, knowledge it could occur does not equal consent to bad treatment.

On intentional infliction of emotional distress, under contemporary standards a jury could find that surreptitiously serving someone dog food is outrageous conduct. Charley may not have intended to cause serious emotional distress, but he was at least reckless that such distress could occur given the history of earlier lawsuits against the county for hazing incidents. The nightmares, loss of job, and therapy are all evidence of Jim's severe emotional distress.

Negligence (in the form of negligent infliction of emotional distress) seems like a strong case here as well. When judged from the perspective of a reasonable person, especially given the history and common sense about surreptitiously serving someone dog food, it is likely that a court or jury would find that Charley's conduct amounts to a failure to use reasonable care. Jim was a foreseeable plaintiff to whom Charley owed a duty. A consent-like assumption of risk argument fails along the same lines as the consent argument in battery.

Actual causation does not appear to be a problem for battery, IIED, or negligence. Nor is there a strong proximate cause policy argument here. There is also no question that Jim has been damaged.

2. (C) It's a Blast. Let's begin by eliminating the clear wrong answers, Choice **B** and Choice **D**. Acme did not have an intent to cause a harmful or offensive contact with Billy, or to put Billy in imminent apprehension of such contact. So there is no battery. Similarly, the suit is not against a product manufacturer or seller for a defect in the product. (That would be the case if, for example, Billy sued the dynamite manufacturer.) So the choice comes down to negligence (Choice **A**) or strict liability for abnormally dangerous products (Choice **C**). Choice **C** is the better answer because the facts tell you that Acme has acted reasonably in its blasting. If Acme has been reasonable, then Billy cannot prove breach and the negligence claim will fail.

3. (D) It's a Blast, Take II. This is a really tricky question, and it requires you to understand the difference between the Second and Third Restatement approaches to plaintiff's conduct and affirmative defenses. Under the Second Restatement, plaintiff's contributory negligence is not a defense to a strict liability for abnormally dangerous activities tort, but assumption of risk is a complete defense. Sometimes, as in the facts of this case (given that the plaintiff is a 10-year-old, which affects both our thoughts about negligence and the knowing and voluntary nature of encountering the risk), it is hard to tell which box this fits into. But under the Third Restatement, both plaintiff's negligence and plaintiff's assumption of risk/consent are factors to be consi-dered in an allocation of responsibility. Both are relevant, and neither is a complete defense. For this reason, Choice **D** is correct, and Choices **A**, **B**, and **C** are incorrect.

4. (D) **Lucky Strike.** It looks like Pat can make out the prima facie case for negligence except for one element, actual causation. But for Dan's actions, Pat's injuries still would have occurred — they were caused by light-ning. Nor is this a case of independent concurrent causation. The lightning fire reached Pat's house *before* Dan's fire, and therefore the doctrine doesn't apply. Without proof of actual causation, Pat cannot prove her prima facie case. Therefore, even if all of the duty, breach, and proximate cause issues were proven by Pat (and given in Choices **A**, **B**, and **C**), Pat will still lose. Dan got very lucky.

5. (C) **Spontaneous Combustion.** It is very difficult under either the Third Restatement or the tougher versions of the consumer expectations test (as in California) to prove that a product is defective without specific proof of defect. Because the car has been destroyed, if there is a manufacturing defect, it would be very difficult, if not impossible to prove that directly. And the question asks you to assume that Veronica has put on no evidence of a design defect. But both tests recognize rare situations, such as brand new cars exploding for no reason, allowing plaintiffs to prove a defect inferen-tially (along the lines of *res ipsa loquitur*). A brand new car exploding appears to be one of those types of rare situations. For this reason, Veronica is likely to succeed under either consumer expectations or the Third Restatement. Choice **C** is therefore the correct choice, and Choices **A**, **B**, and **D** are incorrect.

6. (C) **Per Se? Pourquoi?** The facts tell you to assume that the very same injury would have happened if Ralph had been driving at the speed limit. This fact tells you that Ralph's violation of the statute was not an actual cause of the injury. Choice **C** correctly makes this point. Choice **A** is incorrect because it is not enough for the plaintiff in a *negligence per se* case to prove that the plaintiff was within the class of those protected. Choice **B** is wrong because the question of cost-justified precautions is *not* the way breach is measured under the *negligence per se* test; instead it is through proof of violation of the statute. Moreover, the problem in this fact pattern is not breach, but actual cause. Finally, Choice **D** is incorrect because being hit by a car violating the speed limit is exactly the type of injury one would expect to result from such a violation. There is no proximate cause problem here.

7. (B) Affirming the Defense. Even if Sally can prove all of the elements of *negligence per se* against Ralph, Ralph may still be able to raise an affirmative defense against Sally. In most jurisdictions, proof of that affirmative defense will lead the jury to compare Sally's responsibility with Ralph's responsibility and come up with an allocation of responsibility between them.

In determining whether Sally is negligent or not, the only statute given in the question relates to speeding, not one relating to running into the street. Therefore, Choice **A** is incorrect. Rather than under a statutory standard, Sally's behavior will be evaluated under the standard of a child of similar age, experience, intelligence, and maturity, and not under an adult standard. (There is no possible "adult activity exception" argument on these facts because playing ball in the streets is not an adult activity.) For this reason, Choice **B** is correct and Choices **C** and **D** are incorrect.

8. (A) Per Se? Pourquoi?, Take II. While violation of a statute proves conclusively that a person has failed to use reasonable care in a *negligence per se* case, *compliance* with the statute is not conclusive of a use of reasonable care. Instead, it is simply evidence of reasonable care. Choice **A** is correct, and Choices **B** and **C** are incorrect. Choice **D** is incorrect for a different reason; compliance with a statute does not show evidence of an industry custom.

9. (C) Another Nightmare Question. Because Barry was asleep when he attacked Dave and his property, he cannot meet the act requirement necessary for intentional torts such as trespass and battery. Without the act requirement met, Dave's case for an intentional tort claim against Barry will fail. For this reason, Choices **A**, **B**, and **D** are incorrect.

The best choice is Choice **C**. Dave can argue that Barry failed to use reasonable care because he knew he did some things in his sleep and failed to take any precautions to make sure he did not hurt anyone. It is not a slam-dunk negligence case, but at least it has a chance of success.

10. (C) Slice of the Pie. Under traditional rules of joint and several liability, a successful plaintiff (now referred to as a judgment creditor) may go after either or all defendants (now referred to as judgment debtors) until the plaintiff has recovered full satisfaction, in this case, an additional $55,000. There is no requirement that the plaintiff try to collect equally from each defendant. In addition, under the traditional rules (unlike some changes that states have made by statute), the rule applies whether the damages are economic or noneconomic. For these reasons, Choice **C** is correct, and Choices **A**, **B**, and **D** are incorrect.

Note that the question of who must pay the *plaintiff* is separate from the right of one of the paying defendants to seek contribution, indemnity, or partial equitable indemnification (depending on state laws) from the non-paying defendant or defendants. It could well be that the shop could get full indemnity from Gerald, in the event that Gerald has the assets to pay the judgment.

11. (C) Bouldered Over. If Jane can prove public necessity, it is a complete defense, meaning that she will not have to pay damages. This looks like a decent case for public necessity, as Jane is transporting 48 schoolchildren. Choice **C** is therefore correct. Choice **A** is incorrect because that is the standard for negligence, not trespass. Choice **B** is incorrect because the eggshell plaintiff rule is irrelevant to whether there is or is not a trespass (it is relevant instead to the question of damages). Choice **D** is incorrect because "defense of others" applies when there is a physical attack, not a force of nature.

12. (B) Spit Spat. This is a tough battery question. The claim would be here for an offensive battery, and courts recognize a dignitary harm from an offensive battery whether or not it results in actual damages. For this reason, Choice **C** is wrong. Courts could award nominal damages of a dollar. Phil can prove his case by demonstrating that:

- Harry acted — which he did through the voluntary muscular contraction of the spit;
- Harry intended to cause a harmful or offensive contact (or in some jurisdictions just a contact) — intending an offensive contact seems the only explanation for Harry's "deliberate" decision;
- Contact was with the person of the other — Phil's eye is part of his person;
- Offensive contact resulted — a spit in the eye in front of a group of people will offend a reasonable person's sense of dignity; and
- No consent — nothing indicates that Phil in any way agreed to this conduct.[1]

As you can see, it is not required to prove that Phil was put in imminent apprehension of contact before the contact took place. For this reason, Choice **A** is wrong. Choice **D** is wrong because it is enough that Harry had the intent to make an offensive contact with Phil, which the facts show that he did. Choice **B** is correct; Phil wins, whether or not he saw the spit coming.

13. (C) Spit Spat, Take II. Under the Supreme Court's recent jurisprudence, punitive damages ordinarily cannot exceed more than a single digit ratio (that is, more than 9:1). However, the Court has recognized that in rare circumstances, it may be appropriate to exceed the ratio, such as "a

---

1. This all goes to the tortious conduct portion of the prima facie case. There should also be no problem proving actual causation (but for Harry's actions, the offensive contact would not have occurred) and proximate causation (not a problem to prove when the defendant, as here, intended harm). Damages are discussed in the text. Nor do there seem to be any affirmative defenses that could apply here.

particularly egregious act [that] has resulted in only a small amount of economic damages."[2] This looks like it could be such a case. In contrast, the Court concluded in *Campbell* that a 1:1 ratio seems appropriate in cases involving substantial compensatory damages.[3]

So which is the best answer here? Let's begin by eliminating Choice **D**. Just about all punitive damage cases involve reprehensible conduct. True, some conduct may be more reprehensible than others, but the Court has never said that the single digit ratio rule applies only to cases with little reprehensibility. Choice **B** is wrong, too; it contains a correct statement of the law, but it is not applicable in this case. An award of $1 in compensatory damages cannot be considered substantial.

So how to choose between Choice **A** and Choice **C**? Note that Choice **A** is categorical, saying that punitive damages can *never* exceed the single digit ratio. Choice **C**, the correct choice, recognizes room for discretion in a case such as this one, under the *BMW* dicta discussed above.

14. (B) Bottle Battle. In order to prove *negligence per se*, Mona will need to prove five elements:

- *Ron had a duty to comply with the state labeling statute.* As a pharmacist, he did.
- *Ron breached that duty.* The facts show that he failed to label the medication as poison, as the statute required.
- *Mona is within the class of those whom the statute was designed to protect.* The legislature would have passed the law to protect consumers and those around them from accidentally ingesting poison.
- *The statute was designed to prevent injuries of this type.* No! Mona's case will fail on this element. The statute was not designed to prevent people knocking bottles over and cutting themselves on the container. (Indeed, the statute says nothing about the type of container that must be used.) Mona cannot show that this was a harm within the risk, and accordingly, this proximate cause element of *negligence per se* fails.
- *Ron's failure to comply with the statute was an actual cause of Mona's injury.* As hard as it is to believe, the actual cause element is met in this case. But for Ron's failure to label the poison as poison, Mona would have put the bottle away and it would not have fallen off of her counter.

Because Mona cannot prove the proximate cause element, but can prove the actual cause element, Choices **A** and **D** are incorrect and Choice **B** is correct. Choice **C** gives an irrelevant answer. It is true that Mona's conduct does not

2. *BMW v. Gore*, 517 U.S. 559, 582 (1996).
3. *State Farm v. Campbell*, 538 U.S. 408, 425 (2003).

rise to the level of an industry custom, but that is not part of the *negligence per se* test.

15. (A) Under the Knife. A doctor's compliance with customary practice does not insulate the doctor from liability in an informed consent case (the way compliance with custom in a negligent treatment case does). For this reason, Choice **A** is correct; such an argument would be the least helpful to Dr. Diana. The other three choices would help Dr. Diana win her case. For Choice **B**, the fact that everyone knows of the risk of infection would defeat the requirement to disclose; there is no need to disclose risks everyone knows about. For Choice **C**, the fact that Peter would have had the operation anyway acts to defeat actual causation; if failure to disclose would not have made a difference under the special objective standard, then Peter's case would fail. For Choice **D**, if she actually disclosed the risk of infection, without mentioning it specifically, Dr. Diana would have complied with her requirement to disclose.

* * *

Well, that's it. I hope that I have helped you to understand the Torts material a little better and to feel more comfortable answering multiple-choice questions. If you think I've led you astray or gotten something wrong, please drop me an e-mail. Good luck!

Table of Cases

Table of Restatement Sections Cited

Table of Books and Articles Cited

Akerlof, George, The Market for Lemons, 84 Q.J. Econ. 488 (1970), 352
Ames, James Barr, Law and Morals, 22 Harv. L. Rev. 97 (1908), 189

Calabresi, Guido, The Cost of Accidents: A Legal and Economic Analysis (1970), 107
Coase, Ronald, The Problem of Social Cost (1960), 105
Comparative Negligence Manual (3d ed. 1995), 169

Dobbs, Dan B. & Paul H. Hayden, Torts and Compensation (5th ed. 2005), 224

Eisenberg, Theodore, et al., Judges, Juries, and Punitive Damages: Empirical Analyses
        Using the Civil Justice Survey of State Courts, 3 J. Empirical Legal Stud. 263
        (2006), 391
Ellickson, Robert, Order without Law: How Neighbors Settle Disputes (2005), 262
Epstein, Richard A., A Theory of Strict Liability, 2 J. Legal Stud. 151 (1973), 190
—, Cases and Materials on Torts (9th ed. 2008), *passim*
—, The Path to the T.J. Hooper, 21 J. Legal Stud. 1 (1992), 139
—, Torts (1999), *passim*

Fletcher, George, Fairness and Utility in Tort Theory, 85 Harv. L. Rev. 537
        (1972), 266
Franklin, Marc A., Robert L. Rabin & Michael D. Green, Tort Law and Alternatives
        (Supp. 2008), 337

Hasen, Richard L., Remedies: Examples and Explanations (2007), *passim*
—, The Efficient Duty to Rescue, 15 Int'l Rev. L. & Econ. 141 (1995), 189
Heyman, Steven J., The Duty to Rescue: A Liberal-Communitarian Approach, in
        The Communitarian Reader: Beyond the Essentials (A. Etzioni ed.,
        2004), 189

Keeton, W. Page et al., Prosser and Keeton on Torts (5th ed. 1984), 36
Kircher, John J., The Four Faces of Tort Law: Liability for Emotional Harm, 90 Marq.
        L. Rev. 789 (2007), 207

Laycock, Douglas, Modern American Remedies (3d ed. 2002), 247

Orr, Leila C., Note, Making a Case for Wealth-Calibrated Punitive Damages, 37 Loy. L.A. L. Rev. 1739 (2004), 408

Prosser, William L., Res Ipsa Loquitur in California, 37 Cal. L. Rev. 183 (1949), 151

Rosenthal, A.M., Thirty-Eight Witnesses: The Kitty Genovese Case (1964), 200

Sanders, Joseph, Punitive Damages in Consumer Actions, 8 J. Tex. Consumer L. 22 (Fall 2004), 400

Schwartz, Victor E., Comparative Negligence (2002 & 2007 Supp.), 163

Sheiner, Naomi, Comment, DES and a Proposed Theory of Enterprise Liability, 46 Fordham L. Rev. 963 (1978), 231

Sunstein, Cass, Worst Case Scenarios (2007), 327

Tinney, Richard C., Annotation, Sufficiency of Showing Actual Damages to Support Award of Punitive Damages—Modern Cases, 40 A.L.R.4th 11 (1985 & 2005 Supp.), 392

Weber, Michael J., Annotation, Motorcyclist's Failure to Wear Helmet or Other Protective Equipment as Affecting Recovery for Personal Injury or Death, 85 A.L.R.4th 365 (1991 & Supps.), 374

Weinrib, Ernest J., Corrective Justice in a Nutshell, 52 U. Toronto L.J. 349 (2002), 348

Wiley, Jerry, The Impact of Judicial Decisions on Professional Conduct: An Empirical Study, 55 S. Cal. L. Rev. 345 (1982), 140

Index